Ancient Tyranny

Ancient Tyranny

Edited by Sian Lewis

EDINBURGH UNIVERSITY PRESS

© in this edition Edinburgh University Press, 2006
© in the individual contributions is retained by the authors

Edinburgh University Press Ltd
22 George Square, Edinburgh

Typeset in 11/13 pt Sabon
by Servis Filmsetting Ltd, Manchester, and
printed and bound in Great Britain by
Antony Rowe Ltd, Chippenham, Wilts

A CIP record for this book is available from the British Library

ISBN 0 7486 2125 3 (hardback)

The right of the contributors
to be identified as authors of this work
has been asserted in accordance with
the Copyright, Designs and Patents Act 1988.

Contents

Acknowledgements

This collection of essays had its origin in a conference, 'Tyrants, Kings, Dynasts and Generals: Modes of Autocracy in the Classical Period', held at Cardiff University in July 2003. I should like to thank all those who participated in the conference and made it both valuable and enjoyable. Thanks are especially due to Christopher Tuplin and Roger Brock, for both their contribution to the conference, and their encouragement of the original idea. The conference was generously supported by the British Academy, the A. G. Leventis Foundation, the Society for the Promotion of Hellenic Studies, the University of Wales Institute of Classics and Ancient History, and the School of History and Archaeology at Cardiff University. I would like to thank my colleagues in Ancient History at Cardiff, particularly Louis Rawlings and Nick Fisher, for their support of the project, and the School of History and Archaeology's Departmental Administrator, Elizabeth Walker, for her invaluable assistance in organising the conference and ensuring its smooth running. Finally, my thanks are due to Christopher Smith and John Davey, for smoothing the path to publication with Edinburgh University Press, and to James Dale for his support through the process of preparation.

Sian Lewis
May 2005

Contributors

Dr Ingo Gildenhard is a Lecturer in Classics at King's College London.

Dr Fay Glinister is a Research Fellow in the Department of History at University College London.

Dr Sarah E. Harrell is Assistant Professor of Classics at Trinity College, Hartford.

Professor Simon Hornblower is Professor of Classics and Ancient History at University College London.

Dr Trinity Jackman is a Postdoctoral Fellow at the Society of Fellows in the Humanities, Columbia University.

Dr Kathryn Lomas is a Research Fellow in the Institute of Archaeology at University College London.

Dr Sian Lewis is a Lecturer in Ancient History at the University of St Andrews.

Professor James McGlew is an Associate Professor in the Department of Classical Studies at the University of Missouri-Columbia.

Dr Lynette G. Mitchell is a Senior Lecturer in the Department of Classics and Ancient History at the University of Exeter.

Professor Claude Mossé is a member of the Centre Louis Gernet at the École des Hautes Études, Paris, and Professeur honoraire of the University of Paris-VIII.

Professor Christopher Smith is Professor of Ancient History at the University of St Andrews.

Dr Sławomir Sprawski is a Lecturer at the Institute of History in the Jagiellonian University, Krakow.

Professor Stephen Ruzicka is an Associate Professor in the Department of History at the University of North Carolina, Greensboro.

Dr Alexander Thein is a lecturer in the Department of Classics, University College Dublin.

Dr Matthew Trundle is a Senior Lecturer in the Department of Classics at the Victoria University of Wellington, New Zealand.

Professor Andrew Wolpert is Associate Professor in the Department of Classics at the University of Florida.

Dr Efrem Zambon was recently a Research Fellow in the Department of Classics at the University of Padua.

Abbreviations

ACD	*Acta Classica Universitatis Scientiarum Debreceniensis*
AIIN	*Annali dell' Istituto Italiano di Numismatica*
AJA	*American Journal of Archaeology*
AJP	*American Journal of Philology*
AMI	*Archäologische Mitteilungen aus Iran*
ANSMN	*American Numismatic Society: Museum Notes*
AntK	*Antike Kunst*
ARV	J. D. Beazley, *Attic Red-Figure Vase-Painters*, 2nd edn, Oxford: Clarendon Press, 1963
BCAR	*Bullettino della Commissione archeologica comunale di Roma*
BCH	*Bulletin de correspondance hellénique*
BTCGI	*Bibliographia Topographia della Colonizzazione Greca in Italia e nelle Isole Terreniche*
C&M	*Classica et Mediaevalia*
CAH²	*Cambridge Ancient History*, 2nd edn
CIE	*Corpus Inscriptionum Etruscarum*
CJ	*Classical Journal*
ClAnt	*Classical Antiquity*
CPh	*Classical Philology*
CQ	*Classical Quarterly*
CW	*Classical World*
Dittenberger	W. Dittenberger, *Sylloge Inscriptionum Gracecarum*, 3rd edn, Leipzig: S. Hirzel, 1915–24
DK	H. Diels and W. Kranz, *Fragmente der Vorsokratiker*, 6th edn, Berlin: Weidmann, 1952
FGrHist	F. Jacoby, *Die Fragmente der griechischen Historiker*, Leiden: Brill, 1923– [followed by author number and fragment number]
G&R	*Greece and Rome*
HSCP	*Harvard Studies in Classical Philology*
IG	*Inscriptiones Graecae*
IGA (Roehl)	H. Roehl, *Inscriptiones Graecae Antiquissimae*, Berlin: Berolini, 1882
JDAI	*Jahrbuch des deutschen archäologischen Instituts*

JHS	*Journal of Hellenic Studies*
JNES	*Journal of Near Eastern Studies*
JNG	*Jahrbuch für Numismatik und Geldgeschichte*
JRA	*Journal of Roman Archaeology*
JRS	*Journal of Roman Studies*
KA	*Poetae Comici Graeci*, ed. R. Kassel and C. Austin, Berlin: de Gruyter, 1983–
MGR	*Miscellanea greca e romana*
ML	R. Meiggs and D. M. Lewis, *A Selection of Greek Historical Inscriptions to the End of the Fifth Century BC*, Oxford: Clarendon Press, 1969 [followed by inscription number]
Michel	C. Michel, *Recueil d'inscriptions grecques*, Hildesheim: Olms, 1976
Mus. Helv.	*Museum Helveticum*
NAC	*Numismatica e antichità classiche*
Num. Chron.	*Numismatic Chronicle*
ORF⁴	H. Malcovati, *Oratorum Romanorum Fragmenta*, 4th edn, Turin: Paravia, 1967
P.Oxy.	*Oxyrhynchus Papyri*
PCPS	*Proceedings of the Cambridge Philological Society*
PMG	D. L. Page (ed.), *Poetae Melici Graeci*, Oxford: Clarendon Press, 1962
PP	*La Parola del Passato*
QUCC	*Quaderni Urbinati di Cultura Classica*
RBN	*Revue belge de numismatique*
RE	A. Fr. von Pauly, rev. G. Wissowa et al., *Real-Encyclopädie der klassischen Altertumswissenschaft*, Stuttgart and Munich: Metzler/Drückenmuller, 1894–1980
REA	*Revue des études anciennes*
REL	*Revue des études latines*
RhM	*Rheinisches Museum für Philologie*
RSA	*Rivista Storica dell'Antichità*
Schw. Munz.	*Schweizerische Münzblätter*
SCI	*Scripta Classica Israelica*
SDHI	*Studia et Documenta Historiae et Iuris*
SEG	*Supplementum Epigraphicum Graecum*
SHA	*Scriptores Historiae Augustae*
TAPA	*Transactions of the American Philological Association*

TLE²   M. Pallottino, *Testimonia Linguae Etruscae*,
              2nd edn, Florence: Nuova Italia, 1968
Tod   M. N. Tod, *A Selection of Greek Historical
              Inscriptions*, vol. 2, Oxford: Clarendon Press,
              1950
TrGF   B. Snell et al. (eds), *Tragicorum Graecorum
              Fragmenta*, Göttingen: Vandenhoeck and
              Ruprecht, 1971–
WS   *Wiener Studien*
ZPE   *Zeitschrift für Papyrologie und Epigraphik*

Figures and Tables

CHAPTER 1

Introduction

Sian Lewis

EUPHRON OF SICYON: A CASE-STUDY

Euphron, who held a short-lived tyranny at Sicyon in the 360s BC, illustrates some of the complexities of our understanding of ancient tyranny. Assisted by an Arcadian force, Euphron seized power, taking control of the city's mercenary troops, and establishing a new democratic constitution. He killed or exiled his opponents, seized their property, freed slaves, and took money from the temples. After some time he was deposed by the Arcadians in concert with the Sicyonian aristocrats, but returned with a new mercenary army raised with Athenian money, and recovered the city with the exception of the Acropolis, which was in Theban hands. On going to Thebes to negotiate a settlement of the situation, he was assassinated by a member of the Sicyonian opposition.[1] Xenophon, our sole source for the episode, depicts Euphron as a tyrant of a very recognisable kind: he plotted with outside powers to obtain sole rule at a time of political upheaval, and sought to maintain his power through oppressive and illegal means. Tyranny, on this view, was a disastrous eventuality for a *polis*; it saw both private and civic interests sacrificed to the benefit of a single individual.

Yet Xenophon's account reveals that there was a struggle to define the nature of Euphron's rule even in his own time: although his opponents characterised him as a tyrant of an indisputable type, the citizens of Sicyon brought Euphron's body back to the city and gave him posthumous worship as founder. He likewise had the support of the democratic Athenians, who forged bonds of *xenia* with him and his descendants. Xenophon was in no doubt that Euphron was a 'classic' tyrant, yet his deeds seem to contradict the simple view: he set up a democracy which continued under his rule, was clearly popular with a large section of the citizens, and used the mercenary forces (which he took over from the previous regime) only in external warfare. Euphron cannot easily be accommodated within the traditional model of tyranny, because that model is limited and simplistic; to accept the label of 'tyrant' uncritically when it is applied to a ruler by historians, and to assume that all tyrants acted in the same manner, is to obscure the complexities of ancient political life. Euphron's story, then, illustrates several of the key themes addressed in this collection: the concern for self-definition and struggle to control the vocabulary of sole rulership; the potential benefits to a *polis* of the concentration of power in individual hands; modern historians' tendency to embrace simplifying models of ancient political life; and, most crucially, the role of the historian in the making of a tyrant.

Why study tyranny?

The origin of this collection was a conference, 'Tyrants, Kings, Dynasts and Generals: Modes of Autocracy in the Classical Period', held in Cardiff in July 2003. The conference brought together ancient historians and philosophers to discuss the ways in which individuals held autocratic power in antiquity, the experience of tyranny, and the responses of classical thinkers to the phenomenon. Although tyranny has, thanks to contemporary global events, once more become a fashionable term in modern political debate, in classical studies it had become a rather antiquated topic, conceptualised as a kind of evolutionary dead-end within the Greek *polis*, significant only in its role as precursor to democracy. Through the 1980s and 1990s, the primary focus of British and American scholarship on ancient politics was democracy, and other types of constitution were treated (explicitly or implicitly) as a prelude to, less satisfactory alternative to, or decline from, the democratic ideal.[2] Recently, however, the emphasis on 2,500 years of democracy has begun to fade and scholars have found a resurgent interest in investigating other constitutional forms. As monarchy, oligarchy and non-*polis* forms of organisation have received attention, it seemed equally opportune to revisit tyranny and to open up new approaches to the idea of autocratic power in antiquity.[3]

The study of tyranny, far from being a parade of cruelty and infamy (although it does have more than its fair share of memorable stories), illuminates ancient political culture in several ways. The persistent focus on democracy, and the model in which the *polis* is envisaged as evolving towards democratic rule, distracts us from the realities of ancient political life. Few states enjoyed a settled constitution for long periods and the history of most ancient states was one of constant upheaval as internal and external forces sought to impose their preferred form of rule. Tyrants and monarchic rulers appeared at all periods, some holding power for a short time and others founding long-lasting dynasties. Although our ancient sources adopt an almost universally negative view of tyrants, it is worth making the point that tyranny persisted in most cases because it had several benefits to offer.[4] It could be a centralised and effective form of government, particularly in contrast to a changeable democracy, and allowed organised effort against an outside threat. This is clearly recognised in the Roman institution of the dictatorship, and the principle was explicitly enunciated by Demosthenes, comparing Philip of Macedon's efficient monarchy with the chaotic response in his own city.[5] As well as strong leadership in times of threat, tyrants could impose their will to carry through ambitious building projects, found cities, foster trade and development and make necessary civil reforms – indeed, the Platonic image of the philosopher-king has its roots in the need to grant sufficient power to an individual to bring about radical change in the state. A tyrant also usually (though not inevitably) championed the cause of the poor, as did Euphron, bringing social justice in contrast to a corrupt oligarchy. The significance of this should not be underestimated, because despite its reputation, tyranny was rarely a one-sided venture: it is often represented as an individual impulse – the man who would be king – imposed on an unwilling populace who hunger for freedom (a view undoubtedly sometimes propagated retrospectively by the people themselves), but this is too simple and too convenient. The people's desire for a dictator, for strong leadership, for social control and for security, is at least as strong a factor as the would-be tyrant's desire: consider the enthusiasm of the Roman people for rule by Caesar or by Augustus, the ability of Pericles to control the Athenian state, the role played by Pelopidas among the Boiotarchs at Thebes, or the popular acclaim for Gelon as ruler of Syracuse.[6]

Studying tyrants also requires us to consider a wide variety of states and political systems, including some which are often neglected, and to take a long perspective, from the seventh century to the first. Syracuse has given us the greatest number of well-documented tyrannical rulers, and *poleis* such as Sicyon have histories dominated by tyrants, from the seventh-century Orthagoras to the third-century Nicocles.[7] Thessaly, Ionia and Euboea all produced significant tyrants, and further afield the Clearchids at Heraclea, Hecatomnids in Caria and Battiads at Cyrene demonstrate the range of autocratic rulers, and the very permeable boundary between tyranny and monarchy.

DEFINITIONS

Any study of this kind must begin with the question: what is a tyrant? Xenophon, in his characterisation of Euphron (written in the 350s BC), evidently had some kind of checklist of tyrannical attributes in mind – he used mercenaries to support his rule, enslaved and killed citizens and stole sacred treasures – but this does not add up to a clear constitutional position. Most influential in the way that we define the tyrant is Aristotle's *Politics*: Aristotle identified three fundamental constitutional types, monarchy, oligarchy and democracy, each with a 'good' and 'bad' form.[8] Kingship is the 'good' form of monarchy, where the ruler is subject to law, and tyranny the 'deviated' form, in which the ruler is able to do whatever he or she wishes. Aristotle's definitions, however, are more difficult to maintain in practice – he admits, for instance, that certain types of rule can be characterised as both tyranny and kingship, such as the 'elective tyranny' of the *aisymnêteia* – and the applications of the term by most classical authors are far less clear cut. The figures to whom the term is applied are extremely diverse: Jason and Alexander of Pherae, for instance, were technically *tagoi* in Thessaly, while Euphron held power within a democratic constitution; all the Sicilian tyrants held the role of *stratêgos autokratôr*, to which they were elected by a popular assembly; Mausolus, called both tyrant and king by his contemporaries, was in fact a satrap within the Persian empire, while tyranny was offered by Dionysius of Halicarnassus as an analogy to the Roman dictatorship.[9] It can be surprisingly difficult to be accurate about rulers' constitutional positions: even in archaic Greece, in the so-called 'age of tyrants', the precise distinction between a lawgiver, a tyrant and a king is hard to define in practice, and the more closely one looks at a figure such as Pisistratus, the less sharply defined his power appears.

As a result, trying to define the role of the tyrant in constitutional terms is an activity of limited value; much more useful is to recognise the essential qualities of tyranny, and to examine the boundary points where it overlaps with other constitutional forms. We see oligarchies accused of operating as *de facto* tyrannies, tyrants who became hereditary kings, leaders within democratic states accused of wielding tyrannical power, and tyrants who held power while rejecting the title. Another of the themes running through this collection is the question of where tyranny begins and ends: was it possible for a king to rule without becoming an autocrat? If a leader in a constitutional system effectively commands the state, as did Pericles in fifth-century

Athens, could his power in practical terms be seen as different from that of a usurping tyrant? Many of the Greek political leaders of the fourth century approached this position, often because of the need for effective command of the state in wartime, and their contemporaries, historians and poets alike, show themselves to be uneasily aware of the fluidity of the nature of rule.

We should therefore not be surprised by the rather shifty nature of tyranny, which is a consequence of the evolution of the concept in political thought. The extent of the role of historians in 'creating' tyranny has been the topic of several recent studies, and it is important to understand how different writers used the term. Some have argued that the concept of tyranny itself is no more than a fifth-century invention, imposed first by Herodotus on his account of archaic Greek history in order to provide a context for the great contest between Greek freedom and the tyranny of the Persian king. There is certainly a case for seeing Herodotus as the creator of archaic tyranny; in contrast, Thucydides removed the focus on the individual tyrant in favour of his formulation of Athens as the 'tyrant city', giving the impression that ruling tyrants disappeared from Greece after 480 (his work contains references to only one contemporary tyrant, the mysterious Euarchus of Astacus, as opposed to Herodotus' naming of more than fifty).[10] Tyranny returns as a concept in the works of Xenophon, who took from philosophy an interest in the possibility of the just king, while Plato's formulations about tyranny and the tyrannical ruler were of fundamental importance as the foundations of later thought: Mossé and Gildenhard (Chapters 13 and 14) in this collection show how the Platonic images of the tyrant and tyrannical nature echo through the writings of Cicero and Plutarch. The first-century Diodorus may be responsible for our view of Sicily as home of endemic tyranny; he notoriously described Sicily as 'particularly prone to one-man rule' (19.1, prefacing his account of Agathocles). But how far is the persistence of tyranny in Diodorus' Sicily the product of his own interpretation of, and expectations about, political life? These historians in turn influenced their Roman successors, though the description of tyrant-like kings in early Roman history in the works of Livy and Dionysius of Halicarnassus has often met with suspicion, on the grounds that the events of the first centuries BC and AD, when the histories were written, led writers to cast the archaic period in terms of tyrants and the struggle for the Republic, in order to reflect their own concerns. The question of whether the archaic Roman tyrants were nothing but literary creations is tackled in this collection by Glinister

and Smith (Chapters 2 and 4); certainly Roman writers turned to
Greek models to explain the upheavals of the first century BC.

Almost all of the chapters here treat, at least in part, the process by
which the concept of the tyrant was developed by subsequent writers
into the form most suitable for their ends, and some explore it explicitly, tracing the ideas expressed about, and uses of, tyranny in political rhetoric in periods from the fifth century to the first. Tyranny was
a malleable concept, which could be divorced from or assimilated
with kingship, and conceptualised as either the opposite of democracy or an extreme form of democratic expression, according to the
needs of the time.

SCHOLARSHIP ON TYRANNY

Tyranny was created by ancient writers, but our understanding of it
has been profoundly influenced by contemporary scholarship. The
clearest manifestation of this is the way in which archaic Greek
tyrants like Cypselus and Cleisthenes have dominated studies of
tyranny at the expense of later rulers such as the Dionysii, a consequence of the 'age of tyrants' model – best exemplified by Andrewes'
The Greek Tyrants – which presents tyranny as an (often regrettable)
stage through which a *polis* had to pass in its early years in order
to achieve political maturity, and as a phenomenon confined to
the archaic period in Greece.[11] This model retains a surprising stran-
glehold on Greek history as currently taught, and one reason for its
dominance is the Athenocentrism which marks so many contemporary ancient history courses. The state of the discipline, and the
factors underlying it, have been very well expounded by Brock and
Hodkinson in their discussion of Greek constitutional history, and I
will not repeat their observations here; it is nevertheless worth com-
menting on the specific effects of the Athenocentric focus on our
views of tyranny.[12] The constitutional history of Athens offers a narrative arc whereby the fall of the Pisistratids in 510 marks the end of
tyranny as a practical proposition, and the beginning of an intellectual history of tyranny, which can be traced through fifth-century
drama and into the philosophy of the fourth century. Under the influence of Thucydides' formulations, the figure of the individual tyrant
is replaced by a vision of Athens as the 'tyrant city', and tyranny
becomes a purely abstract concept rather than a practical possibility.
The ideas of political philosophers are discussed with some reference
to Plato's interventions at the court of the Dionysii, but otherwise

tyranny is cast as something comfortably distant from Athens, a primitive constitutional form found on the less-developed margins of the Greek world. The continuing anti-tyrannical legislation passed by the Athenians in the fourth century is taken to be symbolic, or aimed in reality at would-be creators of an oligarchic regime rather than at any real tyrant.[13] Clearly this view ignores the part played by tyranny in the fourth-century Peloponnese and the rest of Greece, but the Athenian model nevertheless tends to dominate non-specialist thinking because of the tempting array of literary sources available, and recent studies follow in this direction, concentrating on the representation of the tyrant in classical drama and the development of the concept of tyranny in fourth-century political theory, with its emphasis on the benefits of wisely applied monarchy.[14] That is not to say that there is no place for studies which look at the representation of tyranny in Athenian literature and thought, since it is Athenian writers who best expose its shifts in meaning and application, shifts which are mapped explicitly by some of the essays here: Mitchell (Chapter 12), in particular, analyses the influence of the revolutions of 411 and 404 on the categorisation of constitutions, and the function of the idea of tyranny in fifth- and fourth-century political discourse. But tyranny cannot be understood by looking solely at Athens, which was in many ways untypical of a Greek *polis*, and a wider view of the scale and function of autocratic rule brings the 'age of tyrants' model under pressure from several different directions.

Of course many historians treat Greek tyranny more broadly, most notably Berve's still fundamental *Die Tyrannis bei den Griechen* and Mossé's *La Tyrannie dans la Grèce antique*.[15] For these scholars, tyranny is best understood in terms of two periods, an archaic age ending with the Pisistratids and Deinomenids, and a classical age from 410 onwards, in which changing political circumstances led to the return of tyranny in the form of rulers such as Jason of Pherae and Dionysius I. Classical tyranny, often identified as qualitatively different from the archaic variety, is then seen to lay the foundations for Hellenistic monarchy, with Dionysius in particular, as ruler over a conquered territory, acting as forerunner to Alexander and the Successor kings. On this view, tyranny looks both forwards and back, to a vanished past and an approaching future, without clear contemporary relevance, although some might find their suspicions aroused by the extremely limited duration of the fifth-century 'tyranny-free' period, from the fall of Thrasybulus at Syracuse in 466 to the accession of Dionysius in 405. A reason for the collapsing of tyranny into

Hellenistic monarchy can perhaps be found in the imbalance of modern historical investigation: fourth-century Greek political history is far less commonly studied within university syllabuses or by researchers, and the 'centre' of fourth-century history is usually held to be the conquest of Greece by Philip of Macedon and the subsequent successes of Alexander, foregrounding the figure of the king. Because figures such as Alexander of Pherae, Callias of Chalcis and Clearchus of Heraclea, and the circumstances in which they took and held power, are less familiar, their importance to their own communities is obscured. It is also relevant that Aristotle himself tended to neglect contemporary rulers in his discussion of the preservation or downfall of tyrannies, reaching instead for archaic or foreign exemplars. He notoriously claimed the three most enduring tyrannical regimes to be the Orthagorids, the Cypselids and the Pisistratids, with an honourable mention for the Deinomenids, inexplicably omitting the claims of the three greatest dynasties of his own time: the Dionysii, Jason's Thessalian dynasty and the Clearchids.[16]

At the same time the certainties of the archaic age of tyrants have come under attack. As debate on the reasons for the 'rise of tyranny' in the seventh century has become more sterile (were the causal factors social, military or political – or an unsurprising mixture of the three?), readings of tyrants and tyranny in the archaic period have become gradually more sceptical. Is it possible to include a group of rulers as disparate as Pheidon, Pittacus and Polycrates under a single title? Can one really accept the sudden appearance of unconstitutional tyrants in previously constitutional states, so early in the history of the *polis*? As Ogden has shown, when one looks before a tyrant such as Pittacus or Cypselus to see what kind of government they replaced, one tends to find not aristocracies or monarchies, but an infinite regress of tyrants, each apparently overthrown by a successor in the name of liberty: at Mytilene, for instance, Pittacus overthrew the tyrant Myrsilus, who had in turn overthrown Melanchrus, and before Melanchrus we hear of Megacles, who put down the rule of the club-wielding Penthelidai.[17] The idea that all Greek states were initially ruled by monarchies, overthrown before the 'age of tyrants', has been called into question by Drews and others, leading studies of monarchy to frame their investigation more broadly, considering a variety of types of monarchic rule, and following themes through the Hellenistic and Roman periods.[18] This too has its effect on the interpretation of tyranny: the more various ancient kingship is seen to be, the less distinct its boundary with tyranny appears, and studies of monarchy have raised the profile of rulers on the fringes of kingship, such as the Battiad rulers of Cyrene, or the Hecatomnids. This collection, then, considers tyranny in all periods, with a concentration on the nature of the personal power such rulers exercised.

THE NATURE OF THE COLLECTION

Some of the chapters in this collection were originally presented as papers at the conference 'Tyrants, Kings, Dynasts and Generals'; others were commissioned later to provide fuller coverage and expand on particular aspects. The papers were chosen with the aim of moving away from well-worn topics and considering how autocracy functioned across a range of societies; they span a period from 500 (the Deinomenids) to 40 BC (Caesar), and a geographical range from Rome and Sicily to Persia. Some focus on individual rulers and dynasties, others on more general features of autocracy and the nature of tyrannical rule.

Two notable features of the book are its exclusion of tyrants and rulers before 500, and its inclusion of figures whom some might hesitate to name as tyrants. It is primarily because of the shape of modern scholarship that archaic tyrannies, including that of the Pisistratids, were excluded from consideration. Rather than revisit existing debates (were archaic tyrants kings? how did tyrants fit into the development of the *polis*?) we aimed to open up new and broader questions. Of course, any ruler stood in the shadow of his predecessors, real or mythological; tyrants themselves looked back to previous rulers and modelled their public image on them (one of the best examples of which is the later tyrant of Syracuse, Hieron II – treated here by Zambon in Chapter 6 – who named his son Gelon and his daughter Damarete after his fifth-century predecessors). Poets and historians too interpreted contemporary tyrants in relation to their predecessors, and indeed vice versa. So 'archaic' tyranny remained present in later periods, as Cicero's reference to Phalaris and Pisistratus as exempla demonstrates (see Gildenhard's study in Chapter 14). For the same reason, instead of understanding tyrants as a distinctive product of a particular era in the development of the *polis*, it seemed more fruitful to compare autocratic rulers across different cultures; therefore rather than focusing solely on those rulers identified as tyrants, this collection considers the whole range of autocratic roles in the classical world: kings, dictators, 'first citizens', generals and satraps, those who were called tyrants but seem to be something else, and those who acted

as tyrants while claiming a different title. So we have Ducetius, leader
of the Sicels in the fifth century, as well as the Dionysii, the Thirty
Tyrants as well as Alexander of Pherae, and the Roman kings as well
as Sulla and Caesar.

The inclusion of figures from Roman history calls for specific
comment. Is it valid to apply the concept of tyranny to either kings in
archaic Rome, or the dictators and dynasts of the late Republic?
Roman writers certainly did, using the term 'tyrannos' to describe the
Tarquins and to explain the nature of Sulla's and Caesar's power, but
in an inversion of Greek historiography this has been seen as the
application of borrowed concepts to a dissimilar context. But as the
authors writing on Rome here emphasise, tyranny was not just an
empty concept inherited from the Greeks; it was instead a means of
describing a real current within Roman society. For the archaic period
archaeological evidence indicates direct contact between sixth-
century Greece and Rome, suggesting that Rome should be seen in the
context of other Italian communities, where Greek-style patterns
of rulership are detectable.[19] Traditions of would-be tyrants persist
throughout the history of the Republic, and hence the contemporary
use of tyranny to explain the nature of Sullan or Caesarian rule can
be seen to be more than simple rhetoric, since it allowed Romans to
name and conceptualise what was going on in their society in the face
of the competing discourse of republicanism.

Other papers focus on Greece and the east; in these, Sicily,
perhaps inevitably, plays the largest part. Tyrant dynasties from the
Deinomenids in the fifth century to Hieron II in the third receive attention, in both their actions within Sicily and their relations to the wider
world. On the mainland, authors look at specific rulers, the Thirty at
Athens and Alexander of Pherae, and also more generally at Greek
constructions of tyranny from the early period through to the fourth
century, in the praise poetry of Pindar, in Attic comedy, and among
political theorists from Herodotus to Plato. Moving beyond Greece,
two chapters focus on the east, on the influence of Persia on power
relations in Greece, and the nature of the power of the Persian king.

In keeping with the aim to expand on the continuities in autocratic
rule across the ancient Mediterranean, these papers are organised in
four thematic sections. The first comprises five chapters concerned
with the ways in which tyrannies came into being and their interpretation by historians. Glinister's examination of the *interregnum* in
Chapter 2, the process of creating kings in archaic Rome, shows that
the last two kings, Servius Tullius and Tarquinius Superbus, despite

their very different reputations, were irregular rulers, defined by their accession as tyrants and comparable to those in contemporary Italy. Hence the Roman anti-monarchical tradition is better understood as an anti-tyrannical tradition. Jackman (Chapter 3) offers a reappraisal of Ducetius, one of the enigmatic figures of Sicilian history, using archaeological evidence to complement the historical accounts and suggest the complexity of fifth-century Sicilian politics. She demonstrates that he is better understood as a self-conscious politician responding to social and political pressures through the creation of a multi-*polis* state, than as a simple ethnic hero. Smith (Chapter 4) gives a fascinating account of the Republican Romans who aimed at monarchy, arguing for the historicity of the *adfectores*, and reading them as an accurate reflection of the archaic period at Rome, similar to the powerful and competing families of sixth-century Greece. The last two chapters in this section look at the later classical Mediterranean: Trundle (Chapter 5) draws a compelling picture of the fourth century in which opportunities for building personal power were created by changes in monetisation (a motif which goes back to the archaic period) and social upheaval, while Zambon (Chapter 6) considers the later rulers of Syracuse, Agathocles and Hieron II, examining the nature and expression of their power, and their role in the development of the concept of kingship within Sicily. All demonstrate that there can be no textbook definition of tyranny, because rulers were forging their own systems and trying to determine how others would respond to their power.

Chapters 7, 8 and 9 form a section discussing the methods by which tyrants adapted themselves to, and influenced, political circumstances, with a focus on questions of interpretation. Lomas analyses the relationship between tyrants and population movement in Sicily from the seventh century to the Roman conquest, arguing that although there is a clear link between tyranny and demographic instability, we can use archaeology to look beyond the mainly negative accounts of mainland historians. A study of events at Messana demonstrates that civic and cultural identities were strong and complex, and able to accommodate or even benefit from interventions by tyrants. Harrell concentrates on a specific period of Sicilian politics, exploring the historiographic tradition created by the Deinomenids around Gelon's victory at Himera, showing how the tyrants negotiated local and panhellenic identities through careful use of history, dedications and poetry. Moving to fourth-century Greece, Sprawski re-examines the reputation of Alexander of Pherae among Greek authors as an archetypally wicked tyrant, showing that his military successes and the good opinion of Isocrates indicate that his support must have been wider than the histories suggest. Although opposition from within and outside Thessaly reduced his chances of building a popular *tageia* of the kind that Jason had, Alexander should still be credited with political vision and aims beyond personal power. All three authors show that stereotyping reactions to the figure of the tyrant can serve to obscure the real circumstances and consequences of their rule.

The third section comprises five chapters examining the ideology of tyranny, from poetic metaphor to political theory. The authors do not confine themselves to Athens, but view the development of the concept from the early fifth century, in the poetry of Pindar, to Cicero's appropriation of Greek ideas to explain the politics of his own day. Hornblower (Chapter 10) explores Pindar's construction of the good and bad ruler, and his ideas about the nature of kingship and the king's relation with the people. These ideas, worked out in practice at the court of Hieron I, find echoes among the fourth-century orators and especially in the works of Plato, as later authors continued debating Pindar's formulations. McGlew and Mitchell (Chapters 11 and 12) both discuss the place of tyranny within Athenian political discourse, McGlew from the perspective of Attic comedy and Mitchell among political thinkers. Both trace the evolution of the idea in the light of changing political events, from the 'first citizenship' of Pericles in the fifth century, through the oligarchic revolutions and into the re-established democracy, and both agree that it was because the idea of tyranny could be constantly reshaped and reinterpreted in its relation to democracy and oligarchy that it remained central to Athenian discourse. Mossé and Gildenhard (Chapters 13 and 14) demonstrate the continuing influence of Platonic ideas in later constructions of tyrants: Mossé shows how Plutarch drew his depiction of tyrants in his *Lives* of Dion and Timoleon from Plato's *Letters*, so that the Dionysii are seen through the prism of Platonic interpretation and Dionysius II in particular is characterised by his brush with Platonic philosophy; Gildenhard traces how Cicero used the formulations of Plato's *Republic* about the nature of tyranny and the tyrannical man to guide his responses and actions at the outbreak of the Civil War in 49 BC, even seeing parallels between his relationship with Caesar and Plato's with Dionysius the Elder.

In the final section three chapters, one each on Greece, Rome and Persia, consider the limitations exerted on autocratic power by the nature of the system itself. Wolpert (Chapter 15) studies the rule of the Thirty at Athens, and the constitutive part played by violence in the government which they created. Violence was not, as the sources suggest, merely opportunism or villainy, but a necessary strategy in allowing the regime to seize and hold power, breaking the will of the people to resist, but also containing the seeds of its own downfall. Ruzicka (Chapter 16) looks at the Persian kings, the ultimate autocrats of antiquity, from Darius II to Artaxerxes III and exposes the limitations of their power, identifying a cycle whereby the king's insecurity led to a dearth of trustworthy commanders. Kings therefore turned to non-Persians to command their campaigns, thus setting in train the effects documented by Trundle in Chapter 5 and simultaneously weakening their own power. Thein (Chapter 17) argues for a similar effect in Sulla's dictatorship at Rome: his political effectiveness, as distinct from his constitutional power, was limited by the nature of his support, which was based on guilt and fear. All three authors echo the critique of tyranny encapsulated in the story of the ruler striking down 'tall poppies': the tyrant who cannot base his rule in justice must constantly narrow and protect his circle of support, and will be weakened by the very actions which ensure his rule.[20]

CONCLUSION

There are other tyrants one could consider who are not included here, other places and periods, other interpretations; a collection of this kind cannot hope to be exhaustive. But it can show what can be achieved by the application of a different model for understanding tyranny. The aim of this project, when it began, was to place tyrannical rule centre stage, and to analyse it on its own merits; to treat autocracy as a positive choice instead of a political failure, and to understand the ways in which ancient writers configured it, using their past to interpret their present. It also aimed to end the artificial separation of a small group of rulers under the name of 'tyrants', recognising that autocratic rulers appear in numerous guises and under different titles, not only in archaic Greece, but throughout classical antiquity. I hope that this collection will encourage a clearer focus on tyranny in all its forms, and its place in the history of political thought, including the cross-cultural comparisons which the ancients themselves made.

It should be obvious that in antiquity tyranny was not a monolithic idea, but an idea created and constantly adapted by historians, with multivalent meaning and application. It might appear that by redefining the tyrant, suggesting that tyranny was not so much a constitutional position as a method of rule, potential within any political system, there is a danger of collapsing the category, or depriving it of meaning, but in fact this collection shows how an understanding of autocracy can cast light on very diverse areas of antiquity. The boundaries between the tyrant, the king, the general and the political leader turn out to be far more permeable than traditional constitutional historians might wish.

NOTES

1. Xenophon *Hell.* 7.1.44–6 and 7.3, with Diodorus 15.70.3. See Lewis 2004 for a full discussion of the episode and bibliography.
2. For example, Ober and Hedrick 1993, 1996; Ober 1996; Morris and Raaflaub 1997; Boedeker and Raaflaub 1998; Connor et al., 1989.
3. Brock and Hodkinson 2000, Ostwald 2000; Morgan 2003.
4. Salmon 1997, Brock and Hodkinson 2000: 14–15.
5. Demosthenes 1.4, 3.4–5, 14, 10.19–20.
6. Caesar: Suet. *Div. Iul.* 73 (on the public response to Caesar's death) and Yavetz 1983: ch. 6; Augustus: *Res Gestae* 5, Suet. *Aug.* 52; Pericles: the famous Thuc. 2.65.9 and the thought-provoking 2.22.1; Pelopidas' re-election to the Boiotarchy: Plut. *Pel.* 24–5, 34.5, Diod. 15.81.4; Gelon: Diod. 11.26.5–6, 67.2–3.
7. Pausanias 2.8.2, Arist. *Pol.* 1315b12–14, Plut. *Mor.* 553a.
8. Arist. *Pol.* 1279a32–b10; on the difficulty of defining the *aisymnêteia* 1285a29–40 and 1295a1–16.
9. *Tagoi*: see Sprawski 1999, 2004 and Chapter 9 in this volume; *stratêgos autokratôr*: Diod. 13.94.5–95.1, 15.20.6, 19.1.4; Mausolus: Hornblower 1982: 59–62, 70–1; dictatorship: DH 5.73.2–3.
10. Parker 1998, Osborne 2003: on Herodotus, Waters 1971, Lateiner 1989: ch. 8, Dewald 2003; Thucydides 2.30; Scanlon 1987.
11. Andrewes 1956, Kinzl 1979, Cawkwell 1995, Giorgini 1993, Barcelo 1993.
12. Brock and Hodkinson 2000: 4–9.
13. Andoc. 1.97, Dem. 24.149, law of 337/6 (Schwenk 1985: no. 6); Giorgini 1993: ch. 6, Rosivach 1988.
14. Giorgini 1993, Morgan 2003.
15. Berve 1967, Mossé 1969, Frolov 1974.
16. Arist. *Pol.* 1315b11–39; Keyt 1999: 181–2, Sprawski 1999: 59.
17. Ogden 1997: 148–9, Arist. *Pol* 1311b23–30, Alcaeus fr. 70, 129, Strabo 13.2.3, Diog. Laert. 1.74.
18. Drews 1983, Carlier 1984, Gruen 1996, Mooren 1983, Martin 1982.
19. Cornell 1995: 145–50, Glinister and Smith, Chapters 2 and 4 in this volume.
20. Herodotus 5.92f–g, Arist. *Pol.* 1284a26–33.

PART I

The making of tyranny

Kingship and tyranny in archaic Rome

Fay Glinister

As ongoing archaeological excavations continue to make ever clearer, sixth-century BC Rome was a major force in Central Italy. It could hold its own with the great Etruscan city-states and was able to conclude with Carthage a treaty that explicitly recognised Rome as the overlord of much of Latium (Polybius 3.22). By this period, Rome was a city-state with a developed urban form, sophisticated communal cults, flourishing markets, and complex political and legal institutions.[1]

Roman society was focused around a ruler whose title, *rex* (attested by contemporary epigraphic as well as later literary evidence), suggests the existence of a formalised monarchical type of government. The Roman literary tradition, however, provides us with contradictory information. On the one hand there appears to be a regular method of making a 'true' king. On the other, the last kings of Rome (those with the best chance of being historical) display 'tyrannical' features in varying degrees (including the illegitimate seizure of power) – as indeed do several of the earlier kings, including Romulus.[2] The aim of this chapter is to explore, and suggest resolutions for, this apparent inconsistency.

This chapter derives from part of my unpublished PhD thesis, 'The Roman Kingship in the Sixth Century BC' (University College London, 1995). Focusing on the *rex sacrorum*, the regalia, the *interregnum*, and the role of women in the succession, the thesis demonstrated the ways in which the kings reinforced and legitimated their power, in response to the demands of a rapidly changing society. I argued that oral tradition could preserve details of the Roman king-ship *system* (as opposed to stories concerning individual kings); there was no cause for such details to be romanticised or exaggerated as the tradition devel-oped (as there might have been with, for example, an important battle), because the institution of kingship was not a central but an incidental part of the story of regal Rome.

CREATING KINGS

According to tradition, almost from the first there was a formal electoral process by which a man became king. The death of the old king
caused an *interregnum*. The power vaccum was filled by an interim
ruler (*interrex*), who possessed the insignia of regal power (such as
the rods: DH 2.57.2). Each *interrex* held office for five days before
handing power over to his successor (Livy 9.34.12). The last nominated the new ruler, who was voted for by an assembly (the *comitia
curiata*). The *patres* confirmed their choice and finally divine sanction
was sought (Cic. *Leg.* 2.8.2).[3] I want briefly to highlight aspects of
this procedure, before offering possible reinterpretations.

In an *interregnum* the auspices are said to have 'returned to the
patres' (*auspicia ad patres redeunt*: Cic. *Brut.* 1.5.4; Livy 1.32.1).
In the Republic the *patres* were a section of the elite with certain hereditary privileges and religious rights. Patrician senators controlled the
auspices under which Republican magistrates were elected and formally ratified decisions of the assemblies concerning elections.[4] It was
by their authority, too, that the new king was installed (according to
Livy 1.22.2, 1.32.1 etc.). Some scholars do not accept that the *interregnum* was a regal institution, arguing instead that it developed
during the early Republic, and believe that the patriciate was formed
only then.[5] It has also been suggested that the concept *auspicia ad
patres redeunt* dates from this time, and would therefore have had no
relevance in the monarchical period.

Evidently there are problems involved in understanding the regal
interregnum; and, as no *interregnum* occurred in the later monarchical period (according to the Roman tradition), there was no direct
continuation of the practice from monarchy to Republic.[6] But the very
existence of the term *interregnum* leaves little reason to doubt that in
archaic Rome there existed some kind of procedure by which a king
was legitimated, and it is not implausible to consider that the *patres*
had a role to play in conferring authority on the king, especially since
interreges were required to be patrician (unlike the king himself).[7]
However, the existence of an interrregnal procedure does not necessarily point to a powerful aristocracy with a controlling interest in the
appointment of a king. Even if a new ruler did seek the approval of
the local aristocracy, it need not mean that the *patres* (probably best
seen at this stage as a kind of council of elders with religious authority) could freely chose a king. In fact it is quite possible that the *patres*
possessed little say over who was to become king: their role may have

been primarily a religious formality, their authority merely an emergency measure.[8] At most, if the *patres* (and/or the people) did confer power on the new king, this 'did not by itself set any limit to that power, it only made the tenure of that power lawful, and marked it off from tyranny, in the sense of unconstitutional seizure of power'.[9]

As well as a role for the Roman elite in the creation of a king, Roman tradition also finds a place for the assembly, in the form of the vote by the *comitia curiata* of a *lex curiata* which confirmed the king's power.[10] (*Imperium*, the power of command, was formally conferred on Republican magistrates by this means.) The role of the *lex curiata* in the monarchical period is open to question (even its function in the Republic is disputed).[11] Certainly, the *interrex* needed no such *lex* to be able to convoke the *comitia*, or to command the army. It may be better to date the introduction of the *lex curiata* to the early Republic.

On the other hand, the involvement of the *curiae* (an important division of society in the archaic and early Republican periods) in the creation of a king seems genuine, as popular assent is a key element in the accession to power of a legitimate ruler.[12] It has been argued that the assembly did not vote or debate, but that the people simply assented to a new ruler by acclamation, a ceremony attested in diverse societies.[13] There is much to be said for this view. Acclamation is attested at various points in the Roman tradition. After the death of the tyrannical Amulius, Numitor is hailed king by Romulus and Remus, and, Livy says, the crowd shout their assent (1.6.2). Romulus and Remus are each acclaimed king by their followers (Livy 1.7.1: *utrumque regem sua multitudo consalutaverat*). Numa, arriving at Rome to take up the kingship, is met by crowds hailing him (DH 2.60.2). The tyrant Tarquinius Superbus, in a striking perversion of the normal manner of acclamation, is first hailed as king by his wife (Livy 1.48.5: *evocavit virum e curia regemque prima appellavit*).[14] It is quite likely that the assembly had no choice other than to accept or reject a candidate. We never hear of more than one candidate; nor do we ever hear of a man failing to become king. This could of course be the result of the poverty of the sources. But in real terms it is unlikely that the people would snub a powerful man, perhaps one who had conquered the city, by refusing to acknowledge him as king.

THE PATTERN OF THE *INTERREGNUM*

The literary sources treat the *interregnum* as a standard event during the monarchical period (e.g. DH 8.90). Ancient authors attribute the

origin of the procedure to the election of Numa after the death of
Romulus (Cic. *Rep.* 2.23, Livy 1.17.7–11, DH 2.57–8, 2.60.3). The
procedure also operates for the elections of Tullus Hostilius (Cic. *Rep.*
2.31, Livy 1.22, DH 3.1.1–3) and Ancus Marcius (Cic. *Rep.* 2.33,
Livy 1.32, DH 3.36.1). It is often assumed that Tarquinius Priscus, as
the first monarch of the so-called 'Etruscan' dynasty, comes to power
in a manner at odds with this established practice. In fact Dionysius
of Halicarnassus' account includes the usual *interregnum*, election
and divine ratification (3.45.1), while an *interregnum* is also implied
by Cicero (*Rep.* 2.35) in the earliest surviving continuous account of
the Roman monarchy. In Livy, too, Priscus is elected by the people,
although a somewhat irregular element is introduced: Priscus is said
to be the first to canvass votes for the kingship amongst the people
(1.35.2), and once in power, he enrols his own supporters in the
senate. Apparently, then, he bases his power on popular rather than
aristocratic support.

Oddly, Servius, the founder of many of Rome's political and religious institutions, is the first king to take power contrary to the 'constitutional' procedure. He obtains power in an abnormal manner,
almost by *usus*.[15] Livy comments:

> There had been no observance of the *interregnum*, as on prior occa-
> sions; no election had been held; not by the votes of the people had
> sovereignty come to him, not with the confirmation of the *patres*, but
> by a woman's gift. (1.47.10)

The tradition on Servius is confused as to whether his power-base was
the senate or the people. In Dionysius the senators plan to make
Servius give up power so an *interregnum* and proper election can take
place (4.8.2). In response Servius immediately bolsters his power
amongst the plebs by paying debts and promising legal reforms, and
has himself elected king by the curiate assembly without obtaining
senatorial ratification (DH 4.12.3). In Cicero's *Republic*, Servius
takes power by a ruse, pretending at first that Tarquin is sick, and that
he himself is governing on Tarquin's instructions. He begins to rule
'without being formally chosen by the people, but with their goodwill
and consent' (*non iussu, sed voluntate atque concessu civium*); he
adopts regal dress, sits in judgement, frees debtors at his own expense,
and generally wins the people over. But, says Cicero:

> He did not put himself in the senate's power (*non commisit se
> patribus*), but, after Tarquin's burial, consulted the people with
> regard to his own power, and when they had bidden him to be king,

> caused a curiate law to be passed confirming his royal authority
> (*se ipse consuluit iussusque regnare*). (2.38)

So here, as a result of Servius' demagogic measures, popular support helps him retain power in the face of a hostile Senate. By contrast, Livy says that Servius at first rules without popular authorisation, but with the consent of the *patres* (1.41.6); only later, in an attempt to secure his power, does Servius court the people, and make them vote him the kingship (1.46.1). The confusion of the sources over whether Servius becomes king with the consent of the *patres*, or of the people, and whether this happens at the start of his reign, or only later, shows that there was no common tradition on this point.[16] What is quite clear is that there is no *interregnum* before he comes to power, making his rule technically illegitimate (so DH 4.31.2, 4.40.1). He is a fondly remembered ruler, but an improperly elected king.

The last king, Tarquinius Superbus, also rules without the consent of the senate or people. He usurps the throne by murdering Servius, and does not bother to obtain the consent either of the people or the gods. He puts senators to death and rules by fear and force (Livy 1.49.1–4). In contrast to Servius, Superbus is portrayed as a tyrant in the worse sense.

Magdelain notes the change in procedure between the early and the 'Etruscan' kings recorded by Livy and Dionysius. He argues that their description of the former was based on the Republican inter-regnal practice, while the latter, in which no *interrex* appears, and in which *auctoritas patrum* plays no part, bears the mark of authenticity.[17] Although he fails to note the tradition that Tarquinius Priscus, the 'Etruscan' king *par excellence*, undergoes an election with *inter-reges*, his belief that the take over of the last two kings is more authentic seems reasonable, since it is difficult to accept many aspects of the tradition on the earlier regal *interregna*.

There is certainly no need to assume that the full technicalities of the procedure date from the regal period, since the complex process described by the literary sources is undoubtedly influenced in part by later Republican practice.[18] Livy's description of the inauguration ritual is very possibly based on that of the *rex sacrorum* in his own day (1.18.6-10; cf. DH 1.86.1–4), while Ogilvie may be right to suggest that the tradition on the monarchical *interregna* was elaborated in consequence of Sulla's revival of the office.[19] But even if the full inter-regnal mechanism of the monarchy was largely reconstructed by the annalists on the assumption that it was the same as that of the consuls, the very name of the institution is surely enough to demonstrate its regal origins.[20] It is reasonable to assume that the *patres* and other representatives of the community played a part in the interregnal procedure of the regal period, and the concept of acclamation may also be genuine.

The existence of an *interregnum* also demonstrates that the death of one king did not mean the immediate creation of another – the process of obtaining the kingship was more complicated than that. Moreover, it suggests that in archaic Rome something akin to the widespread theory of the king's 'Two Bodies' existed: the king might die or be deposed but the kingship, symbolising the state, endured. The Romans had a concept of kingship that was separate from the person of the king.

WHY AN *INTERREGNUM*?

Various interpretations of the function of the *interregnum* are possible. It could be seen as an emergency measure to ensure the succession and the internal stability of the state on occasions when the king died with no obvious successor (as it worked in the Republic, only coming into operation when consuls died or resigned). It could be argued, then, that the literary sources were wrong to assume that the *interregnum* was a permanent feature of the accession process. Alternatively the *interregnum* could be seen as a standard feature of the succession (as it was viewed in the sources). If we accept that the *interregnum* was a regular procedure, we then have to determine its true importance. Was it a key part of the accession process, and one in which the *patres* exercised a controlling interest? Or was it merely a formality whereby the interest groups of the Roman state formally acknowledged the power of a new ruler?

The literary sources portray the *interregnum* as the means by which the *patres* installed the man of their choice as the new king. Several factors, however, suggest that ancient writers fundamentally misunderstood the archaic reality. Notably, the actual choice of the new king is never clearly defined, and there is no obvious mechanism for making such a choice; that there was only ever one candidate strongly suggests that the *interrex* did not himself have a free choice (as is hinted at by the tradition).[21] All this probably indicates that kings often imposed themselves on Rome rather than being elected voluntarily by the Romans. Typically the kings of Rome are outsiders (perhaps conquerors) and never patricians. Some kings are killed by their successors:

Ancus, for example, is said to have killed Tullus (DH 3.35.2). Only Numa dies in his bed.

The kingship is usually regarded as elective, the chief evidence for this being the ancient descriptions of the *interregnum* procedure.[22] However, the king's 'election' is better viewed as a ceremony whereby the new ruler accepts the homage of his new subjects, receives the approval of the gods, and thereby legitimates his authority. The ceremony reconciles the chief elements of society (elders, religious authorities, army and so on) to the new order, and creates the basis for a working relationship between ruler and ruled. It would have been rational and convenient for many new rulers to maintain the traditional hierarchy, and it is not hard to understand why even a conquering king might submit himself to the usual procedures for obtaining the kingship proper. Equally, it is obvious why a tyrant might choose to spurn election rituals, and instead look to other methods of reinforcing his power.

In side-stepping the normal rituals of election Servius and Superbus are, plainly, 'unconstitutional' rulers, despite the fact that they appear in the king-list. They may have felt politically and militarily secure enough to ignore the procedure entirely. The fact that no *interregnum* is recorded for them is not the only indication of their unconstitutional, 'tyrannical' status: note also their attempts to enhance their charisma and legitimate their regimes by associating themselves with particular deities (best seen in the case of Servius and the goddess Fortuna).[23] That Servius and Superbus both successfully hold on to power for years demonstrates that in practice the *interregnum* is an option and not a prerequisite.[24]

KINGSHIP AND TYRANNY IN THE LITERARY TRADITION

It has long been argued that in the Republic the Romans were neurotically obsessed with the idea of kings. According to Mommsen, Superbus' behaviour caused the name of king to be regarded thereafter with 'blind hatred' in Rome.[25] Walsh speaks of Livy's 'almost pathological abhorrence of kingship at Rome'; Andrewes writes that 'the mere word *rex* aroused prejudice, and the first emperor had to pretend that he was no more than an unusually influential citizen'.[26] There is some support for this view in the sources. For example, Cicero writes that when Superbus was banished, the title of king came to be as bitterly hated by the Romans as it had been desired after the death of Romulus (*Rep.* 2.52, cf. Livy 1.17.6–9). However, Roman anti-monarchism may be interpreted in another way, as the well-known cases of *adfectatio regni* suggest.

Spurius Cassius was put to death in 486 BC after sponsoring an agrarian law. Spurius Maelius was killed in 439, following a grain distribution to the plebs during a famine. Manlius Capitolinus was executed in 384 BC after paying the debts of the poor.[27] To these semi-legendary stories we may add, for example, those of Caesar, and the Gracchi. Plutarch records that when Attalus Philometer of Pergamum died in 133 BC, naming the Roman people as his heir, Tiberius Gracchus offended the senate by proposing that the king's money should be distributed among the citizens who received public land; it was claimed there that Eudemus of Pergamum had given Gracchus a diadem and purple robe, 'believing that he was going to be king in Rome' (*Ti. Gracchus* 14.1–2). The common theme of all these cases is a presumed attempt at obtaining the kingship via the 'purchase' of popular support. To be the champion of the populace is the traditional role of the tyrant. Is not the Roman anti-monarchical tradition better seen as an anti-tyrannical tradition? We should recall that because Latin has no native word for 'tyranny', the term *regnum* ('kingship') was employed to express this concept. The characteristic features of (bad) tyrannical rule are *vis*, *superbia*, *libido* and *crudelitas*, all vices which threatened aristocratic *libertas*.[28] Thus it could be argued that the Roman aristocracy feared not so much kingly, as popular and anti-aristocratic, rule, which would have cut into their jealously guarded powers and privileges.[29] They were right to be afraid: the Augustan monarchy brought the end of aristocratic *libertas*, and emperors often found it politically advisable to pander to the Roman mob.

The Romans did not remember their kings unkindly. Statues of the kings stood on the Capitol in the late Republic (Dio 43.45, Livy 6.41.3). Every king but the last was viewed favourably and openly recognised as having benefited the state, a tradition which can be traced back to our earliest literary sources. Romulus is the founder of the city itself, and revered as a god (certainly in the later Republic; perhaps also much earlier); Numa is the creator of Rome's ancient priestly colleges. The warrior Tullus Hostilius subdues Rome's mother-city Alba Longa; Ancus Marcius enlarges the city and creates a port for Rome at Ostia. Tarquinius Priscus expands the senate, and builds the Circus Maximus and the Roman Games; Servius reorganises Roman social and political structures. In the Roman tradition, then, '*every king contributed many good and useful institutions*' (Cic. *Rep.* 2.37).

Only Tarquinius Superbus is consistently abhorred (although, Livy grudgingly admits, he is a pretty good general: 1.53.1). He is an acknowledged tyrant (DH 8.5.4). *His* behaviour, Cicero says, made the title of 'king' hateful to the Romans (*Rep.* 1.62, cf. 1.64). Even his name, Superbus, is a deliberately constructed aspect of the tradition: *superbia*, or *hubris*, is the standard characteristic of a tyrant.[30] In Livy, the references are not to bad kings but to bad old Tarquinius Superbus. The good citizen Tarquinius Collatinus is sent into exile, merely out of hatred for his name (Livy 4.15.4, DH 8.49.6, Cic. *Rep.* 2.53); Augustine comments that a change of name might have done just as well (*Civ. Dei* 3.16). Here it is clearly possession of the name of Tarquin which causes problems for its bearers.[31] The name becomes a slur: Livy records that the decemvirs were punished for their kingly arrogance (*ob superbiam regiam*, a pun on the name of Superbus), and calls them 'ten Tarquins' (not kings) (3.39.3, cf. 3.43.1; DH 10.60.1). Sextius and Licinius are 'Tarquin-tribunes' (Livy 6.40.11).

Superbus' characterisation in the tradition as a tyrant is important because it specifically distances him from the legitimate, honoured kingship of Numa and the rest. Erskine suggests that the tradition on Superbus' tyranny was worked up in the late Republic.[32] It is, however, quite possible that the historical Superbus was indeed a tyrant, and that his nickname could have arisen at an early date, perhaps even during his reign. We know that other tyrants were operating in Italy at about this period, in Magna Graecia, and probably in Etruria, if we can interpret Thefarie Velianas of Caere as such (see further below). Moreover, Superbus behaves much like a Greek tyrant. He is credited with a large-scale building programme, including the erection of seats in the Circus Maximus, and the construction of the Cloaca Maxima (Livy 1.55.1–56.2). The building of the Capitoline temple (confirmed by recent archaeological work as dating to the second half of the sixth century BC) is conceived in part as a memorial to Superbus' reign (Livy 1.55.1: *monumentum regni sui nominisque relinqueret*). Greek tyrants also encouraged the development of urban structures such as temples, public buildings and markets; if Ure is to be believed, they were early capitalists.[33] It is surely no coincidence that early Rome's development into a *polis*-type community reached a peak during Superbus' reign. Some scholars attribute this feature of the tradition to annalistic invention on the basis of Greek models, but the archaeological record strongly supports the idea that Rome in the late sixth century was developing in this way. Later annalists did not invent all this.

The fall of the monarchy, whether we interpret it as a revolution or as a palace coup, is entirely an aristocratic movement, stemming from the fears and ambitions of the nobility. It includes no real elements of popular resentment. Indeed the evidence for popular hatred of monarchy is limited.[34] Even amongst the nobility, it was generally accepted that the kings had presided over the infancy of the state to its advantage. The significance of anti-monarchism at Rome seems to have been exaggerated by modern scholars (though there is no doubt that anti-monarchical feeling did exist in certain spheres). To counter the idea of the hatred of the title *rex*, we need only note that this was an honoured title of Jupiter. We may also cite the respect with which a supposedly anti-regal historian like Livy can treat foreign kings such as Massinissa (e.g. 28.35.12). The Roman state was happy to deal with client kings, acknowledging their right to *be* kings; there are even instances in which the triumphal gear (insignia of the Roman kings) was awarded to foreign rulers as a mark of honour. Some *gentes* were proud to claim descent from a Roman king, and the Marcii Reges held that name without any apparent trouble during the Republic. Moreover, at the very moment when Rome reverted to monarchy, Virgil in his *Aeneid* could refer to kingship frequently and positively, without strongly contrasting *regnum* and *libertas*.[35]

Although anti-monarchical feeling is primarily an aristocratic construct, and one to which undue emphasis has been given, to some extent it probably did have a bearing on the tradition. The problem is to determine how far our evidence has been affected, and whether we can identify and deal with the distortions thus created, in order to discover the 'reality' of kingship at Rome.[36] I would argue that these distortions are limited, and on the whole easily identifiable. Antipathy towards monarchy (or tyranny) seems to have affected the tradition on the famous examples of *adfectatio regni* (which supposedly threatened aristocratic *libertas*) more than it affected the tradition on the regal period. Aristocratic manipulation may, however, have affected the tradition on the fall of the monarchy, perhaps in order to credit the nobility with the creation of *libertas* at Rome. A variant tradition, for example (Tacitus *Hist.* 3.72; cf. Pliny *NH* 34.139), has led some scholars to suggest that monarchy was brought to an end by Lars Porsenna's brief conquest of Rome (this is hinted at even in the Livian version). Yet other aspects of the tradition on the kings appear free from anti-monarchical contamination, for example the basic features of the king's role (such as his military functions and supervision of the state's religious and administrative system).

A further problem is to what extent Roman awareness of contemporary and near-contemporary kingship affected the tradition on Rome's own kings. According to Erskine, who sees Roman hatred of kingship as derived from contact with Hellenistic monarchs, the latter 'were fundamental in forming the conception of kingship held by Romans in the late Republic. Indeed they even affected Roman perceptions of their own kings'.[37] However, the nature of the Roman kingship as portrayed in the literary tradition suggests that this system of kingship was not invented by the annalists on the basis of their knowledge of Hellenistic monarchies, which bear little resemblance to the Roman model. Moreover, in the accounts of the Roman monarchy we find unusual elements which cannot have been copied from Hellenistic models. Encoded in stories of the regal period, the tradition has preserved at least in part the authentic pattern of Roman kingship.

CONCLUSION

Examination of the literary tradition shows that there is a clear pattern to the election of the kings, which is distorted in the later monarchy. Contrary to the common view, it is not the last three 'Etruscan kings' who are thus highlighted as 'unconstitutional rulers', nor merely the last, avowedly 'tyrannical' ruler. Instead, both (good) Servius Tullius *and* (bad) Tarquinius Superbus are tyrants rather than kings. The quite different attributes, and levels of respect, awarded to these two figures highlights the widely differing nature of archaic tyranny, which is far from being a standardised 'negative' construct: Servius is a tyrant (by and large) without the tyranny. Instead, tyranny can be viewed as one of the responses made towards a rapidly changing, urbanised society, with competing class and status interests.[38]

Contemporary responses were emerging across the Mediterranean. In Italy at the turn of the sixth/fifth century BC we see a number of rulers who can plausibly be interpreted as tyrants. In inscriptions set up at the emporion sanctuary of Pyrgi, the port of Caere, Thefarie Velianas describes himself as *zilath* (in Etruscan) and *melek* (in Punic) of Caere.[39] This is one of the earliest occurrences of the title *zilath*, which normally signifies a magistrate, and while *melek* can refer to a magistrate, it generally means 'king'. If Velianas was a magistrate, he was not annually elected (the the text informs us that he has already been in power for three years), and he seems to lack colleagues.

All this suggests that he was the holder of power for life, and that his rule represents some sort of intermediate (tyrannical?) stage between monarchical and magisterial government.[40]

Leaving aside this important independent evidence, the ancient literary sources provide further evidence of a phase of tyranny in archaic Central Italy. It seems likely, for example, that the men who are said to have assisted Superbus in his struggle to regain power at Rome were themselves tyrants. First there is Octavius Mamilius of Tusculum, who commands Superbus' troops at the battle of Lake Regillus (Livy 2.19.3–20.13) and who is characterised by our sources as the most powerful of the Latins (Livy 1.49.9; DH 4.45.1, 4.47.4). Mamilius is, furthermore, Superbus' son-in-law. Superbus can be seen to be acting in a way similar to contemporary Greek tyrants, who tend to marry into the families of other tyrants, creating defensive alliances in order to maintain dynastic power in the face of rising aristocratic opposition.[41] Alongside Mamilius, Superbus is aided by Lars Porsenna of Clusium (DH 5.21.3; Livy 2.9.1), a figure who dominates the history of late sixth- early fifth-century Central Italy, operating as far afield as Northern Etruria and Campania. Although it is hard to make firm statements about the nature of power in archaic Etruscan cities, Porsenna may very well have been a tyrant.[42] Another likely candidate is Superbus' own son Sextus Tarquinius, said to have become chief magistrate (according to Livy 1.54.4; cf. 1.60.2), *stratê-gos* (general, according to Cassius Dio 2 = Zonaras 7.10) or supreme commander (*autokratôr*, according to Dionysius 4.55.4, 4.58.4, 4.85.4) of Gabii. Finally, there is Aristodemus, explicitly described as the tyrant of Cumae (DH 6.21.3), at whose court Superbus ends his days.

Rome's last kings, like Velianas and the other figures mentioned above, can be seen as forming part of a brief phase of tyranny, a transitional stage of government in a period of rapid social and political change, when 'the state' was a comparatively weak entity. The Roman context is one of contest and negotiation between social groupings, in which, ultimately, one-man rule lost out to the Republican aristocratic consensus.[43] It is an open question whether Rome's tyrants were directly mimicking their Greek counterparts, or whether instead, and as a result of its well-documented interactions with the archaic Mediterranean world, the city shared in the kinds of social and political trends that formed the Greek experience of tyranny.

NOTES

1. The clearest treatment of the period is provided by Cornell 1995; for the size of Rome, its population and its territory, and the level of Roman power during the sixth century BC, see his chapter 8.
2. See e.g. John Lydus, *Mag.* 1.5 on Romulus as a tyrant, among other reasons, 'because he killed his brother'.
3. Livy 1.32.1: *regem populus creavit*; 1.22.1–2: *regem populus iussit, patres auctores facti*. In fact the ancient sources differ as to whether the senate or people effectively elect the king. In Dionysius, for example, the people usually vote to ratify the decision of the senate; in Livy, the people vote and the *patres* afterwards give their confirmation.
4. Livy 6.41.5–6. See Cornell 1995: ch. 10 for this view, following Magdelain and Momigliano. Cf. Linderski 1990.
5. Ogilvie 1965: 87–8, comments that the *interregnum* was 'doubtless first created on the expulsion of the kings'; on the patriciate, see e.g. Leifer 1931: 90. That the patriciate existed under the monarchy is also denied by Magdelain 1964, who argues that the patriciate was formed c. 509–433 by the *gentes*, who provided chief magistrates. Cf. Last 1945; Momigliano 1967. Cornell 1995: 251–2 believes that the patriciate existed in some form in the regal period.
6. The *interregnum* was supposedly restored in 509 BC, when Brutus appointed Sp. Lucretius as *interrex* to preside over the election of the first consuls, 'following ancestral custom' (DH 4.76.1, 4.84.5).
7. Dionysius 2.58.1 is concerned to offer a rationalising explanation as to why the *patres* chose as king a neutral candidate from outside their own number.
8. Mitchell 1990: 130 sees the *patres* as hereditary priests who found a place in the senate only as the king's advisers.
9. Wirszubski 1950: 111.
10. Cic. *Rep.* 2.25, 2.35; cf. *Leg. Agr.* 2.20, 2.26 ff.
11. Coli 1951 argued that the *lex curiata* was Republican because *imperium* was not a monarchical power; Magdelain 1968: 30, 33 suggested that the *lex* was attributed to the kings because it operated for the magistrates, and the Romans saw consular *imperium* as following on from that of the kings. Cf. Nichols 1967; Staveley 1954 (with bibliography); Staveley 1972: 123; De Martino 1972: 156.
12. On the *curiae*, see Smith 2005.
13. Coli 1951: 385. Also suggested by Botsford 1909: 183–4; Staveley 1972: 122.
14. Cf. Caesar's acclamation as 'king': Cassius Dio 44.10.1, Plut. *Caes.* 60.1, Suet. *Caes.* 79. Magdelain 1968: 32–3, argues that acclamation is particularly a feature of the election of the 'Etruscan' kings, where the *interregnum* is absent, but my examples show how common acclamations are prior to this.

15. Livy 1.46.1: *Servius quamquam iam usu haud dubie regnum possederat*. On Servius' election, see Thomsen 1980: 10, 108–12.
16. De Francisci 1959: 726.
17. Magdelain 1968: 31–2.
18. Guarino 1948, for example, argued for a Republican origin; cf. Staveley 1956: 83.
19. Ogilvie 1965: 88.
20. There is no need to assume, with Magdelain, that the regal *interregnum* was totally different from that of the Republic. Magdelain 1968 argued that the monarchical *interrex* took the place of the king after the Regifugium (24 February) and held office as 'king' for the five supernumary days separating the end of the old year and the beginning of the new one. However, it is difficult to see how the Republican *interrex* could have grown out of this hypothetical sacral replacement for the king.
21. Several rulers act as the advisers or military aides of their predecessors. Tarquinius Priscus becomes the trusted adviser of Ancus Marcius (Livy 1.34.12); Servius serves in Priscus' army (DH 4.3.2); Brutus, the first consul, is tribune of the *celeres* under Superbus (Livy 1.59.7). Cf. Aeneas, who holds sacred power alongside Latinus; and Numa Marcius, son-in-law of Numa and father of Ancus: Martin 1982: 117. On this basis it is sometimes argued that each king nominated his successor. If so, it is noteworthy that the choice of 'heir' is never a son, even when the king has sons living (as with Ancus). Clearly the monarchy is not inherited, at least not in direct succession from father to son.
22. See e.g. Botsford 1909: 183. This has given rise to the idea that the king was a magistrate, but this need not be the case even if the kings were routinely elected. In early medieval Europe, for example, election and inheritance often went hand in hand. In any case, the 'election' of Rome's kings may have represented the confirmation of a *fait accompli* rather than the outright creation of a new king.
23. This is related to ideas in many cultures concerning kingship, power, female divinity and cult practice, and should not be lightly dismissed as a late myth manufactured on the basis of Greek models. Note the association of Thefarie Velianas of Caere (below) with Uni, the Etruscan Juno, a goddess raised to great prominence at Rome with the foundation of the Capitoline temple by his contemporary Superbus.
24. The *interregnum* does not prove that any particular sector of society could choose the king, or have any real say in the government. It could simply be seen as a process whereby the major power groupings in the state, the *populus* and the *patres*, publicly acknowledged their submission to the new ruler.
25. Mommsen 1908: 316.
26. Walsh 1961: 16; Andrewes 1956: 21.
27. See Smith, chapter 4 in this volume, for these and other examples.

28. See Dunkle 1967. On the concept of *libertas*, see Brunt 1988; Wirszubski 1950. The *libido* connected with the name of Tarquin belongs to Superbus' son, Sextus, the rapist of Lucretia – perhaps himself a tyrant (see below).
29. Cf. for example Andrewes 1956: 7; White 1955: 8–9; Béranger 1935.
30. Ure 1922: 8.
31. Similarly possession of the Claudian name causes Appius Claudius difficulties in 310 BC, when a tribune declares: 'This name is far more hostile to your liberty than that of the Tarquins' (Livy 9.34.5). A. Griffiths, 'Where did early Roman history come from?', http://www.ucl.ac.uk/GrandLat/people/griffiths/collatin.htm may be right to point out the parallel ('rip-off') with the story of the ostracism of Hipparchus son of Charmus (*Ath. Pol.* 22.4), whose native deme was Kollutos, but the fact is that the name of Tarquin *does* have clear negative associations in our literary sources.
32. Erskine 1991: 120.
33. Ure 1922, *passim*. Cf. White 1955: 10–11.
34. Although Livy remarks of Spurius Cassius that the people rejected his offer to repay money due to them as an attempt to buy regal power, 'so much did their inherent suspicion of monarchy make them scornful of his gifts' (2.41.9).
35. Of course, that could be because of Virgil's relationship to the new monarch, Augustus. See Cairns 1989: 1ff.; Murray 1964–5; Venturini 1988: 466.
36. On kingship in the Roman tradition, see Classen 1965; Giua 1967; Bellen 1991; Grimal 1986.
37. Erskine 1991: 120.
38. A further response is the separation of the religious and politico-military authority of the ruler, which can be dated to the sixth century BC; for further discussion and bibliography, see Glinister 1995: Pt 2, ch. 1, and cf. Cornell 1995: 232–6.
39. *TLE*[2] 874–6; *CIE* 6314–16. On the inscriptions, see e.g. Pfiffig 1965: 29 ff.
40. His tenure in power and his ambiguous regal or magisterial status calls to mind P. Valerius Publicola, whom Roman tradition credits with a string of consulships at the end of the sixth century. Note that monarchical government seems to have continued at Caere longer than in many other Etruscan and Latin centres: one of Thefarie's successors, Orgulnius, is described in a Latin Julio-Claudian honorific inscription as a *rex*, whom Spurinna, a Tarquinian magistrate, seems to have expelled from power, probably in the fifth century (the date is disputed): see Torelli 1975: 39–42, 71–2; cf. Cornell 1978.
41. Tyrants also tend to marry within their own family circle, within degrees of relationship that would in ordinary circumstances be considered incestuous (Gernet 1981). Thus at Rome the daughters of Servius marry close relatives, who are either their uncles (mothers' brothers) (e.g. Livy 1.46.4–5, 1.42.1, representing the majority of the sources, including Fabius Pictor) or their first cousins (DH 4.7.5, 4.28.1, following L. Piso Frugi). On either view, the

marriage of Tullia and Superbus falls within the customary six degrees of relationship within which marriage at Rome was normally strictly prohibited: Bettini 1988.

42. Latin and Greek literary sources are ill-informed about Etruscan rulers (at any rate ones that look historical), although in the 430s BC a king of Veii is named as Lars Tolumnius (Livy 4.19.5, 4.17.3, 8, 4.19.5, 4.32.4; Cassius Dio 44.4.3; 51.24.4). The Veientes are said to have reverted to (elective) monarchy in 403 BC after series of annual magistracies (Livy 5.1.3–7 – the sole reference to the creation of an Etruscan king).

43. Under Servius in particular Rome is said to have undergone radical social reorganisation (Livy 1.42–3); see e.g. Smith 1997. The origins of the change from monarchy via tyranny to oligarchy seem rather similar across Central Italy (economic problems, social discontent, and increasing aristocratic power), although the timescale varies from city to city.

CHAPTER 3

Ducetius and fifth-century Sicilian tyranny

Trinity Jackman

INTRODUCTION

From Hippocrates to Dionysius, fifth-century Sicily produced some of the most powerful tyrants of the Greek world. This autocratic tendency was not limited to the Hellenic populations of the island: Ducetius, a native Sicel, created a Sicel *synteleia*, or federation, that at its height controlled a large portion of east-central Sicily. Despite a classical historiographical tradition that generally had little interest in Sicily's native peoples, Ducetius, in his territorial conquests, shifting alliances and conflicts with the Greek colonies, emerges as a major political actor in Diodorus Siculus' Sicilian narrative for the years 466–440 BC.[1] The figure of Ducetius provides a brief glimpse into the Sicel world and it is rare to encounter a discussion of Sicel identity, culture or 'Hellenisation', without at least a passing reference to his life. Yet, although the corpus of work that aims to decipher Ducetius' ethnic identity continues to grow, political historians – who generally pass over Ducetius completely in discussions of Sicilian tyranny – have ignored the broader implications of his territorial and political conquests.[2]

Explaining Ducetius' actions exclusively through the framework of Greek-native identity underestimates his importance within the wider socio-political realities of fifth-century Sicily. Ducetius' career highlights both the dense web of interconnections between native and Greek elites and how each group responded to the territorial pressures of a landscape populated with aggressive and expansionist states. Moreover, this analysis of Ducetius within his socio-political context can help illuminate some of the cultural questions that dominate current scholarship of the 'Hellenisation' of the native peoples

I would like to thank the participants at the conference 'Tyrants, Kings, Dynasts and Generals: Modes of Autocracy in the Classical Period' for their comments and insights. I am also grateful for Ian Morris and Jack Mitchell for reading earlier drafts of this paper.

of the Greek colonial world. Rather than a political oddity of limited
interest, Ducetius was one of the more powerful autocratic rulers of
fifth-century Sicily, and hence deserves a place in any discussion of
classical tyranny.

My chapter is divided into four sections. In the first I give a brief
account of the life of Ducetius as recounted by Diodorus Siculus. In
the second section, I examine the nature of Ducetius' *synteleia*, as well
as his role in Sicel political development more generally, arguing that
his importance in Sicel state-formation is often overemphasised. In
the third section, I place Ducetius in the context of current discussions
of the 'Hellenisation' of native peoples, suggesting that although his
actions are normally interpreted through the spectrum of ethnic identity, this is not the most fruitful way of understanding his political
motivations. In the fourth section I locate Ducetius' *synteleia* within
the trend towards the creation of multi-*poleis* states and alliances in
Sicily, and suggest that redistributing land, relocating populations
and refounding cities were not actions limited to Greek tyrants, but a
response to the political realities of fifth-century Sicily.

LIFE OF DUCETIUS

Ducetius emerged on the political arena of eastern Sicily during a
period of immense social change. Two years earlier, the last Deinomenid tyrant, Polyzelus, had been expelled from Syracuse. Polyzelus'
brothers, Gelon and Hieron, had followed aggressive territorially
expansionist policies, absorbing previously autonomous cities into an
empire centred on Syracuse. Under their successive rules, Syracuse
grew to be one of the largest Greek cities in the Mediterranean,
absorbing parts of the populations of Gela, Camarina, Euboea,
Leontini and Megara Hyblaea, as well as 10,000 resettled mercenaries. Gelon's successor and brother, Hieron, had transferred the populations of Naxos and Catana to Leontini. In 476 BC, he refounded
Catana, renaming the city Aetna, and annexed land from Sicel territory to create allotments for 10,000 settlers composed mostly of his
former mercenaries.[3]

Diodorus writes that after the fall of the Deinomenids the Greek
city-states regained their autonomy and instituted democratic regimes.
Greeks who had often been forcibly transplanted began returning to
their home cities, whereas at Syracuse mercenaries enrolled as citizens
under the tyrants were expelled (11.76.4–6). In 461 BC, the new
Syracusan state turned its attention to the mercenaries-turned-settlers

Figure 3.1 Map of ancient Sicily

at Aetna, one of the few groups that had remained loyal to Polyzelus. The Syracusan forces met up with a Sicel army led by Ducetius, which aimed to reclaim the territory Hieron had taken from the Sicels.[4] Victorious, the Syracusans and Sicels divided the territory of Aetna between them (11.76.1–4). Next, Ducetius refounded his native city of Menai, as well as founding a settlement near the important Sicel cult centre of Palike. He then went on to redistribute land within the territories of both cities.[5] It was during this period that Ducetius presumably consolidated his power as leader of a Sicel *synteleia*, a federation of Sicel cities and towns. Apparently, Ducetius' federation met with some opposition, as Hybla refused to join and a series of unknown events led to Ducetius' destruction of Morgantina (11.78.5, 88.4–5).

Ducetius soon turned his attention to the hinterlands of the Greek colonies. In 451 BC, he seized Inessa, a Sicel town where the refugees from Aetna had fled. He then attacked Motyum, a garrison of Acragas. The Acragantini, allied with the Syracusans, marched out against Ducetius' forces. They were unsuccessful, and the Syracusans executed their general, Bolcon, under the suspicion that he had had secret dealings with Ducetius. The next campaign went more smoothly for the Syracusans. When the tide of battle turned against the Sicel forces, many of Ducetius' soldiers deserted, fleeing back to their home cities in the interior (11.91.1–4). When defeat seemed inevitable, Ducetius himself fled, not to Menai or Palike but to Syracuse, where he seated himself as a supplicant at the altar in the agora (11.92.1). A meeting of the Syracusan assembly was called to decide his fate. Those accustomed to speak at the assembly called for punishment, but the 'better sort of men' (*charientes*) called for moderation, arguing that they should spare a supplicant at their altars. These men persuaded the people, and Ducetius, with an allowance, was exiled to Corinth (11.92.2–4).

This is not the end of Ducetius' remarkable story. Diodorus writes that in 446 BC a war broke out between the Syracusans and Acragantini over the return of Ducetius and his foundation of a colony called Cale Acte. On the urging of an oracle, Ducetius had apparently left Corinth with a group of Greek colonists, to found a new city on the north shore of Sicily. He was joined by Sicel colonists, including Archonidas, ruler of Herbita. The details of the ensuing battle are vague, although the fighting seems to have drawn in many of the cities of Sicily, and the Acragantini sustained heavy losses (12.8.1–4). Ducetius remained at Cale Acte until his death in 440 BC (12.29.1).

DEFINITIONS AND SOURCES

Is Ducetius the equivalent of a Greek tyrant? The use of the term *tyrannos*, from its emergence in the lyric poets, through the classical period, has been well documented.[6] Although both Thucydides (1.13.1) and Aristotle (*Politics* 1279a32–b7) stress the unconstitutional nature of tyranny, such straightforward definitions belie the fact that the term was so embedded in popular discourse by the classical period (at least in Athens) that there was considerable doubt over who could be called a tyrant, what sort of actions were considered tyrannical, and whether such actions in fact were always so terrible.[7] Generally, the term *tyrannos* was pejorative; Pindar calls Hieron by the more flattering *basileus* (*Pythian* 1.60) and early in the fourth century the Athenians called Dionysius I by the term *archôn* (*IG* II² 105.32–4). Definitional ambiguities surrounding the term *tyranny* have been further magnified by some scholars' reluctance to include the immensely powerful and chronologically late fifth-century Sicilian tyrants in the same category as those of the archaic Aegean.[8]

Although Diodorus never calls Ducetius *tyrannos*, the latter is referred to variously as *dynastês*, *hêgemôn* and *basileus*.[9] Even the name Ducetius may not be a real name but rather a title similar to the Latin *dux*.[10] He is further described as making himself the leader of a *synteleia*, a federation of Sicel towns. Judging from Diodorus' use of this term elsewhere, the Sicel *synteleia* was a hierarchical federation that may have given a privileged role to Ducetius' home city of Menai.[11]

There is the problem of how much trust historians can place in Diodorus' narrative. Diodorus' monumental *Bibliotheke* do contain inconsistencies and anachronisms, although his reputation among modern historians has improved significantly in the past twenty years.[12] In Ducetius' refoundation of cities, transplantation of populations and redistribution of land, he employed strategies akin to those of the Deinomenid tyrants and of the later Dionysius I. This raises the possibility that Diodorus or his earlier sources were eliding the exploits of Ducetius with these Greek tyrants. Yet Diodorus appears to draw on both Ephorus and Timaeus for the Ducetian episode, and as he shows no particular interest in the Sicels elsewhere in his narrative (they usually appear as an amorphous mass of cities referenced only when at war with the Greeks), it seems unlikely that Diodorus would fabricate this episode.[13] It was undoubtedly Ducetius' tyrannical behaviour that interested Diodorus in the first place, as Diodorus details the exploits of the Deinomenids and Dionysii, while giving only a brief account of the period of Syracusan democracy.

Diodorus' narrative seems corroborated (or at least not contradicted) by the archaeological evidence. Fieldwork at Palike has shown that although there is evidence of an earlier archaic occupation at the summit of Rocchicella, there was a large-scale refoundation of the site, connected by the excavators to the activities of Ducetius.[14] A similar refoundation appears to have occurred at Menai.[15] There is also a destruction level from this period in the Citadella settlement at Morgantina and a subsequent refoundation.[16]

There are good reasons to see Ducetius as a genuine autocrat. Yet
it is impossible to tell from Diodorus' narrative whether Ducetius'
role marked a significant point of departure from previous Sicel
social relations. Archaeologically there is evidence for Sicel elites in
the archaic and classical periods. Mortuary remains suggest significant social complexity at Sicel sites, with 'elite' burials found at
Morgantina, Sant'Angelo Muxaro, Polizzello, Mt Adranone and
Menai, although mortuary data alone can be a dangerously one-sided
way of measuring social complexity.[17] The fragmentary epigraphic
record may provide some illumination; a monumental inscription
from Mendolito, dating to the second half of the sixth century, suggests the presence of a large assembly with a smaller group within
it.[18] In his discussion of the founding of Cale Acte in 447–6 BC,
Diodorus also refers to a Sicel leader (*dynastês*) named Archonidas of
Herbita. Thucydides would later mention another Archonidas, who
in 413 was a *philos* of the Athenians (Thuc. 7.1.4), and was referred
to as *basileus* of the Sicels. The recurrence of this name may suggest
a potential dynasty among some Sicel groups, and an aristocratic
society.[19] Ducetius himself was, as Diodorus notes, from a famous
family (Diod. 11.78.5). Combined, these various strands of evidence
point to a Sicel society that was hierarchical and possibly oligarchic
and suggest that Ducetius, in the same manner as many Greek tyrants,
extended his own personal authority by carving out for himself a new
position in Sicel society.

However, because the source material for Ducetius is so exceptionally rich compared to what we know for any other native figure
in Sicilian ancient history, there is a danger of overestimating his significance for fifth-century Sicel society. Galvagno has claimed that
through his population transfers and refoundation of cities, Ducetius
transformed Sicel society from a series of loosely connected villages
to a *polis*-type society, ushering in a 'political phase' of Sicel state formation.[20] Hence Ducetius not only acted in the same manner as a
Greek tyrant, but in fact remade Sicel society, using a Greek political
mould. Yet, it is suspicious that Sicels underwent a profound political
transformation the moment details of internal Sicel political dynamics appear for the first time in the textual record. Ducetius was probably less of a bridge between two types of Sicel society than a figure
who stands at a disciplinary divide between the prehistorians who
study the archaeological remains of Sicily's native populations and
classical historians who study the island's political history based on
textual and epigraphic evidence.[21] Archaeological evidence does not

lend itself to the study of the issues that dominate Greek political history, such as the development of constitutions, citizenship and political institutions. The internal political dynamics of Sicel states may be lost to us, but this does not mean that they never existed. The apparent gulf between Greek and Sicel polities may not be a gulf between societies, but rather between the types of evidence used to describe them.

Yet archaeological and historical accounts are not incompatible. Instead, the archaeological record from sixth- and fifth-century Sicily should not be used just to verify Diodorus' account, but rather to understand long-term changes in Sicel culture. During the initial period of Greek colonisation, in the eighth and seventh centuries BC, some indigenous settlements close to the coastal regions were destroyed or abandoned. However, many inland settlements, such as Grammichele, Ramacca-Montagna, Morgantina, Paternò, Mendolito and Butera, saw continuous habitation throughout the archaic period and increased nucleation in the sixth century.[22] Although few field surveys have been undertaken in Sicily, a survey conducted around Morgantina shows infilling of the landscape and intensified land-use, particularly intensifying in the early fifth century.[23] Western Sicily saw similar processes of site nucleation in the late sixth century, with the abandonment of sites coinciding with the growth of larger urban centres.[24]

Ducetius came to power in a world that was already rapidly trans-forming. His actions were part of a wider pattern of the nucleation of native sites in the interior that had been accelerating since the sixth century. The changes in Sicel society were a lot bigger than Ducetius; attributing its transformation to the charismatic leadership of one 'Hellenised' individual is not only an oversimplification but also casts the Sicels in a passive, imitative role.

DUCETIUS AND HELLENISATION

Was Ducetius acting like a Greek tyrant? Early scholarship on Ducetius saw him as emblematic of the process of Hellenisation of the native Sicels; not only does Ducetius act like a Greek tyrant, but his adventures at Syracuse and Corinth show that he can obviously speak Greek and was familiar with Greek social customs.[25] Ducetius' Hellenised nature was seen as the natural outcome of a process which began at the start of Greek colonisation and which saw the native peoples of Sicily irresistibly drawn to a superior Hellenic culture.

In this model of cultural interaction, little distinction was made between the spread of Greek culture and the direct control of Sicel sites by Greeks, and often the presence of Greek material culture on archaeological sites was considered to indicate the presence of Greek colonists or rulers.[26]

This notion of Hellenisation has been increasingly problematised. Greek colonisation is no longer generally seen as analogous to the modern colonial experience.[27] At the same time, earlier interpretations of European colonisation themselves have been reformulated by the deep influence of postcolonial theory in the humanities and social sciences. Since the 1990s current events have been dominated by discussions of ethnic relations and globalisation, creating an intellectual environment where scholars have become more interested in the native populations with which the Greeks came into contact.[28] Hellenisation as a concept has been shown to be inadequate for its assumptions that cultural change was a one-way process, with the native populations as passive subjects. Scholars have turned their focus to the agency of native populations in their selective adaptation of Greek material culture to fit within their own internal social dynamics.[29]

For scholars who are anxious to demonstrate the agency of native groups, Ducetius' federation of Sicel towns has often been described as an 'ethnic revolt'. Undoubtedly claims to common ethnicity played a role in uniting Sicels in a federation, just as claims to a common Greekness may have served to unite at times the belligerent Greek colonies.[30] Yet it is unlikely whether 'freedom for the Sicels' was the rallying call for the Ducetian *synteleia*. First, although some Sicel communities may have paid tribute to the Deinomenid tyrants, many Sicel towns retained their autonomy. Although generally a poor source for internal Sicel dynamics, Diodorus does write that the city of Trinacria, identified by Galvagno with Palike, had never been conquered until its sack by Syracuse, in 440 BC.[31] Thucydides writes that the Sicels of the interior who sided with the Athenians against Syracuse in 425 BC had always been free, as opposed to the subjugated Sicels in the coastal regions (4.25). Rather than clamouring for their liberation, Ducetius' forces should be seen as taking advantage of a period of weakness and social unrest within the Greek city-states to carve out a greater territory for themselves. Second, the notion of a Sicel revolt reintroduces the Greek–Sicel binary that many critics of Hellenisation want to avoid. The Sicels themselves were not totally unified: the Sicel settlement and major cultic centre of Hybla refused to join Ducetius' *synteleia*. The establishment of Palike may have been an attempt to create a rival centre of power within the Sicel interior. The sacking of Morgantina again shows tensions between Sicel settlements. The Greek sources' presentation of the Sicels as a unified group may result more from ignorance or lack of interest on the part of Greek authors than a transcendental Sicel solidarity. Presumably the Sicels, like the Greeks, had a stronger allegiance to their home community than to their ethnic group. The sources are silent on inter-Sicel relations, although scholars may be presumptuous in assuming that even sacked native sites must have met their fate at the hands of the Greeks and were not products of inter-Sicel strife. Arguing that Ducetius' *synteleia* was a revolt again places the Sicels in a reactive role. Sicel towns were players in the shifting military alliances of the island well after the death of Ducetius.[32]

Ducetius was neither a freedom fighter nor a mimic of Greek tyrants. Both interpretations are opposite extremes that look to his ethnic identity to explain his political motivations. Rather, Ducetius was a player in a landscape composed of a series of polities bristling with territorial tensions. He could march against Syracuse and not be making a statement about opposition to Greekness; he could be on comfortable terms with Syracusans and Corinthians without being a Hellenised 'sell-out'. I am not downplaying the frequent violence involved in Greek colonisation and expansion; undoubtedly many Sicels met extremely unpleasant ends, yet their fates were not necessarily worse than those met by Greeks under both the tyrants and the subsequent democracies. Whatever the motivations of his followers, Ducetius' actions after the failure of the siege of Motyum suggest that he was no martyr for the Sicel cause; in the manner of most successful autocrats, Ducetius' ambition was tempered by a healthy dose of self-preservation.

Ducetius must be placed in his elite social context. A network of ritualised friendship linked the elites of the Greek *poleis* with each other and with the elites of the non-Greek world.[33] These inter-elite links were governed not by the claims of the *polis*, local community or ethnic group but rather by aristocratic values. Perhaps the embodiment of this tension of loyalties is found in the figure of Alcibiades, whose defection to the Spartans in the middle of the Peloponnesian War was probably smoothed over by his ancestral *xenos* Endius, son of the Spartan Alcibiades.[34] In turn, Alcibiades' flight to the Persian court would seem even more remarkable, although he was simply following in the footsteps of Pausanias, Demaratus and Themistocles.

The textual sources for *xenia* between the Sicilian elites are poor, although this is not surprising, given the nature of the source material; Herodotus and Thucydides both mention incidents from Sicilian history, but other sources which detail Aegean relations of guest-friendship, namely Xenophon and the Attic orators, barely touch on the island. Despite this, there are examples of Sicilian Greek relations of *xenia* with non-Greeks. The Battle of Himera was, according to Herodotus, brought on partially because of the friendship of Terillus, tyrant of Himera, with Hamilcar, king of Carthage (6.88). A Syracusan in Thucydides is called Sicanus, evocative of the practice of *xenoi* naming their children in honour of each other.[35] Archonidas of Herbita is called a *philos* of the Athenians perhaps in his role as *proxenos*.[36] But there is no greater illustration than Ducetius of the ease with which members of the Sicel elite could move within the Greek city-states. The death of Bolcon on accusations of treacherous dealings with Ducetius may mask a relation of *xenia*, as such relationships were often interpreted as treasonous.[37] Ducetius' support from the *charientes* in the Syracusan assembly again suggests he had personal relations with members of the Syracusan elite. His exile to Corinth and subsequent return show him to be a true native Alcibiades, able to smoothly negotiate Sicel and Syracusan political milieux.

Archaeologically the presence of Greek drinking vessels associated with the symposium has often been marked as an indicator of Hellenisation. The bulk of inscriptions in native languages are scratched on sympotic vessels; this phenomenon has been noted at Morgantina, Castiglione, M. Casasia, Ramacca and Montagna di Marzo, suggesting that the symposium was an important sphere of linguistic interaction.[38] One such vessel from Morgantina has the Sicel imperative to drink, 'Pibe', written in Greek retrograde letters, perhaps a play on the common Greek sympotic practice to exhort one's fellow symposiasts to drink, while a krater proclaims 'I am Kypara', perhaps the name of a native woman or nymph, but also a pun on the Greek word *kyparos*, which can refer to the shape of a large vessel such as a krater.[39] Antonaccio suggests that such verbal play is indicative of a cultural bilingualism and of complex interactions between Greeks and Sicels.[40] Albanese-Procelli has gone further, to argue that there developed in Sicily and Magna Graecia a new cultural *koinê* among the elites that was neither truly Greek nor native, as evidenced by the spread of orphism (or at least orphic paraphernalia) among both elites in southern Italy and Sicily.[41]

POLITICAL LANDSCAPES

Both the Deinomenid tyrants and Ducetius redistributed land, trans-ferred populations and refounded cities. Yet to argue that Ducetius was copying the Syracusan dynasts ignores evidence that such activ-ities were ongoing throughout the fifth century in Sicily and Southern Italy and were connected with tyrannical, oligarchic and democratic regimes. The intensification of Sicel state formation under Ducetius was part of a wider fifth-century trend which saw the constant con-quest and absorption and (often) the return to independence of indi-vidual city-states within the Sicilian and South Italian landscape.

Agitations for land redistributions were frequent in the archaic and classical periods throughout the Greek world. Finley argued that dis-putes over land and debt-bondage were the closest the Greco-Roman world came to class warfare and social revolution.[42] Although in Aristotle's ideal society each settler received one lot in prime land and one lot in marginal land (*Pol.* 1330a14–16; cf. 1265b24–6), and colo-nial foundation stories told that each colony was founded with equal allotments of land (ML 5, Diod. 9 fr. 2, 1; Diod. 12.11.2; 10.6–7; D.L. 1.75), that this was actually true seems increasingly improbable, as the highly organised nature of colonisation has been vigorously cri-tiqued.[43] Certainly by the fifth century, *stasis* over inequalities in the holdings of land was endemic on the island as well as in Southern Italy. Such inequalities caused or exacerbated the differences in wealth between elite and non-elite; Diodorus describes the extrava-gant households at Acragas (Diod. 13.81–4), while Nicias marvels at the riches of the island, including the personal wealth of some Sicilians (Thuc. 6.20.4). Resentments over landholdings could arise very quickly: within a decade of its foundation in Southern Italy, Thurii had to be refounded because of unrest over unequal divisions of land (Diod. 12.11.1–4).

Land distributions were often connected to tyrants; rallies for the redistribution of land among the general populace could open the door for tyrants to foment social unrest, a trend seen frequently in the Aegean. However, Gelon's land distributions did not follow these precedents; when there was civil unrest in Syracuse between the landowning Gamoroi and an alliance of the *dêmos* and Kyllyrioi, the Syracusan serf population, Gelon took the side of the oligarchs and returned them (and himself) to Syracuse. His subsequent land distri-butions, refoundations and relocations entailed the removal of the elite of neighbouring cities to Syracuse, whereas the urban poor were

Figure 3.2 Map of ancient Southern Italy

sold into slavery and the farm workers remained to work the land.[44] This policy disrupted local loyalties and alliances while at the same time making aristocrats increasingly beholden to the ruling tyrant. Whether Ducetius had similar goals in his redistribution of land is unclear from Diodorus' narrative. There is, however, no reason to believe that Ducetius needed the model of the Deinomenids to inspire such reforms; the internal socio-political dynamics that made landownership the driving factor for political agitation in Greek *poleis* were undoubtedly present in the similarly agrarian-based Sicel communities.

The consolidation of the territory of south-eastern Sicily under the Deinomenids has been well documented: these tyrants directly controlled Gela, Camarina, Catana, Megara Hyblaea, Euboea and Leontini, and their influence reached into South Italy, with their political alliance with Locri.[45] The trend towards multi-*polis* states ruled by tyrants extended beyond the Deinomenids to the conquest of Messana by Anaxilas, tyrant of Rhegium (Thuc. 6.4.6), and the meddling in the north coast of Sicily by Theron, tyrant of Acragas, who by driving Terillus, the tyrant of Himera, from his city instigated the Carthaginian invasion of the island.

The territorial policies of the tyrants meant that increasingly independent *poleis* were less able to defend themselves. Yet, tyranny was not necessarily the only socio-political response to the intense escalation of state-formation in the early fifth century. In the Aegean, Athens also extended her influence through the Athenian naval alliance, which would turn into the Athenian Empire. Nor was such expansion limited to the Greeks: Carthage had been asserting her grip on the western part of Sicily through the control of the Phoenician colonies of Motya and Solunto, as well as over much of Sardinia and southern Spain.[46]

In southern Italy, contemporaneous to the tyrants in Sicily, an oligarchic group identified as the Pythagoreans took power in Croton. These oligarchs are described by Diodorus as urging the Crotonites to war against the Sybarites, in 510 BC, on behalf of the Sybarite oligarchs, who had been driven from the city because of land disputes (Diod. 12.9; Iambl. *Vit. Pyth.* 255). It is with the subsequent destruction of Sybaris that Crotonian hegemony in Southern Italy began, with numismatic evidence suggesting that the Crotonite sphere of power extended over several cities in Southern Italy, including Caulonia, Temesa and Terina.[47] Whether Croton exercised direct control is uncertain, but it is clear from Polybius' description of a mass uprising against the Pythagoreans in the 450s that the leading men of each city were killed at a meeting in Croton (2.39.1–2). Through ruling Pythagorean groups, the oligarchic rulers of certain South Italian cities could become part of a larger and more defensive alliance, while not relinquishing completely their political autonomy. Even though not all states fell under Crotonite hegemony, few remained completely independent: Locri turned to the protection of Syracuse and her tyrants in what Redfield has termed a 'Finlandization' of Locrian foreign policy.[48] Likewise the Tarantini removed the inhabitants of Siris and added them to their own colonists to found Heraclea (Diod. 12.36.4), presumably to create a stronger and more defensive state against the growing power of the local native populations.

Democratic states were also clearly interested in territorial expansion. The reasons for Syracuse and Acragas going to war over

Ducetius' foundation of a colony at Cale Acte suggests that neither city had ceased their attempts to gain influence on the north side of the island.[49] Diodorus recounts frequent incursions by the Syracusans into the Sicilian interior, and Syracuse became active in the 440s in the Tyrrhenian Straits.[50] Syracuse's neighbouring state of Leontini regained its independence after the fall of Polyzelus, but the Syracusans never ceased eyeing its territory. Leontini went into alliance with Athens, probably by 432, but the congress of Gela meant that the Athenian navy was forced to leave the island and once again made Leontini vulnerable. When a *stasis* broke out in Leontini, in 424–422, over the redistribution of land, Syracuse intervened and dismantled the *polis*, transferring the elite to Syracuse (Thuc. 5.4.1–5).[51]

Tyrants such as the Deinomenids were unusually powerful compared to their Aegean counterparts of the archaic period (Thuc. 1.17). Their vast financial resources and mercenary armies endowed them with the means of coercion to accelerate socio-political changes. Yet tyrannies were just part of a tendency towards multi-*polis* states which characterised so much of Sicilian history. By the classical period, independent *poleis* were particularly vulnerable to the territorial ambitions of their neighbours. The result was either absorption into a larger state or entry into an alliance. While Ducetius' policies are commonly associated with those of the Deinomenids, his *synteleia* may have been closer to the model of the Pythagorean federation, based on a multi-state alliance centred on Croton. When placed within their wider fifth-century context, Ducetius' actions seem less dependent on Deinomenid inspiration and more a variation on the trend towards types of states which moved beyond the *polis* in its traditional sense.

CONCLUSION

In the 1990s a renewed interest in the native populations of Sicily coincided with a shift towards cultural history within the discipline of classics. Although this led to significant advances in the study of the native cultures of the island, it has also meant a near de-politicisation of these non-Greek populations. Yet the territorial ambitions and tensions of Sicilian polities crossed ethnic lines, and Sicily's non-Greek populations should be included in the island's political histories. The native elites of Sicily were affected by the socio-political realities of the fifth century, where we see the surge and ebb of small territorial empires, be they Greek, Punic or Sicel. Leaders such as Ducetius were necessary not just for Sicel autonomy, but also for the autonomy of any community, regardless of ethnicity.

NOTES

1. 11.76.3, 78.5, 88.6, 90.1–2, 91–92.4, 12.8.1–4, 29.1.
2. For recent major works on Greek tyranny in Sicily see Luraghi 1994; Braccesi 1998.
3. Hdt. 7.153–5; Diod. 11.48.3–4; 11.72.3. For discussions of territorial ambitions of Deinomenids see Demand 1990: 45–54; Luraghi 1994: 273–374.
4. For a discussion of Sicel–Syracusan relations at this time see Musti 1992: 218–20.
5. There has been considerable debate as to the locations of the sites mentioned by Diodorus Siculus. Adamesteanu 1962: 122–52; Galvagno 1991; Rizzo 1970: 43–9; Chisoli 1993: 24.
6. Surveys on archaic Greek tyranny in the Aegean include Andrewes 1956; Mossé 1969; Berve 1967. More recent critiques include Osborne 1996: 192–7. See also notes 2 and 7.
7. See papers in Morgan 2003, particularly those by Raaflaub, Kallet and Henderson.
8. Luraghi 1994: 5–6; Lewis 2000: 97–8.
9. For Diodorus' sources for this period see Meister 1967: 50–2; Pearson 1987: 140–2; Chisoli 1993: 22. Chisoli argues that Timaeus refers to Ducetius as *hêgemôn* (11.76.3 and 88.6) and Ephorus as *basileus* (11.76.3) and *dynastôs* (12.8.1).
10. Agostiniani 1992: 192.
11. Cusumano 1996: 306–11.
12. Ibid. 304.
13. See note 9.
14. Maniscalco et al. 2003: 153.
15. Galvagno 2000: 71, with references.
16. Antonaccio 1997: 186–7.
17. Ross Holloway 1991: 64–6; Albanese-Procelli 1996: 173; Maniscalco et al. 2003: 171; De Angelis, 2003: 26–7, with references; on mortuary data, see Leighton 2000: 18.
18. Maniscalco et al. 2003: 170, with references.
19. De Vido 1997; Galvagno 2000: 87–9.
20. Galvagno 2000: 71–3.
21. For the divide between history and prehistory generally in classics see Morris 1994: 14–15.
22. Albanese-Procelli 2003: 146.
23. Thompson 1999: 387.

24. Vassallo 2000; Morris et al. 2003.
25. Freeman 1891: 359–61; Adamesteanu 1962: 169; Demand 1990: 55–8.
26. See Antonaccio 1997 for a description of the debates surrounding the competing identifications of Morgantina as a Greek or native settlement.
27. De Angelis 1998.
28. For a discussion of how ancient ethnicity has been made more pressing by modern problems see Hall 2002: 1–4. For a connection between the rise in interest in ethnicity in scholarship and ascension of ethnicity as 'the major global challenge' in the aftermath of the collapse of the Soviet Union, see Garnett 2004: 11. For globalisation: Morris 2003.
29. Lyons 1996, De Angelis 2003, Antonaccio 1997: 167–94; Dietler 1989; Dietler 1999; Albanese-Procelli 1996: 167–76.
30. Antonaccio 2001.
31. Galvagno 1991: 110–12.
32. See Thucydides 3.115.1; 4.25.9; 6.88.3; 6.103.2; 7.57.11.
33. Herman 1987.
34. Ibid.
35. I would like to thank Simon Hornblower for drawing this reference to my attention. Other incidences of *xenoi* naming their children after or in honour of each other: Lacedaemonios, the son of Cimon (Thuc. 1.45.2) and Thessalus, the son of Pisistratus (Thuc. 1.20.2). Herman 1987: 18–21.
36. IG I^3 228; Walbank 1978: 354, n. 66.
37. Herman 1987: 156–61.
38. Albanese-Procelli 1996: 183.
39. Antonaccio 1997: 183; Antonaccio and Neils 1995: 261–77.
40. Antonaccio and Neils 1995: 261–77.
41. Albanese-Procelli 2003: 243; Mele 1981: 61–96; Small 2004: 267–85.
42. Finley 1981: 162–3.
43. Osborne 1998: 251–67.
44. Demand 1990: 48.
45. Redfield 2003: 207, 279.
46. The nature of the Carthaginian *eparchia* is disputed. See references in Morris et al. 2002: 191 n. 85.
47. Dunbabin 1948: 366–8, with references.
48. Redfield 2003: 207.
49. Galvagno 2000: 37.
50. Consolo Langher 1992: 252–8.
51. Berger 1991: 135–7, with references.

CHAPTER 4

Adfectatio regni *in the Roman Republic*

Christopher Smith

INTRODUCTION

In his article 'Roman history and the ideological vacuum', Peter Wiseman argued powerfully for a return to a reading of Roman history which acknowledges the political gulf between *optimates* and *populares*.[1] Wiseman made a brief reference to one story which illustrates his point. In 439 BC, Spurius Maelius supplied corn to the people and was suspected of aiming at tyranny; the dictator Cincinnatus ordered Servilius Ahala summarily to execute Maelius, an act often compared to the murder of Tiberius Gracchus.[2] There were two ways (at least) of telling the story. Dionysius describes Maelius as cut down 'like an animal', but in Livy, Ahala is praised for saving the Republic, and it is a notable fact that Marcus Junius Brutus, in addition to being descended from the Brutus who expelled Tarquinius Superbus, was descended from Ahala on his mother's side, and drew inspiration from his ancestors for his own act of assassination.[3]

It has long been recognised that the historical accounts of those who aimed at tyranny, Spurius Cassius, Spurius Maelius and Manlius Capitolinus, were heavily influenced by events contemporary to the writers.[4] There is a substantial body of writing which demonstrates how, in each case, both the issues which inspired them and the fates which befell them were related to the problems of the late Republic. In this chapter I wish to review the accounts of the three canonical would-be tyrants. By setting these stories in a wider context, I wish to make some suggestions about early Rome, and some observations about these stories as *exempla*, as a contribution to a wider argument about the nature and purpose of Roman historical thinking.

SP. CASSIUS

Sp. Cassius had a significant and important military and political career prior to his downfall, despite the fact that his family was plebeian.[5] He was consul in 502, 493 and 486, and in 501 was *magister equitum* to the first Roman dictator T. Larcius. He celebrated one triumph and demanded a second, and (perhaps) dedicated a temple to Ceres. Cassius was thus one of the most significant figures of the early Republic, and his career spanned its first quarter of a century. There even appeared to be physical evidence for his activity in the form of treaties, inscriptions and statues, though none of these bears much scrutiny.

In his third consulship, Cassius and his fellow consul Proculus Verginius struck a treaty with the Hernici, who had been defeated in the operations which followed the collapse of Coriolanus' treachery. At this point, Cassius proposed a *lex agraria*, the first at Rome, and a dangerous dispute arose. Livy and Dionysius tell slightly different stories about how the matter proceeded, but in both accounts the influence of the debates over the Gracchan land laws is palpable in the suggestion that the distribution of land involved the *socii et nomen Latinum*, the selfish rhetoric of Cassius' opponents, and the ineffectual commission.[6]

This leaves the issue of Cassius' condemnation and death. Here there are two conflicting versions, and both are given by Livy and Dionysius. In one, Cassius was charged by two quaestors, Kaeso Fabius and Lucius Valerius Publicola; in the other, he was tried in his home by his father. Both sources prefer the first explanation, which must be wrong. The formal charge of *perduellio* will have been administered by *duoviri*, though Cicero in the earliest surviving account speaks of one quaestor. Whether there was a trial before the people is disputed.[7] The form of execution is also variously reported; Cicero uses the verb *mactare*, which implies a kind of sacrifice, and perhaps survives in Livy's account of the private version of the trial after which Cassius' father beat him to death. Dionysius says he was hurled from the Tarpeian rock. The sources do agree that Cassius' property, or more accurately that of his family, since he was not *sui iuris*, became forfeit to Ceres.[8]

Dating the various strands of the tradition is difficult. The solution which has found the most favour is as follows; first we have a story of someone who aspires to tyranny and is killed by his own father.[9] The aspiration may have been fuelled by a shortage of corn, which was resolved by import. It is intriguing that the corn comes from tyrants, Aristodemus of Cumae and Gelon of Syracuse, and there may have been corroborative Greek evidence concerning this transaction.[10] Conceivably, Calpurnius Piso Frugi, consul of

133, introduced the issue of agrarian reform, and Dionysius of Halicarnassus reflects a *popularis* account, perhaps that of Licinius Macer, whilst Livy demonstrates a more conservative attitude sometimes attributed to Valerius Antias, whose hand is suspected because one of the quaestors is named Valerius.[11] Whilst the Gracchan echoes are evident, Dionysius (8.80) also gives us a debate over the proscription of Cassius' children, which must post-date the Sullan proscriptions. There are also similarities with the *lex Julia agraria* of 59 BC.[12] As for the trial, Lintott and others have supposed that Piso is a good candidate for the author who, notwithstanding the difficulty of Cassius' juridical status, prefers a public condemnation as opposed to a private affair, but Ogilvie took the trial back to Fabius Pictor, and suggested that Piso's view was that Cassius dedicated a statue in the temple of Ceres to himself, which formed the basis for the suspicion of his motives. The *iudicium domesticum* is a dramatic but not trustworthy fable; Cicero and Dionysius knew an intermediate version in which the father was chief witness at his son's trial.[13]

Why was there this substantial rewriting of Cassius' career? One way of approaching this is purely historiographical. Each transformation of the tradition relates solely to the working out of internal contradictions, or to the elaboration of the story. This is often represented by the attempt to indicate what the ancient writers had as their evidence; so Lintott writes, 'The original annalistic tradition was derived from a basic notice in the *Fasti* together with the evidence of the inscriptions and perhaps some oral tradition connected with them.'[14] If the ancient historians were genuinely disinterested in political terms, then one might suppose that the twists and turns of *Quellenkritik* are nothing more than the traces of determined efforts to write a good story. If, however, when we read Dionysius' account of an intellectually vigorous and bold plan of agrarian reform, we are reading a justification of Cassius' reform and simultaneously a defence of agrarian and frumentary reform in the light of the events surrounding G. Gracchus, C. Fannius and Marcus Drusus, then this and other stories are not simply dramatic tales but inspired by and productive of political debate.

Some indication of the extent to which Cassius' political activity could be woven into a particular kind of story is given by Dionysius of Halicarnassus at 10.38 in a speech delivered in 453 BC by the great plebeian hero L. Siccius Dentatus. Although almost entirely absent from the text of Livy, Siccius is a hugely important figure in

Dionysius. In a speech in favour of agrarian reform, Siccius refers directly to Spurius Cassius:

> They accused Spurius Cassius, who first proposed the allotment of land, a man who had been honoured with three consulships and two most brilliant triumphs and who had shown greater ability in both military undertakings and political counsels than anyone of that age – this man, I say, they accused of aiming at tyranny and defeated him by means of false testimony, for no other reason than because he was a lover of his country and a lover of the people, and they destroyed him by shoving him over the cliff.

Dionysius is wholly positive about Siccius. He is brave, resourceful and his murder at the hands of the decemvirs (which Livy does relate) is one of the most dramatic and damning events of that period. Praising and defending Cassius through an entirely positive character is therefore striking. Running through Dionysius' account therefore is the trace of a very different and very positive version of the agitation surrounding Spurius Cassius, which suggests a history dramatically different from that of Livy, and different not merely in the odd detail or element of style, but in terms of basic political outlook.

This would explain why some authors who would have been in favour of the Gracchan reform may have chosen to use Spurius Cassius as the protagonist of the movement, notwithstanding his conviction and death. Cassius is the first in a line of Romans whose actions on behalf of the people resulted in their death. The aftermath proves the senate duplicitous, and the Fabii invincible – and the people regret their condemnation of Cassius, just as they will regret the loss of Manlius Capitolinus.[15]

SP. MAELIUS

The account of Sp. Maelius' alleged bid for power rests within the context of growing difficulties over supplying the city of Rome.[16] Livy prefaces his account with a dramatic picture of desperate famine, with plebeians committing suicide by throwing themselves into the Tiber. An *eques*, Sp. Maelius, who had used his own money to buy up grain in Etruria, began to distribute it for free. Knowing that he had little chance of getting a consulship, he set his sights on sole rule, but the elections returned two stern foes of revolution, Titus Quinctius Capitolinus and Menenius Agrippa. The prefect of the corn supply was Lucius Minucius, apparently for a second year, and he reported to the senate that weapons were being collected at Maelius' house and there was talk of a revolution. The consul named his relative L. Quinctius Cincinnatus as dictator, and he named Servilius Ahala as *magister equitum*. Servilius attempted to arrest Maelius in the Forum, and when the terrified knight tried to run away, Servilius overtook him, killed him, and returned to the senate, guarded by a band of young patricians, to be welcomed and praised by the dictator.

Cincinnatus summoned the assembly and justified the action; Maelius had refused the summons of the dictator, and had been guilty of the greater crime of attempting to gain sole power, by trying to purchase the favour of the people. Minucius was rewarded, but Maelius' house was razed to the ground, and the land named the Aequimaelium. Dionysius' account is very similar to that of Livy, but he also knew an alternative and very different version, which he attributes to L. Cincius Alimentus and L. Calpurnius Piso Frugi. In this account, when the senate hears Minucius' evidence, one of their number proposes that Maelius should be put to death without trial, and appointed Servilius Ahala to do the deed. He hid a dagger in his armpit (hence his name), assassinated Maelius, and fled, claiming to have acted at the command of the senate, which was sufficient to make the pursuing mob desist.

The key aspect of this must be the legitimacy of the murder of Maelius. Indubitably Maelius is a *privatus*, but what of his assassin? Two suggestions have been made; Münzer thought that pro-Gracchan writers insisted that Ahala was a magistrate in order to make a distinction between Ahala and Scipio Nasica, the murderer of Tiberius Gracchus; Piso appears to have been using Ahala as an *exemplum* to justify the actions of his fellow senator. Lintott argued that the intervention was by senatorial historians, not necessarily supportive of what Nasica had done, who wished to assert the importance of constitutional legitimacy for such assassinations. The matter is clouded further by the layers of significance added by Cicero, who used the case in connection with Milo's assassination of Clodius, and Dionysius' use of elements of the murder of Caesar.

Once again, the story is versatile and the treatments of it powerfully polemical. Roman writers used the story to examine and to take up positions on the issue of state-sponsored murder and assassination. The debate is really about Maelius' death; it is for his ending that the story is told, quite as much as for his actions in life. The focus rapidly shifts to the debate over whether Maelius was *iure caesum*, and Cincinnatus has a hard time persuading the people that he was.

Moreover, implicit in the way in which Cicero uses the *exemplum* is the assumption that his audience will immediately both remember the story and follow the way in which it is being used. He may not have been the first; a fragment of Fannius' speech against Gaius Gracchus' grain law compares Gaius' *largitio* with that of other tyrants and puts it down to the same desire for domination.[17] *Mutatis mutandis*, Fannius' rhetoric and Cincinnatus' self-justification are identical.

M. MANLIUS CAPITOLINUS

Of the three aspirants for sole rule, M. Manlius Capitolinus is the most fully rounded in the historical sources, but the loss of the relevant portion of Dionysius of Halicarnassus renders us more reliant on Livy's version.[18] Consul in 392, Manlius was renowned for a remarkable action in holding the Capitol against the Gauls.[19] They had made a night-time attack, and had escaped notice of the guard (who was subsequently thrown from the Capitol) and the dogs, but not the geese, who woke Manlius; he dislodged the first of the Gauls, and was joined by colleagues who repulsed the attack. In their gratitude the soldiers gave him a equal portion of their own slim rations at his house on the Capitol.

We see Manlius next as *interrex* in 387, but then his pride and his envy of Camillus' achievements take root. Manlius' own version of the salvation of Rome is that his was the key intervention, a view which contradicts the massive emphasis in Livy's own version on Camillus.[20] He became the first patrician to support the aims of the plebeians, first by proposing agrarian legislation and then by attacking the problem of debt. So serious was the concern over domestic unrest, coupled with the threat of the Volscians, that a dictator, Aulus Cornelius Cossus, was appointed. He returned from success against the enemy to find the city in turmoil. Manlius' popular appeal, and his use of his house as a political centre led first to his imprisonment, and ultimately to his conviction and death, thrown from the Tarpeian rock.

There is much that is odd in this story, and it has clearly undergone a series of changes and revisions. Briefly, an early version in which Manlius, oppressor of the people, is prosecuted and flogged to death, perhaps in the plebeian assembly, becomes overlaid with contemporary reference. Manlius could be an oppressor, and a victim of the tribunes, or a more sympathetic character, and after 63 and the trial of Rabirius, the whole paraphernalia of *perduellio* could be brought in. Gradually the attack of the Gauls was shifted from an ascent via a tunnel, to the shrine of Carmenta, and ultimately to the Tarpeian rock, to allow for the sententious moral of the man thrown from the place where he had earlier saved Rome. At the same time, a good deal of Catilinarian rhetoric is inserted, and Manlius becomes an early foreshadowing of that other great patrician demagogue and revolutionary. There are other echoes too; the *perduellio* trial makes one think of Rabirius on trial for the murder of Saturninus in 63 BC, but the case was not exactly analogous. What would have been analogous, and what may have crossed some readers' minds, is that this was precisely the kind of formal trial which might legitimately have brought the end of Catiline. Instead, his murder was rushed through senate, and carried out in the dark of the prison, not in the light of day. The early Republic knew better than the later how to kill a would-be tyrant – Cicero was no Camillus.

OTHER WOULD-BE TYRANTS

By the time of Cicero, the three individuals we have considered could be regarded as a trio of malefactors who threatened the *libertas* of the Roman people. Whether Cicero was the first to combine them we simply cannot tell, but certainly after him the tradition is secure and lasts right through to Ampelius, and beyond. However, the focus on the three individuals deprives us of the wider context, for there were in fact a number of individuals who from different directions threatened to exceed the limits of constitutional power.[21]

There are the great leaders of the people, such as Volero Publilius and Gaius Laetorius, and Licinius and Sextius who have an extraordinary tenure of the tribunate for some ten years. There are foreign adventurers, Porsenna, Appius Herdonius and Vitruvius Vaccus, the latter notable for having had a house in Rome which was razed to the ground exactly as the more famous Roman examples. Finally there are the dangerous patricians, the Fabii, who take unprecedented control in Rome, as far as we can tell from the Fasti, shortly after Cassius' downfall, Coriolanus, and Ap. Claudius the decemvir, who took his own life before the inevitable outcome of his trial. Another excellent example is Kaeso Quinctius, leader of the *adulescentes nobiles*, who opposed a law intended to constrain the power of the consuls; he was forced into exile in 461 BC, and his family's property was confiscated, which meant that his father was forced to live in a hut across the Tiber.

Nor should we forget the wider context. The early fifth century sees tyrants in Sicily, and the reign of Aristodemus of Cumae.

Porsenna's actions in Etruria were not isolated; one may compare Thefarie Velianas at Caere, or the frequent mentions of kingship in various Etruscan towns, not all of them wholly popular either with their own populations, or with their neighbours. We are accustomed to think of sixth-century Greece as an age of tyrants, but we should contemplate the record of central Italy and Magna Graecia at the same time. The historical record of early Republican Rome is full of such figures not just because it was the expected historiographical pattern, but because the rise of powerful individuals was common in the period, and the state's capacity to constrain them was relatively weak.

If this is true, we need to ask why Rome was so successful, apparently, in avoiding the descent back into individual rule after the expulsion of Tarquinius Superbus until the late first century BC. One might add that this success, unless it is illusory, will have had its own consequences, and here I would mention a provocative question posed by Martin. He refers to the idea that tyranny was an indispensable transition from an aristocratic to a democratic regime (a view which is not uncontroversial), and suggests that the *leges sacratae* which protected the tribunes and the repression of *adfectatio regni* were the two decisive factors in preventing Rome from ever trying out democracy.[22] In the light of the recent debate over the extent to which Rome experienced either genuine democratic politics, or sophisticated democratic ideology, the attempts to establish a *regnum* at Rome occupy a key part. They become part of a way of writing history which Wiseman has characterised as ideological, and so are integral to an understanding of the kinds of debates which engaged late Republican thinkers, but at the same time, it is at least worth asking what they might tell us about earlier Rome.

ARCHAIC REALITIES

The complexity of the source tradition, the absence of contemporary evidence which can be trusted, and the influence of Greek historiography on the nature of the Roman historical imagination makes it hard to be certain about early Roman history, and the subject naturally invites scepticism. Recently, scholars have given more positive assessments, and Cornell expresses a limited confidence in the tradition about the individuals we have discussed. Cassius and Manlius at any rate will have been in the Fasti, though that in itself would not be a sufficient reason for believing in details about them.

The best statement about the historicity of archaic Rome is, in my opinion, that offered by Purcell in a recent article where he discusses the Roman phenomenon of 'becoming historical'.[23] Purcell's argument is that Rome was not as isolated and disconnected from the Greek world as even later Romans thought, and that if we take seriously all the manifold ways in which Roman historical memory operated, whilst we will not have an account of early Rome which was in all cases purely factual and straightforwardly credible, we can believe in a sophisticated interpretative milieu. Purcell characterises the historical consciousness as 'a web of intercommunicating discourses – exegetic, epigraphic, archival, dramatic, pictorial, narrative, poetic, moving in and out of different layers of literacy and orality, and, constantly, intertextually linked with outsiders' oral and written descriptions and contributions'. From this point of view the topographic aetiologies, the dramatic construction of the stories and the possibility of multiple media of transmission allow us to speculate about a set of discourses within which the theme of *adfectatio regni* may have developed before the later Republic.

Purcell also refers to a relevant case-study, the dedication of the temple of Juno Moneta. Whilst some sources, probably wrongly, attribute the temple to the great Furius Camillus, others, including Livy, prefer his son or grandson, who vowed and built the temple in the 340s as a thanksgiving for victory over the Aurunci. This throws into question the tradition about Manlius' house, but at the same time it may suggest that the Camilli had a tradition about their own connection with Juno on the Capitol – the great Camillus famously evoked Juno Regina from Veii.[24] Similarly Fabius Pictor himself wrote that when M. Regulus vowed a temple to Jupiter Stator, he claimed to do so in imitation of Romulus, which pushes the idea of reference to the past in the course of contemporary action back into the third century BC, and intimates that it may well have preceded historical writing, rather than being a product of it.[25]

In our tendency to downdate as far as possible the specific historiographical circumstances which surround the three claimants of tyranny, we overlook problems much closer to the beginnings of the process of writing down Roman history. We have seen three individuals who were concerned with the distribution of land and frumentary laws, and who called into question the senate's handling of the Roman economy. The Gracchi were not the first to propose agrarian legislation, nor to worry about grain distribution; indeed without looking too hard one may clearly see in the case of C. Flaminius in the later third century a very similar set of ideas and actions, and similarly strong reactions from the senatorial elite.[26] With the example of Regulus before us, we might wonder whether Flaminius ever referred to his predecessors among the champions of the *plebs*.

On the specific issue of the key themes which characterise the actions of popular leaders (and in the case of Coriolanus and other champions of the opposition, are the focus of resistance), distribution of grain and land stand out. These themes had currency in the late Republic. It is difficult, however, to deny their relevance at an earlier stage.[27] Cato the Elder indicates that shortages of food were recorded in the *annales maximi*; they are also an endemic feature of antiquity, and few states were entirely buffered against short-term fluctuations in the availability of staple foods. The agrarian issue is more difficult because we do not understand the regime of landownership in early Rome; nevertheless, it is worth restating Cornell's important observation that the kinds of land reforms attributed to Licinius and Sextius in particular are not identical to those we know of in the late Republic. Moreover, the expansion of Roman territory is one of the most credible aspects of early Roman history, and the tradition that the reorganisation by Servius Tullius of the citizen body through a reform of the tribes goes back to Fabius Pictor, and is, as I have stated elsewhere, entirely plausible as a sixth-century reality.[28] Momigliano may have been right, as long ago as 1936, to have argued that food shortages not land redistribution were at the root of the historical reality of Cassius and Maelius, but until we have a better understanding of early Republican land tenure we cannot be sure.

However, whilst it is possible to argue that the issues are entirely the product of later historical reconstruction, the other main concern of these stories, the suppression of someone who aspired to power by murder, is a somewhat different matter. My tentative suggestion is that one very important aspect of the Roman historical self-consciousness revolved around the limits to which resistance to the state was to be permitted. Whilst this had obvious later significance, if one adds these *exempla* to tribunician *sacrosanctitas*, the secessions of the *plebs*, the resistance to overweening aristocratic behaviour such as that of Coriolanus or the decemvirs, and the diminution of patrician monopolies over political and priestly office, one finds a rich vein of political thought in action. The fact that the would-be tyrants are subject to a kind of religious sanction is not proof of antiquity but places the discourse in the same realm as the oath which L. Junius

Brutus placed upon the people after the expulsion of the kings not to permit a return to monarchical power.[29]

Within the context of Central Italy, the rise of powerful individuals and their suppression is neither implausible nor unexampled in the fifth and fourth centuries. The ways in which those attempts were made can be disputed, and it should be stressed that the enemies of Roman *libertas* were not simply the champions of the *plebs*, but also the champions of elite power. Cornell has shown how the story of Coriolanus can be accommodated within 'a world of aristocratic adventurers, of private armies, of youth-groups, and above all of movement'; just so the story of Manlius Capitolinus can be accommodated in a Rome of deep internal divisions, held together by a complex and sophisticated political system, in which military glory was a route to power, but individual prowess, as at Sparta, could be seen as threatening to the state. The evidence Cornell can muster is almost exactly the same for warrior-hero Coriolanus as it is for the warrior-hero Manlius, and observed from a slightly different angle, the dominance of Camillus, like the dominance of the Fabii after the death of Spurius Cassius, looks very much like the triumph of one powerful individual or family over another. Camillus, we should remember, spent the period before the sack by the Gauls in exile, charged with crimes relating either to his misuse of the Veientine booty, or the nature of his extraordinary triumph; had he not returned gloriously to Rome, he could easily have been made to fit the pattern of his opponent.

I want briefly to return to Martin's question about Rome and the resistance to tyranny. The accounts of the last two kings at Rome, Servius Tullius and Tarquinius Superbus, attribute characteristics to them which are very similar to those of Greek tyrants. This has long been recognised, and indeed has been adduced as clear evidence of the later invention of Roman history. As archaeological evidence has built up, however, this has become less plausible. The existence of a sixth-century statue of Hercules and Minerva in the Forum Boarium, by the temple of Fortuna attributed to Servius Tullius, paralleling the use by Pisistratus of Heracles and Athena at almost the same time in Athens, is extremely hard to argue away. The contacts with the Greek world as indicated by imported pottery and the adoption of a Greek mythological framework, attested epigraphically by such finds as the Castor and Pollux inscription at Lavinium and the presence of a representation of Hephaestus at the Volcanal in the Comitium, all point to a profound understanding of the Greek world in late sixth-century Rome, just as the Pyrgi tablets which refer to Thefarie Velianas demonstrate the depth of contact with the Phoenician world. The *Elogia Tarquiniensia* demonstrates that the Etruscans at least knew about the Sicilian expedition, and the erection of a statue of Alcibiades in the Forum has been linked to the same stratum of knowledge.[30]

This does not mean, of course, that there was no subsequent elaboration, but it is not necessary to deny the possibility of an influence on Rome of Greek models, and not merely on the creation of the tradition but also on the practice of politics. Servius Tullius and Tarquinius Superbus are not unfamiliar kinds of figures, and their role in the formation of the Roman constitution is not disproved by the historiographical games Romans played. One might turn Martin's question around entirely. The actions and experience of kingship in the later sixth century at Rome may have been precisely analogous with the experience of some Greek cities, where a period of tyranny is productive of a constitutional settlement which establishes boundaries between elite power and popular representation, though the boundaries remain contested. The actions of Cassius and Maelius take place against the backdrop of the emergence of the tribunate, and the secessions of the *plebs*. Manlius is executed in 384; if the Fasti are to be believed, in 376 Licinius and Sextius hold the first of ten successive tribunates during which there is an intense fight to introduce land reform and the breaking open of the consulship to plebeians. Throughout the century or so between Cassius and Manlius, as is frequently overlooked, patricians held office only through the medium of the electoral assemblies.

What we have consistently underestimated is the complexity of the problems facing Rome in the early Republic and the sophistication of the answers which were provided. The problems over land and debt, and the issue of plebeian access to office, come together definitively in the Licinian-Sextian legislation, but are predicated on a fundamental question of exactly what the *plebs* at Rome was, and what were its rightful powers, and that is the question which underlies the entire debate about democracy at Rome. We owe in part to Cicero the isolation of three figures, Cassius, Maelius and Manlius, as *adfectores regni*; the historical tradition elaborated and argued over their significance. Yet in context, they are merely a part of a far more complex political situation, and one in which the role of the Roman community is crucial. As Martin elegantly demonstrates, for leading plebeians, handing over a leadership role to individuals was a threat to the alternative solution of collectively bursting in to power for themselves. The tension between individual power and communal responsibility seems to me one of the most interesting aspects of Roman Republican history, and one which requires much more careful consideration.

We have seen briefly the way in which the *adfectores regni* later became *exempla*, both for reformers and their opponents. We have seen Brutus contemplating his murderous ancestor Servilius Ahala, and Cicero defending Milo by reference to the past. We have seen historians defining a golden thread that linked the Gracchi to their predecessors. We have been able to trace the use of the actions of the past to justify the present at least to the third century in terms of temple foundations, and we have seen how buildings, or their destruction, are intimately connected with the fates of those who challenge the state. If we accept the fundamental historicity of the existence of individuals who attempted by various means and for various purposes to take a position of pre-eminence at Rome, and consider Mary Beard's contention that at Rome, history replaced the mythical discourse that dominated in the Greek world, might we not take more seriously the stories of the *adfectores regni* as *exempla* whose relevance was almost immediately recognised, and not newly discovered by Fabius Pictor and his successors?[31] Such a suggestion would fit perfectly with Purcell's 'resilient mesh for retaining ideas about the past'. Moreover, if justification of present action by reference to past precedent were to be identified as a profound motivation in the Roman *mentalité*, we should at least allow that the flexibility and adaptability of this discourse could have been an original feature, and a vehicle from the outset of political debate. Tyranny at Rome, and more importantly its suppression, was a real phenomenon, and part of a political discourse in its own time.

I would like to take one last step. Mary Beard demonstrated the way that history was used in declamation, and she argued that 'declamation was one important means of turning dead and buried myth-history into an issue of the present: constant re*present*ation.'[32] This chapter has argued that we have enough evidence to suggest that this was traditional; the open-ended debating of the past itself had a long history, and is part of the context within which we can situate a number of what one might call 'para-historical' discourses, notably the funeral, but also the dramatic tradition which Wiseman has endeavoured to discover.[33] The importance of rhetoric is evident in all the accounts which we have discussed, and in the way their authors construct alternative visions of the world, drawing upon the experiences of others and their own past. This is an exercise in self-redefinition, or re*present*ation, or (to use a phrase of Quentin Skinner) 'rhetorical redescription', in which the discussion of virtues and vices is in effect a challenge to the society to reconsider and perhaps transvalue some of its moral values. One of the greatest exponents of this art was Machiavelli, and it is therefore entirely unsurprising that Cassius, Maelius and Manlius reappear in his *Discorsi*.[34] I would suggest that Machiavelli has taken not simply the names from Roman history, but an entire intellectual endeavour, in which the *adfectores regni* and the rhetorical redescriptions employed by their historians have a central and still not fully explored role.

NOTES

1. Wiseman 2002.
2. For general accounts see Mommsen 1864–79; Lintott 1970; Gutberlet 1985; Mustakallio 1994; Turchetti 2001: 125–64; Panitschek 1989; Martin 1990; Martin 1982–94; Liou-Gille 1996; Chassignet 2001; Vigourt 2001a; Vigourt 2001b.
3. Wiseman 2002: 296 with reference to Cic. *Att.* 2.24.3, 13.40.1, *Phil.* 2.26; Plut. *Brut.* 1.3; and Ahala on Brutus' coin issue of 54, in Crawford 1974: 455–6.
4. The earliest important contribution is Mommsen 1864–79.
5. Sources: Livy 2.41; DH 8.68–80; Temple to Ceres: DH 6.94.3, Tac. *Ann.* 2.49 (but often doubted as a piece of excessive dramatic irony). Treaty: DH 6.95 and Festus 166L; Livy 33.9 *foedus . . . in columna aenea insculptum*; Cic. *Pro Balbo* 53 indicating that it no longer stood in 56 BC. Statues: Livy 2.41.10, cf. Pliny *NH* 34.15 for the statue with the inscription *ex Cassia familia datum*; Pliny *NH* 34.30 for the statue erected to himself; see Forsythe 1994: 296–301. Trial and death: Val. Max. 5.8.2, 6.3.1b, 6.3.2; Dio fr. 22; Cic. *Rep.* 2.60. Destruction of house: Cic. *Dom.* 101. For an excellent summary of his career with references to the sources, see Münzer, *RE Cassius* 91 and Ogilvie 1965: 337–45. In addition to the sources in n. 2, see Gabba 1964; Basile 1978; de Cazenove 1989; de Cazenove 1990.
6. Cornell 1995: 271 for a recent interpretation of the historical reality, challenging the specifically Gracchan echoes; cf. Gutberlet 1985.
7. Cic. *Rep.* 2.60. The literature on *perduellio* is vast; see Magdelain 1973; Oakley 1997: I.563–5.
8. On Cassius' death see Mustakallio 1994: 36–8; on the forfeited property see Spaeth 1996: 71–3.
9. Lintott 1970.
10. DH 7.1.6; 8.70.5; Livy 2.34.

11. Livy 2.41.11.
12. Panitschek 1989.
13. Lintott 1970; Ogilvie 1965: 338, 344–5.
14. Lintott 1970: 20.
15. Livy 2.42.1; DH 8.81.
16. Sources: Livy 4.13–16; DH 12.1–4 (citing Cincius F6 Peter; Piso F24 Peter; on Piso's version, see Forsythe 1994: 301–10); Livy's mention of the *libri lintei* in relation to Minucius' position indicates some reference to Licinius Macer; see Walt 1997: 255–9, 319–24. Cic. *Sen.* 56; Cat. 1.3; *Att.* 2.24.3, 13.40.1; Val. Max. 5.3.2g; Quint. 5.13.24; *Vir. ill.* 17.5. Aequimaelium: Livy 2.16; Cic. *Dom.* 101; Varro *LL* 5.157; Val. Max. 6.3.1c. Reward of a statue to Minucius: Pliny *NH* 18.3.15; 34.5.21; DH 12.4. For parallels with Milo, Cic. *Mil.* 72; cf. also *Cat.* 1.3; for Dionysius and the death of Caesar see Valvo 1975; Mustakallio 1994: 42–3. For a defence of historicity see Cornell 1986: 58–61; cf. Wiseman 1996.
17. Fannius *ORF*⁴ fr. 6–7 *ap.* Iul. Victor 11.
18. The story of the *seditio* dominates Livy book 6; see Bayet 1966: 106–26; Oakley 1997: I.476–568. Other sourcess: Val. Max. 6.3.1a; Gell. 17.2.14 (= Claudius Quadrigarius F7 Peter); 17.21.24 (citing Varro F2 Peter and Nepos F5 Peter); Plut. *QR* 91; App. *Ital.* 9; *Vir. ill.* 24; Amm. 21.16.13 (citing a lost letter of Cicero to Nepos: *feliciorque meo iudicio Camillus exsulans quam temporibus eisdem manlius, etiam si (id quod cupierat) regnare potuisset*); Serv. *A.* 8.652. Wiseman 1979; Jaeger 1997: 57–93; Valvo 1983. On Juno Moneta see Gianelli 1980–1; Ziolkowski 1993; Meadows and Williams 2001. Sources which refer to all or some of the above: Cic. *De amicitia* 28, 36 (Cassius and Maelius); *Dom.* 101; *Phil.* 2.87, 114; *Rep.* 2.49; Quint. 3.7.20, 5.9.13 (Maelius and Manlius); Flor. 1.17.(26) 7 (certainly Cassius, but the text is corrupt); Ampel. *Lib. memorialis* 27 (all three with Coriolanus and Catiline).
19. Livy 5.47; Diod. 14.116.6; DH 13.8; Plut. *Cam.* 27, and many incidental references.
20. Livy 6.11. Jaeger and Oakley both lay emphasis on Manlius' unsuccessful attempt to interpret history, and see Feldherr 1998 for the larger theme of *imperator* as historian.
21. Coriolanus: Cornell 2003. Volero Publilius: Livy 2.55–6, 58; DH 9.39, 41. G. Laetorius: Livy 2.56; DH 9.46–8; Licinius and Sextius: Livy 6.34–42; DH 14.12. Lars Porsenna: Livy 2.8, 11–15; DH 5.21–2, 27–35. Appius Herdonius: Livy 3.15; DH 10.14. Vitruvius Vaccus: Livy 8.19; DH 14.13; Cic. *Dom.* 101. Kaeso Quinctius: Livy 3.11–14, 19, 24–5; DH 10.5–27. Tyrants in Sicily: Asheri, *CAH* IV² 753–80; *CAH* V² 147–61. Aristodemus of Cumae: DH 7.3–11; Frederiksen 1984: 95–9 ('in the accounts of the social revolution which was so closely connected with Aristodemus' success we have a detailed, fascinating and wholly credible account of an episode of the unrest which seems to have characterised many of the cities of the

west at the end of the sixth century'). Thefarie Velianas: Smith 1996: 146 with references. Kingship in Central Italy: Glinister 1995.

22. Martin 1990.
23. Purcell 2003.
24. Livy 7.28; Bruun 2000.
25. Livy 10.37 = Fabius Pictor F19 Peter (Regulus).
26. Von Ungern-Sternberg 1986.
27. Cornell 1995: 327–40; Garnsey 1988: 167–81; for grain supply rather than agrarian legislation as the motivation of Cassius and Maelius, see Momigliano 1936. Agrarian reform at Rome, Hermon 2001.
28. Smith 1997.
29. Livy 2.2.
30. Forum Boarium: Cristofani 1990: 111–30; Coarelli 1988. Castor and Pollux: Cristofani 1990: 190. *Elogia Tarquiniensia*: Torelli 1975, rev. T. J. Cornell 1978. Statue of Alcibiades: Plut. *Num.* 8.20; Plin. *NH* 34.26 (coupled with Pythagoras).
31. Beard 1993.
32. Ibid. 62.
33. Flower 1996; Wiseman 1998.
34. Skinner 2002: 31.175–87; Coby 1999.

CHAPTER 5

Money and the Great Man in the fourth century BC: *military power, aristocratic connections and mercenary service*

Matthew Trundle

Great men thrived in the Greek world of the fourth century BC. Money, mercenaries and aristocratic connections augmented and supported their power. The Athenian Empire had monetised the Aegean basin in the previous century due to naval warfare's dependence on coinage. The fall of the empire left a vacuum in the Aegean. Powerful individuals and their families from the wider Greek world, the Persian Empire, Sicily and Macedonia, filled this vacuum. Money facilitated the power and influence of these dynasts. Money bought friends and eroded the independence of the civic communities of the Greek *poleis*. Money and mercenaries led the way towards the hegemony and dominance over the eastern Mediterranean of the Macedonian and Hellenistic kings.

Autocrats (*tyrannoi, dynastai, mounarchoi, basilêes*) were a feature of early *poleis*. These had disappeared from almost every state in the Greek world by the middle of the fifth century BC.[1] This century saw the rise of the Athenian naval *archê* and with it the domination of the Aegean Basin by a single controlling authority. The Athenians controlled their empire with a navy that consumed vast quantities of coined silver for payment of crews, rowers and ships. Naval warfare, unlike land warfare, was massively expensive. Its cost monetised war and society to an extent previously unsurpassed. The Athenian navy's use of money resulted in increased use of coins in other areas of society, most noticeable in payments for land warfare and political services within the state. In order to sustain payments in what was fast ceasing to be a purely agricultural economy, the Athenians controlled the resources of silver for the minting of coins and particularly the management of silver bullion, mints and mines in the Aegean Basin. This is most famously illustrated by the coinage decree, perhaps from the first five years of the 440s BC, in which the Athenians appear to regulate how their allies paid tribute in Athenian coin.[2] The importance of revenues is well attested in Thucydides and his obsession with the relationship between finances and power is a subject highlighted in recent research.[3] Thucydides wrote (1.10) that prior to his time empires were unable to sustain campaigns, not from a lack of men, but from a lack of *chrêmata*. *Chrêmata*, literally the tools by which ends were achieved, meant money.[4] Money in the Aegean was central to the maintenance and spread of power on a sustained and grand scale.

Several related and significant things occurred as a result of Athens' defeat. Autocracies re-emerged within many communities as powerful individuals dominated Greek politics in a way they had not previously. Tyranny reappeared in Sicily, most famously at Syracuse, in the wake of the Athenian and Carthaginian invasions. Several tyrannies appeared in the Aegean. These tyrannies fed off the development of a destabilised and war-torn environment. The power of money in the Greek Mediterranean was a feature of this environment. Another was the increased role of non-Greek intervention in the region. Powerful individuals promoted non-Greek interests, those of the rulers of the barbarian world, offering money and friendship in return for alliance and aid. Thus, Thracian monarchs and princes played a bigger role in Greek affairs. The satraps of the western Persian Empire emerged as significant players on the international stage in their own right. The reassertion of Egyptian independence from Persia enabled several Pharaohs to contest Persian control. The Greek communities, warlike and interested in money, offered these individuals a product that stemmed naturally from the ubiquity of money and warfare: the professional soldier. Consequentially, the period witnessed an explosion in the number of foreign hired soldiers, Greek mainlanders, in the service of the autocrats of the Mediterranean.

The ancient sources love to demonstrate that money fed the beast of tyranny and destabilised democratic or oligarchic, particularly aristocratic, power in the classical Mediterranean. State controls on money increased at the end of the fifth century. The Athenians had something akin to a tyranny over their empire, according to Thucydides' Pericles (2.63.2; also 1.122.3, 124.3, 3.37.2), and the *dêmos* could be likened to a tyrant (Ar. *Eq.* 1111–14, 1229–30, 1333; Arist. *Pol.* 1275a5–7).[5] Radical democracy could be like a tyranny (Arist. *Pol.* 1296a1–5). Attic Old Comedy portrayed the *dêmos* as a consumer of the resources of the empire (Ar. *Vesp.*

667–94). The Ionians in the fleet served the Athenian cause for payment in coin. Thucydides (1.143.1) has Pericles allay fears that Sparta will outbid Athens for rowers with Delphian treasury money. Later, Xenophon (*Hell.* 1.5.4) cited Lysander's hopes of attracting rowers to the Spartan–Persian cause by offering higher payments than the Athenians could. National sentiment never stood in the way of mercenary-oarsmen's ambitions in the classical age. The defence of Polycles (Dem. 50) illustrates well the difficulties of Athenian tri-erarchs in keeping Athenian crews loyal while on campaign in the face of offers of higher pay and rewards.[6]

Money provided a stimulus for the growing numbers of mercenar-ies in the later fifth and fourth centuries BC. Some associate the inven-tion of coinage with mercenary service.[7] Certainly, the widespread use of coinage was a *sine qua non* for the appearance of large-scale mer-cenary armies.[8] Money enabled individuals and communities to corner necessary resources, such as grain supplies or expertise. For ancient autocrats it was essential to control the military resources of the state, often by bringing men in from outside the state in order to control the citizen population. For this they needed a surplus, ideally in money. Aristotle (*Pol.* 1311a) recognised the role of money and mercenaries and their relationship to tyranny when he stated that:

> Tyranny, as has repeatedly been said, pays regard to no common interest unless for the sake of its private benefit; and the aim of tyranny is what is pleasant (*hêdus*), that of royalty what is noble (*kalos*). Hence even in their requisitions, money is the aim of tyrants (*chrêmata tyrannika*), but rather marks of honour (*timê*) that of kings; and a king's bodyguard consists of citizens, a tyrant's of foreign mercenaries (*xenoi*).

The citizens must be kept poor (Arist. *Pol.* 1313b), their resources channelled towards the tyrant's friends, such as the soldiers on whom the tyranny is based, while conversely the citizens' poverty keeps them powerless. Greek traditions associated many of the archaic tyrants with coinage, and as in the case of early lawgivers, who were them-selves autocrats, with weights and measures. Thucydides (1.13.1) thought the earlier tyrannies were a result of increasing amounts of wealth (*chrêmata*) accrued in the various *poleis*.[9] Even family members of the tyrannies can be associated with money. After Himera, Demarete, the wife of Gelon, minted high value coins (*nomisma*) (Diod. 11.26.3). Pheidon of Argos was credited with the first stan-dardisation of weights and measures and the earliest money on the

Greek mainland (Hdt. 6.127.3).[10] Money is a predominant feature of
Herodotean tales about the tyrannies of Polycrates (3.123.1) and
Maeandrius (3.142). Polycrates is the only Greek to mint coins in
Herodotus (3.56), and worthless coins at that. He craved great wealth
and he died when Oroetes lured him across to the mainland with
promises of *chrêmata* (3.122–5). According to Herodotus, the money
was to provide the foundations for Polycrates' control of all Hellas,
which was what made it attractive (3.122). The word *chrêmata* is
emphasised throughout the story: Herodotus wanted his audience left
in no doubt about the root cause of Polycrates' fall. This is reminiscent of Thucydides' maxim (1.10) that prior to his generation states
were incapable of greater power not because of a lack of manpower
(*oliganthrôpia*), but because of a lack of *chrêmata*. Maeandrius,
Polycrates' successor, found money was the sticking point when nego-
tiating his abdication with aristocrats who demanded an account of
his treasuries (Hdt. 3.142–3). No doubt this was not the truest cause
of their concerns, but a significant point upon which Herodotus
focuses.[11] Finally, Herodotus (1.61.3–4) and Aristotle (*Ath. Pol.*
15.1–3) both associated the power of money with the final establishment of Pisistratus as tyrant in Athens. His control of metals in the
north Aegean around Pangaeum was particularly important.[12]

   Money and the tyrannies of the later fifth and fourth centuries BC
are associated. Tyrants required wealth and demonstrated their superiority by display and consumption, none more so than Dionysius of
Syracuse.[13] Tyrants, like Dionysius, were painted as evil, and even
ludicrous, in their garnering of financial resources. Thus they killed
or exiled the rich within their communities and seized their resources.
They levied enormous taxes to keep those around them poor and so
provided themselves with revenues. Aristotle (*Pol.* 1313b16) relates
how Dionysius of Syracuse levied heavy taxes on the people. In his
Economics (1349a–b) he tells nine stories of how Dionysius raised
money, often from the hapless Syracusans; in one he defrauded them
of their silver and used it to repay his debts with coins to which he
gave an arbitrarily inflated value. Like the overvalued ratio of genuine
silver to the value of a coin, the tyrant has no intrinsic value himself.
Dionysius is a typical tyrant, who, when not killing, defrauding and
taxing his own citizens, raised money for mercenaries by looting
temples and their sacred treasuries (Diod. 15.13.1, 14.3; Livy, 24.3.8;
Strabo 5.226). These are all common to the negative traditions concerning men like Dionysius and other military dynasts. There may be
another side to men like Dionysius and these negative traditions

often take us from the sublime to the ridiculous, well illustrated in the *stratêgêmata* of Polyaenus (6.1.2–3), where for example Jason of Pherae raised money for mercenaries by playing tricks on his wealthy mother.[14]

The money raised by these schemes supported ancient tyranny by several methods. Mercenaries were a necessary expense. Hired help from outside the state's boundaries supported autocratic regimes and provided men whose loyalty to the autocrat and position was guaranteed. Autocrats styled as tyrannical or tyrants by the sources regularly gathered foreign military support against the citizens they ruled. Sicilian tyrants, most notably Hieron (Diod. 11.48.3), gathered *xenoi* about their persons: Thrasydaeus (Diod. 11.53.2–3), having become *biaios phonikos* and therefore *tyrannikos*, hired *misthophoroi*, and Thrasybulus (Diod.11.67.5), was *kakos* and *biaios* and enrolled a large number of mercenaries (*plêthos misthophoros*) to secure his position. To return once more to Aristotle (*Pol.* 1285a, 1311a), the philosopher noted that a state's citizens protected legitimate monarchs, while tyrants needed outsiders to protect them from their own people. Mercenaries were, therefore, central to his definition of a Greek tyrant.

Military coups in which support came from hired assistance from outsiders established several important tyrannies. Dionysius ruled through his mercenaries, disarming the citizen body and turning Ortygia into a fortified palace for his hirelings. According to a hostile Diodorus, he had gathered 'a multitude of mercenaries (*misthophoroi*) . . . to hold the Syracusans in slavery (*douleia*)' (Diod. 14.65.2–3). Clearchus at Heraclea in the 360s (Polyaenus 2.30.2; Justin 16.4.1) and Timophanes at Corinth (Arist. *Pol.* 1306a19) both reflect Aristotle's belief that military leadership and political power are never far removed. Other tyrants are associated with mercenary troops through the establishment and maintenance of their power and with their own ability to pay desperate non-citizens. Thus Dionysius broke certain conventions in providing arms to men who could not arm themselves, the lower classes of society, and employing them in his service (Diod. 16.41.1–43.2). This was also the case with Theron of Selinus (Polyaenus 1.26) and Phalaris of Acragas (Polyaenus 5.1), who armed slaves to secure their power.

There are many examples of revolutions based on mercenary support, resulting in tyranny. Euphron at Sicyon in about 367 BC made himself tyrant through such a revolution.[15] He established a democratic government in opposition to the Spartan-supported oligarchy, appointed his son Adeas to command the mercenary troops and then proceeded to win over the loyalty of these troops by judicious use of public treasuries and sacred funds (*tôn dêmosiôn* . . . *tôn hierôn chrêmatôn*). He was then able to kill and banish his enemies, bring everybody (*pas*) under his control, and, in the words of a very hostile Xenophon, established himself as manifestly a tyrant (*saphôs tyrannos*). The use of the combination of money (*chrêmata*) and a mercenary force (*xenikon*) underpinned the anti-oligarchic and anti-Spartan revolution. The generals of Phocis became *tyrannoi* in the minds of certain contemporaries because they commanded mercenary armies, behaved sacrilegiously at Delphi and dictated Phocian policy towards the shrine.[16] Demosthenes (23.124) perhaps more accurately called Phayllus a *dynastês*. Jason of Pherae, *tagos* of Thessaly, established himself as master of central Greece in the later 370s largely through a highly professional army described in approving terms by Xenophon (*Hell.* 6.1.6); Kraay illustrates what might be a coin of Jason.[17] Jason and the Phocians attracted men to them because of their generosity. Their money enabled them to reward their troops handsomely. Jason even rewarded his men on merit. Xenophon (6.1.6) records that Jason expelled the soft or weak (*malakos*) from his armies, but gave to men who were most fond of toil (*philoponos*) and danger (*philokundinos*) double, triple and even quadruple rewards (*moiria*) and gifts (*dôron*).

The Phocian generals went further than other Greek mainlanders during the Third Sacred War in their association of money and mercenaries with their power. Diodorus (16.28.2, 36.1, 56.5) attests that several of the Phocian leaders minted coins from melted-down dedications taken from the sanctuary. Onomarchus was one of these. His coins bore the legend of his name alongside the usual symbols of Apollo and the oracle.[18] The attribution to a single person on the legend illustrates a new style of autocracy on the Greek mainland, reflecting the growing influence of the dynasts of the east in Greek affairs. Coins of the Thebans display the personal names of the rotating magistrates, Boeotarchs, from the mid-390s.[19] The metal for these came from Tithraustes, the Persian successor of Tissaphernes (Xen. *Hell.* 3.5.1). Like Jason, Alexander of Pherae minted coins with his personal legend in the early 360s BC.[20] Previously the legends of Greek coinage referred to the coining community, the Athenians, the Corinthians or the Syracusans. Not even Dionysius of Syracuse broke this tradition despite his reliance upon money and mercenaries to support his regime. Only the Great King of the Persians and other barbarian rulers, including Alexander I of Macedonia who coined in the 460s BC, had placed their personal symbols on coins.[21] In the later fifth century this habit was becoming more widespread as less powerful dynasts amongst the non-Hellenes minted their own coins in imitation of Athenian and Persian models. This was due to the more monetised nature of the Greek world and its environs, but also to the need of these men to hire Greek mercenaries from the mainland and to keep such mercenaries loyal in the more disparate political world of the late classical age. Thus coinages with images of the heads of Persian satraps on the obverse, men like Tissaphernes and Pharnabazus, produced in the latter stages of the Peloponnesian wars, appear to be mocking Athenian issues with owls, olives and the legend BAS for the Greek word for the Great King (*Basileus*) on the reverse.[22] The identity of the men on these coins has been challenged, but they are certainly eastern dynasts.[23] All these coins must be for a Greek audience. They illustrate eastern interest in Greek military personnel and show the trend by which individual paymasters (*misthodotai*) commanded troops in the eastern Mediterranean. Cyrus the Younger, who hired some 13,000 Greeks for his coup against the Great King, minted special imitation darics with a beardless and youthful Great King-like figure on the face of the coin for his cause. Non-Greek coins for a Greek audience appeared in other parts of the Mediterranean, like Egypt and Thrace.[24]

The symbolic, as opposed to the purely economic, importance of coinage in establishing relationships should not be overlooked. By his victory in the Sacred War Philip made possession of any coinage of the Phocian generals illegal (Diod. 16.60.1). The coins were made from stolen dedications from the sanctuary at Delphi, at least according to the propaganda of the victors. Coinage in this instance demonstrates complicity in an illegal action, and also with an enemy of Philip. Diodorus (16.8.6–7) knew well that Philip's fortunes rested heavily on his coinages; he transformed Macedonia completely when in 356 BC he gained control of Amphipolis and with it the mines at Pangaeum in a manner somewhat reminiscent of Pisistratus. Philip's coins, the Philippeioi, dominated the Aegean in the 350s and 340s BC.[25] As a king Philip had few qualms about stamping his legend and symbols, though not his own image, on these coins and he used them to pay a professional army, hire mercenaries and bribe the Greeks.[26] Coins attracted men to his cause and went hand in hand with war, marriage and diplomacy. Theopompus' (115 F 225) hostility extended to Philip's friends: dissipated by Philip's money, they became common

prostitutes, indeed brothel-men or ground-thumpers (*chamaitypoi*).
Money was a sure way of bringing men together and keeping them in
service. Coin became a potent symbol of power and of paymaster.

Coinage was only one of many tools by which Philip augmented
his power abroad. It remained an instrument that facilitated the
decline of the *polis* and enabled influential and well-connected men to
spread their influence beyond the boundaries of their own communities. But the success of autocracy in the late classical period rested on
related phenomena as well. For the growth and maintenance of the
power of the great man, the importance of friendship networks across
community boundaries was of equal significance in the late classical
period. The powerful men in the Greek mainland and Sicily had, for
a brief time in the fifth century, to live within the growing social isolation of their democratic communities. This was particularly true of
Athens, where democracy had limited opportunities for and benefits
gained from the friendship of great and powerful men in the rest of
the world. Athenian statesmen had to function within an Athenian
sea. Even had they wished to maintain strong links with aristocrats
from other communities, several factors limited the appeal of such
connections, not least being Pericles' citizenship law of 451 BC, which
made marriage to non-Athenian women unattractive (Arist. *Ath. Pol.*
26.3). There was also a lack of opportunity to command large forces
for others, to colonise wealthy lands outside the Athenian sphere of
influence, or to obtain greater rewards than one's own state could
provide. It is almost impossible to find an Athenian in service abroad
under any authority other than the Athenian state during the last two-
thirds of the fifth century. After the collapse of the Athenian Empire
we find various Athenians in service to others including with the
Thracians, Persian satraps and Egyptians, not to mention the Great
King himself.

One of the mainstays of non-democratic government, not necessarily limited to autocracy, was the cultivation of aristocratic networks of
friendship across community boundaries. The early tyrants seem to
have supported each other with military and other traditional features of ritualised friendships (*xeniai*). Lygdamis of Naxos supported
Pisistratus, who also, as we have seen, received help from Argos
and Thebes (Hdt. 1.61–4).[27] Polycrates and Amasis the Egyptian were
xenoi (Hdt. 3.39). More democratic Greek governments feared these
relationships as potentially dangerous to their own socio-political
structures. Thus Sparta felt threatened enough by the relations of
Pausanias son of Cleombrotus with those outside Spartan boundaries,

that they accused him of plotting a marriage-alliance with the Great King (Thuc. 1.128–35). Athenian democrats nurtured social isolation within the community to the detriment of both panhellenic policies and friendships with non-Hellenes. As the Peloponnesian War came to an end and the Persians played an increasingly important role in Greek affairs, powerful friendships began to resurface among the elite. Alcibiades was the first of the Athenians to utilise these friendships in his activities outside the Athenian sphere of influence: among the Spartans as a guest-friend of the Spartan king (Thuc. 6.88) and then with the Persian nobility in western Asia Minor (Thuc. 8.45–52). Persian friendship enabled him to return to Athenian politics in the hope that he might be able to make the Athenians the friends of the Great King (Thuc. 8.47.2).

At the end of the war the dynasts of the east influenced the Greek communities and fostered ambitious individuals. Their money travelled across political boundaries to their traditional ritualised guest-friends and associates. *Xenia* and *philia* amongst aristocrats now played their part in creating anti-democratic structures within the Greek world. This is well illustrated by Cyrus the Younger's revolutionary war against his brother, Artaxerxes II. Cyrus had links with Greek communities and with individual Greeks, in part because he had facilitated Persian aid to Sparta and its allies (Xen. *Hell.* 3.1.1). Several friendships went back some time (Xen. *Anab.* 1.1). In 402 BC he laid his plans for war against his brother, sending money to his friends to raise troops. In at least one case on the Greek mainland, involving Aristippus in Thessaly, this money and the troops it raised fed a local political revolution (Xen. *Anab.* 1.1.10). The Spartan renegade Clearchus established himself as tyrant in the Chersonesos with the money he received from Cyrus and with this he hired mercenaries (Xen. *Anab.* 1.1.9; Diod. 14.12.9). Eventually, Cyrus called on his Greek friends to help in his war, and Sparta and many of his *xenoi* duly sent troops. Many went in hopes of rich rewards from the Persian prince. Xenophon (*Anab.* 3.1.4) couched his own reasons for going on the expedition in terms, not of greed or of monetary interest, but of aristocratic friendship. He stated of himself:

> There was a man in the army named Xenophon who was neither general nor captain nor private, but had accompanied the expedition because Proxenus, a ritualised friend (*xenos*) of his, had sent him at his home an invitation to go with him. Proxenus had promised that if he would go, he would make him a friend (*philos*) of Cyrus, whom he himself regarded as being worth more to him than was his native state.

This says much about Proxenus' feelings towards Boeotia and the power of Cyrus. Nowhere is the importance of such trans-community friendships better illustrated than in the speeches of Clearchus the Spartan in the opening stages of Xenophon's *Anabasis* (1.3.1–6, 1.3.9–12, 2.5.14). He said to Tissaphernes that 'the reason I wanted to become the friend of Cyrus was that I thought of all his contemporaries he was best able to help those he wished to help' (Xen. *Anab.* 2.5.13). Clearchus having turned his back on Sparta owed everything to Cyrus. The ten thousand darics that Cyrus provided had enabled him to thrive in Thrace as tyrant. Cyrus was bigger than Sparta or indeed any state in Greece and his friendship and money enabled ambitious men to break their city's social, political and economic constraints. Eastern despotism enabled the rise of powerful individuals in the Greek world in the later classical period. The *xenoi* of the wealthy and the men who followed them were attracted to powerful men of the east by hopes of wealth and patronage. The friends of the Great King and his associates became great men in their own right. Money and mercenaries were the tools that drove their power.

For many talented Greeks in the fourth century BC provenance ceased to be paramount as *poleis* lost ground to the dynasts on the periphery of the Greek world. Inscriptions and other evidence show all manner of Greeks in service of great men in this period.[28] Greeks found service with dynasts in the east, with princes in the north and with tyrants in the west. The attractions of the wealth of eastern rulers had long been a topos of Greek literature. Fragments of Antiphanes' fourth-century play *The Soldier* (Athenaeus 6.258) indicate that the allure of the wealth of individuals was strong in 350 BC. In the fourth century many were seeking mercenary associations outside Greece with powerful autocrats.[29] The Rhodian brothers Mentor and Memnon are a case in point.[30] They rose to positions of authority in the Persian Empire that no other Greek had ever achieved. They were not just the friends (*philoi*) of the Great King himself, but each man in turn was as powerful as Cyrus had been in the western empire. These Rhodians were more than mere mercenary commanders, though among the services they provided were recruitment and command of mercenaries for the Persians. In this world of great men they had married into the Persian nobility and become part of a world broader than the city community, the boundaries of which they had crossed long before.

Memnon of Rhodes was a product of his fourth-century context. He had grown powerful through marriage into the Persian nobility, had recruited and commanded mercenaries for the Persian satraps, and had become the *philos* of the Great King, rising above all other friends of the King. He was a great man in his own right, in a way reminiscent of the world before the Athenian Empire. That was a world of aristocratic chieftains and tyrants interacting through friendships, military alliances and marriages across city, community and national boundaries. In the sixth century, the Cretan Hybrias could sing a drinking-war song typical of the time before the Athenian hegemony.[31] He praised his arms for his food and his drink. He was a mercenary and his trade enabled his status. He is called master and Great King, alluding to a deep desire for prestige among all Greek citizens. Hybrias would have found mercenary mobility more difficult in the fifth century. The Athenians had briefly submerged their elite within the socially exclusive *polis*. They had for a short time turned their wealthy citizens to look inward and away from friendships outside the state. In the process they had monetised Athens and accustomed the Aegean to coin. The collapse of Athens re-opened the world of the cities to the elite's quest for friends outside their communities. This included the world of the Persian elite. Now the aristocrats of Greece re-emerged from their cities and re-established ancient associations among their friends abroad.

The chaos of the fourth century BC was a product of competing political interests. No one power or person controlled the resources of the eastern Aegean, let alone the Mediterranean. Philip and Alexander's success lay in their control of a large part of the mineral resources of the region. Amphipolis produced as many as thirteen million coins, producing 700 obverse and 1,300 reverse dies in the eighteen years prior to Alexander's death.[32] This money did much to help him pay his friends in a world in which friendship and alliance were more fluid and less constrained by provenance. Money made the kingdom and the man at the same time, as money, friends and mercenaries underpinned success. All supported the great men. The Macedonian kings were among the principal beneficiaries of these new relationships. Alexander realised all men's ambitions when he became Great King of the Persian Empire, actualising an age-old topos of Greek imagination whether it be in an archaic poet's drinking songs or in Spartan and Athenian fears that one of their own might marry the daughter of the king of Persia. He made himself King of All. He and his successors were the last act in this triumph of the individual over the state.

NOTES

1. Andrewes 1956: 20; Salmon 1977: 93–101 and 1997: 60–73; Luraghi 1994.
2. Figueira 1998: 3–13, 175–9; Meiggs 1972: 167–72; Starr 1982: 129–34.
3. Kallet-Marx 1993: 23, 28–32.
4. Von Reden 1995: 173–5; Kallet-Marx 1993: 29–30.
5. Kallet 2003: 137–42; Raaflaub 2003: 77–84.
6. See Gabrielsen 1994: 105–25.
7. Cook 1958: 275–92; see Wallace 1987: 385–97; Knapp 2002: 183–96.
8. De Ste. Croix 1981: 171.
9. See Kallet-Marx 1993: 30.
10. Also Arist. *Pol.* 1310b; Ephorus 70 F 115, 176; Andrewes 1956: 39–42.
11. See McGlew 1993: 124–5; Roisman 1985: 257–77; Shipley 1987: 103, who speculates that Maeandrius was complicit in Polycrates' fall.
12. See Seltman 1955: pl. 3 nos 16 and 17 for what might be coins of Pisistratus.
13. Kallet 2003: 122–6; Seaford 2003: 95–115; on Dionysius, Andrewes 1956: 137–42.
14. Sanders 1987: 176 no. 3.
15. Xen. *Hell.* 7.1.44–6; Andrewes 1956: 143–4.
16. Aesch. 2.130–1; also Polyaen. 5.4.5; Plut. *Mor.* 249f and 401f; Athenaeus 6.231d.
17. Kraay 1976: pl. 21, no. 387.
18. Carradice and Price 1988: pl. 10, no. 142; Williams 1976: 22–56.
19. Carradice and Price 1988: pl. 10, no. 140.
20. Seltman 1955: pl. 34, nos 14 and 15; Kraay 1976: pl. 21, nos 388–89; see Sprawski, Chapter 9, this volume.
21. Seltman 1955: pl. 27 no. 13.
22. Tissaphernes: Carradice and Price 1988: pl. 11, no. 159; Jenkins 1972: 103 nos 218–19; Pharnabazus: Carradice and Price 1988: pl. 11, no. 158.
23. Harrison 2002: 302–19.
24. Kraay 1976: pl. 12, no. 217 (Tachos), Youroukova 1976: no. 13 (Cotys) and no. 17 (Seuthes).
25. Martin 1985: *passim*.
26. Seltman 1955: pl. 46, nos 7–14.
27. See Andrewes 1956: 112–13.
28. *CIG* 3.4702; Miller 1984: 153–60; Trundle 2004: 44–6.
29. Pritchett 1974: 56–112; Herman 1987: 97–102; Mitchell 1997: 188.
30. Diod. 16.42.3, 45.2, 52.1–8, 17.7.1; Parke 1933: 166–9, 178.
31. Parke 1933: 4.
32. Seltman 1955: 207 no. 1.

CHAPTER 6

From Agathocles to Hieron II: *the birth and development of* basileia *in Hellenistic Sicily*

Efrem Zambon

The kingships of Agathocles and Hieron II in Syracuse are often seen not as monarchies of the Hellenistic kind, but as a continuation of the type of tyranny held by Hieron I and Gelon in the fifth century, and Dionysius the Elder in the fourth. In this chapter I will argue that, on the contrary, the historical evidence plainly shows them to be true kingships.

Institutional change in Sicily in the first decades of the Hellenistic age was undoubtedly a slow and difficult process. From the fifth century Sicily had undergone a peculiar historical evolution, which reached its height in the age of the elder Dionysius, the distinctive features of which – the autocratic form of power, the creation of an extensive state, colonisation in the Adriatic and the development of urban buildings – are similar to many in the Hellenistic age. Conditions in Sicily allowed the adoption of political solutions which the Greeks of the mainland and the eastern Mediterranean basin were to test later, with Alexander the Great and especially the Successors; the most important of these developments was the birth of *basileia*.

Timoleon, who arrived in Sicily in 344 BC to mediate among the struggling parties in Syracuse, succeeded in remedying not only the problems of that city-state, but also those of many other Sicilian *poleis* which were at that time dominated by tyrants and threatened – as usual – by military and political pressure from Carthage. He first defeated the Punic troops at the River Crimisus and confined the Carthaginians to the western part of Sicily; this was achieved with the support of the Sicilian tyrants, who subsequently became his new enemies. Hicetas of Leontini, Mamercus of Catane and Hippo of Messina were overthrown and driven out from their towns, where Timoleon encouraged the establishment of new democracies. The *poleis* organised themselves into an alliance (*symmachia*) under the leadership of Syracuse. Nevertheless, after Timoleon's death in

337 the political and social concord he had created in Sicily immediately collapsed, primarily due to the lack of a new leader: tyrannies returned in many *poleis* and the Carthaginians renewed their aims of eastward expansionism, trying as always to complete the conquest of Sicily. In Syracuse the democratic system established by Timoleon was replaced by an oligarchic government of six hundred Syracusan nobles, led by Sosistratus and Heracleides; they unsurprisingly faced opposition from the democratic party, together with representatives of the impoverished social classes, who very soon found a new leader and spurred him on to aim at tyranny.[1]

Agathocles' early political career was spent mostly in exile from Syracuse, which allowed him to gain support elsewhere in Sicily, for example at Morgantina and Leontini, where he was able to hire many mercenary troops.[2] When he was recalled to Syracuse in 319, he still acted as popular leader and succeeded in winning back the support of many people through his deeds and his eloquence. Diodorus Siculus (19.5.4–5) states that Agathocles won the favour of the Syracusan people by his populist approach (δημαγωγήσας), saying that he wanted to protect democracy, and so he was elected as general and protector of the peace (στρατηγὸς κατεσστάθη καὶ φύλαξ τῆς εἰρήνης). A different definition of Agathocles' first office appears in the *Marmor Parium* (*FGrHist* 239 F 12), where Agathocles is said to have been appointed by the Syracusans as *stratêgos autokratôr* (αὐτοκράτορα στρατηγόν). The whole colour of Diodorus' passage seems to be favourable to Agathocles; we can conjecture that his source changed the title of *stratêgos autokratôr* to the simple *stratêgeia* and guardianship of the peace, in order to support Agathocles' propaganda; nevertheless, the nature of the power was exactly the same, and the position offered an excellent opportunity for a coup d'état. Because the office was an extraordinary one, as the terminology of the *Marmor* clearly indicates, with the specific aim of bringing about a reconciliation among the political parties, it was not annual but of indefinite term. No doubt this was the first step towards monarchic government, and the autocratic *stratêgeia* of Agathocles was 'officially' renewed after the coup of 316/15.[3]

In declaring that he was happy to accept the decision of the popular assembly, provided no colleagues were appointed with him (as he did not wish to take responsibility for their illegal acts), Agathocles was behaving in a similar way to Dionysius I or Pisistratus. Although Diodorus emphasises the role of the assembly in his election, it is meaningless to stress its lawful aspect; indeed, the elimination of his political challengers, through murder or exile, had paved the way for Agathocles' election. The assembly continued to exist in Syracuse as a political institution, but it was deprived of its powers and became simply a means to carry out the general's (or the king's) wishes.[4] Undoubtedly, after such tyrannical acts, the oligarchs and their supporters found it difficult to show open opposition; certainly at the time of his election the assembly was full of Agathocles' followers and the representatives of the poorest classes (indeed, Diodorus says that the greatest part of those sitting in the assembly had been responsible for the massacre of the oligarchs). Even if Diodorus says that Agathocles did not have a bodyguard, he could rely on his loyal army and mercenaries, and such conditions should not lead us to see his election to the autocratic *stratêgeia* as legal: his coup has the distinctive features of the beginning of a tyranny. The parallels between Agathocles and Dionysius at this stage can be seen from a careful reading of Diodorus' account of events (19.9.1–7): he describes the rule of the Six Hundred in Syracuse as an oligarchy, but then says that Agathocles freed the town from people who were planning to seize absolute power, using the term *dynasteia* (usually used to describe Dionysius' rule), meaning absolute power of a tyrannical kind.[5] In describing Agathocles' government, Diodorus says that when the people made him sole leader of the city (the verb used here is *monarchein*), and after he had been appointed *stratêgos autokratôr*, it was clear that he held absolute power: here, once again, Diodorus' historical source used the word *dynasteia* to denote supreme authority, like a tyranny. At the end of the chapter Diodorus says that although Agathocles held absolute power (*dynasteia*), he never wore the diadem, nor did he have bodyguards, or think it advantageous to make himself unapproachable, as most tyrants used to do. Two things can be understood from this narrative: first, that at the end of his paragraph Diodorus must have changed his source, because his remarks are undoubtedly favourable to Agathocles, and secondly that for a Greek of the fourth century, *dynasteia* was something different from a simple tyranny. The authority of Agathocles looks a lot like the power of the older Dionysius: a monarchic power, though still not a modern 'monarchy' or kingship.[6]

The turning point, for both Agathocles and his subjects, was the military campaign in Africa in 310–307, when the Sicilian Greeks first encountered the new ideology of the Hellenistic world. It cannot be doubted that this campaign prompted Agathocles to establish a new kind of kingship, in accordance with precedents from both the east and from Africa itself.[7] He decided to assume the royal title in

the year 307–306, at the end of the African venture, in imitation of
the Successors. But we can assume that this was not a spur-of-the-
moment decision, since Diodorus (20.34.3–5) describes a significant
episode in the expedition, which he dates to 309. After his first victories, Agathocles faced a dangerous mutiny of some of his officers
and troops in Tunis, and decided to meet his own soldiers face to
face. His actions were similar to his performance in the Syracusan
assembly in 316/15, when he took off his traditional Macedonian
cloak (*chlamis*), and donned a simple *himation*. But in Africa, something had changed: Agathocles wore a purple robe (τὴν πορφύραν),
which he took off to dress up in a simple *himation* before facing his
soldiers. Now purple robes could be worn by other people besides
the king, but from Hellenistic times onwards it became a symbol of
royal power.[8] We do not know exactly what Agathocles intended
by wearing purple in Africa, but Diodorus says that the soldiers
regarded the purple robe as royal clothes (τὴν βασιλικὴν ἐσθῆτα)
and that it was appropriate for their commander (τὸν προσήκοντα
κόσμον). Of course, this does not mean that Agathocles was thinking of himself as a typical Hellenistic king in 309 – his claim to the
title came a few years after – but certainly something had already
changed in the view of his subjects.

The decisive event of Agathocles' political career is dated by
Diodorus to 307–306, the year in which Demetrius freed Greece from
the influence of Ptolemy, after his success in the naval battle fought near
Cyprus. When he received news of his son's triumph, Antigonus the
One-Eyed wore the diadem and adopted the royal title, together with
Demetrius. His rivals, Ptolemy, Seleucus, Lysimachus and Cassander,
did the same soon after.[9] Diodorus says (20.54.1) that Agathocles,
not to be inferior to them, also began to call himself king (ἑαυτὸν
ἀνηγόρευσε βασιλέα). This act marked the end of a process which had
begun with Dionysius the Elder, and which had made Sicily a new kind
of state, in which the traditional political significance of the Greek *polis*
began to fade away. Diodorus seems to emphasise the change: he says
that Agathocles decided not to wear the diadem, but just a wreath,
which he never abandoned throughout his political career, either as
tyrant or as king.[10]

The plentiful Syracusan coinage of the Agathoclean period offers
further strong evidence for the gradual evolution of his political
career.[11] All the coins of the first period (from 317/16 to 310) carry
the inscription ΣΥΡΑΚΟΣΙΩΝ: although the devices of the gold
series resemble the *Philippeioi*, the name of Agathocles does not

appear. He was at that time *stratêgos autokratôr*, but officially the minting authority was the city of Syracuse. The first signs of change appear on the coins of the second period (310–306). Two series of silver tetradrachms carry a new-style head of Persephone on their obverse, and on the reverse Nike raising a trophy (symbolising Agathocles as victor) and the legend *ΑΓΑΘΟΚΛΕΟΣ*. The first issue still bears on the obverse the inscription *ΣΥΡΑΚΟΣΙΩΝ* as the issuing authority, which may indicate a second stage of political development, with Agathocles as *stratêgos autokratôr*, but officially acknowledging the role of his fellow-citizens. The second issue of tetradrachms have the inscription *ΑΓΑΘΟΚΛΕΟΣ* without the *ΣΥΡΑΚΟΣΙΩΝ*, and additionally there is a monogram AN, which scholars agree is an abbreviation of the name Antander, the brother of Agathocles who was appointed as governor of Syracuse while Agathocles was in Africa. One may suppose that from this time Agathocles assumed the right to mint the silver coinage, and in his absence the duty was assigned to his brother (who signed his name with a monogram); the disappearance of the *ΣΥΡΑΚΟΣΙΩΝ* hints that Agathocles' transition to monarch was imminent. In contrast, the bronze coinage of the period 310–306 bears only the ethnic inscription *ΣΥΡΑΚΟΣΙΩΝ*, which may imply that the Syracusans retained the right to issue some coins in their own name, even if only in bronze. This seems to support the hypothesis that Agathocles gradually took over minting rights.

A gold stater from the same period (of which only three examples are known) has on the obverse a head wearing an elephant scalp, with Ammon's horns, and aegis; on the reverse there is a winged Athena, wearing a helmet and holding a shield and spear.[12] At her feet is an owl, and behind her the inscription *ΑΓΑΘΟΚΛΕΟΣ*. The coin is usually connected with Agathocles' African campaign and therefore dated between 310 and 307; scholars have rightly noted its imitation of Ptolemy's tetradrachms of 314/13.[13] The legend *ΑΓΑΘΟΚΛΕΟΣ* provides a cross-check for the chronology, given that it overlaps the second stage of the silver coinage, but one can be more precise thanks to the representation of the winged Athena and the owl. Since the African campaign ended in defeat, there would have been no reason for Agathocles to issue a victory-coin in 307. But Diodorus described the first great success of the Syracusan leader in North Africa: when the Greeks were outnumbered three to one by the Punic troops, Agathocles suddenly roused their bravery by releasing some owls, which settled on their helmets and shields.[14] If the winged Athena (who has to be considered an Athena Nike) and the owl refer to the victory outside Carthage, the coin was probably minted in the summer of 310. But whose is the head portrayed on the obverse? Some scholars suggest Agathocles himself, others a personification of Africa or of Sicily.[15] The device, however, clearly reproduces the portrait of Alexander the Great on the tetradrachms of Ptolemy, and therefore I suggest that we should identify Alexander on Agathocles' gold staters too, an image with a political message. Not only was Agathocles performing a feat to rival Alexander's in daring, he was in fact fulfilling one of the last plans of the Macedonian king – the conquest of Carthage. Furthermore, the image of Alexander on the gold staters is a sign of Agathocles' monarchic intentions; none of the Diadochoi had the title of king in 310, but all of them claimed to be the rightful successor of Alexander. This, I suggest, was what Agathocles meant by striking this coin after defeating the Carthaginians in their homeland.

The inscription *ΑΓΑΘΟΚΛΕΟΣ ΒΑΣΙΛΕΩΣ* duly appears on the gold and bronze coins of the third period (305–289), while the silver staters have no legend at all. This is strange; many years ago, Head observed that the devices on these silver coins are typical of the Corinthian tradition (head of Athena wearing a Corinthian helmet; flying Pegasus), and had been imported into Sicily by Timoleon; no doubt they suggested to the Syracusans the democratic institutions that the Corinthian leader established in their city.[16] Perhaps Agathocles wanted to give a minor recompense to those citizens who had supported him in seizing the power in Syracuse; even so there is no reappearance of the legend *ΣΥΡΑΚΟΣΙΩΝ*, and Agathocles still found a way to sign those coins with his symbols (the *triskelês* and, especially, the winged thunderbolt).

The emergence on the coinage of the royal title without any ethnic specification – as on contemporary Ptolemaic and Cyrenean issues – meant that the authority of the king had no territorial limits, covering all the areas under direct control of the ruler, as in the other Hellenistic states. Every new monarch repeatedly claimed the principle of a never-ending authority over the so-called *doriktêtos chôra*, the spear-won land, and Mørkholm rightly pointed out that the representation of Athena holding a thunderbolt or a spear, recurrent on the coins of several Hellenistic kings, evokes this ideology.[17] Agathocles' devices on both his gold staters and on the bronze *hêmilitra* minted in the period 305–289 exhibit the same ideology: it is very significant that Agathocles, perhaps even before Demetrius the Besieger, used (as did Ptolemy and Lysimachus) the designs of Athena wearing a Corinthian helmet, Athena standing holding a spear, and the thunderbolt. No doubt this was calculated, since those figures had appeared previously on the coinage issued by Alexander the Great. They are in all probability indicative of a 'personal' kingship, claiming possession of the countries conquered through the army.

In conclusion, the numismatic evidence shows the evolution towards the establishment of the first kingship in Sicily. Agathocles thought of himself as a counterpart of the Successors, who had (or acted as if they had) the right to be the Successors of Alexander: by assuming the royal title, Agathocles gave his own authority a new significance, which integrated him – and his homeland as well – in the new world which had been created by the conquests of Alexander.

Agathocles organised his new kingship with formal procedures (he was surrounded by a group of Friends), minting privileges and royal propaganda (such as the paintings in the temple of Athena in Syracuse, mentioned by Cicero).[18] Some institutions continued under the kingship, particularly the popular assembly, whose activity is attested from the literary sources in foreign and domestic policy. As regards the dynastic succession, for instance, a fragmentary passage of Diodorus relates Agathocles' decision to appoint his son, Agathocles junior, as successor to his kingship. He wanted to introduce his son in the popular assembly, intending that the Syracusans should confirm his choice.[19] This demonstrates that Agathocles did not simply imitate the other Successors (as Diodorus himself seemed to believe) but carefully reorganised the Greek areas of Sicily into a real kingdom, through a meticulous regulation of the cooperation between the king and the popular assembly.

How should one compare Agathocles' kingship with his contemporary eastern Mediterranean autocratic rulers? Berve, focusing only on the formal aspects of the institution, makes a distinction which seems difficult to accept: the kingship of Agathocles was a 'personal' monarchy which had no relation with the city of Syracuse (where he continued to hold the offices of *stratêgos autokratôr* and administrator, as a kind of governor of the city), but only with the rest of Sicily and the other countries he had conquered in his own name. Consequently Agathocles made his conquests in the name of Syracuse, since he was the highest executive officer of the city, but then, as king, added them to his possessions as spear-won lands.[20] But this view of Sicily does not stand up to scrutiny. Agathocles' royal title was not connected with a specific territory; its meaning was absolute, in a political sense, even if in Sicily it seemed to have been tempered, at least officially, by the popular councils of the Greek communities. Agathocles' kingship might be considered as a middle course between so-called 'national' monarchy, like the Macedonian kingship which coexisted with the Macedonian assembly, and 'personal' monarchy, with no territorial limits (like the kingships of the Ptolemies or the Seleucids). The decisions of the king were endorsed – at least formally – by the popular assembly, while all the members of Agathocles' family received royal honours; privileges for Theoxene, the Egyptian wife of Agathocles, Lanassa and his son Agathocles junior are all mentioned by the surviving historical sources.[21]

Some may say that many of these features can already be found in the political tradition dating back to the Deinomenids, but the cultural setting and the ideological background of the period were completely different. The innovations of Agathocles' age include the establishment of the monarchic territorial state as a new political institution; the close dynastic and economic interactions with the other Successors; the transformation of the Sicilian *poleis*, which had been affected since their foundation – and sometimes still were – by social struggles and civil wars, but which had been renewed through ethnic mixing; the innovative organisation of commercial exchanges between the cities; the interaction of communities with their rural areas; and last but not least, equality for all before the king and the duties that had to be paid to him. The establishment of the kingship and changes to these institutions made Sicily for the first time similar to the other Hellenistic kingdoms, in that both the Greek city-states and the native communities of the Sicels were linked to the king; they retained their own institutions, like the popular councils, even if not the same power. It is not clear whether the subject cities were controlled by occupying forces, or whether they were ruled by the king through the election of a local administrator; they did, however, lose the right to issue coinage because Syracuse became the exclusive mint for the whole of Greek Sicily.[22]

When Agathocles neared the end of his life, he initially decided to leave the kingship to his son, Agathocles junior, but once his heir had been murdered by Archagathus, his son-in-law, Agathocles decided to restore the democracy in Syracuse, and to give the popular assembly the task of taking revenge for him against Archagathus.[23] What followed was a period of great political uncertainty and unrest, leading to two major events: the new military offensive of the Carthaginians in Sicily, and the rise of new tyrannies in the Greek city-states.[24] This latter event seems to show that the *basileia* invented in Sicily by Agathocles had not had enough time to become rooted in the political thought of the Siceliotes. Evidence that the Greeks of Sicily were still uncertain about the political innovation of the monarchy is provided by Phintias of Acragas, who was tyrant in the city after the death of Agathocles and before Pyrrhus' arrival in Sicily. The few literary passages concerning Phintias portray him as a typical tyrant: Diodorus reports that he was a bloodthirsty man who put to death many wealthy citizens and behaved so violently against the cities under his control that they rose up and expelled the garrisons settled there by him, forcing him to change his methods of government and to act with more temperance. Diodorus' source designated him Ἀκράγαντος τύραννος, but the numismatic evidence shows a different perspective: only bronze coinage minted in Acragas in the period of Phintias' government survives, and for the most part the coins bear on the reverse the inscription *ΒΑΣΙΛΕΩΣ ΦΙΝΤΙΑ*, '(coin) of king Phintias': there is no doubt that, following the example of Agathocles, after seizing power in Acragas Phintias decided to assume the royal title, and wanted to be considered as king of Acragas itself and of all the cities under his control, although it is less certain that he meant to be king of Sicily as well.[25] At least once (22.2.2) Diodorus' source characterises Phintias as a Hellenistic king: it is not surprising that Phintias should have founded a city, transplanting the population from the devastated Gela to a new settlement, but it is astonishing that he gave his own name to the new city, which was called Phintias. This was a typical action for a Hellenistic king, and Phintias was the first to perform it in the West. In this case, one cannot say that he was imitating Agathocles; rather, he had heard of the foundations made by the Successors in the east and was trying to follow their example in the west.[26]

Basileia next appeared in Sicily with the military expedition of Pyrrhus, king of Epirus. When he settled in Syracuse to organise the military advance westwards against Carthage, he received diplomatic representatives from other Sicilian *poleis*, who wanted to place their hometowns' trust in him.[27] Polybius (7.4.5) said that Pyrrhus was the only man whom all the Siceliotes accepted as their *hêgemôn* and king. It has been suggested that Pyrrhus' role was that of *hêgemôn* when in the autumn of 278 he became commander-in-chief of all the Siceliotes, while *basileus* was his real political title.[28] But there must be a connection between the two titles; indeed, when the representatives entrusted complete jurisdiction over their communities to Pyrrhus, the

cities immediately became components of a single kingdom, the Sicilian
kingdom, which was later joined with the other two kingdoms – Italy
and Epirus – which Pyrrhus assigned to his two sons. Once again,
Pyrrhus achieved the territorial and political unification of Sicily
(except, of course, the territories still under Carthaginian control) in
the mode of a 'personal', absolute, Hellenistic monarchy. Justin
(23.3.2) says that 'after his arrival in Syracuse, Pyrrhus was hailed as
both king of Sicily and king of Epirus'.[29] Bengtson has rightly pointed
out that in Epirus the royal authority was not absolute, because of the
restrictions on the king's decisions from the federal assembly of the
Epirotes (the Epirote monarchy was hardly of the Hellenistic kind).[30]
Pyrrhus made several attempts to strengthen the king's position in
Epirus: his basic objective seems to have been to found a purely
Hellenistic kingship there as well as in Sicily. Pyrrhus' contemporaries
saw him as a Hellenistic monarch; as Bengtson notes, both the Roman
literary sources and the Greek writers who were favourable to the
Romans always designated Pyrrhus as *rex Epiri*, equating him with the
other Hellenistic kings.

In time, events drove Pyrrhus to take absolute and despotic decisions, which very soon stirred up rebellion among those same natives
who had welcomed him enthusiastically just two years before; the
rupture with the Siceliotes happened when Pyrrhus planned a new
expedition to Africa. Plutarch (*Pyrrhus* 23.3–4) says that at first he
behaved with an extreme – and perhaps not disinterested – courtesy,
but then there was a progression of brutal and violent deeds, which
in all probability began once he attained the kingship and supremacy
over the Greek city-states. As Plutarch's source maintains, he changed
from king to tyrant. The nature of Pyrrhus' measures makes plain that
the hatred of the Siceliotes was deep-rooted; Pyrrhus' political choices
could only be seen by the Greek city-states as deliberate violation
of their independence. But this was natural in the perspective of a
Hellenistic monarch. So Plutarch's words γινόμενος ἐκ δημαγωγοῦ
τύραννος do not mean that Pyrrhus, after being the leader of the
democratic party, became a tyrant with the support of the aristocracy;
they mean that, after being the king of all the Siceliotes, he became
their tyrant. Once again, the controversy between the Hellenistic
meaning of kingship and Greek ideas about it can be seen: Dionysius
of Halicarnassus (20.8.1) said that it had become evident to the chief
cities of Sicily that Pyrrhus' leadership was not that of a king (διὰ τὸ
μὴ βασιλικὴν φανῆναι τὴν ἡγεμονίαν) but of a despot (δεσποτικήν).
Dionysius' source (Timaeus?) emphasised the clear-cut definition of a

Hellenistic ruler, who would consider both Sicily and the Greek city-states not as allies (as a *hêgemôn* might) but as subjects.[31] The Siceliotes did not entirely realise the consequences of their willing submission; the struggles that broke out after the first year of victorious operations against the Carthaginians originated in the difference between the Greek idea of royal power and Pyrrhus' own. The Siceliotes still understood royal power in a 'Greek' way, as they had previously done with Agathocles and the fourth-century dynasts, who had been characterised as tyrants and had to face fierce rebellions either because they seemed to behave as monarchs or because they wanted to give their rule the typical features of the Hellenistic kingships.

Pyrrhus' coinage in Sicily has some features which further emphasise his political position.[32] The iconography of the gold and silver coinage is part of a planned celebration of the king, with detailed allusions to his heroic ancestry (the head of Achilles, wearing a Corinthian helmet, coupled with his mother Thetis sitting on a hippocampus), his divine descent and, of course, his Epirote origin. The silver tetradrachms bear on the obverse the head of Dodonean Zeus, crowned with oak leaves, and on the reverse his wife Dione; the meaning of the devices is clear, because Dione was not only a 'national' goddess of Epirus but was widely celebrated in Sicily, so the representation was useful to show the Siceliotes that they were related to Pyrrhus' homeland through religion.[33] Pyrrhus used other symbols to connect himself with his predecessors in the Sicilian kingship and with the Successor kings: on the reverse of the silver octobols, for instance, a standing Athena is represented holding a shield and throwing a spear, the same model of Athena Promachos as represented on several coins of Ptolemy and Agathocles.[34] But for his political propaganda Pyrrhus especially used devices typical of the Syracusan minting tradition, such as the head of Persephone with long hair, the head of Artemis with curly hair and the winged thunderbolt. The iconography of the gold coinage is particularly evocative: the staters bear on the obverse the head of Athena wearing a Corinthian helmet, and on the reverse a standing Nike, holding trophies in her hands and crowned with oak leaves; the drachmas have on the obverse the head of Artemis, and on the reverse the same standing Nike. No doubt the coins were issued after the arrival of Pyrrhus in Syracuse in 278, as the meaning of the Nike Trophaiophora is clearly to celebrate the first victories of the king in Sicily. The most important element of the coins is the legend, which is always *ΠΥΡΡΟΥ ΒΑΣΙΛΕΩΣ*, and since they were minted in Sicily, for the most part in the official mint of Syracuse, the reference is to the Sicilian kingship. Pyrrhus minted coins in Sicily with his own name because the Greeks gave him this privilege when they appointed him as their own king and *hêgemôn*.

But the monarchic experience of Pyrrhus in Sicily finally proved to be a failure, and after his departure the same unrest ensued in Syracuse as after Agathocles' death; the aristocracy theoretically held power, but were opposed by the people, supported by the troops. The soldiers put forward two of their leaders, Hieron and Artemidorus, both of whom were nominated *archontes* by the people, an office that had never appeared in Syracuse before the Hellenistic age. While Artemidorus simply disappeared from the scene, Hieron on the contrary established a personal sovereignty very similar to contemporary Hellenistic kingships.[35] He immediately tried to settle the civil struggles, and for the first time achieved it without massacres, proscriptions or confiscation of properties: the people were on his side, and to ensure the support of the upper and wealthy classes, Hieron married Philistis, a descendant of the historian Philistus and a member of a prominent family of the Syracusan oligarchy. Like many other absolute rulers before him, he understood that a state of war could strengthen his political power; he therefore got from the popular assembly the office of *stratêgos autokratôr* for the war against Carthage (like Agathocles), which he retained until he assumed the royal title.

The primary feature of Hieron's kingship is his relationship with Rome: the king was faithful to the Romans throughout his long reign, but never accepted their domination, and maintained diplomatic relationships or commercial exchanges with the main powers of the Mediterranean, including Carthage.[36] Those activities assured him international authority and economic prosperity, which made possible several modernising projects. Both agricultural and commercial activities were subject to the payment of a toll; all the goods that arrived in the harbours of Syracuse paid a tax, the exact amount of which is unknown, probably not less than the so-called *portoria* of the Roman age (5 per cent of the value of the merchandise). Other taxes were established through the *lex Hieronica*, which regulated the collection of a tithe of all agricultural products. Those payments were collected in enormous warehouses in Syracuse, and Hieron used them to support his great philanthropy, a trait that he shared with many other Hellenistic kings. The accomplishment of great public works, in Syracuse and elsewhere in the kingdom (for example at Morgantina), may be ascribed to his age.[37]

The prosperity of the Syracusan kingdom is illustrated by Hieron's new coinage, which he aimed to introduce into all the commercial markets of the Mediterranean.[38] He abandoned the customary weight system based on the Attic drachma, and began to use the native weight system based on the *litra*: the basic coin was the four-litrae piece, the so-called *tetralitron*, which had a weight very similar to a light drachma in circulation all around the Mediterranean. A coin of five litrae was compatible in weight with the Attic drachma, and the fractions of this coin could be easily compared with the new Roman coin, the *denarius*. The heaviest issues were destined for international commerce, and were the main instrument of royal propaganda, since Hieron and his wife Philistis were portrayed magnificently on them, the first representation of a king of Sicily on coins. Hieron tried to complete his ideological propaganda by establishing a relationship with the Syracusan autocratic tradition: with the Deinomenids (he named his children Gelon and Damareta), with Dionysius the Elder (by marrying Philistis, who was a descendant of Philistus, he could claim to have some relationship with the Syracusan *dynasteia*), and with Pyrrhus (his son Gelon married Nereis, Pyrrhus' daughter).[39]

At home, Hieron wanted to appear as a king whose authority originated from the people; at several points he even offered to hand over his power, to gain the people's backing. Polybius writes that 'actually on several occasions when he wished to lay down his authority (*dynasteia*) he was prevented from doing so by the common action of the citizens'.[40] Hieron needed the support of the *dêmos*, and his kingship, at first centralised and autocratic, became more concerned with of the needs of his subjects. The turning point in this political evolution came in 241, when Hieron decided to associate with himself in power his son Gelon, who was inclined to satisfy the claims of the Syracusan people.[41] Afterwards, the Syracusan *dêmos* was mentioned in the official documents as a legal authority and with a constitutional meaning.

In his old age, Hieron decided (as had Agathocles) to name as his successor his young grandson Hieronymus, and appointed as supervisors his sons-in-law, Adranodorus and Zohippus, together with a board of thirteen Syracusan aristocrats, who were favourable to the Romans. The new king reversed his grandfather's style of government; his first concern was to highlight the his royal authority (by employing bodyguards, like former Syracusan tyrants).[42] At home, Hieronymus put an end to the power of the popular assembly, which until then had cooperated with and supported the king. Furthermore, he sided with the Carthaginians against Rome and thus Latin authors could not but be hostile to him, although their views are counterbalanced by those of some Greek historians.[43] The last king of the Syracusans ended his days in a way more appropriate for a tyrant than for a king, since he died in 214, killed by some Syracusan oligarchs in Leontini. Adranodorus tried then to seize power but was in turn assassinated; soon after, all members of the royal family were brutally slaughtered.

Sicilian kingship thus came to an end; Marcus Claudius Marcellus arrived in Sicily and the following year began the siege of Syracuse. Syracuse lost her freedom two years after, in 211; her past glory, her tyrants, her dynasts and, finally, her kings were no more than a memory for the new conquerors, as Livy wrote:

> Marcellus, on entering the walls and from the higher ground viewing one of the most beautiful of all cities in that age lying before his eyes, is said to have wept, partly for joy over his great achievement, partly for the ancient glory of the city. The sinking of the fleets of the Athenians and the destruction of two mighty armies along with two very distinguished generals came to his mind, and so many wars waged with so great risk against the Carthaginians; tyrants and kings, so many and so wealthy, above all Hieron, a king vividly remembered and also, above all that his own merit and success had given him, conspicuous for his favours to the Roman people.[44]

NOTES

1. A general account of Timoleon's Sicily is offered by Westlake 1952; Orlandini 1958; Sordi 1961; Talbert 1974. Agathocles' seizure of power in Syracuse has been described by Consolo Langher 1980; Mossé 1999.
2. The most recent wide-ranging work on Agathocles' age is Consolo Langher 2000, which offers an extensive bibliography. For the political meaning of Agathocles' rule, see Berve 1953; Mossé 1969; Meister, 'Agathocles', *CAH*[2] VII.384–411.
3. Consolo Langher 1976; Amado Araceli 1991.
4. A fragment of a lost historian who wrote about Agathocles' times and career, *P.Oxy.* XXIV, 2933, clearly shows that there was no freedom of expression in the popular Assembly: Huss 1980, 64–6; Berger 1988: 93–6; Raffone 2001.
5. Stroheker 1958; Sanders 1987; Caven 1990; Sordi 1992; Braccesi 1998: 69–86.
6. The resemblance between Dionysius the Elder and Agathocles was celebrated by the ancient historical sources: Polyb. 15.35.3–4 wrote that they

both became in their times tyrants of Syracuse (τύραννοι Συρακουσῶν) and were then recognised as kings of the whole of Sicily (βασιλεῖς).

7. Consolo Langher 1996a.
8. Meyer 1970: 35–6; Blum 1998: 98–9.
9. Gruen 1985.
10. The diadem was clearly meant to be a symbol of royal power: Ritter 1965, Virgilio 1998, 2003: 38. It was represented on the portraits of the kings and on the coinage: Smith 1988: 34–8.
11. The best dicussion of Agathocles' plentiful coinage is provided by Buda 1969–70; Ross Holloway 1979; Borba Florenzano 1993; Consolo Langher 1993; Garraffo 1995; Rutter 1997: 172–5.
12. The best analysis of the coin is offered by Stewart 1993: 266–9.
13. Kuschel 1961.
14. Diod. 20.11.3–5.
15. Stewart 1993: 268, n. 15 gives references for the various suppositions.
16. Evans 1894. More recently, Cantilena 1993; Castrizio 1995.
17. Mehl 1980–1; Virgilio 2003: 72–3. The idea has been represented in the paintings of a Roman villa: Mørkholm 1991: 26; Smith 1994; Moreno 1998: 37–40; Torelli 2003.
18. Coarelli 1982; Consolo Langher 1999a; Cic. *Verr.* 2.4.122–3.
19. Diod. 21.16.3.
20. Berve 1953: 62–8. His assessments have been rejected by Consolo Langher 2000: 258–61.
21. Just. 23.2.6 (Theoxene: see Manni 1984, 1990); Plut. *Pyrrh.* 10.5; Diod. 21.4.1 (Lanassa); Diod. 21.16.3 (Agathocles jr).
22. Diod. 20.56.3 maintains that in 307 BC, after conquering the city of Kephaloidion, Agathocles left his companion Leptines there as *epimelêtês*.
23. Diod. 21.16.3–4.
24. Zambon 2004.
25. Zambon 2001.
26. Zambon 2000.
27. Diod. 22.8.5 refers to an embassy sent to Pyrrhus by Heracleides, the tyrant of Leontini. For the political and social background to the Sicilian venture of Pyrrhus, see Zambon forthcoming, esp. ch. 2: 'The expedition of Pyrrhus in Sicily: military events, political meanings and ideological implications'.
28. A point of view expressed by Beloch 1927: 553, and shared by many other scholars.
29. Berve 1954 (but see Nenci 1953: 84–7), followed by Bengtson 1956; Bengtson 1975: 102; La Bua 1980: 215–21.
30. Bengtson 1956: 166–7: 'Wenn ihn die römischen Quellen *rex Epiri* nennen, so zeigt dies, daß ihn die Römer mit den anderen hellenistischen Königen auf eine Stufe stellten – eine Auffassung, die natürlich den wirklichen Verhältnissen *nicht* gerecht wird'); Hammond 1967; Cabanes 1976; Corvisier 1999; Davies 2000.

31. The source is still difficult to identify (a view endorsed by Prof. Simon Hornblower): some scholars suggest Timaeus (for example, La Bua 1980: 218–19 and 244–5). However, there can be no doubt that the same source was used by Dionysius of Halicarnassus and by Appian (*Samn.* 12.1), who said that Pyrrhus was a burden for the Greeks of Sicily, owing to the hospitality, the supplies, the garrisons and the tributes (ἤδη καὶ τοῖς Σικελιώταις βαρὺν ἐπί τε ξενίαις καὶ χορηγίαις καὶ φρουραῖς καὶ εἰσφοραῖς γενόμενον).

32. Useful general surveys of the topic in Head 1911: 322–5; Giesecke 1923: 105–11; Nenci 1953: 74–80; Lévêque 1957: 464–74; Babelon 1958; Borba Florenzano 1992; Rutter 1997: 175–8; de Callataÿ 2000.

33. Mildenberg 1985 nos 1117–22, rightly comments that the portrait of Zeus derives from that on the tetradrachms of Alexander the Great.

34. The hypothesis that the Athena Promachos of the coins is a reproduction of the statue of Athena Alkis in Pella was proposed by Head 1874, and has been universally accepted; see Brett 1950; Jenkins 1972: 217; Davis and Kraay 1973: no. 122; Garraffo 1995: 460–1.

35. De Sensi Sestito 1977; Prestianni Giallombardo 1995.

36. Eckstein 1980; Millino 2003.

37. Bell 1999.

38. Carroccio 1994; Caccamo Caltabiano et al. 1995; Garraffo 1995; Caccamo Caltabiano et al. 1997.

39. Polyb. 1.9.2–3 (marriage of Hiero with Philistis); Paus. 6.12.3; Polyb. 7.4.5; Liv. 24.6.8; Just. 28.3–4 (Nereis, daughter of Pyrrhus).

40. Polyb. 7.8.5.

41. De Sensi Sestito 1980; 1995.

42. He underlined the royal signs on his coinage: Ross Holloway 1969; Massner 1973.

43. The least favourable reference to Hieronymus' kingship is offered by Liv. 24.5.2–5; compare the positive assessment of Polyb. 7.7.1–4.

44. Liv. 25.24.11–13.

PART II

Tyranny and politics

CHAPTER 7

Tyrants and the polis: migration, identity and urban development in Sicily

Kathryn Lomas

In his account of the debate leading up to the Athenian expedition to Sicily in 415 BC, Thucydides stated:

> The Sicilian cities have enlarged populations made out of all sorts of mixtures, and there are constant changes and rearrangements in their citizen bodies. The result is that they lack the feeling that they are fighting for their own country. (Thucydides 6.17)

This passage – the significance of which is hotly debated – identifies one of the most prominent features of the development of the Greek-colonised areas of the western Mediterranean, namely that the conceptualisation of *polis* membership, citizenship and territory, may have developed along significantly different lines from those of the rest of the Greek world.[1] The Greek cities of the mainland and the Aegean underwent a period of social and political upheaval in the archaic period, leading to the establishment of tyrannies in many communities in the seventh and early sixth centuries BC, before developing various forms of representative government – whether oligarchic or democratic, in conventional Greek terminology – in the late sixth century. In the west, in contrast, and particularly in Sicily, the tyrant remained a prominent feature of the political scene from the seventh century right down to the period of Roman conquest, with only relatively brief interludes of representative government. The nature of tyranny and kingship in the western Mediterranean, and the possible reasons for the prevalence of tyranny as a political system, are contentious issues. This chapter,

I would like to thank Prof. T. J. Cornell and Dr J. R. W. Prag for comments and discussion on various aspects of this paper, especially on the material from Messana, and Prof. M. H. Crawford for access to epigraphic data from Messana included in the *Imagines Italicae* database.

however, will focus on one particular aspect of tyrants and their deeds – an examination of the demographic changes and instability to which Thucydides refers (albeit in the loaded context of a speech urging the invasion of Sicily). These have frequently been linked to tyranny both as symptom and potential cause but the relationship between these two phenomena remains unclear and requires much more exploration. [2]

Even a very brief survey of the ancient evidence shows that a high proportion (although not all) of the enforced demographic movement which took place in Sicily between the sixth and third centuries BC took place as a result of direct political and/or military intervention by tyrants.[3] The sources are, of course problematic and our understanding depends on unpicking the complex structure of Diodorus' narrative and his possible underlying sources – in particular the Sicilian, but deeply anti-tyrannical and anti-Syracusan, historian Timaeus[4] – but this chapter will examine the possible connections between tyrants and population change, and the social and cultural effects of such change. Superficially, the sources suggest that there is a strong connection between tyrannical regimes, and the sort of loose linkage between land, *polis* and people on which Thucydides comments. Forced migration and the encouragement of immigrant groups such as mercenaries become a stock feature of tyrant personae in Greek literature, something discussed further below. They are, however, a prominent feature of Sicilian history, and the impact of such policies on the development of Sicily requires further examination. There is considerable debate about the relationship between population movement and tyranny, and about the causes and effects of such movements in both Italy and Sicily.[5] It is unclear, for instance, whether all tyrants were alike in pursuing this policy. Even if this were the case, their motivations for doing so may have been significantly different. In addition, such large-scale demographic changes would have had a significant impact on both the displaced populations and the areas they moved to. Ultimately, this type of demographic engineering is likely to have had a major impact on concepts of citizenship and on the culture and identity of the *polis* in Sicily. The purpose of this chapter is to explore more fully the patterns of such mobility in Greek Sicily, their implications for *polis* development, and their impact on the cultural and ethnic development of both Greeks and non-Greeks.

Even a very basic examination of the chronological and geographic patterns revealed by the available evidence shows very widespread and long-term demographic change in Greek Sicily, and indicates that it may have had connections, though not exclusive ones, with the phenomenon of tyranny (table 7.1). Greek historians from the fifth century BC onwards consistently focus on this as an aspect of tyranny or of other types of autocratic regime in Sicily.

This interest in the phenomenon of large-scale forced migration and the manipulation of the composition of the citizen body, usually by tyrants, begins with Hippocrates of Gela and his attempts to establish Gela as a major power in south-east Sicily, and with the attempted domination of Zancle by his relative by marriage, Anaxilas of Rhegion.[6] In 494, according to both Herodotus and Thucydides' *Archaeology* of Sicily, a group of Samian mercenaries took over Zancle with the assistance and support of Hippocrates of Gela. Hippocrates handed over 300 of the leading citizens of Zancle to them, on the assumption (false, as it turned out) that the Samians would execute them. The Samians remained in control until 489, when, also according to Thucydides (Hdt. 6.24–6, Thuc. 6.4.6) they were ejected by Anaxilas and the depleted city was repopulated with settlers from various parts of Greece, including Messenia. This account brings together three consistently linked aspects of archaic tyranny: aggressive expansionism, attempted control of other cities by the selective expulsion or execution of all or part of their elite, and the use of mercenaries to enforce this policy or replace the displaced population of the cities affected. Clearly, there is a possibility that this relates more to the image of a tyrant in fifth-century literature than to reality – something which is discussed further below – but it cannot be dismissed out of hand as a mere literary topos.

Hippocrates' successor Gelon undertook a more large-scale and systematic programme of resettlement, in both his initial capacity as tyrant of Gela and his later and more prominent position as tyrant of Syracuse. In the 480s he destroyed the city of Camarina and absorbed the entire population into Syracuse.[7] He also transferred half of the population of Gela to Syracuse, but it is not clear from Herodotus' account how this group were selected, what their social profile was, and whether they represented any particular political group. Demand suggests that the use of *astoi* rather than *politai* to describe this group

Table 7.1. Population redistribution in Sicily, 494–289.

Date	From	To	By whom	Reference
494 BC	Zancle/Messana	300 leading men handed over to Samian mercenaries	Hippocrates of Gela	Hdt. 6.24–6
489 BC	Various places	Zancle/Messana: Samian mercenaries replaced by Greeks of various origins	Anaxilas of Rhegium	Thuc. 6.4.6
488–484 BC	Camarina	Syracuse	Gelon	Hdt. 7.156
488–484 BC	Gela	50 per cent of population moved to Syracuse	Gelon	Hdt. 7.156
488–484 BC	Megara Hyblaea	*Aristoi* made citizens of Syracuse, *dêmos* sold as slaves	Gelon	Hdt. 7.156
488–484 BC	Euboea	*Aristoi* made citizens of Syracuse, *dêmos* sold as slaves	Gelon	Hdt. 7.156
488–484 BC	Various places	10,000 mercenaries made citizens of Syracuse	Gelon	Diod. 11.72–8
476 BC	5,000 Peloponnesians and 5,000 Syracusans	Naxos and Catania; territory of Catane and Sicels allotted to settlers and name of Catane changed to Aetna	Hieron	Diod. 11.49
476 BC	Naxos and Catane	Population of Naxos and Catane moved to Leontini	Hieron	Diod. 11.49
476 BC	Greece	Himera repopulated by a general invitation to Dorian colonists to settle there	Theron	Diod. 11.49
461 BC	Catane	Inessa: Catanians eject colonists; Aetna refounded at Inessa	—	Strabo 6.2.3, Diod. 11.76
461 BC	Syracuse and other cities	Gela, Acragas, Himera: original populations return home. Territory of Camarina reallocated	—	Diod. 11.76
427 BC	Leontini	Population forced to leave by Syracuse and disperses to other cities	Syracuse	Diod. 12.53, 12.83
409 BC	Various places	Himera: city repopulated with recalled exiles	Syracuse (Hermocrates)	Diod. 13.63

Date	Place	Event	Syracuse	Source
409 BC	Various places	Selinous: city repopulated with recalled exiles	Syracuse (Hermocrates)	Diod. 13.63
406 BC	Acragas	Gela	——	Diod. 13.89
406/5 BC	Gela	Agrigentine refugees migrate to Leontini, Syracuse and Italy	——	Diod. 13.89
405 BC	Gela and Camarina	Syracuse and Leontini; allowed to return by treaty of 405	Dionysius I	Diod. 13.111
405 BC	Various places	Acragas, Himera, Gela and Camarina: exiles return but pay tribute to Carthage	Dionysius I	Diod. 13.114
404 BC	——	Slaves made citizens of Syracuse and given land	Dionysius I	Diod. 14.7
404 BC	Aetna	Entella: Campanian mercenaries ejected from Aetna take over Entella	Dionysius I	Diod. 14.9
403 BC	Catania	Citizens sold as slaves; land distributed to Campanian mercenaries	Dionysius I	Diod. 14.15
403 BC	Naxos	Citizens sold as slaves; land distributed to Sicels	Dionysius I	Diod. 14.15
403 BC	Herbite	Mercenaries, exiles and refugees from Herbite found colony of Halaesa	Archonides of Herbite	Diod. 14.16
397/6 BC	——	Adranum	Dionysius I	Diod. 14.37.5
396 BC	Catane	Campanian mercenaries moved from Catane to Aetna	Dionysius I	Diod. 14.58
396 BC	Naxos	Tauromenion: Sicels occupying Naxos move to Tauromenion	Dionysius I	Diod. 14.59
396 BC	Locri, Medma, Zacynthos and Naupactos	Messana: 1,000 Locrians, 4,000 Medmans, 600 from Zacynthos and Naupactos	Dionysius I	Diod. 14.78.3–6
396 BC	Messana	Tyndaris: new colony by exiles from Zacynthos and Naupactos	Dionysius I	Diod. 14.78.3–6
396 BC	——	Leontini given to mercenaries	Dionysius I	Diod. 14.78.3–6
396 BC	——	Campanian mercenaries settled at Messana	Dionysius I	Diod. 14.78.3–6

Table 7.1. (continued)

Date	From	To	By whom	Reference
394 BC	Rhegium	Mylai: Naxian and Catanian exiles assisted to found new city	Rhegium	Diod. 14.87
392 BC	—	Tauromenion – Sicels ejected and colony of mercenaries founded	Dionysius I	Diod. 14.96
369/8 BC	Messenia	Messana: exiles from Greece migrate to Sicily	—	Diod. 15.66.5
346/5 BC	Various places	Various: cities damaged by war with Carthage repopulated	Timoleon	Diod. 16.65, 16.69, 16.73
343 BC	Aetna	Various: Campanians ejected from Aetna and dispersed	Timoleon	Diod. 16.69
339/8 BC	Greece	60,000 settlers from mainland Greece settled at various cities	Timoleon	Diod. 16.82–3
339/8 BC	Leontini	Syracuse: population removed from Leontini as punishment for support of Hicetas	Timoleon	Diod. 16.82–3
307 BC	Various places	Solus: Sicilian exiles return and settled near Panormus	Agathocles	Diod. 20.69
307 BC	Segesta	Various: female population enslaved and men killed or exiled. Resettled with mercenaries and renamed Dikaiopolis	Agathocles	Diod. 20.71
288–285 BC	—	Messana: Campanian mercenaries take over the city	—	Strabo 6.2.3, Diod. 22.13.2, Polyb. 1.7–11

may indicate that it was composed of a lower socio-economic group, and that Gelon was therefore favouring the elite at the expense of the rest of the population, but this is not certain.[8] It is unclear what the reaction of the elite would have been to such a policy, or whether there were penalties for the citizens left behind, although his actions elsewhere suggest that there might have been. At Megara Hyblaea and another city identified as Euboea, however, he was definitely more selective, enslaving the poorer citizens and granting Syracusan citizenship to the elite (Hdt. 7.156). He further expanded the population by awarding Syracusan citizenship to up to 10,000 mercenaries of unspecified provenance (Hdt. 7.156, Diod. 11.72.3), if Diodorus' figures can be believed. Some care was taken to formally mark these changes and to make provision for the new citizens. There was a major programme of temple-building and public works at Syracuse, designed to further emphasise Gelon's munificence, and housing was provided for the new population in an area of the city known as Neapolis.[9] A number of the new citizens, mainly resettled mercenaries, can be identified from inscriptions at Olympia and Delphi which include a dual ethnic, including Astylos of Croton and Syracuse, Phormias and Agesias of Arcadia and Syracuse, and Praxiteles of Mantinea, Camarina and Syracuse.[10]

By 476 Gelon's brother Hieron was implementing an even more ambitious policy of expansion and relocation. He moved the populations of Naxos and Catane en masse to Leontini, just north of Syracuse. He also replaced the people of Catane with 10,000 settlers from Syracuse and from the Peloponnese, changing its name to Aetna and celebrating the 'foundation' of the new city with honours granted to himself as oikist and a lavish ceremony.[11] Much, although not all, of Hieron's settlement seems to have involved mercenaries, and also to have involved substantial changes to the communities affected. Changes to the urban layout of Naxos may date to the period of Hieron's settlement; Chalcidian law-codes, such as that found at Monte S. Mauro, were symbolically destroyed; coins bearing Deinomenid and Syracusan symbols – notably a quadriga driven by Nike or a horseman on the obverse and a seated Zeus on the reverse – were minted at Aetna.[12] Elsewhere in Sicily, the population of Himera was boosted by an invitation by the tyrant Theron to Greeks in general – and more specifically, Dorians – to migrate and settle there (Diod. 11.49). Even allowing for inflated figures and a possible anti-Deinomenid (or more general anti-tyrannical) slant, there is clearly still a substantial amount of non-voluntary migration and resettlement of population during the early fifth century, affecting south-east Sicily in particular.

The period after the fall of the Deinomenid tyrants is not entirely free from large-scale demographic movement, giving the lie to the idea that it was something entirely promoted by tyrants in support of their regimes, but it fits into a rather different pattern. The emergent democratic regime of 466–405 at Syracuse was not averse to demographic manoeuvring to consolidate territorial interests and settle old scores, but much of it took the form of reversing the actions of the Deinomenids and promoting the return of exiles displaced by them.[13] In 461 the original population of Gela, Acragas and Himera were permitted to return to their home cities, but the territory of Camarina was carved up and reallocated to new settlers. The population of Catane also returned home, ejecting Hieron's colonists, who refounded Aetna at Inessa, several miles inland (Strabo 6.2.3, Diod. 11.76). In 427, the population of Leontini was forcibly dispersed and in 409, the Syracusan general Hermocrates initiated a programme to repopulate Selinous and Himera with recalled exiles.[14] Some of these measures were essentially a means of reversing the population redistributions of Hieron and others and were duly celebrated by new issues of coinage, such as the replacement of the Syracusan quadriga with the head of Apollo on that of Leontini, and the use of the local river-god Amenanus on that of Catane.[15] Other initiatives, however, indicate some degree of continuity with Syracuse's policy of undermining the Chalcidian presence on the island – something which can be seen particularly in the continued manipulation of the demography of Leontini and Camarina.[16]

Much larger population movements and mass displacement occurred under Dionysius I and his successors.[17] At Syracuse in 405–404 there were large-scale redistributions of land to favour Dionysius' supporters and reward his mercenaries, and also major changes to the composition of the citizen body.[18] Land was allotted not just to existing citizens, but also non-Syracusan inhabitants (*xenoi*) and freed slaves, whom he enfranchised and termed *neopolitai*. In 403 Enna, Naxos, Catane and Leontini all fell under Dionysius' control. Catane and Naxos were acquired after he suborned members of their elite, and suffered widespread enslavement or displacement of their populations; the land was then distributed to Campanian and Sicel mercenaries. Leontini surrendered and the population was ordered to move to Syracuse, where it was absorbed into the citizen body.[19] Meanwhile, another group of Campanian mercenaries, which had taken over Aetna, was ejected and went on to take Entella and settle there. Further major realignments occurred after the Carthaginian defeat of 396 (Diod. 14.77.5–78.6). Leontini was resettled with discharged mercenaries, the land being offered in lieu of pay, and population displaced from Locri and Medma in southern Italy was settled at Messana. A group of exiles from the Peloponnese were also placed there but later moved to Tyndaris, after protest from Sparta. Further groups of Campanian mercenaries and Messenian exiles from Greece were settled at Messana (Diod. 14.96, 15.66.5) and another colony of mercenaries was established on the highly strategic site of Tauromenion (Diod. 14.96). Although the pattern of mobility within the Greek population in Italy was rather different and less dramatic in its effects, both Dionysius I and Dionysius II wreaked a fair amount of havoc during their campaigns in Calabria, in particular on the populations of Locri and some of the smaller settlements of the region (Diod. 14.78.5, 14.106.3–107.3, 16.11.3). Medma lost some of its population to Messana (Diod. 14.78.5), and Caulonia was partially destroyed (Strabo 6.1.10). Many of these cities – notably Locri – recovered and went on to play a significant role in the later Hellenistic period, but some of the smaller ones, such as Medma, were seriously weakened.

Further demographic movement was occasioned by the activities of Dionysius' successors in the fourth century, some of which was directly inspired by a wish to overturn Dionysius' actions. Dion's revolt against Dionysius II was supported by many of the displaced citizens of Camarina and Leontini, possibly in the hope of securing a return, as well as by exiled and disaffected Syracusans (Plut. *Dion* 27). Between 346 and 339/8 Timoleon undertook his own programme of demographic change, although he presented it as an anti-tyrannical programme to counter the actions of Dionysius I and II and also those of Dion. He dispersed some of the settlements of mercenaries, notably those from Aetna (Diod. 16.69) and invited new colonists from Greece to migrate to Sicily to rejuvenate depopulated cities, in a measure which was viewed as a re-Hellenisation of Sicily, to counter the effects of Dionysius' settlements of non-Greek mercenaries. In all, he is said to have settled 60,000 new inhabitants (Diod. 16.82–3) and to have encouraged major investment in urban renewal in order to make good the devastation caused during the previous fifty years. However, Timoleon also used relocation as a punitive act, removing the population from Leontini as punishment for their support of his opponent, Hicetas (Diod. 16.82–3).

Finally, to conclude this survey of demographic movement, Agathocles (who called himself *basileus*, not tyrant) killed or exiled the male population of Segesta in 307 and enslaved the female population. He then settled some of his mercenaries there and renamed the Elymnian city with the Greek name Dicaiopolis (Diod. 20.71). In the same year, he allowed Sicilian Greek exiles who had left under previous regimes to return to Solus and settle there (Diod. 20.69). At the end of his reign, some of his Oscan-speaking Italic mercenaries created more mayhem by invading Messana, after his death in 289.[20] They slaughtered the Greek rulers of the city, and settled down to form their own community there, an episode which poses considerable historical problems and will be discussed in more detail below.[21]

TYRANNY AND DEMOGRAPHIC CHANGE

In many – although not all – of the cases cited so far, there is a common factor: a tyrant. It was not invariably the case, but tyranny and demographic mobility (voluntary or enforced) tend to go together. The link was not exclusive – political regimes which were not tyrannies also undertook similar programmes – but a comparison of the numbers is instructive. There are ten known instances of forced migration and displacement under the Deinomenids and fourteen under Dionysius I and Dionysius II, as compared with only six in the intervening years of non-tyrannical rule. Demographic engineering of the type undertaken by Dionysius I, particularly if it involved destroying the political identity of a city, as at Leontini, or the admixture of non-Greek elements into the population, as at Entella (non-Greek mercenaries settled there in 397; Diod. 14.9), was regarded as typically tyrant-like behaviour. In particular, the creation of settlements of mercenaries, either as new foundations or as additions to existing cities, is regarded as particularly unacceptable and tyrant-like, partly because it frequently involved the settlement of non-Greek population and therefore raised the question of 'barbarisation'. Conversely, refounding destroyed cities, either with new population or by recalling the exiled citizens, can be presented as symptomatic of a move away from tyranny.[22] It can, however, be difficult to differentiate absolutely between a variety of causes and motivations, and also between tyrants and other forms of political government. Hermocrates' repopulation of Selinous and Himera involved recalling exiles, but his role at Syracuse was so ambiguous that it has been argued that he shows many characteristics of an actual or aspiring tyrant.[23] It has been argued strongly by several scholars, notably Vattuone, that these displacements and demographic movements were not connected with tyranny as such but had other, practical, motivations such as a need to consolidate Syracusan domination in the face of challenges from the Carthaginians and others, or a wish to assert a Dorian ethnicity against challenges from neighbouring Chalcidian colonies, but these factors need not necessarily exclude a link with tyranny.[24] On the whole, there seems to be too much evidence for the general phenomenon of large-scale demographic change in Sicily to dismiss this as a generic tyrant-topos or literary construct.

One question which must be considered is how far the actions of the Sicilian tyrants can be reconstructed from our sources, or whether we are looking at evidence which is simply a reflection of later Greek anxieties and of the literary stereotypes and personae of tyranny. The persona of the tyrant was one which was of strong interest to the Greeks, and particularly to writers of the fifth and fourth centuries, who were examining the phenomenon from the standpoint of the emergence of democracy, particularly at Athens. There has been vigorous debate about whether Herodotus presented an objective view of tyrants and their deeds, or whether he was more concerned to create for them a persona which would defined them as 'other' vis-à-vis the Greek coalition against Persia.[25] In the case of Gelon, it is clear that he took a hostile view, and Vattuone's argument that Herodotus was concerned to present him in a bad light as a way of undermining his achievements and with them, his stature as a possible member of the coalition against Persia, highlights the extent to which later preoccupations shaped the persona of the tyrant in Greek literature.[26] Thucydides and Xenophon are equally concerned to present tyranny in a bad light, as were later writers (for Plato, Plutarch and the persona of the tyrant, see Mossé, Chapter 13 of this volume) but this does not provide a conclusive reason for dismissing the evidence for land redistribution and forced migration and settlement as a literary construct. There are stereotypical aspects of tyrannies, such as the employment of mercenaries as bodyguards (e.g. Xen. *Hieron* 6.3–8, 10.1–6), which are clearly related to this issue – particularly in the context of Hellenistic Sicily – but no obvious reason why we should dismiss the link between migration and tyranny, and considerable amounts of evidence for the presence and impact of mercenary settlements.[27]

Greek perceptions that demographic movement was a bad thing were influenced not just by its connections with tyranny, but by a series of more general anxieties in the Greek world centring on citizenship, landownership and levels of population. Many Greek writers of the classical period identify *politographia* (revision of citizenship lists) and *oliganthrôpia* (decline in population) as phenomena which could potentially undermine the state.[28] A paucity of urban population and/or decrepitude of urban physical structures was equated with moral and political decadence and weakness of the political community. Similarly – and particularly with reference to Sicily – *politographia* was regarded with suspicion as it involved changes to the formal composition of the citizen body, whether these entailed the admission of new citizens or the expulsion of existing ones. Population was, therefore, a sensitive topic, particularly viewed from a mainland perspective, and may have led to exaggeration of the themes of migration and demographic change. Plutarch, for instance, refers to Sicily at the end of the reign of Dionysius II as being without cities (*apolis*, Plut. *Timol.* 1.1), which is clearly an overstatement of the case. Archaeological evidence for Sicilian cities in the fourth century does indeed show periods of change and disruption, but not the wholesale disappearance of the *polis*.

If examined from the Sicilian point of view, however, this outlook may not have quite so much force. The cities there, formed in a non-Greek – and sometimes hostile – environment at a time when the very notion of the *polis* was not yet fully developed, may have developed rather differently from the cities of the mainland in their ways of handling citizenship and land-tenure.[29] There are, therefore, several reasons – anxieties about land and citizenship, and objections to tyranny – which might cause Greeks writing from within Athens and other mainland democracies to view the demographic shifts and political developments of Sicily negatively. However, this is not sufficient grounds on which to dismiss the connection between tyrants and migration as purely the result of constructed tyrant personae.

What is less clear, however, is whether demographic movement and the consequent social re-engineering of communities were specific characteristics of all Greek tyrants, or whether it was a peculiarly Sicilian phenomenon. A study of urban relocation and refoundation in the Greek world argues that, far from being a phenomenon particularly characteristic of tyranny in general, it was something peculiar to Sicily and to other specific peripheral areas of the Greek world such as parts of Asia Minor.[30] However, there seems to be strong evidence for a general preoccupation by tyrants with retaining control over the population and its location, although this took different forms in different areas of the Greek world. Both Plato and Aristotle identify the need to control populations, where they live and what land they own, and to bring in foreigners and mercenaries, as essential to the power-base of tyrants.[31] A number of the earlier mainland tyrants, such as Periander at Corinth and Pisistratus at Athens, emphasised the virtues of life in villages and the territory of the city, and tried to keep the population dispersed in traditional settlements rather than moving it around and concentrating it.[32] In Sicily, in contrast, tyranny resulted in a preoccupation with moving population around, for a variety of reasons – to assert Syracusan dominance, particularly over her near neighbours in south-eastern Sicily and over the Sicels of the interior, to concentrate Greek population in strategic areas, and to secure territory against possible Carthaginian incursion. Viewed from this angle, it seems possible that the need to control the whereabouts of the population was a general factor in Greek tyranny, in order to prevent the formation of opposition, but that the specific form of mass migration and frequent land redistribution and *politographia* found in Sicily was the result of the specific circumstances of the colonial world.[33]

There also seems to be a considerable difference between the strategies to control the population adopted by Gelon and those of the later tyrants. Gelon's most frequent policy was one of selective movement, removing the elites of cities which he wished to dominate to Syracuse and absorbing them into the citizen body there, whereas tyrants from Dionysius I onwards tended to promote much larger-scale demographic movements. It can also be argued that population mobility in a very wide sense was a key characteristic of the tyranny of Dionysius I in particular.[34] His policy of enforced demographic change had the effect of concentrating the Greek population in Syracuse; this, along with large-scale use of mercenaries and imported 'specialists' (including artists and philosophers as well as architects and engineers), and the creation of a large *clientela* loyal to himself rather than the city, was a central element in the establishment of his tyranny. His reorganisation of Syracuse was thorough and wide-ranging, with a reorganisation not just of the citizen body but also of the city's urban space and territorial resources. Landholdings were reorganised to favour his supporters and urban property was redistributed to concentrate his supporters and mercenaries on Ortygia, which was fortified and turned into a military/industrial complex; by extension, this presumably excluded any possible opponents from this strategically sensitive area. Once the best land had been used to reward supporters, the bulk of the territory was divided into equal lots and distributed amongst the rest of the population. This, according to Diodorus, was taken to mean not just existing Syracusan citizens, but also non-Syracusan inhabitants of the city (*xenoi*) and freed slaves, whom he enfranchised and termed *neopolitai*. This, however, also seems to be a fairly typical strategy for securing power, rewarding a core of loyalists and ensuring that new population was integrated into the city in ways which made them beholden to Dionysius.[35]

What seems to underlie this evidence is a complicated pattern of demographic change which can be broken down into several strands. One is the extreme prominence given to the phenomenon, and the negative spin placed on it, by ancient authors, which can be seen in the context of construction of the persona of the tyrant as a type, and in more general anxieties about landownership and citizenship. Another is that demographic change was not solely, or even primarily, a device to secure the power-base of a tyrant or provide a means of controlling a population; the concentration on the south-east of the island suggests that it has a stronger connection with Syracusan attempts to dominate the region by re-engineering either whole populations or the ruling classes of the neighbouring cities. It is clear that there are several different mechanisms at work, which are not all employed by all tyrants.

THE IMPACT OF DEMOGRAPHIC CHANGE

One of the most important aspects of this entire topic, but one of the most difficult to assess, is the impact that these demographic changes may have had on communities and on their sense of identity. There is a temptation to assume that these displaced populations became, and remained, outsiders. Some studies, for instance, construct a model of the outsider (defined as somebody outside the citizen body of a *polis*, either as an exile, a mercenary or an itinerant artist or craftsman) as both endemic in Sicily, and as integral to the undermining of the *polis* as the primary form of social and political organisation in the Greek world.[36] This posits the forced dispersion of urban populations and the growing numbers of people living outside their home cities as crucial factors in the ability of rulers, particularly in the Hellenistic era, to construct a personal power-base independent of the structure of the *polis*. However, it is unclear to what extent displaced populations actually stayed displaced in the long term, integrating into the citizen body of their adopted *polis*, or returned home. There are many instances, particularly in the fifth century, in which some sections – although not all – of exiled populations returned home once the regime responsible for the exile had been removed, and indeed were encouraged to do so as a way of marking a symbolic break with previous authority.[37] Repopulation, however, could mean just that – recruitment of new population but not necessarily from the displaced former citizens. Timoleon, for instance, was keen to repopulate and 're-Hellenise' Sicily as a way of distancing his rule from that of his tyrannical predecessors, but did so by recruiting new settlers from Greece as much as (if not more than) by restoring displaced Sicilians.[38] It is also unclear what sweeping statements about destruction of cities and removal of populations actually mean. Do they all, for instance, assume the removal of the entire population of a city, or do they actually mean political and social 'decapitation' – removal of the social and political elite in the interests of domination and 'regime-change', to use a current terminology?

In the case of the early incursions of Hippocrates and Gelon on Zancle, Gela, Megara and other communities, Herodotus is very clear that we are looking at the removal of the ruling class – 300 of the leading men of Zancle were handed over to the Samians, and the leading men (*aristoi*) of other cities were removed in circumstances which were in some cases (although by no means all) honorific, involving absorption into a new city. On occasions (as in the 460s–50s) when they returned home, this was part of a complex and structured process which involved the formal redistribution of land and revision of citizenship registers in order to dissociate them from their adopted *polis* and reintegrate them into their former one.[39]

The dynamics of population change and its effect on the *polis* also depend on a number of other factors, such as for how long a population is displaced, and what provision is made for integrating them into other communities. Under Hieron, and even more so under the fourth-century tyrants, population displacement tended to be more widespread – often involving thousands rather than hundreds of migrants – and resettlement of returning populations more problematic. Various strategies were adopted to solve these problems. Some of the cities destroyed by Dionysius were refounded by means of recalling the original, exiled, population, for instance Hipponion in Italy (Diod. 14.107.2) and Acragas and Gela in Sicily (Plut. *Timol.* 35.2). In fact, some populations which were ejected from their home cities were able to return within a relatively short space of time.[40] Other cities, however, were effectively refounded as new communities with the admixture of new colonists from different areas of Sicily or beyond (e.g. Diod. 16.65–83, 16.82–3; Plut. *Timol.* 23.6, 39.4). The other significant fact is that many of those displaced from other *poleis* did not remain outsiders but changed status and were absorbed into other cities, most notably Syracuse. The people of Catane and Naxos were enslaved and dispersed, thus losing the ability to be a part of any *polis*; the people of Leontini were not left as outsiders but given Syracusan citizenship and were thus absorbed into the body politic of a different state. At an earlier date, Gelon used the same tactic, giving Syracusan citizenship to the ruling elite of Megara. Comparative evidence from outside Sicily also supports a potentially complex interrelation between displaced or exiled people and their host city. The people of Cumae were ejected permanently from their city by the Campanians in 421, and many of them fled to Naples (Diod. 12.76.4; Strabo 5.4.4). They seem to have been admitted to the citizenship of Naples, but their descendents retained their own identity within the citizen body of Naples for many years to come. Livy and Dionysius of Halicarnassus, describing the war between Naples and Rome nearly a century later, in 327, note that some of the descendents of Cumaean refugees still felt tempted by a chance to return to Cumae, and the phratry of the Kumaioi was still in existence as late as the second century AD (*IG* 14.721). Clearly, displaced populations could retain a high level of identification with their original community while at the same time occupying a role as citizens of another *polis*.[41]

Traces of the impact of demographic change, sometimes explicitly linked to the persona of a tyrant, are sometimes discernible in the inscriptions, coinage and urban fabric of some Sicilian cities. Hieron's spectacular attempt to refound Catane as Aetna, with himself as oikist, is the best documented, reflected in a new coinage, a new city name, and iconography equating Hieron himself with Zeus. The whole package was showcased in a grand foundation ceremony and festival, commemorated in a new tragedy by Aeschylus. At Rhegium, the tyrant Anaxilas issued new coinage which celebrated both his own rule and the identity of the city.[42] In the later fourth century, many cities marked changes in their population and civic identity by instituting significant rebuilding programmes, some of which involved wholesale changes to the street pattern, the development of completely new areas of the city, and shifting of the focus of communal activity to new buildings or quarters of the city. These are frequently associated with Timoleon's programme of repopulation and urban renewal, but not all of them can be directly linked to his regime, and there is evidence that major changes to urban space were a characteristic of many other fourth-century regimes as well. Dionysius I, for instance, developed new areas of the city to house his new citizens, designated certain areas as housing for his close supporters, and developed Ortygia as the centre of his military power.[43]

These processes can be traced in the archaeological record, but only up to a point. Archaeological evidence for the fourth century BC is not plentiful at some sites, and dating it sufficiently accurately to match it with the activities of individual regimes is not always possible – or even, from an archaeological point of view, methodologically advisable. However, there is evidence of Dionysius' reconstruction at Syracuse and many other cities show signs of extensive new building, often of a type designed to implement new aspects of urbanism in the later fourth century.[44] At Acragas the walls were rebuilt and new civic buildings, including a *bouleutêrion* and *ekklêsiastêrion* were added, at Gela there was extensive construction in a new area of the city to the west of the archaic centre, and at Camarina the street-plan was remodelled on the lines of Hellenistic cities such as Priene, and a new public/ceremonial area was developed close to the temple of Athena.[45] The impact of Dionysius I on Naxos and the aftermath of his activities can also be seen in a phase of destruction in the centre of the city and major redevelopment in the later fourth and third centuries BC on the north side of the harbour, moving the centre of gravity of the city away from the archaic centre.[46]

The complexity of the cultural and, in some cases, ethnic interaction which resulted from mass population movement can be clearly illustrated by examples from both Sicily and Italy. In 282 or thereabouts, the city of Rhegium – whose history and development are closely linked with that of northern Sicily – was garrisoned, at its own request, by Campanians serving in the Roman army in order to protect it from Pyrrhus. In 279, however, the Campanians rose against the government of the city, slaughtered the Greek citizens, and took the city for themselves.[47] The sources paint a harrowing picture of the extermination of the Greek population, but the archaeological and epigraphic evidence contradicts this, indicating a continuation of Greek language and culture until well into the early empire.[48] Similarly, Paestum, which was overrun by the Lucanians in 410, is described by later sources as being entirely Oscanised – the Greek population having been killed, driven out or enslaved.[49] In fact, both Greeks and their culture remained alive and well at Paestum until well after this date. Greek inscriptions, Greek names, production of Greek vases and other forms of material culture, and the co-existence of

Greek and Lucanian burials all attest to the fact that the Greeks still existed there in significant numbers.[50] What seems to have happened in both these cases is not mass slaughter and displacement of the population, but the removal and replacement of the ruling elite, or particular factions of it.

Returning to focus on Sicily, the most complex example of the impact of demographic change, and of the strategies used by tyrants involving shifts in population, is that of Messana. It is worth examining in detail for what it can tell us about the cultural and ethnic changes which could result from the mass migrations instigated by tyrants. A complex interplay can be traced between the original identity as Chalcidian Zancle, the various manifestations of Greek Messana, and the later, partially Oscanised, identity forged after the takeover by Agathocles' Campanian mercenaries early in the third century BC. The city had a multi-layered identity from an early stage in its history. It was initially a Chalcidian colony, but in the early fifth century it suffered incursions from a group of Samian mercenaries, and then had a group of Doric Messenians settled there after an intervention by Anaxilas of Rhegium.[51] The ethnic divisions between the Ionian Chalcidians and the new Dorian settlers from the Peloponnese seem to have become entrenched within the city, and may have been influential in determining the political allegiances of Messana at certain crucial points in the fourth century BC.[52] In the fourth century it was a focus of mercenary settlement and acquired a substantial Campanian minority even before the events of the 280s. In 396 Dionysius I settled around 5,000 Greeks from Italy there, as well as some of his Campanian mercenaries, and some additional settlers from Greece migrated there in 369/8.[53] At some point in the 280s, there was a decisive change when the Mamertines – Campanian mercenaries brought to Sicily by Agathocles – attacked the city and took it over. The dating is problematic, and it is unclear whether this happened in 286/5 or as late as 282, but it is presented in the sources as a decisive and traumatic event involving the slaughter of the Greek population.[54]

When other evidence for the fourth- and third-century development of the city is examined, however, a very complex cultural identity emerges and it is clear that the Campanian settlements of both the fourth and third centuries did not by any means wipe out Greek culture. Much of the identity of the city remains Greek and there must be a strong suspicion that, as at Rhegium, there were many more Greeks left at Messana than the ancient sources admit. There is also evidence that the new Campanian settlers developed an identity which blended both Greek and Oscan elements.

The topography of the city shows major changes dating to the fourth and third centuries, reflecting the presence of new population and hinting at changes in civic identity. Buildings in the centre of the archaic and classical areas of settlement fall into disuse and usage of this area declines, while new areas of housing and artisan activity (represented by a large concentration of kilns active from the fourth to the first centuries) develop to the west and south-west of the original settlement, and there is a major expansion of habitation probably connected with the Mamertine take over to the north.[55] This coincides with a major expansion of the south-western cemeteries of Orto della Maddalena and S. Cecilia and the construction of new fortifications, attributed to the Mamertines.[56] There is some debate about whether these changes in urban topography and use of urban space should be associated specifically with the Mamertine conquest, or with earlier cultural, demographic and political changes in the later fourth century.[57] Whichever interpretation is accepted, they remain a graphic illustration of the impact which the various population movements associated with tyranny and its overthrow could have on a community.

The wider culture of Messana, however, presents a more complex picture of interaction between the various groups of inhabitants in the fourth and third centuries. Greek language is still widely used for inscriptions until well into the Roman period and the majority of personal names attested in the epigraphy of Hellenistic Messana are Greek, although there are a number of Oscan or Italic ones present too.[58] A fourth-century chamber tomb found in Via C. Battisti contained a vase with a dipinto, written in Greek but naming its owner as the Oscan Pakia Pompeia.[59] In particular, the cemeteries to the south of the city, in Via S. Cecilia and Via S. Marta, and at Orto della Maddalena, show continuity from the fourth to the first centuries BC and have produced Greek inscriptions and tile stamps, some of which carry the word *MAMEPTINΩN*.[60] A second-century reference in the lists of Thearodokoi at Delphi refers to the city by its Greek name, Messana, and indicates that the city was still part of the wider Greek cultural community.[61] In the initial stages, therefore, the presence of the Campanian mercenaries seems to have had relatively little cultural impact, and there is evidence that Greek language, script and other cultural indicators were used even where the Mamertines were presenting their own collective identity. The coinage of Hellenistic

Messana is a similar mixture of cultural types. Some of the coin types, such as an issue bearing the head of Zeus on the obverse and a trident and dolphin on the reverse, are clearly echoing the coinage of fifth- and fourth-century Messana.[62] Others introduce new designs, but the vast majority combine a generically Greek iconography, use of Greek script, and use of Greek names where the legends identify individuals, with the Greek legend *MAMEPTINΩN* to denote the identity of the community.[63]

This merging of Greek and Oscan culture and adoption of many aspects of Hellenism can also be seen at several other sites settled by Campanian mercenaries in Sicily. Both Entella and Nakone also show the same pattern of adoption of Greek script and Greek language to a large degree, and the use of Greek-style coinage.[64] At Messana, however, there was a marked phase of 'Oscanisation' which seems to be datable rather later than the Mamertine take over of the city – probably to the late third century.[65] This is marked by the appearance of Oscan inscriptions, most notably a dedication to Apollo, written in Oscan but in Greek script.[66] The dedicators – two magistrates, making the dedication on behalf of the community – are Oscan *meddices* rather than Greek magistrates.[67] Hellenistic brick and tile stamps similarly use the Oscan *mamertinos* (*IG* 14.2400.7, 2394.3) to identify the community but write the inscription in Greek characters, while some later examples use the Oscan *MAMEPTINOYM* instead.[68] The exact nature, date and cause of this new cultural phase is a matter of intense debate, although there is a strong likelihood that it was triggered by the cultural and political challenges posed by the First Punic War and the arrival of Rome.[69] What is clear, however, is that demographic change – while destabilising to a community – did not involve the destruction of that community's entire identity and sense of self, but could entail an absorption of the new elements of population (even those which were the result of a traumatic take over) into the pre-existing culture, or the interplay of several cultures to produce a new civic identity.

CONCLUSIONS: TYRANNY, POPULATION AND CULTURE IN GREEK SICILY

In conclusion, demographic movements in Sicily have a strong, but not exclusive, connection both to the actual actions and policies of tyrants, and to the literary and philosophical persona of the tyrant-figure. Some aspects, in particular, come to exemplify the unacceptable face of the tyrant, especially the use of mass relocations as a means of suppressing dissent and opposition, and the displacement of Greeks to allow for the settlement of 'barbarian' mercenaries of Campanian or Sicel origin. These relocations and shifts of population tap into a number of Greek anxieties about identity, 'barbarisation' and the nature of 'The Other', and about depopulation and the nature of citizenship. These were fundamental concerns for Greek authors of the classical period, but they may reflect the concerns of Greece and the Aegean – and of disaffected exiles such as Timaeus – to a greater degree than those of most Sicilian Greeks. The fluid nature of settlement and colonisation in the west, highlighted in studies of both the early foundations and the later political development of the western colonies, suggests that they did not develop the very strong bonds between population, land and citizenship which was characteristic of the core areas of the Greek world.[70] There may be a case for viewing the demographic history of Sicily as a process of constant flux and successive waves of colonisation and re-colonisation prompted by its situation on the edge of the Greek world and in constant contact and dialogue with non-Greeks.

Despite the prejudice of most Greek writers against this process, an examination of the evidence for urban development – especially in the Hellenistic period – suggests that demographic movement and displacement was not necessarily the catastrophe for the cultural identity of the cities involved which it is sometimes portrayed as by our sources. It clearly had an impact on the internal organisation of cities. The most successful initiatives are those which involved detailed plans to integrate the displaced population into their new communities via provision of land and housing, new cults to provide a focus for their communal loyalties, and programmes of public building to reaffirm civic identity. The cultural identity of the Sicilian city, however, is not straightforwardly determined by ethnic composition or demographic change, and attempts to map these changes onto such identities runs the risk of oversimplification. Case-studies – in particular those which involve the addition of non-Greek population to Greek communities – indicate that cultural identity is the result of a series of negotiations and interactions between different cultural elements within a community. It is not something which is simplistically determined by changes in population and ethnicity. The evidence for the interplay of Greek and Oscan elements in the identities of communities such as Messana and Entella illustrates very clearly the extremely complex relationships between different groups of citizens and their cultures in forging an overall civic identity.

This chapter began with the assertion that the connections between tyranny and demographic change were open to question and in need of re-examination. Despite the fact that forms of government other than tyrannies also initiated mass movements of population in Sicily, the preponderance of such relocations was undertaken by tyrants, and many of those that were not were undertaken as a direct reaction to the policies of tyrants. There does, therefore, seem to be a strong correlation between tyranny and population displacement in Sicilian history – a connection which is much closer than it is in many other areas of the Greek world. The factors underlying this are many and various, and have their roots in the specific nature of Sicilian and colonial society. Ethnic difference and conflict (both between Dorian and Chalcidian Greeks and between Greeks and non-Greeks), the strategic needs of Syracuse, the political needs of the tyrants, and the unique nature of citizenship and landholding in the western colonies all contributed to this link between autocracy and relocation of populations, and the relative significance of each individual element is often impossible to disentangle. It seems possible to conclude that in Sicily, at least, the connection between autocracy and demographic movement is both real and substantive, supported by enough epigraphic, numismatic and archaeological evidence to indicate that it is not just part of the literary persona of the tyrant. In order to take the debate forward, however, and to examine the effects of the actions of tyrants on their own cities and others, it is necessary to move away from the analysis of the historical sources and political motivations in isolation and to attempt to place the actions of tyrants in their material contexts. Further archaeological examination of cities and their territories may throw more light on the problem of how this demographic fluidity impacted on the development of the Sicilian *polis*, but for the moment, the evidence available for communities such as Messana suggests that it did not have the disastrous consequences for the culture of Greek Sicily that the more apocalyptic rhetoric of our Greek sources would suggest.

NOTES

1. Berger 1992: 1–2; Finley 1979: 48; Lomas 2000.
2. Andrewes 1956: 128–42; Berve 1967: I.128–63; Demand 1990: 10–12; against this, see Vattuone 1994: 89–95.
3. Demand 1990: 10–12.
4. Pearson 1987; Talbert 1974; Sordi 1980.

5. Lomas 2000; Vattuone 1994: 89–95; Asheri 1980; Vanotti 1995.

6. Hdt. 6.24–6, Thuc. 6.4.6, Arist. *Pol.* 1316a34–7; Heraclid. Pont. *FHG* 2.219, Justin 4.2.4, DH 19.4.

7. Hdt. 7.156; Demand 1990: 45–50.

8. Demand 1990: 45–50.

9. Plut. *Apophth. Gelon* 2, Diod. 11.73.1–3, Polyaen. 1.27.1; Demand 1990: 49.

10. Paus. 5.27.2, Pind. *Olymp.* 6.6; Dittenberger 266; Moretti 1953: 186–7, 196–7, 219.

11. Diod. 11.49; Vanotti 1995: 91–5; Pind. *Pyth.* 1; Aesch. *Women of Aitna*, *ap.* Macrob. *Saturnalia* 5.1.9.24; *TrGF* 3, *Vita* 9; Dougherty 1993: 83–102; Harrell, Chapter 8 this volume.

12. Naxos: Asheri 1966: 39–40; Pelagatti 1972; Demand 1990: 50–1; Di Vita 1996: 296–9; lawcodes: Vanotti 1995: 91; Cordano 1986; coinage: Boehringer 1968: 76–9.

13. Diod. 11.72.3–73.3, 11.76.4–6; Asheri 1980.

14. Diod. 12.53, 12.83; Vanotti 1995: 97; Diod. 13.63.

15. Kraay 1976: nos 835 and 839; Jenkins 1966: 16–17 and 24–5; Jenkins 1972: 368–9; Demand 1990: 54–5.

16. Vanotti 1995: 90, 97–102.

17. McKechnie 1989: 34–43; Krasilnikoff 1995: 174–82; Giuliani 1995; Sordi 1980.

18. Diod. 14.7.1–5; Sordi 1980: 213.

19. Diod. 14.14.4–15.4; Sordi 1980: 214.

20. See Dench 1995: 55 and Herring 2000. 69–71 for the debate on whether they were of Campanian or Samnite origin.

21. DH 20.4.8; Strabo 6.2.3; Diod. 22.13.2; Polyb. 1.7–11; Alfius *ap.* Festus 150L; Dio fr. 40.8; Zonaras 8.8.

22. Pl. *Epist.* 3.315c8–d7, 8.353a4–8; see also the symbolism of coin issues at Aetna, Leontini and Catane, pp. 110–11.

23. Sordi 1981.

24. Vattuone 1994: 81–9; Vanotti 1995; Raccuia 1981.

25. Waters 1971; Gammie 1986; Gray 1996.

26. Gammie 1986: 22; Vattuone 1994: 96–104.

27. Tagliamonte 1994: 91–102, 136–7, 191–8.

28. Alcock 1993, 24–32; Gallo 1980, 1233–70; Vattuone 1994: 108–9.

29. Berger 1992: 58–9; Lomas 2000: 168–73, on a possible link between the colonial environment and the prevalence of tyranny, see De Angelis 2003: 38–40.

30. Demand 1990: 10–12.

31. Pl. *Rep.* 9(8) 562–7; Arist. *Pol.* 1275b34, 1310b40, 1313a34, 1313b4–5, 1311a8–14.

32. Arist. *Pol.* 1313a34, 1313b4–5, 1311a8–14.

33. Berger 1992: 62–5.

34. Krasilnikoff 1995.
35. Diod. 14.7; on the general tendency of tyrants to adopt these policies, cf. Pl. *Rep.* 9(8) 566, Arist. *Pol.* 1313a34; McKechnie 1989: 39; Krasilnikoff 1995: 171–4.
36. McKechnie 1989: 6–11, 34–45.
37. Asheri 1980; Vanotti 1995: 96–102.
38. Diod. 16.65–9, 73, 82–3; Plut. *Timol.* 23.6; Talbert 1974.
39. Asheri 1980: 145, 154–5.
40. McKechnie 1989: 39–42.
41. Livy 8.25–7; DH 15.5.1–9.2; Frederiksen 1984, 210–11; Lomas 1993: 45–7.
42. Rutter 2001: 187–92; discussed with reference to Messana in Consolo Langher 1996b, 409–18 and 1999b: 34–5.
43. Diod. 14.7; Di Vita 1996: 273–5 and 2002.
44. Di Vita 1996 and 2002.
45. Di Vita 1996: 300–4.
46. Lentini 2002.
47. Polyb. 1.7.1; App. *Samn.* 7.1, 9.1; Livy 31.31.6–8; DH 20.4; Livy *Per.* 12.
48. Lomas 1993: 33–4.
49. Aristox. *ap.* Ath. *Deip.* 14.632a–b.
50. Pedley 1990: 97–112.
51. Hdt. 6.24–6, Thuc. 6.4.6; Consolo Langher 1999b: 33–8.
52. Mafodda 1979; Raccuia 1981: 19 and 25.
53. Diod. 14.78.3–6, 15.66.5; on the mercenary settlement, see Tagliamonte 1994: 191–8.
54. Tagliamonte 1994: 191; Pinzone 1999.
55. Bacci and Tigano 1999, 53–4.
56. Ibid., 54–5.
57. Bacci 1995: 427–30; Scibona 1986: 446; Bacci and Tigano 1999: 53.
58. Bitto 2001; Fraser and Matthews 1997; Pinzone 1999; Orioles 1992.
59. Tagliamonte 1994: 196.
60. *IG* 14.2394; Bitto 2001: 120–2 and 125–8.
61. *IG* 5.1504, 24; *SEG* 22.455; *BTCGI* 10: 10–11.
62. Lehmann 1981; Arnold-Biucchi 1983.
63. Orioles 1992.
64. Tagliamonte 1994: 136–7.
65. Pinzone 1999: 134–42; Orioles 1992: 333–6; Parlangèli 1956: 28–9.
66. Vetter 1959: no. 197.
67. Costabile 1978; Pinzone 1999: 121–34, 154–65; Orioles 1992: 333–6.
68. Bitto 2001; Vetter 1959: no. 198; Pinzone 1999: 159.
69. For the various hypotheses, see Orioles 1992; Pinzone 1999.
70. See especially Osborne 1998; Berger 1992.

CHAPTER 8

Synchronicity: the local and the panhellenic within Sicilian tyranny

Sarah E. Harrell

My title, 'synchronicity', alludes to the Sicilian claim, recorded in book 7 of Herodotus' *Histories*, that the battle between the Greeks and Carthaginians at Himera, in Sicily, occurred on the very same day as the battle between the Greeks and Persians at Salamis in 480 BC (Hdt. 7.166). Herodotus has just noted that (again according to the Sicilians), Gelon would have aided the Greek alliance at Salamis if the two battles had not been simultaneous (7.165). While accepted by some ancient authors as fact, the idea of such a 'synchronicity' appears highly improbable to modern eyes.[1] My purpose here is not to investigate the historicity of this aspect of Herodotus' text. Instead I will examine how the synchronicity represents a tension within Herodotus' Sicilian narrative between the local and the panhellenic nature of the fifth century Deinomenid tyranny.[2] Herodotus introduces his account of the Deinomenid Gelon and his family background by describing a Greek embassy that has been sent to Sicily to seek help against the Persians. The account of the embassy leads Herodotus to explain how Gelon came to power as tyrant first of Gela and later of Syracuse. The Sicilian narrative culminates with the victory at Himera of Gelon and Theron, Greek tyrant of Acragas, over the barbarian forces led by the Carthaginian king Hamilcar. Herodotus therefore does not describe the battle of Himera in isolation. It is an integral part of his representation of Sicilian tyranny. He also clearly relates the battle to the allied Greek defence of their homeland against the barbarian attack led by the Persian king Xerxes.

I contend that the very same tension between the local and the panhellenic that we see in Herodotus' account plays a prominent role in the representations of Himera generated by the tyrants themselves. Roughly fifty years before Herodotus wrote his *Histories*, the Deinomenids, Gelon and his younger brother Hieron, celebrated their martial victory through monuments in the panhellenic sanctuaries and through the commission of epinician poetry. Some have suggested that Herodotus' Sicilian narrative demonstrates his awareness of local traditions that grew out of this 'Deinomenid propaganda'.[3] While this seems likely to me, it is difficult to prove definitively. Nevertheless, the contemporary and near-contemporary representations of Deinomenid tyranny display a similar pull between the tyrants' local identities and their significance in the panhellenic sphere. The representations of the battle of Himera composed by Herodotus and by artists hired by the Deinomenids provide a revealing case-study of what I see as a larger trend. These sources continuously represent Deinomenid tyranny from both local and panhellenic viewpoints.

HERODOTUS' NARRATIVE

As I have said, Herodotus places Gelon's tyranny firmly within a panhellenic context by associating it with a wider Greek and international arena. Sicily is one of the regions that Greek messengers approach in order to ask for contributions to the Greek force that is being assembled to ward off the Persians. According to Herodotus, the messengers come 'intending that somehow there might be a Hellenic collective, and that acting together they all might somehow accomplish the same thing, since the enemy was attacking all Greeks alike' (φρονήσαντες εἴ κως ἕν τε γένοιτο τὸ Ἑλληνικὸν καὶ εἰ συγκύψαντες τὠυτὸ πρήσσοιεν πάντες, ὡς δεινῶν ἐπιόντων ὁμοίως πᾶσι Ἕλλησι, Hdt. 7.145.2). Yet, with the very next sentence, Herodotus suggests why Gelon in particular might have trouble blending into a panhellenic alliance. He states that 'the power of Gelon was said to be great; that of no other Greek was any greater' (τὰ δὲ Γέλωνος πρήγματα μεγάλα ἐλέγετο εἶναι, οὐδαμῶν Ἑλληνικῶν τῶν οὐ πολλὸν μέζω, 7.145.2). Just after he has explained that the ambassadors have come with a message of Greek commonality, Herodotus marks Gelon as different from all other Greeks. We already sense that the embassy's message will not have much resonance with the Sicilian tyrant.

Later, Herodotus describes the failure of the embassy's plea. Gelon responds to the ambassadors with his own counter-offer. He promises to help the Greeks on the condition that 'I will be both general and leader of the Greeks against the barbarian' (τε στρατηγός τε καὶ ἡγεμὼν τῶν Ἑλλήνων ἔσομαι πρὸς τὸν βάρβαρον . . ., 7.158.5). Gelon formulates his offer with such stark boldness that it appears intended to be rejected. Moreover, he explains his terms only after he has expressed anger at his past treatment at the hands of the mainland

Greeks. Gelon recalls that on several occasions the Greeks ignored his requests for help: when he entered a dispute (or *neikos*) with the Carthaginians, when he wished to punish the Segestans for the murder of the Spartan Dorieus, and when he proposed to liberate trading posts (*emporia*) from a barbarian force. Gelon concludes that for the Greeks 'these things are controlled by the barbarians' (τάδε πάντα ὑπὸ βαρβάροισι νέμεται, 7.158.2). His local 'barbarian conflicts' in Sicily did not move the mainland Greeks, and now Gelon has no reason to help them resist their own barbarian attack. Several scholars have questioned the historicity of Gelon's speech because it takes place before the battle of Himera and refers to episodes that are difficult to confirm with external evidence.[4] Leaving aside the issue of historicity, this speech signals an overall theme in Herodotus' narrative. Gelon's reply to the mainland Greeks reflects the limitations of a panhellenic ideal when it is placed alongside local realities. In contrast to the messengers for whom the Persians constitute the barbarian, for a Sicilian Greek the barbarian has several identities. Gelon specifies two barbarian peoples in the course of his response to the Greek ambassadors. He mentions the 'Segestans', who were Elymians, a non-Greek people of uncertain origin who lived in western Sicily. In addition, Gelon speaks of a conflict with the Carthaginians, the inhabitants of the dominant city on the north coast of Africa, originally founded by Phoenicians. Herodotus already has made clear that other non-Greek peoples dwelled alongside the Greeks on the island (Hdt. 7.154.2, 7.155). We know that these peoples included the indigenous Sicels and Sicans, and the Phoenicians who set up colonies in Sicily.[5] Herodotus includes Gelon's speech in his narrative in part to demonstrate that Gelon's own experience with the 'barbarian' prevents him from entering easily into the Greeks' alliance against the Persian. Local identity outweighs panhellenism.[6]

At the same time that he emphasises the nature of Greek–barbarian relations in Sicily, Herodotus goes out of his way to associate a local Sicilian conflict, the battle of Himera, with the Persian wars. Himera was a Greek city with great strategic importance within Sicily. It formed the northern point of an imaginary boundary that separated 'Greek' from 'non-Greek' Sicily (figure 8.1). While Greeks and non-Greeks intermingled throughout the island, the Greeks controlled the eastern portions of Sicily, starting from Himera in the north and Acragas (Agrigento) in the south. Non-Greeks (especially the Phoenicians and Elymians) were dominant in western Sicily. In his account of the battle of Himera, Herodotus records that the 'Sicilians'

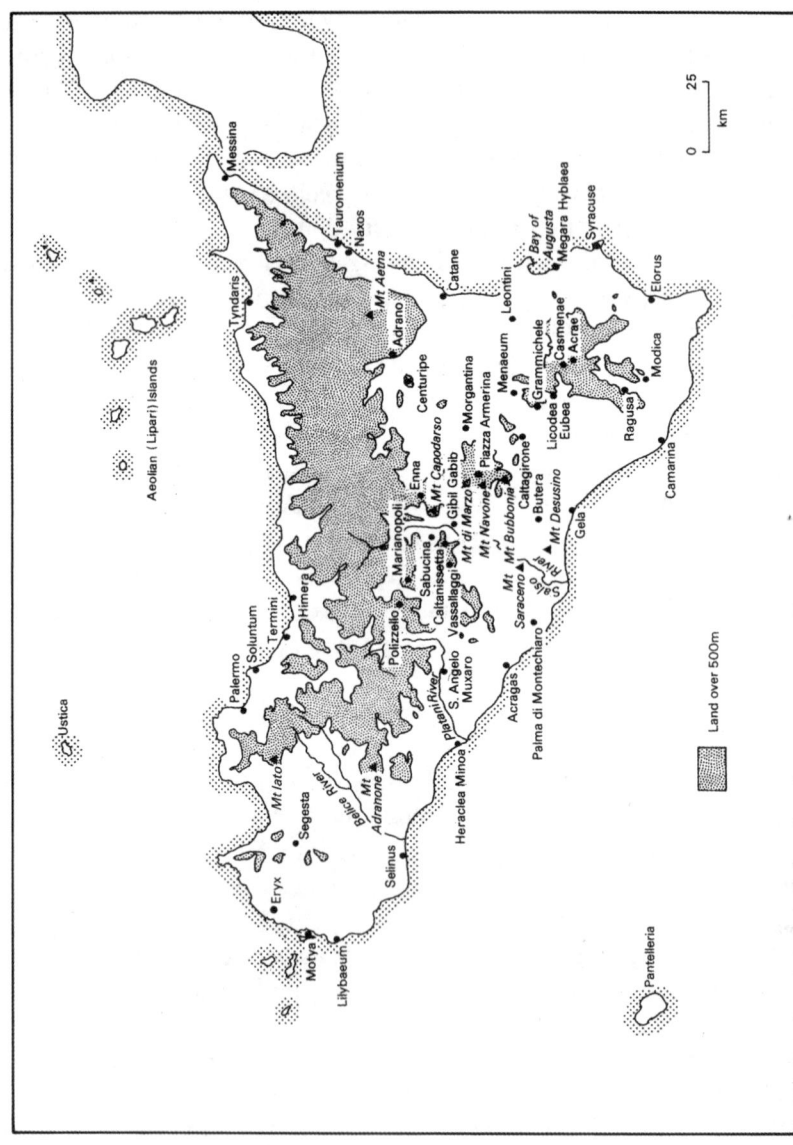

Figure 8.1 Map of Greek and Phoenician sites in Sicily (after Holloway, *Archaeology of Ancient Sicily*)

say 'that it turned out that on the same day in Sicily Gelon and Theron conquered Hamilcar the Carthaginian, and in Salamis the Greeks conquered the Persian' (ὡς συνέβη τῆς αὐτῆς ἡμέρης ἔν τε τῇ Σικελίῃ Γέλωνα καὶ Θήρωνα νικᾶν Ἀμίλκαν τὸν Καρχηδόνιον καὶ ἐν Σαλαμῖνι τοὺς Ἕλληνας τὸν Πέρσην, Hdt. 7.166). While Herodotus does not comment on the veracity of the Sicilian claim of synchronicity, by including this claim without direct comment he implies at the very least that Himera and Salamis form a significant pair.[7]

Herodotus also strengthens the parallel nature of Salamis and Himera by posing Hamilcar as a figure similar to Xerxes. Herodotus' brief description of the army that Hamilcar leads recalls on a smaller scale his lengthy account of Xerxes' force at the beginning of book 7 (7.61–99). Both accounts exaggerate the number of troops assembled by each leader, and include a list of subject nations from which the troops were drawn. Hamilcar's army includes: Phoenicians, Libyans, Iberians, Elisycans, Sardonians (from Sardinia), and Cyrnians (from Corsica) (7.165).[8] These peoples roughly represent the western region that the imperial force of Carthage controlled in this period. Even more striking is Herodotus' presentation of Hamilcar as an eastern 'king' (*basileus*: 7.165, 166).[9] Whatever the actual nature of Carthaginian kingship, Herodotus' use of this title reminds the audience of Carthage's inextricable ties to the east, and in particular to Phoenicia, where cities were ruled by hereditary monarchs. Moreover, the title of king strengthens the parallel between the two barbarian leaders, Hamilcar and Xerxes. In the *Histories*, Herodotus clearly depicts Xerxes as the great eastern 'king' (7. 4–5). Herodotus suggests the 'eastern' and 'royal' nature of Hamilcar most vividly when he records the Carthaginian explanation for Hamilcar's disappearance from Himera. Without fully endorsing this story as fact, Herodotus indicates some preference for the Carthaginian version. He refers to it as 'reasonable' or 'likely' (οἰκότι χρεωμένων, 7.167.1). According to the Carthaginians, as the battle of Himera raged on:

> Hamilcar, remaining in the encampment during this time, sacrificed and obtained favourable omens by offering up whole bodies on the great pyre. But when he saw the flight of his own troops, while he was in the act of pouring libations upon the sacrifices he threw himself into the fire. Thus, having been burned completely, he disappeared. (7.167.1)

ὁ δὲ Ἀμίλκας ἐν τούτῳ τῷ χρόνῳ μένων ἐν τῷ στρατοπέδῳ [ἐθύετο καὶ] ἐκαλλιερέετο ἐπὶ πυρῆς μεγάλης σώματα ὅλα

καταγίζων· ἰδὼν δὲ τροπὴν τῶν ἑωυτοῦ γινομένην, ὡς ἔτυχε
ἐπισπένδων τοῖσι ἱροῖσι, ὦσε ἑωυτὸν ἐς τὸ πῦρ· οὕτω δὴ
κατακαυθέντα ἀφανισθῆναι.

This manner of death has clear parallels with recorded self-immolations of eastern monarchs. For example, later traditions tell us that Elissa, or Dido, the first Phoenician queen of Carthage, died in this manner, as did Sardanapallus, ancient king of Nineveh.[10] Herodotus himself provides two additional accounts of similar events. In book 1 of the *Histories*, we learn that the king of Lydia, Croesus, almost dies on a pyre after being defeated by the Persians (1.86.2). Contemporary traditions record that he in fact threw himself on the pyre.[11] In book 7 of the *Histories*, Herodotus recounts how Boges, the Persian ruler of Eion, throws himself on a pyre when facing defeat by the Greeks (7.107). When Herodotus depicts Hamilcar dying in a manner fit for an eastern monarch, he links the Carthaginian to the great eastern king, Xerxes.

On the one hand, Herodotus' narrative suggests that Carthage was a foreign, royal power like Persia that suffered a crushing defeat, similar to Salamis, in a failed attempt to gain control over Greek territory. Modern historians have noted, however, that there is no external evidence to support the view that the battle of Himera was a grand imperial invasion on Carthage's part. Instead the battle more likely was a local conflict between neighbours with limited goals that, in the end, did not greatly affect Carthage's power.[12] Herodotus himself hints at the local nature of this battle, and the fact that it was not a clear-cut Greek versus barbarian standoff. Hamilcar leads a military force into Sicily only at the request of Terillus, the Greek tyrant of Himera. Again making clear that he is recording a Sicilian version of events, Herodotus reports that Gelon would have helped the Spartans face the Persians if not for this power struggle between the Greek tyrants Terillus and Theron. After Theron drove Terillus out of Himera, Terillus turned to two allies for help. One was the tyrant of the Greek colony of Rhegium in Southern Italy, Anaxilas, with whom Terillus was aligned through marriage. The other was the Carthaginian Hamilcar. Herodotus explains that Terillus persuaded Hamilcar to intervene because of their *xenia* (or guest-friendship) (κατὰ ξεινίην, 7.165) In addition, Anaxilas hands over to Hamilcar his own children as hostages in order to ensure the Carthaginian's help in restoring power to his father-in-law Terillus (7.165).[13] The use of the term *xenia* is significant here. It shows that Sicilian Greeks and Carthaginians, in

some cases at least, had cooperative relationships, determined by aristocratic and diplomatic alliances.[14] A Sicilian Greek tyrant invites a
Carthaginian to help him regain his city in the face of the growing
desire of rival Greek tyrants, Gelon and Theron, to control the eastern
portion of Sicily. In the midst of representing the battle of Himera as
an invasion of a massive barbarian force, Herodotus makes clear that
local Greek rivalries began the conflict, and that aristocratic bonds of
friendship induced the Carthaginians to enter it.

Herodotus shows the battle of Himera to be more nuanced than a
confrontation between Greeks and a generic barbarian enemy. His
account reinforces analyses of the region by historians and archaeol-
ogists. Clearly relations between Greeks and non-Greeks in the
western Mediterranean were complex.[15] Herodotus provides a striking indication of this complex reality in his brief description of
Hamilcar's family background. He tells us, without editorial
comment, that Hamilcar was: 'Carthaginian on his father's side and
Syracusan on his mother's' (Καρχηδόνιον ἐόντα πρὸς πατρός,
μητρόθεν δὲ Συρηκόσιον, 7.166). The marriage of a Carthaginian
and a Syracusan further suggests the links between Sicilian and
Carthaginian aristocrats.[16] Proximity must have played some role in
creating such bonds, which have left only faint traces in our Greek
sources. Despite the relative silence of Greek authors on this issue,
peaceful interactions may have been just as common as the hostilities
that receive more attention, especially after the Persian wars.
Herodotus includes both aspects of this western reality in his account
of Gelon's victory at Himera.

DEINOMENID SELF-REPRESENTATION

When we turn to representations of the victory at Himera that the
Deinomenids themselves commissioned, we see a similar recognition
of the local and panhellenic significance of the battle. Here I will
focus on monuments placed within the panhellenic sanctuaries of
Olympia and Delphi and on epinician poetry. It is necessary to view
this evidence in terms of the audiences for which it was originally
intended. While dedications at Olympia and Delphi were set up to
be seen by a larger Greek and international community, epinician
poetry celebrated athletic victories at these sanctuaries, but generally was performed for a local audience.[17] Thus these two types of
representation, by their very nature, reveal both panhellenic and
local perspectives.

Diodorus Siculus mentions that the tyrant Gelon dedicated a golden tripod at Delphi to commemorate his victory at Himera (Diod. 11.26.7). The base of this tripod stands partially preserved *in situ* at Delphi today, with a clear inscription identifying it as the dedication of Gelon, as can be seen in figure 8.2. The tripod monument contains two bases. The base on the right is badly damaged, but it most likely identified as its dedicator Hieron, Gelon's younger brother who succeeded him as tyrant of Syracuse. Both bases appear to have been part of the original plan of the monument, with Hieron's added later.[18] This was an elaborate monument, probably consisting of two gold tripods standing atop statues of Nike. Gelon's inscription identifies both dedicator and artist, reading 'Gelon, the son of Deinomenes, the Syracusan, dedicated this to Apollo. Bion, the son of Diodorus, the Milesian, made the tripod and the Nike' (*Γέλον ὁ Δεινομέν[εος] / ἀνέθεκε τὸπόλλονι / Συραϙόσιος. / τὸν τρίποδα καὶ τὲν Νίκεν ἐργάσατο Βίον Διοδόρο υἱὸς Μιλέσιος*, ML 28). No contemporary documentary evidence explicitly connects this dedication with the victory at Himera. But scholars agree that the monument whose remains we possess is in fact the same one that Diodorus describes.[19]

Figure 8.2   Deinomenid Tripod Monument (Gelon's tripod base). (author photo)

Gelon managed to make his monument impossible to miss, placing it in a prominent position on the Sacred Way at Delphi. As can be seen in figures 8.3 and 8.4, anyone following the path of the Sacred Way toward Apollo's temple, the site of Delphic oracle, had to pass by the Deinomenid dedication. Moreover, its scale and materials (gold and bronze) would have caught the notice of all who saw it. While the inscription does not mention Himera explicitly, it is safe to say that visitors to Delphi knew about the battle, or at least came to know about it through this magnificent display. A tripod situated atop a statue of Nike may have prompted the association between the dedication and Himera in the minds of viewers. Perhaps the inscription's silence about the battle made an even louder statement. The victory at Himera was so important that it did not need mentioning, even to the wider Greek and international audience that visited Delphi. Gelon's inscription asserts that the glory of this achievement belongs to him (and by extension to his family and to the city of Syracuse). Unlike the nearly contemporary Plataean victory monument at Delphi (ML 27), this dedication provides no listing of allied states that participated in the victory at Himera or its commemoration. A clear message is sent

Figure 8.3 Deinomenid Tripod Monument, foreground, viewed from the north (Sacred Way centre, terrace of Apollo's temple to right) (author photo)

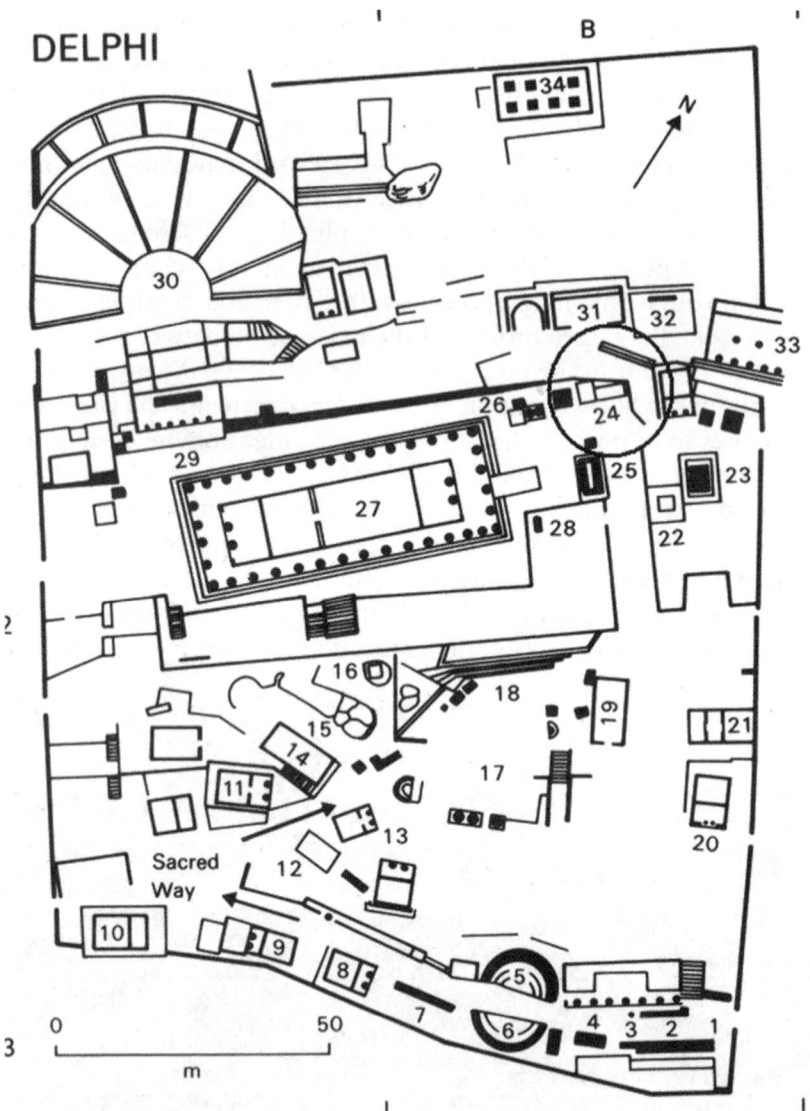

Figure 8.4 Plan of the sanctuary at Delphi, showing site of the Tripod Monument (24, ringed) (after Talbert, *Atlas of Classical History*)

to the double audience of Sicilians and non-Sicilians who saw or heard about the monument. The Deinomenids alone are responsible for this great victory and the magnificent display in its honour.[20]

I now turn to the sanctuary of Olympia, where Gelon also commemorated the victory at Himera. Only the foundations remain

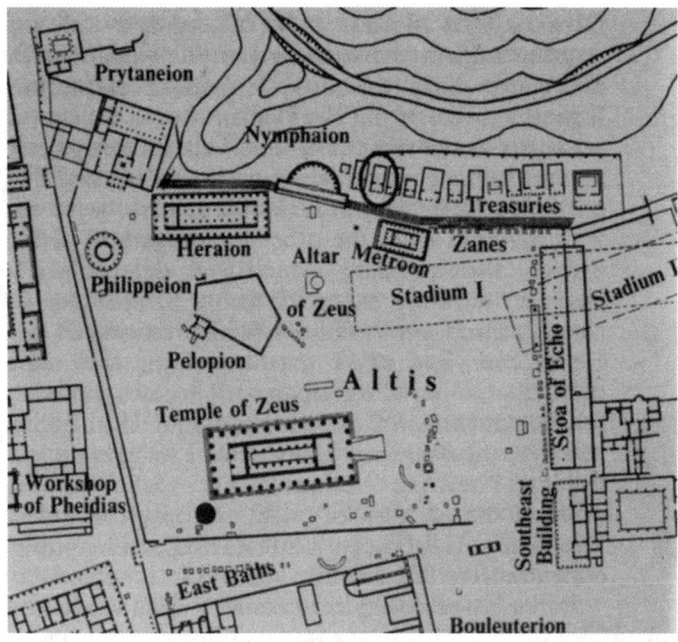

Figure 8.5 Plan of the sanctuary at Olympia, showing site of the Syracusan treasury (ringed) (after Mallwitz)

today of the Syracusan treasury on the Treasury Terrace at Olympia (figure 8.5). Pausanias describes its location and calls it 'the Treasury of the Carthaginians'. He does not state explicitly that the treasury was built to commemorate the victory at Himera, but this can be the only explanation for his use of the title. Pausanias also describes the offerings housed within the treasury: a statue of Zeus, and three linen breastplates, 'the dedication of Gelon and the Syracusans after overpowering the Phoenicians either in a land or sea battle' (Γέλωνος δὲ ἀνάθημα καὶ Συρακοσίων Φοίνικας ἤτοι τριήρεσιν ἢ καὶ πεζῇ μάχῃ κρατησάντων, Paus. 6.19.7). Pausanias may have seen an inscription on the objects housed in the treasury, which marked them as war spoils taken from the 'Phoenicians' (i.e. the Carthaginians). Thus the treasury itself and the offerings inside would have celebrated Gelon and the Syracusans as victors over the Carthaginians.[21] Again we have a prominently placed monument within a panhellenic sanctuary that draws attention to Gelon's status as the victor at Himera before a wide Greek audience. The treasury suggests that the victory over a barbarian force has relevance to Greeks in general.

In this instance, unlike in the case of the tripod monument at Delphi, the inscriptions on the objects housed within the treasury seem to give credit also to the Syracusans for the defeat and the offerings to Zeus. If Pausanias' account reflects the actual wording of the inscriptions on the dedications within the treasury, they would resemble helmets that Hieron later dedicated after his victory at Cumae over the Etruscans, in 474. These helmets have been found at Olympia, and they name both Hieron and the Syracusans as dedicators of the war spoils seized from a non-Greek opponent (ML 29). Perhaps these dedications were aimed at a Sicilian as well as a wider Greek audience at Olympia. Philipp has argued convincingly that Olympia in this period had a particularly strong western colonial presence and orientation.[22] Sicilians and Sicilian tyrants were especially prominent among known Olympic victors and dedicators. Thus the more inclusive form of the dedicatory inscriptions would have appealed to Syracusan visitors, who were more likely to have travelled to Olympia than to other panhellenic sanctuaries. At the same time, this inclusiveness is limited. The objects from Himera, again if we follow Pausanias' account, are marked clearly as a Deinomenid and Syracusan gift. Here, as at Delphi, we have no mention of other Sicilian participants in the victory, including the Emmenid tyrants. The treasury and the objects that it holds assert Deinomenid and Syracusan pre-eminence over a barbarian enemy. Again, Gelon and the Deinomenids appear to have taken sole credit for this victory at home and abroad. Perhaps they wished to remind their Emmenid allies that they were in reality the supreme Greek power in eastern Sicily.[23] By building a treasury at the popular sanctuary of Olympia, Gelon made this position clear also to an audience beyond Sicily.

The contemporary genre of epinician poetry celebrates Deinomenid athletic victories at Olympia and Delphi. At the same time, it commemorates the family's martial conquests. We possess epinician poems commissioned by Hieron, Gelon's younger brother, and by his associates. They date to a period slightly later than Himera, after the death of Gelon, when Hieron had risen to prominence as the new tyrant of Syracuse. The most relevant poem with regard to Himera is Pindar's *Pythian* 1.[24] It was occasioned by Hieron's chariot victory at Delphi in 470; it also honoured his foundation of the city of Aetna in Sicily.[25] *Pythian* 1 praises Hieron as an athletic victor at Delphi, the founder of a new city, and a just and excellent ruler. In addition, it represents Hieron as a great warrior, not only at Cumae but also at Himera:

I pray, son of Cronus, grant that the war cry of the Phoenicians and Etruscans may remain tamed at home, since they have seen arrogance bringing sorrow to their ships before Cumae. They suffered such things, having been subdued by the ruler of the Syracusans, he who hurled their youth into the sea from their swiftly moving ships, and who drew Hellas out of heavy slavery. I shall receive gratitude as a reward from the Athenians because of Salamis, in Sparta because of the battles before Cithaeron, in which the Medes of the curved bows were defeated, and also beside the well-watered shore of Himera, having made payment of a hymn to the sons of Deinomenes, which they received for their excellence, after the enemy had been defeated (Pind. *Pyth.* 1.71–80).

λίσσομαι νεῦσον, Κρονίων, ἥμερον
ὄφρα κατ᾽ οἶκον ὁ Φοίνιξ ὁ Τυρσα-
     νῶν τ᾽ ἀλαλατὸς ἔχῃ, ναυ-
σίστονον ὕβριν ἰδὼν τὰν πρὸ Κύμας,
οἷα Συρακοσίων ἀρχῷ δαμασθέντες πάθον,
ὠκυπόρων ἀπὸ ναῶν ὅ σφιν ἐν πόν-
     τῳ βάλεθ᾽ ἁλικίαν,
Ἑλλάδ᾽ ἐξέλκων βαρείας δουλίας. ἀρέομαι
πὰρ μὲν Σαλαμῖνος Ἀθαναίων χάριν
μισθόν, ἐν Σπάρτᾳ δ᾽ <ἀπὸ> τὰν πρὸ Κιθαιρῶ-
     νος μαχᾶν,
ταῖσι Μήδειοι κάμον ἀγκυλότοξοι,
παρὰ δὲ τὰν εὔυδρον ἀκτὰν
     Ἱμέρα παίδεσσιν ὕμνον Δεινομένεος τελέσαις,
τὸν ἐδέξαντ᾽ ἀμφ᾽ ἀρετᾷ, πολεμίων ἀνδρῶν
     καμόντων.

The beginning of this passage implicitly aligns Hieron's victory over the Etruscans at Cumae with the battle of Himera by expressing the hope that both local barbarian enemies (Phoenician/Carthaginian and Etruscan) will not dare to rise again (71). Before the local audience of Aetna, Pindar not only gives Hieron sole credit for defeating the Etruscans at Cumae (73–5). He also implies that Hieron helped crush the barbarian enemy at Himera as well. He names the 'sons of Deinomenes' as those who deserve a hymn celebrating their victory at this site, and Hieron, the recipient of the present ode, is one of these children (79–80). Pindar's inclusion of Hieron as one of those responsible for the defeat of the Carthaginians is significant, since we do not have direct evidence for his participation in the battle. In Herodotus' account of Himera, Hieron is not mentioned. In fact, Herodotus only names Hieron once within his Sicilian narrative: 'although he [Gelon] controlled Gela, he considered it to be of less importance and turned it over to his brother Hieron, while he strengthened Syracuse' (Hdt. 7.156.1). For Herodotus at least, Hieron is not a player during the period before he succeeded his brother as tyrant of Syracuse. Of course, Pindar has a very different focus than Herodotus, since it is Hieron who commissioned *Pythian* 1 and who was its primary audience.

Perhaps Pindar's boldest claim in the poem is that Hieron has saved Greece (*Hellas*) from the threat of slavery to a barbarian master (75). Hieron is a tyrant who has ensured the freedom not only of Sicily, but also of Greece. Hieron freed all of Greece through the battles of Cumae and Himera. This is quite an elevation in status for two battles that had local significance in the west, but which must have impacted the rest of the Greek world only minimally. Before the home crowd in Sicily, Hieron is proclaimed to be a true panhellenic hero. Pindar reinforces this message when he joins together the battles of Cumae and Himera with Salamis and Plataea. Just after describing Hieron's single-handed defeat of the Etruscans at Cumae, the poet imagines the reward or payment (*misthos*) that he will receive in return for the hymns that he will compose in honour of the victories at Salamis, Plataea ('before Mt Cithaeron') and Himera (75–80). Pindar makes no mention of the Greek alliance against the Persians, from which the Deinomenids were notably absent. Instead, Salamis and Plataea are credited to Athens and Sparta respectively. In the case of Himera, Pindar does not offer the hymn to a state, but to the Deinomenids as a family. This draws attention again to the tyrants as those primarily responsible for the victory. In Pindar's telling, this battle was a family effort, rather than a victory belonging only to Gelon. It clearly was on the same level as the battles at Salamis and Plataea, in which the great Persian empire was defeated.

Pindar does not align Salamis and Himera by stating that they occurred on the same day, as Herodotus does. Yet this poem is our earliest evidence for a connection and implied comparison between the two battles. It is an obvious statement of the panhellenic significance of the battle of Himera and of the Deinomenid tyrants.[26] According to Pindar, the Sicilian battle is just as relevant to the whole Greek world as Salamis and Plataea. The threat posed by the Carthaginians, and Etruscans, was just as great as that of the Medes, or Persians. The defeat of the western barbarians brought freedom to all of Hellas. This strongest and most explicit characterisation of Himera's panhellenic significance occurs in a text composed in honour of the Deinomenid Hieron. It was performed initially before a local audience in a city firmly under the tyrant's control. We can be sure that this is no coincidence.[27]

NOTES

1. Ephorus, the fourth-century BC historian, in a lost work appears not only to have considered the synchronicity to be factual, but also to have attributed it to a conspiracy between the eastern and western barbarians (Schol. Pind. *Pyth.* 1.146b). See Gauthier 1966: 25–31; Asheri 1991/2: 56–8.
2. I expand on this argument, and the evidence presented here, in a forthcoming book. See also Harrell 2002.
3. e.g. Gauthier 1966: 8–11; Asheri 1991/2: 57.
4. Treves 1941; Asheri, 'Carthaginians and Greeks', *CAH²* IV.739–80, at 767; Luraghi 1994: 278–81.
5. See Thuc. 6.2.3–6 for a brief summary of the non-Greeks who inhabited Sicily. Many scholars have pointed out that it is difficult to confirm the accuracy of accounts provided by Greek historians of the origins, cultures, and sometimes even the names of early non-Greek inhabitants of Sicily. Very little material evidence remains of their pre-Greek existence. Yet, as both Herodotus and Thucydides make clear, Greek settlers lived side by side on the island with non-Greeks, many of whom could claim a longer presence in Sicily (Dunbabin 1948: 20–2, 40–3, 335–7; Bernabò Brea 1966; Sjöqvist 1973: 28–35; Asheri *CAH²* IV.742–3; Niemeyer 1990; Antonaccio and Neils 1995, Garbini 1996; Shepherd 1999; Antonaccio 2001; Aubet 2001: 231–4; Jackman, Chapter 3, this volume).
6. Lomas 2000 discusses the situation for Greeks in Italy, where proximity to their own non-Greek neighbours contributed to their unique local identity.
7. See Dewald 1987, 2002 on Herodotus' use of the authorial voice, and the varying degrees to which he comments on the truth-value of statements that he records.
8. Asheri *CAH²* IV.773 and Ameling 1993: 23–5 note the similar exaggerations of troop numbers in both passages. Ameling suggests that Herodotus' description of Hamilcar's force is meant to recall the earlier account of Xerxes' army.
9. It is unclear in what sense the historical Hamilcar was 'king' of Carthage, since the colonial city Carthage probably did not possess a traditional hereditary monarchy, as its mother city, Phoenician Tyre, did (Bunnens 1979: 287–9; Ameling 1993: 67–97).
10. Burkert 1985: 4–10 summarises the known examples of this type of self-immolation. On Dido/Elissa see Bunnens 1979: 369–74; on Sardanapallus see Weissbach *RE* 'Sardanapal'.
11. e.g. the so-called Myson amphora (Paris Louvre G197, *ARV* 238.1) and Bacchyl. 3. 23–62. The latter was composed in honour of the Deinomenid

tyrant Hieron in 468. On the relationship between these versions of the Croesus myth and Herodotus' narrative, see Segal 1971; Burkert 1985: 12–15; Crane 1996.

12. Whittaker 1978: 64–6; Luraghi 1994: 308–9.
13. Luraghi 1994: 305–6.
14. Whittaker 1978: 76–8; Ameling 1993: 36–9.
15. See Shepherd 1999; Lomas 2000.
16. Freeman 1891: 184; Ameling 1993: 37.
17. On the original performance context of epinician poetry, see Mullen 1982: 23–31; Heath 1988; Morgan 1993.
18. According to Athenaeus, it took Hieron some time to gather the funds necessary to complete his portion of the dedication (6.232b).
19. On the form, placement and significance of the Deinomenid tripod monument, see Homolle 1897, 1898; Gentili 1953; Amandry 1987: 81–92; Krumeich 1991; Luraghi 1994: 314–17; Harrell 2002: 453–4.
20. Luraghi 1994: 320 argues that in their celebrations of the victory at Himera the Deinomenids consistently and deliberately downplayed the role of the Emmenid tyrants of Acragas.
21. Dyer 1905: 299–300; Mallwitz 1972: 169; Luraghi 1994: 317–18.
22. Philipp (1994).
23. Luraghi 1994: 320.
24. Bacchylides *Ode* 3, composed in honour of Hieron in 468, is also relevant since it describes the tripod monument at Delphi that celebrated the Deinomenid martial victories (17–21). But this poem, unlike *Pythian* 1, does not mention Himera explicitly. I discuss this ode and its relationship to *Pythian* 1 and Delphi in a forthcoming book.
25. Kirsten 1941; Trumpf 1958; Dougherty 1993: 93–8 discuss the connection between this ode and the foundation of Aetna.
26. Gauthier 1966: 8–11.
27. I would like to thank Sian Lewis for her generosity and care both as the organiser of a stimulating and enjoyable conference and as the editor of this volume. I owe thanks also to the other participants in the conference for their comments and suggestions, as well as to Carla Antonaccio, Denis Feeney, Nino Luraghi and Gary Reger.

CHAPTER 9

Alexander of Pherae: infelix *tyrant*

Sławomir Sprawski

> Hoc rege infelicior Alexander, cuius praecordia hinc amor, hinc metus torserunt. (Valerius Maximus, 9.13 ext. 3)

A book on Greek tyranny should not lack a chapter on Alexander of Pherae, a man who was remembered throughout antiquity as one of the most ferocious and wicked tyrants. The atrocities he committed and the tragic end of his life were familiar not only to Roman scholars such as Cicero and Valerius Maximus, but also to the poet Ovid, to the great Christian theologian Origen and to the Byzantine Emperor Constantine VII. His ill fame was even longer-lived; he is most likely the Alexander 'indulged in blood, and rapine', whom Dante met, next to Dionysius, in the circle of the *violenti* in his *Inferno* (12.107).

He came to power in 369 BC as a tyrant slayer, murdering Polyphron, his uncle and *tagos* of the Thessalians (Xen. *Hell.* 6.4.34). He slew him to avenge his father Polydorus, who had died a few months earlier, probably murdered by Polyphron. In 358 or 357 Alexander met his tragic end murdered by his own wife Thebe and her brothers.[1]

The longest description of Alexander can be found in Plutarch's *Life of Pelopidas*, but our other sources are almost univocal in their presentation of his vicious character. Plutarch presented Alexander as an incurably brutish man, full of savagery, strong sexual desire and cruelty (26.2). Alexander tortured and slew innocent citizens 'day by day' and behaved like a beast. He sometimes buried men alive, and sometimes dressed them in a bear's or boar's skin, and then baited them with dogs, or shot them for his amusement. Alexander's

I would like to thank the conference participants who took part in the discussion of my paper and kindly contributed their comments, some of which influenced the final draft of the text. I am very grateful to Dr Argyroula Doulgeri-Intzesiloglou and Dr Massimo Di Salvatore who were kind enough to share their knowledge of Pherae with me.

brutality could be directed not only towards individuals but also towards whole cities. He attacked the allied and friendly Thessalian cities of Meliboea and Scotoussa. At Scotoussa, he called all the inhabitants to an assembly and then, with the help of his guards, surrounded them and cut them into pieces (*Pel.* 29). To his description of Alexander, Plutarch adds the information that he consecrated the spear with which he had killed his uncle Polyphron and honoured it as a god, giving it the name Tychon. Plutarch must have seen something insane in this act. He also related how the tyrant was so moved by the performance of Euripides' *Troades* that he left the theatre in order not to be seen weeping. It is no accident that the tyrant was presented weeping over the sorrows of Hecuba and Andromache rather than over someone he had murdered (*Pel.* 29; *De Alexandri Magni fortuna* 334a).[2]

In Plutarch's account Alexander's actions earned him the hatred of the gods (*Pel.* 28.3). When Pelopidas was killed in the battle against the tyrant at Cynoscephalae in 364, his death 'was revenged by Heaven' (*Pel.* 35) and Alexander was murdered in his bed by his own wife and her brothers. Plutarch provides a detailed description of the conspirators capturing the sleeping tyrant and cutting his throat. According to him, although this death was speedier than was fit, the tyrant got what he deserved. He adds with some satisfaction that his body 'was cast out and trodden under foot by the Pheraeans' (*Pel.* 35.7 trans. B. Perrin).

There is no doubt that Plutarch's description of Alexander is exaggerated and flawed by prejudice. To the author, the tyrant was not only an enemy of Pelopidas and the man responsible for his death but also a villain, the opposite of all the positive features of a Theban hero.[3] No other author paid so much attention to Alexander and none was quite as unambiguous in his appraisal. Naturally, Alexander's negative image is not solely the work of Plutarch. The tyrant's contemporary, Xenophon, presents him as responsible for the decadence of the Thessalian *tageia*, contrasting this with the respect in which Alexander's great predecessor, Jason, was held by his contemporaries (*Hell.* 6.4.28), and the mildness of his government to the harsh ruling of Alexander (*Hell.* 6.4.33–5). For Demosthenes he was a tyrant responsible for the subsequent violence and brutality and was worthy only to be killed (23.120). Diodorus presents Alexander in very similar way to Plutarch and it is likely that both used the same pro-Boeotian tradition transmitted through works of Callisthenes and Ephorus. It has been proposed that the portrayal of the tyrant's brutality may have been derived from Theopompus' remarks on

Alexander in his *Philippica*. Later authors such as Pausanias or Constantine Porphyrogenitus maintain the similar negative attitude towards Alexander.[4]

It is impossible to discard such a clearly negative judgement of Alexander's nature and behaviour, but it is difficult to determine to what extent it is based on true events and to what extent on rumours and slander. One cannot fail to notice the discrepancies between various accounts. Xenophon, a contemporary of Alexander, reports (*Hell.* 6.4.37) that there were various opinions on the reasons for Thebe's hatred for her husband. Xenophon shows her as an unloved wife and Plutarch as a victim who sought the comfort and support of Pelopidas. Cicero (*Off.* 2.25) and Valerius Maximus wrote on the contrary that Alexander dearly loved his wife but feared an assassination attempt by her (9.13 ext.3). Plutarch (*De mal. Herod.* 856a), who shows Thebe in a very favourable light, was irritated with some authors who doubted the nobility of her intentions.

Plutarch reports that the death Alexander suffered at the hands of his wife was the only or the first such case among the tyrants (*Pel.* 35.7). This fact in itself must have made the case highly intriguing and seems to be the main reason for the interest which Alexander commanded. It is probably not an accident that Conon in the first century BC included this story in his collection *Narrations* among forty-nine other stories on bizarre, mostly mythical events (Photius 186). A vision of the tyrant killed at the hands of his own wife was very impressive and could be regarded as a result of an intervention of the gods. In any event it was a good subject for tragedy and as early as the fourth century BC the Athenian poet Moschion wrote a tragedy called *Pheraeans*. Unfortunately, all that is preserved of Moschion's tragedy is a short fragment. Although it is impossible to determine, we may wonder to what extent the poet's imagination might have influenced the image of Alexander and his wife. As H. D. Westlake noted, Moschion could have modified the story to suit his dramatic purpose, so we cannot fully accept the negative opinion of Alexander's nature presented in the ancient sources and transfer it to an evaluation of his politics.[5] Although these issues have been given attention, the negative judgement of Alexander's actions persists; he is perceived as a politician who introduced chaos rather than one who was capable of building something positive. His role in Thessalian history was often limited to a persistent struggle to maintain what remained of his power as *tagos* and to impose tyrannical power over Thessaly. His only positive impact was, by creating a continuous threat for the cities, to force them to carry out a reform of the Thessalian *koinon*, which was done with the help of Pelopidas. [6]

This picture, however, must arouse doubts. It is difficult to see how Alexander could have fought off almost all the Thessalians for so many years, especially as they were backed by the Thebans, who were at the peak of their military and political power. It is not easy to explain how, relying mainly on mercenaries and controlling a small territory, he could have gathered such large armies. It seems that Alexander must have had some wider support in Thessaly and have been regarded at least by some in Greece as an excellent general and politician, if Isocrates saw him as a candidate for the leader of a joint expedition of all the Greeks against Persia, thus equating him with Agesilaos, Dionysius I and Philip of Macedon (*Epistolae Socraticorum* 30.13).[7] Naturally, it is possible that Alexander caught Isocrates' attention after 368, when the tyrant was allied to Athens and his relations with the city were so friendly that the Athenians erected a bronze statue of him (Dem. 23.120; Plut. *Pel.* 31.4). However, Isocrates, who was a friend of Jason of Pherae and later wrote a letter to Thebe and her brothers, knew the situation in Thessaly very well and must have known much more about Alexander than the average Athenian (Isoc. *Letter* 6; Ephippus fr. 1; Plut. *Mor.* 193d). Isocrates' opinion of Alexander induces us to attempt to present a more favourable picture of Alexander as a Thessalian leader and author of innovative political conceptions.

According to Xenophon, when Alexander murdered Polyphron (early summer 369 BC) he took over his power soon after and became *tagos* of the Thessalians. It seems that this office had been created few years earlier by Jason of Pherae to conceal the tyrannical power he had won over the whole of Thessaly. He did not rely on strength alone; he also tried to win the trust and support of the Thessalians by means of clever diplomacy and the art of rhetoric, conceiving political plans which were attractive for them. Jason devoted a lot of effort to making sure that his rule would not be regarded as tyranny and strove to legitimate it. He was likely to remember the unsuccessful efforts of his predecessor, Lycophron, who had tried to seize power over all Thessaly by force at the turn of the fourth century.[8] We may presume that at that time the Thessalian *koinon* was headed by an official called an *archon*, but Jason was not interested in this title as it did not give him the power he desired. Instead, he brought about his election as the *tagos* of the Thessalians. He created this office and endowed it with rights which ensured his advantage over any competitor – the right to mobilise and command the Thessalian army and the right to control the *perioikoi*, including the collection of tribute from them. To make the title easier to accept, Jason may have tried to appear as if he was resuming the power and rights consistent with Thessalian *nomos*, and once held by the Thessalian generals at the time of the state's greatness. But in essence *tagos* was a new office, legitimating the extraordinary position Jason had achieved in the state as a result of his military power and diplomatic talents. [9]

Jason probably started to revamp the Thessalian *koinon* in an attempt to create an efficient centre of power and a well-organised system of army mobilisation and collection of tribute from the *perioikoi*. His efforts, however, were brutally interrupted by assassins. The system he created survived him and the office of *tagos* was taken up by his two brothers, Polydorus and Polyphron. It seems likely that, like Jason, they were both elected to this office with all the appearance of legality. In a passage on Thessalian events, Xenophon emphasises that it was only after Polydorus' mysterious death, when Polyphron became the sole *tagos*, that the latter's behaviour made *tageia* similar to tyranny. He reportedly murdered Polydamas, the ruler of Pharsalos, and the eight most powerful citizens of this city and forced many influential residents of Larissa into exile.

Alexander took a stand against Polyphron, put an end to his tyranny and took the office of *tagos*. It seems not improbable that he became *tagos* like Jason by consent expressed by the Thessalian cities. But very soon it became impossible for him to follow Jason's policy of mildness and observing Thessalian *nomos*, because he had to face the opposition of the Aleuads of Larissa and Macedonian intervention. Although Diodorus (15.61.2–3) states that the tyrant was 'hated for his violent and severe rule' and the Aleuads decided to seek help 'in fear of his lawlessness', it seems that it was not the *tagos*'s behaviour that prompted them to act. The Aleuads turned for help to the king of Macedonia almost immediately after Alexander took power; it seems that they did so irrespective of what kind of *tagos* Alexander might turn out to be. The Aleuads' dislike of Alexander may have resulted from reasons of both ambition and economy. Larissa was the most important political centre of Thessaly and its elite, the Aleuads, who traced their origins back to Heracles, traditionally led the country, probably treating other cities as inferior. It is not surprising, therefore, that the leadership of Pherae, even if it could have been beneficial for them, was difficult to accept. Economic reasons could also have been essential. Larissa's location in the central part of the country gave it control over vast, fertile lands and enabled it to benefit considerably from grain production. The income of the people of Larissa certainly increased when there was a demand for Thessalian grain. However, the sea trade took place in the port of Pagasae controlled by Pherae. If Jason, once made *tagos*, seized the profits from port tolls to finance his own undertakings, it definitely could not have met with the enthusiasm of the Larissans, who paid the expenses.

To regain their old influence in the state, the Aleuads turned for help to their traditional friends, the Macedonian royal family. Perhaps they decided to take this step because, almost simultaneously, king Amyntas III died, and his son Alexander II ascended the throne. Perhaps the old king could not or would not become involved in Thessalian affairs, while his successor was easier to persuade to intervene in Thessaly, even though the situation in Macedonia was uncertain as well. The Macedonian intervention surprised Alexander, who did not manage to organise his defence or launch an attack on Macedonia in time. The Macedonian king deprived Alexander of Pherae of control over Larissa and Crannon but, against the Thessalians' will, kept his garrisons there. Although this move has sometimes been interpreted as an act of treachery on the part of the Macedonian king, it seems to have agreed with the Aleuads; at least there is no mention of the influence it might have had on their relations with the Argeads. In Thessaly dynasts quite often paid little attention to the will of the majority of the Thessalians (Hdt. 7.6; 7.130.3; 7.172.1; Thuc. 4.78; 4.132).

At the same time some unknown Thessalians supposedly called for the Thebans to intervene in Thessaly against Alexander (Diod. 16. 67.2; Plut. *Pel.* 26.1). It is difficult to tell which Thessalians could have done this, but it seems unlikely that it was the Aleuads, who had been associated with the Macedonians. They had numerous reasons to suspect the Thebans, especially Pelopidas who was sent as general, of an affinity for Jason's family. We can only suppose that the invitation for Thebans came from the leaders of Pharsalus instigated by the action of Aleuads. [10]

The motives of the Theban intervention in Thessaly are not altogether clear. Diodorus (15.67.3) reports that the Thebans ordered Pelopidas 'to arrange Thessalian affairs in the interests of the Boeotians' and Plutarch emphasises the personal ambitions of the Theban general.[11] Having entered Thessaly, Pelopidas came to an agreement with the Macedonians and took over Larissa and other Thessalian cities they were holding. When Alexander came to Larissa, Pelopidas 'tried to make him, instead of a tyrant, one who would govern the Thessalians mildly and according to law'. It is likely that Pelopidas proposed to Alexander that he should assume the office of *archôn*, traditional head of the confederation, instead of the role of *tagos*, which was unconstitutional and no longer accepted by the Thessalians.[12] It seems, as Buckler suggests, that Pelopidas was willing to recognise Alexander as a constitutional ruler, but in that case we might be suspicious as to whether Pelopidas originally intended to intervene against him.

Alexander did not want to be only nominal leader of the Thessalians and unwilling to accept such a limitation of his power; he broke off talks and left Larissa. It follows from Diodorus' (15.67.4) and Plutarch's (*Pel.* 26.3) accounts that Pelopidas managed to arrange Thessalian affairs in accordance with the interests of the Boeotians, although there are mentions of military operations which he led against Alexander that can only be dated to this year.[13]

The next year Alexander reportedly started unrest in the Thessalian cities, probably trying to win control of them, but the Thebans were not convinced that the situation in Thessaly demanded military intervention. Instead of this they sent an embassy consisting of Pelopidas and Ismenias in order to restore tranquillity in Thessaly by diplomatic means. In Thessaly Pelopidas won the support of some Thessalians, recruited mercenaries, and with these forces carried out a successful intervention in Macedonia. However, his Thessalian mercenaries betrayed him and when he returned to Thessaly to take revenge on their families who remained in Pharsalos, he encountered Alexander, who approached the city at the head of his troops. He took Pelopidas and Ismenias prisoner and captured Pharsalos.[14] Afterwards, the Thessalian support for the Thebans quickly decreased. When the Thebans sent an army to free the prisoners, it was soon abandoned by the Thessalian allies who did not even provide the Thebans with food supplies (Diod. 15.71.2–6). This badly commanded expedition managed to leave Thessaly with extreme difficulty, chased by Alexander's cavalry. The next expedition was commanded by Epaminondas himself. Although Plutarch (*Pel.* 29.2) writes extensively about the great hopes and enthusiasm that it woke in the Thessalians, he is silent about the sore disappointment which soon ensued. The prisoners were freed in return for a thirty-day truce and although the Thebans refused to make friendship with Alexander and recognise his position in Thessaly, the truce was a real victory for him. The Thebans left his power intact and abandoned their Thessalian allies for the next three years.[15]

Having defeated the pre-eminent military power that was Thebes and remaining a close ally of Athens, Alexander reached the peak of his power. In the course of the struggle with the Thebans, Alexander had probably regained control of the majority of the country, but after an open war was started by the Aleuads and his position as the legitimate Thessalian leader was negated, it was difficult for him to return to Jason's policy of mediation and keep up the appearance of the legitimacy of power, symbolised by the office of *tagos*. Alexander decided to crack down on his enemies and to show his force, an example of which was the destruction of Scotoussa and Meliboea.[16] He also decided to build a new ideology of power, in which the emphasis was shifted away from the office of *tagos* and adherence to tradition towards building his personal authority.[17]

The most explicit example of the change of Alexander's attitude to tradition was his minting of coins whose legends included his name. Coins in Thessaly were minted by cities and, with the exception of Larissa, in small quantities. Placing one's name on a coin was extremely rare at this time in the Greek world and was certainly very important to Alexander in terms of propaganda. There were no coins of Jason but it was consistent with his policy of respect for Thessalian *nomos*. It was the cities that had the privilege of striking coins and placing images on them. Alexander broke this tradition to promote and enforce his position. On some coins, the tyrant even placed his image as a horseman attacking with a spear. The coins he minted bore a resemblance to earlier coins from Pherae and showed the image of the goddess Ennodia, worshipped in a sanctuary in Pherae, and the nymph Hyperia, associated with a famous spring in the city. Just like earlier coins from Pherae, Alexander's coins also showed a lion's head, which refers to the water spout of Hyperia's spring. Some researchers believe that on Alexander's coins the lion's head was endowed with a new meaning, a symbol of strength and power.[18] Another design used on coins of various denominations is the double-axe. It has been suggested that the double-axe symbolised the office of *tagos*. Alexander supposedly used it as a propaganda element at the time when Larissa questioned his position. But there is no direct evidence to connect this symbol to the office of *tagos* and we may suspect that it was a more universal symbol of power, since it also appeared on the coins of the Thracian kings of the Odrysae,

Amadocus I and Teres II.[19] It has also been suggested that the double-axe or *pelekys* was a religious symbol and was associated with the cult of Dionysus, which originated in Thrace and was widespread particularly in Pherae and Pelasgiotis, Phthiotis Achaia and Magnesia.[20] Sources do mention the special reverence that Alexander had for Dionysus, worshipped in Pagasae (Theopomp. 115 F 352). The tradition is that the god reportedly rewarded Alexander: when the murdered Alexander's body was thrown into the sea, Dionysus appeared in a fisherman's dream and ordered him to recover the tyrant's body so that it could be buried according to custom. Perhaps this tradition referred to Alexander's efforts to present himself as someone under the god's special care.

Alexander's coins differed from other coins minted in Pherae in that they were very carefully crafted. They were recognisable and also enjoyed a good reputation outside Thessaly, as can be deduced from the remarks of Diogenes Laertius (5.18). It was no doubt very important to Alexander that the coins should be willingly received. He could have supported his diplomacy financially, like the Phocian tyrant Onomarchos after him, who, according to Diodorus, 'having struck coinage from silver and gold distributed it among the allied cities and chiefly gave it as bribes to the leaders of those cities'; in this way 'he persuaded even the Thessalians, who were held in highest esteem amongst the allies, by bribes to maintain the peace' (16.33.3 trans. Sherman). Money could have helped him build a more positive image among the Athenian elite. The account of Diogenes Laertius says that Plato bought a book by the Pythagorean Philolaos for forty Alexandrian *minae* (8.85), probably received from Alexander of Pherae, like the 100 *minae* which he obtained from Dion for purchasing Pythagorean books (DL 8.15; 8.84–5). A visit to Pherae by the philosopher Eudemos shortly before the tyrant's death has been interpreted as a trace of Alexander's contacts with Plato and his disciples raising funds for Dion's expedition to Sicily (Cic. *Div.* 1.53; Plut. *Dion* 22.5). [21]

Minting one's own coins must have been important mostly for practical purposes. What is notable is the large number of denominations (didrachm, drachm, semidrachm, triobolon), unusual for Thessaly and unheard of before. It could have been related to the diverse needs of Alexander to pay his people. The tyrant maintained a large mercenary army consisting of cavalry and infantry, and also kept a fleet.[22] According to Demosthenes (23.162) in the end of his life he tried with some success to recruit the gifted mercenary commander Charidemus. Having control over Thessaly, according to Diodorus, he called up more than 20,000 people against Pelopidas in 364, though some Thessalians fought on the Theban side (Diod. 15.80.4). Even if the number of Alexander's soldiers quoted by Diodorus is exaggerated Alexander had an army strong enough to force the Thebans to send against him an army of about 8,000 hoplites (15.71.3; 7,000 in 364: 15.80.2).

Minting a large number of coins of various denominations could also have been related to the strengthening of the fortifications of Pherae. In the fourth century the city was surrounded by new, carefully built fortifications, which turned it into a mighty fortress. We can only speculate as to the time these defences were erected, but certainly the period of Alexander's rule seems very probable. Under his rule the position of Pherae changed; it became the tyrant's main base, his headquarters, which was supposed to give him a sense of security while reflecting his power to the outside world. It is interesting that the extension of the walls of Pherae could have been an element of a broader programme of building a system of defences to ensure that the city had full control over the surrounding territory and communication trails. Plutarch (*Pel.* 31) says that he fortified the cities of Magnesia and Phthiotian Achaea, and in this context the destruction of Scotoussa in Phthiotis and Meliboea in Magnesia might have been of strategic importance, aimed at eliminating the cities which could have served as bases for his opponents.[23]

Alexander needed large sums of money. Its main source seems to have been harbour tolls which were probably collected in Pagasae. We know that later they were a substantial source of income for Philip II when he took the port. The income from the tolls must have varied but when trade bloomed, it could have been very high. We may only speculate that in the 360s Thessaly could have profited from the grain trade, which had to go through Pagasae (Xen. *Hell.* 5.4.56). Alexander could also have benefited from the meat trade. Plutarch (*Apoph. Reg. et imp.* 70.17) reports that having made an alliance with the Athenians, Alexander committed himself to delivering them meat at the attractive price of a half-obol a mina. Finally, Pagasae was famous as a centre for the slave trade, as documented by the poet Hermippos (fr. 63.19).

Alexander, however, did not manage to hold on to his power. In 364, the Thessalian opposition managed to persuade the Thebans to intervene. Although the Theban army, ready to march off, was stopped by a bad omen (an eclipse of the sun), Pelopidas himself came regardless. In Pharsalos he managed to gather together his Thessalian allies, with whom he fought a battle at Cynoscephalae against Alexander's overwhelming forces. The tyrant apparently underestimated the strength and skill of Pelopidas and lost the battle despite the death of the Theban general. Weakened by the defeat and left without the help of the Athenians, he was defeated by a second Theban army sent to deal him a final blow (Diod. 15.80; 81.3; Strabo 9.5.6; Nepos *Pel.* 5.2–4; Plut. *Pel.* 32). After the defeat he was forced to relinquish his control of the Thessalian cities, to return the Magnesians and Phthiotian Achaeans to Theban control and 'for the future to be the ruler over Pherae alone as an ally of the Boeotians' (Diod. 15.80.6 trans. Sherman).[24]

In this way Alexander turned from the *tagos* of the Thessalians to the tyrant of Pherae, forced to send levies at the call of the Thebans. He never gave up attempts to strengthen his position and in 362, almost immediately after the battle of Mantinea, he undertook a sea expedition to the Cyclades and issued a challenge to the Athenians, his former allies. Jason had already established a fleet (Xen. *Hell.* 6.4.21) but Alexander was the first to be capable of using it efficiently. His fleet attacked the Cyclades and seized Tenos, conquered Peparethos, was successful against the Athenian fleet and even made a successful attack against Piraeus ([Dem.] 50.4–5; Diod. 15.95.1–3). Polyaenus' *Strategemata* (6.2.1–2, 6.46) gives evidence of the tyrant's creativity in waging war at sea. Never before or after was Thessalian maritime policy so active. He must have remained a threat for the Thessalians to the end of his days; in 361 they contracted a defence alliance with the Athenians aimed against Alexander.[25]

Despite a clearly negative image of Alexander passed on in the historical sources, he was more than a bloody tyrant. He tried to follow in Jason's footsteps and maintain a strong, autocratic power over Thessaly, which possibly could have turned this country into a military and political superpower. A similar process of strengthening monarchic power occurred in the neighbouring Macedonia and Epirus, but with more success than in Thessaly. The reasons for Alexander's failure may be ascribed to his nature and style of politics, which were reportedly fundamentally different from Jason's. It seems, however, that the decisive factor was the political situation around Thessaly, which had changed since the reign of Jason, who brilliantly took advantage of the balance of forces in order to separate internal opposition from external help. Alexander did not have this opportunity, and with the active help of the Macedonians and the Thebans it was easy to build a strong Thessalian opposition against him, particularly among the aristocracy, for which the strengthening of monarchic power meant permanently limited influence.

NOTES

1. On the reign of Alexander see: Kaerst, Alexandros (5), *RE* I.1408–9; Westlake 1935: 126–59; Sordi 1958: 193–234; Buckler 1980: 110–29, 175–82, 245–9; Berve 1967: I.290–3, II.670–1; Gehrke 1986: 192–4; Wartenberg 1994: 151–9; Frolov 2001: 184–97. The chronology of Thessalian events in the 360s is discussed by Spoerri 1966; Buckler 1980: 245–9; Buckler 2003: 320 n. 27; Stylianou 1998: 446–55.
2. Compare Aelian *Var. Hist.* 14.40; Cary, *CAH* VI.85.
3. Westlake 1935: 156–7; Fuscagni 1975: 49–51; Prandi 1985: 71; Georgiadou 1996: 81–5; Georgiadou 1997: 24–5 and 192–3.
4. Diod. 75.1; Plut. *Pel.* 29.7; Paus. 6.5.2. See also Westlake 1935: 31; Stylianou 1998: ad loc.
5. *TrGF* 1.97.3; cf. Ribbeck 1875: 156–9.
6. Westlake 1935: 134–8; Buckler 2003: 322.
7. See Signes Codoñer 2002: 96–8.
8. Sprawski 2004.
9. For discussion see Sprawski 1999: 15–23 and 2003: 62–4.
10. Sordi 1958: 203–4; Buckler 1980: 113–15; Stylianou 1998: 455–6.
11. Buckler 2003: 322–3.
12. Helly 1995: 352–3.
13. Polyaenus 2.4.1–2; Frontinus 1.5.2; 3.8.2; 4.7.28. Theopompus F 409. See Buckler 1980: 115 and 247.
14. Diod. 71.2; Plut. *Pel.* 27; Polyb. 8.35.7–9; Buckler 1980: 119–29; Stylianou 1998: 466–8; Georgiadou 1997: 196–9.
15. Diod. 15.71.3–6; 75.2; Plut. *Pel.* 28–9; Paus. 9.15.1–2; Sordi 1958: 210 n. 2 and Buckler 1980: 247.
16. Diod. 15.75.1; Plut. *Pel.* 29.7; Paus. 6.5. 2; Constantinus Porphyrogenitus *De virtutibus* 1.240. Westlake 1935: 144–5. Sordi 1958: 215 dates the massacre of Scotoussa before the expedition of Epaminondas. See also Frolov 2001: 191, Stylianou 1998: 480.
17. There is no information as to whether the sons of Jason aimed at the title of *tagos*. The coins bearing name of one of them, Teisiphonus, suggest that they followed the example of Alexander rather than Jason. See Head 1911: 308–9.
18. Head 1911: 308; Wartenberg 1994: 153–4. For Thessalian coinage see also Martin 1985: 34–59.
19. Wartenberg 1994: 154–5.

20. Chrisostomou 1994: 124–5. Compare Maas 1888: 70–80.
21. Spoerri 1966: 46; Le Rider 1981: 43–4; Knoepfler 1989: 224–30.
22. Wartenberg 1994: 153. Martin 1983: 28 argues that the issue of didrachms seems to be related to a standard cavalryman's pay at that time.
23. Westlake 1935: 145; Di Salvatore 1994: 100–1 and 108; Doulgeri-Intzesiloglou 1994: 79–80.
24. On the battle of Cynoscephalae see Pritchett 1969: 112–19; Buckler 1980: 175–82.
25. *IG* II² 116, 175; Westlake 1935: 154–5; Sordi 1958: 223–30; Frolov 2001: 194–5; Buckler 2003: 371.

PART III

The ideology of tyranny

CHAPTER 10

Pindar and kingship theory

Simon Hornblower

PART 1

The structure of this chapter is simple. Part 1 looks at kingship in Pindar and glances at his models or predecessors. Part 2 asks how, if at all, he influenced kingship theory in the fourth century BC and the post-classical period. I anticipate an obvious objection at the outset and say that I use the term 'theory' loosely. Pindar is not Aristotle, and we cannot expect systematic tabulated exposition of doctrine. Aristotle himself says it is the mark of a cultivated person to expect the amount of precision that the subject allows (*Nic. Eth.* 1095b25). Nor do I confine myself to hereditary one-man rule, *basileia* as at Cyrene or Macedon. Pindar's vocabulary is fluid, and he can talk approvingly, as we shall see, of a 'people-guiding *tyrannos*', said of Hieron of Syracuse. I would even be happy to allow in the *collective* rule of the Aleuads of Thessaly, who 'uphold and exalt the state of the Thessalians', in the closing words of *Pythian* 10. The poem ends: 'with good men rests the governance of cities as a cherished inheritance'. So 'Pindar and the good ruler' might be a better title for my chapter. There are, however, some distinctions to be made. Where the upstart Sicilian tyrants are concerned he naturally stresses inherited excellence less on the whole. But even this has to be qualified in view of *Pythian* 6 for Xenocrates of Acragas, brother of the tyrant Theron. The poem has much in praise of Xenocrates' son Thrasybulus and here the hereditary element does feature (lines 15–16).

At first sight my title may seem ridiculous: what sane person would look for anything so prosy and pedestrian as political theory of any sort in a poet such as Pindar, the eagle in the stratosphere? In prose authors, comparative political theory begins with the debate on the

I am grateful to Sian Lewis for the opportunity to explore this topic in the context of her 2003 conference on monarchy and one-man rule in Greece. This chapter (especially in Part 2) develops ideas argued for more briefly in Hornblower 2004, esp. 63–6 and 367.

constitutions in book 3 of Herodotus.[1] This elegantly sorts the possible constitutions into the minimum three: rule by the many, rule by the few, rule by the one. That is simple and exhaustive: they are the only three logical possibilities. As Tacitus put it: 'nam cunctas nationes et urbes populus aut primores aut singuli regunt' (*Annals* 4.33). But Herodotus was not the first so to sort the possibilities, because as good students of Greek politics have noted, Pindar got there half a century ahead of him, in the closing passage of *Pythian* 2. For this reason Pindar makes a single surprising appearance in the *index locorum* to that excellent handbook by M. H. Hansen, *Athenian Democracy in the Age of Demosthenes*. The same point about Pindaric priority has been correctly and separately made by Peter Rhodes and Andrew Lintott in a recent edited collection of essays.[2] These are not scholars whose names are normally associated with Pindar. What does Pindar actually say?

> ἐν πάντα δὲ νόμον εὐθύγλωσσος ἀνὴρ προφέρει,
> παρὰ τυραννίδι χὤπόταν ὁ λάβρος στρατός,
> χὤταν πόλιν οἱ σοφοὶ τηρέωντι.

> 'under every regime the straight-talking man excels:
> in a tyranny, when the boisterous people rule,
> or when the wise watch over the city'. (*Pyth.* 2.86–8)

The date of this poem is much disputed. But the range of serious possibilities extends only from 477 to 467, the death-year of the honorand Hieron. This makes it far earlier than any remotely conceivable 'composition date' of Herodotus, so for the present purpose the precise date is immaterial. Can we extract anything about Pindar's own preferences from the vocabulary he uses? There is scholarly argument about whether λάβρος, 'boisterous', 'turbulent', is or is not pejorative.[3] It is not the worst word you could use about the 'people' or 'host' (στρατός, more normally 'army'), not least because of its – possibly deliberate – instability of meaning. By 'possibly deliberate' I mean that there may be no single definite answer to the question 'what did Pindar mean by λάβρος?' That, *mutatis mutandis*, is what Adam Parry suggested about the equally problematic ἐλευθέρως in Thucydides' final assessment of Pericles at 2.65 (κατεῖχε τὸ πλῆθος ἐλευθέρως: either he 'restrained the people as if they were free men' or 'he restrained them as a free, i.e. liberal, man would lead them'.) Parry's conclusion about ἐλευθέρως was reached after considering various possibilities: 'did Thucydides, by the word translated as *freely*, mean any single one of these things, or even merely a combination of them?' It is notable that the examples we have considered are both political. Ambiguity, and choice of inherently fluid terminology, is one way of avoiding commitment, and offence; it may also indicate that one finds an issue particularly tormenting and profound. Dictionaries can hardly do justice to this common phenomenon. This is a stylistic feature which the Pindar commentator Ilya Pfeijffer calls 'polyinterpretability'. It is a good way of offending no one. Alan Sommerstein has identified an Aeschylean example which is also political, 'fear of the citizens', ἀστῶν φόβος, used of the changes to the Areopagus in 460. It can mean either fear felt by the citizens for the Areopagus or fear felt for the citizens by the Areopagus, and is thus acceptable both to radicals and conservatives. To return to λάβρος, it could be ruder but it is not exactly polite; the essential ideas are noisiness plus violence (it is used of wind and sea), and as between these two notions, scholars place the emphasis according to their own sympathies. The reference to the 'wise', σόφοι, might be thought favourable enough to make Pindar an oligarch. But the truth is that none of the three regimes is being endorsed: what is praised is straight speaking, and the enumeration which follows is just a paratactic strengthening device.

This passage, then, for all its importance in the history of political theory, does not tell us what Pindar personally preferred. Perhaps that quest is futile. Work since Bundy on the conventions and traditions lying behind Pindar's art has taught us to be careful about his seemingly authorial and first-person statements. A much-discussed Pindaric example, very relevant to my theme, is in *Pythian* 11, μέμφομ' αἶσαν τυραννίδων, 'I deplore the condition of tyrannies'.[4] This was once seen as an apology for the poet's involvement with the Sicilian tyrants (Wilamowitz), then when the poem was reassigned to a later date it was reinterpreted as a rejection of Athens the tyrant city (Bowra). But David Young has shown that the remark really belongs in a poetic tradition which begins with Archilochus and ends with Euripides' *Ion* in 412, not 'I disapprove of particular tyrants' but 'I reject the hateful dangerous life-style of tyrants'. Pindar warns against athletic arrogance, which is a sort of quasi-tyrannical behaviour. Nothing follows about his political preferences, though the remark is a sort of contribution to kingship theory.

Explicit advice to rulers is not the only technique available to a poet. Pindar is an oblique author who uses metaphor richly, sometimes packing several metaphors into a single short sentence. One way of offering kingship advice was by professional analogy, which is a sort of extended metaphor. The medical analogy is a favourite one because the doctor is an authority figure like the ruler. And medicine is a favourite topic with Pindar generally, not just as a vehicle for ruler-advice.[5] There are many relevant passages: *Pythian* 3 is the most obviously 'medical ode' in Pindar. But like Thucydides, who registered the powerlessness and ignorance of doctors in face of the plague, Pindar was realistically aware that medicine has what have been called 'crucially limited capabilities', which contrast with the immortality conferred by praise poetry.

Medical metaphors are natural in all genres of literature. One application of the medical metaphor deserves special attention here. Both Pindar and Thucydides, or at least a Thucydidean speaker, treat politics as a kind of medicine: ruler as doctor. The idea of the body as vulnerable organism goes back to Solon, 'an unavoidable wound, ἕλκος ἄφυκτον, comes to the whole city' (F4W line 17). But Pindar is more specific. Urging Arcesilas king of Cyrene to restore the exiled Damophilus, Pindar says:

> ἐσσὶ δ' ἰατὴρ ἐπικαιρότατος, Παιάν τέ σοι τιμᾷ φάος.
> χρὴ μαλακὰν χέρα προσβάλλοντα τρώμαν ἕλκεος ἀμφιπολεῖν.

> but you are a most fitting healer, and Paian [Apollo the healer]
>   honours your saving light.
> One must apply a gentle hand to tend a sore wound . . .
>   (*Pyth.* 4.270–1)

So too Thucydides makes Nicias say to the *prytanis* in the debate before the Sicilian expedition that he should be 'doctor of the city when it has taken bad advice', and that he should 'help his country as far as possible or at least not willingly harm it', a Hippocratic principle.[6] This is a modest view of the art of politics as of medicine, but Thucydides and Pindar were realists about what could be achieved by practitioners of both skills. Thucydides had limited, intellectual, non-moralising views of how the study of the past, and the activity of historically aware politicians, can make people better.

So there is kingship advice, if not much actual kingship theory, in Pindar. Examples are *Pythian* 1, 'guide your people with a rudder of justice, forge your tongue to bronze on an anvil of truth' (lines 86–8),[7] or the praise of Arcesilas of Cyrene at the end of *Pythian* 4 (line 262), 'you [plural, i.e. Arcesilas' family] who have devised policy based on right counsel', ὀρθόβουλον μῆτιν ἐφευρομένοις. This theme involves a favourite political concept of Pindar, that of ἡσυχία, because in

Pythian 1 Pindar observes that with the help of Zeus a man who is ruler and instructs his son can in honouring his people turn them to harmonious *hêsychia* (lines 69–71). Zeus's help is important; we recall that for Hesiod (*Theog.* 96) princes are from Zeus, ἐκ δὲ Διὸς βασιλῆες. As for *hêsychia* in Pindar, much has been written about it. An invocation to Hesychia opens the last poem Pindar wrote, *Pythian* 8, and is commonly taken to mean oligarchic quietism, the opposite of Athenian *polypragmosyne*. That interpretation goes hand in hand with a very political interpretation of the poem which is for a man of Aegina. It is held to be a warning to the Athenians in 446 BC not to commit excesses against the Aeginetans, whose independence had already been reduced, and whose very existence was now threatened, by the meddlesome Athenians. I have discussed this more fully else-where.[8] In a Pindar fragment quoted by Polybius (F109) the noun refers to Theban medism in the Persian wars. Elsewhere, as we have seen, it is something that kings should foster. It has in fact no single simple message. That does not reduce its importance for understanding Pindar's outlook. It is one of what John Davies has well called 'the various personified abstractions which are Pindar's nearest approach to a systematic moral theology'.[9] (He instances not only Hesychia but also Themis, for which compare the very Homeric 'themis-wielding sceptre', θεμιστεῖον . . . σκᾶπτον, of *Olympian* 1 line 12, for Hieron.) I suggest, then, that Pindar's preoccupation with *hêsychia* should not with Polybius be seen narrowly and inaccurately in terms of Theban medism, nor too exclusively in terms of Athenian imperialism and its critics, but also as part of the vocabulary of 'advice to princes', a genre with a long future ahead of it. Pindar's 'people-guiding *tyrannos*' (λαγέτας τύραννος, *Pyth.* 3. 85), an expression which surely implies beneficent care, looks forward to Hellenistic conceptions of the good ruler for whom kingship is 'noble servitude', εὔδοξος δουλεία. But it also and more obviously looks back to Homer, who, as Aristotle noted (*Nic. Eth.* 1161a15f.), calls Agamemnon 'shepherd of the people', ποιμένα λαῶν, because the good king studies to promote the welfare of his people as a shepherd studies the welfare of his sheep.[10] Aristotle's comment suggests that Homer's 'shepherd of the people' metaphor was to Greek ears not as 'dead' a metaphor as Michael Silk believes.[11]

Hellenistic writers who took it on themselves to offer advice to kings had to be careful how they expressed themselves. The written word was safer than the spoken – 'what friends do not dare to say to kings they write in books', as Demetrius of Phaleron said to Ptolemy

Philadelphus (*FGrHist* 228 T6b). But even when writing to a man like Hieron, it was a good idea to be oblique. So the bronze of Pindar's anvil metaphor conceals, it has been said, a warning against the 'destructive violence inherent in all absolute power'.[12] Bronze is associated at the poem's end with the wicked Phalaris of Acragas and his brazen bull, a Greek tyrant contrasted as negative role model with the kindly excellence of the Lydian king Croesus, a reversal of the usual Greek–barbarian opposition.

Let us pursue the implications of this idea. Pindar does not just praise but may warn against, and even disapproves of, certain sorts of behaviour by one-man rulers. He advises tyrants, but, as we have seen, he draws distinctions between good tyrants and bad ones, between Croesus and Phalaris. Cicero, who later applauded the great tyrannicide of his own century (in a letter written just after the Ides of March when Caesar was assassinated), did the same when Caesar was alive. He asked 'will Caesar take Phalaris or Pisistratus for his model?' (*Fam.* 6.15; *Att.* 7.20, cf. 8.16.2). Pindar's *Olympian* 12 is not as explicit as Cicero's letter after the Ides of March, but it does begin by invoking Zeus the liberator, and the whole short ode has been seen as a celebration of the fall of Sicilian tyranny.[13] The implication of this for Pindar's own politics has been clearly drawn by Lloyd-Jones: Pindar was not always a praiser of one-man rule but here celebrates its downfall. We can add that in *Olympian* 4 Pindar praises a private citizen victor from Camarina at a time when the city had, as we now know, recently undergone a democratic reform.[14]

Bacchylides has less advice to offer Hieron than Pindar has for his tyrannical patrons; but Bacchylides does naturally offer politically expressed praise as well as praise for athletic success. Thus Hieron ὃς παρὰ Ζηνὸς λαχὼν πλείσταρχον Ἑλλάνων γέρας, that is, he 'got from Zeus the privilege of ruling over the greatest number of Greeks' (3.1–12). The thought and language here anticipate Thucydides' Pericles about his fellow-Athenians: ἢν καὶ νῦν ὑπενδῶμέν ποτε (πάντα γὰρ πέφυκε καὶ ἐλασσοῦσθαι), μνήμη καταλελείψεται, Ἑλλήνων τε ὅτι Ἕλληνες πλείστων δὴ ἤρξαμεν, 'if our empire ever yields a little – and everything is born to decline as well as to grow – still we shall be remembered as the Greeks who ruled over the largest number of other Greeks' (Thuc. 2.64.3). That was said about another, collective, tyrant, namely the 'tyrant city' Athens.

The cynic may say that Pindar and Bacchylides would say anything for money, and that *Olympian* 12 for Ergoteles of liberated Himera must have been paid for, like *Olympian* 1 for Hieron. To that there is no real answer, except perhaps to wonder if Ergoteles needed to be celebrated by quite so politically specific an opening flourish.

P. W. Rose has approached the problem of the 'ideology' of Pindar in a slightly different, in fact in a specifically Marxist (and Freudian) way, which he calls a 'dialectical hermeneutic'.[15] Rejecting the eclectic approach of Norwood, which assembles gnomic utterances in the poems, he asks what are the general implications of the verbally virtuosic praise of rich sportsmen found in Pindar (and presumably Bacchylides). Rose's answer is that by the very act of conferring such highly crafted praise on rulers and elites, a literary and linguistic feat quite beyond the intellectual range of his patrons, the poet asserts his own superiority to those patrons. There is in fact a sort of menace involved: freely to confer a gift implies the possibility of withholding it. Also, by helping the ruling class in this way the epinician poets were proving that 'the ruling class needed help'. This is a refreshing approach. It is, however, frustrating that we cannot be certain how important this help actually was. Something of the same sort applies to the prose writers of the fourth century: did Philip II of Macedon care what Isocrates wrote about him? 'Needed help' is a strong expression. That a Pindaric ode, like the panhellenic athletic or equestrian victory it commemorated, gave *kudos* is certain. In the case of rulers or elites in fringe areas of the Greek world – Cyrene, Macedon and Sicily – it might also be a politically valuable way of asserting Hellenism under pressure. But on the whole it is the singer who has an occupational interest in emphasising the 'power' of song. Homer (*Iliad* 9.443) makes Phoenix say that the good leader should aim to be μύθων τε ῥητῆρ' ἔμεναι πρηκτῆρά τε ἔργων, 'a speaker of words and a doer of deeds', in that order, a line echoed by Thucydides when he says Pericles was 'very able in speech and action', again in that order. Those are fine tributes to rhetoric, and the Homer passage in particular shows that rhetoric was recognised as a political force well before the intellectual innovations of the fifth century. But the order of words is the poet's order, or the historian's order. The other thing that 'helped' keep tyrants in power was military force, and the 'doing of deeds' by killing people if necessary if they got in your way. If we ask what kept Theron of Acragas in power it is hard to get the precise balance between *Olympian* 2 and the massacre of his opponents which Diodorus (11.48.2) says he ordered at Himera.

Nevertheless the idea that the epinician poet is not altogether servile (roughly the Moses Finley position) is an interesting one. It is not quite new. Alan Cameron in his recent book on Callimachus, noting what he calls the 'independence of Pindar, an aristocrat patronized by aristocrats', quotes Gildersleeve a century earlier.[16] Gildersleeve wrote 'there was a strain of familiar banter in [Pindar's] poems that would not have been tolerated or tolerable in any ordinary man'. (Cameron suggests that Callimachus' relations with his patrons were not so different.) But later writers made a distinction between Pindar and his predecessor Simonides: Simonides was thought greedy, and that may be why Xenophon chose him and not Pindar as the interlocutor in the *Hieron*. The athletic and equestrian examples and expressions in the treatise are striking and I feel confident that Xenophon knew Pindar's poetry.

Finally, Thucydides. In my recent book *Thucydides and Pindar: Historical Narrative and the World of Epinician Poetry*, I argued that Thucydides knew and was in subtle ways influenced by Pindar's poetry and that ancient literary critics were right to compare the two as examples of the severe style. I also examined their views, making allowance for the problems posed on the one hand by the disputed status of Thucydides' speeches, and on the other by the disputed status of first-person pronouncements in Pindar. What of kingship?

In general, Homeric, Pindaric, Aristotelian, and Hellenistic reflections on how autocratic power should be used are absent from Thucydides, though he listed the achievements of Archelaos of Macedon, was aware of the power of the Deinomenid rulers of Sicily, and may even have glanced forward to the tyranny of Dionysius. Persia and the satraps featured increasingly as his work went on and would surely have featured even more in 411–404; but unlike Herodotus or Xenophon he never had, or would have had, occasion to reflect on issues like the difference between good king Cyrus and bad king Cambyses, good Croesus and bad Phalaris. Thucydides' prime concern is rather with the coercive power exercised by the citizens of one *polis* against those of another *polis* or against each other, and it is in these areas that we have to look for political reflections of a Pindaric sort.

So Thucydides, unlike Plato and Aristotle, does not offer political theory as such, in this or any other area. Nor does he offer advice to kings like Pindar or his prose successors of the fourth century. Did he admire tyrants? He praises the *aretê* and intelligence, ξύνεσις, of the Pisistratids (6.54.5), and the combination of the two qualities is high praise; they are otherwise used *together* only of Brasidas (also authorial: 4.81.2). Thucydides also perhaps implies that the Athenian oligarch Antiphon had both qualities, but he does so at different points

in the relevant chapter: the active oligarchs of 411 collectively, including Antiphon, are said to be ξυνετοί (8.68.1 and 4). The word *aretê*
is hard to pin down; sometimes, as when used of Antiphon in my
view, it does not carry much or any ethical weight but denotes little
more than functional excellence, 'good at' doing something. But
praise for the Pisistratids' behaviour and policies is not the same as
praise for all tyrants. Nor is it the same as a liking for tyranny as a
form of government, in the manner of Thucydides' imitator Philistus:
'Philistum . . . hominem amicum non magis tyranno quam tyrannidi'
(*FGrHist* 556 T5d).

PART 2

In this second section I shall discuss the post-classical reception of
Pindar's views on kingship. In one of his aspects Pindar can be seen
as a precursor of fourth-century and Hellenistic writings 'On kingship'. Hellenistic writers like Diotogenes, a neo-Pythagorean of disputed date, wrote specialist treatises *peri basileias*, 'On kingship'. But
it is the fourth century which sees the emergence and separating out
of this as of many literary genres; historiography is the most obvious
parallel example. The general idea that the fourth-century epideictic
orators were the most relevant artistic heirs of Pindar is old; it
goes back at least as far as Croiset in 1880, who wrote, 'Simonide
et Pindare ont pour légitimes successeurs les Lysias et les Isocrate.'
Croiset cites Ps.-Dion. Hal. *On oratory*, section VII of which is called
προτρεπτικὸς ἀθλητῶν, i.e. how to write speeches encouraging ath-
letes, including advice to include a section on the athlete's *polis*. 'Bien
avant les Lysias et les Isocrate, le lyrisme employait à profusion toutes
les figures et des pensées que la rhétorique devait cataloguer.'[17] Bundy
was aware of this aspect. He compared Lysias 2.2 (the preamble to
the Funeral Speech) with *Isthmian* 4.2ff., 'as perfect a prose equivalent . . . as we could hope to find'.[18] My point is, however, a more specific one, to do with the prose orations best exemplified by the
'Cypriot' orations of Isocrates (Isoc. 2, 3 and 9), and perhaps also by
the lost orations delivered by Greek orators at the funeral *agôn* held
for the dead satrap Mausolus by his sister-wife Artemisia. I once
suggested that parts of Isocrates 9, *Evagoras*, give the flavour of
these Mausolan orations.[19] On the one hand, Pindar is conspicuously
absent from *To Nicocles*, whereas Hesiod, Theognis and Phocylides
are specifically recommended, as are Homer and 'the first inventors
of tragedy' (Isoc. 2.43 and 48). On the other hand, note how in the

Evagoras, Isocrates traces the king's royal virtues to his Aeacid ancestors from Aegina, above all Teucros son of Telamon and cousin of Achilles; Aegina itself features (Isoc. 9.12–20). We are right in Pindar's world here, above all the odes for men and boys of Aegina, which regularly extol the whole Aeacid family. I think of many *Isthmian* and *Nemean* odes but also of *Olympian* 8. In *Nemean* 4 Pindar speaks of 'Cyprus where Teucros rules in exile' (lines 46–7). So I wonder after all if Isocrates had Pindar in mind in these Cypriot orations on kingship. For such legitimation through myth we may compare the *Archelaos* of Euripides.

Xenophon I have glanced at already. He does not mention Pindar and in the *Hieron* chooses Simonides instead as the tyrant's interlocutor. Isocrates mentions Pindar specifically only once – for the story that the Athenians rewarded Pindar for praising them as the 'bulwark of Greece', Ἑλλάδος ἔρεισμα (Isoc. 15.166). Lysias does not mention him, nor does Demosthenes. We shall get nowhere by merely looking for mentions of Pindar in these orators, though I have already suggested that there is a generic debt.

The great exception is Plato. Plato loved to quote Pindar and does so often, indeed we owe to him some important fragments like the 'ancient grief of Persephone' poem which features in the *Meno* and is important for students of Orphism (F133).[20] Sometimes Plato quotes Pindar to create literary atmosphere and raise the tone. Thus in the *Euthydemos* (304b) he quotes Pindar by name from *Olympian* 1 for the opening words 'water is best'. (Compare Aristotle, who has only two trivial mentions, both in the *Rhetoric*: 1364a28, 'water is best' again; and 1401a18.) Another category of intertextual relation between Plato and Pindar is allusion without actual citation. Michael Silk, in a recent article, has brilliantly identified a sustained and important example from the *Republic*.[21] Part of the Myth of Er is in this view a head-on argument with the closing section of *Pythian* 8, the great final poem we have already discussed. Pindar is not mentioned by name but the passage shouts out the identity of its intended interlocutor by a series of linguistic and literary allusions. These culminate in the magnificent metaphor of athletic prizes, which forms the closure to the entire *Republic*. The subject is as solemn and great as it could be: no less than the nature of human destiny. But even that is still not a Pindaric contribution to the kingship theories of Plato. For that, we must go to the *Gorgias* and the *Laws*.[22] Plato re-quotes a fragment (169) of Pindar already used by Herodotus (3.38): *nomos* is *basileus*, Law or custom or convention or what is generally accepted, has absolute power. In *Gorgias* he puts it into the mouth of the brutal realist Callicles for whom might is right; and he quotes more of the poem than Herodotus had done: Heracles violently stole the cattle of Geryon and this shows that Nomos makes just what is most violent. Forty years or so ago even more of the original poem was discovered on papyrus; this has helped with some of the problems but unfortunately we still do not know what kind of poem it was. Notoriously, Plato makes very different use of the poem from Herodotus, for whom *nomos* just meant custom. More important, Plato's – or rather Callicles' – use is different from Pindar's own. Dodds's remark, in his *Gorgias* commentary, is still worth quoting: 'We can hardly credit the pious Pindar with this shocking opinion' – that is, a belief in the 'right' of the stronger. How was the error possible? In between Pindar and Plato there was the *nomos/physis* debate, and most Platonists now accept Ostwald's view that this explains the mistake. So we have an odd situation in two ways. First, the poem of Pindar which in antiquity was most influential on the subject of kingship is not from any of his epinician poems celebrating kings or rulers, but from a poem whose genre is uncertain and which may not have been written for or about a one-man ruler at all. Second, Pindar was either misinterpreted by Plato or else Plato artfully made Callicles misinterpret him.

It may be asked why I have treated the 'might is right' doctrine of the *Gorgias* as kingship theory rather than just political extremism generally. My answer is that the context is quite certainly kingship: the dialogue has just addressed the problem of Archelaos who was king of Macedon from 413 to 399 BC, and Socrates has just rejected the idea that he was an ἄδικος εὐδαίμων, a happy unjust man whose absolute power allowed him to do what he felt like. There is a dialogue going on here not just with Pindar (who celebrated Macedonian kings in fragmentary encomia) but also with Thucydides, who famously admires Archelaos at the end of book 2, though not, it must be said, for his ethical qualities (2.100.2).

At first sight it might seem that the conclusion must be negative: Pindar is not much cited in the fourth century. But since Pindar was so powerful an influence on Plato, and not just as literary decoration, I hardly need to prove further that Pindar was of indirect importance for kingship theory. I see Plato's relation to Pindar as like that of Thucydides to Herodotus: great admiration and strong reaction. But Plato, who plays with genre, as Andrea Nightingale has shown, is subtle and ludic in his use of predecessors and of other genres of literature.[23] Nevertheless, we should hold on to one experience Pindar and Plato had in common: first-hand knowledge of Sicilian tyranny. Plato, whose presentation of tyranny in the *Republic* is coloured by his own Sicilian experience, surely read the Sicilian odes of Pindar from this aspect.

Space forbids me to go further into the post-classical period except to say that we should not confine ourselves to direct literary citation. Alexander spared the house of Pindar, who counted as a benefactor of the Macedonian royal family – the family of Archelaos whom Plato had denounced (Arr. *Anab.* 1.9.10). What did Plato's pupil Aristotle teach his own royal pupil about the argument between Plato and Pindar? In his second Preface to the *Anabasis*, Arrian noted that Alexander lacked a Homer – but also that he lacked 'choral lyrics such as were written for Hieron, Gelon, Theron and many others not to be compared with him' (1.12.2). The allusion to Pindar and the other epinician poets is clear. Philip no less than his son Alexander lacked a Pindar, and Philip, unlike Alexander, engaged in precisely the sort of activities Pindar had celebrated, winning an equestrian victory at Olympia. Callimachus revived epinician poetry and was well aware of Pindar; but as Cameron has noted he uses hexameters instead of Pindar's complex rhythms and poem-types. I leave the question there.

NOTES

1. Hdt. 3.80–2 with Pelling 2002.
2. See Hansen 1999: 66; Brock and Hodkinson 2000: 124 (Rhodes) and 153 n. 4 (Lintott).
3. On λάβρος see Carey 1981: 60, citing Burton, Lloyd-Jones et al. On the instability of ἐλευθέρως: Parry 1989: 144ff.; Pindaric 'polyinterpretability': Pfeijffer 1999: 25ff., also 156 on *Nemean* 5 line 32; Aesch. *Eum.* line 691, with Sommerstein 1989: 215–16.
4. *Pythian* 11 line 53, with Young 1968: 1–26, who discusses earlier views.
5. On this topic see generally Brock 2000: 24–34.
6. Nicias to the *prytanis*: τῆς δὲ πόλεως <κακῶς> βουλευσαμένης ἰατρὸς ἂν γενέσθαι, and that he should 'help his country as far as possible or at least not willingly harm it', τὴν πατρίδα ὠφελήσῃ ὡς πλεῖστα ἢ ἑκὼν εἶναι μηδὲν βλάψῃ: Thuc. 6.14. Cf. Hipp. *Epidemics* 1.11.
7. For good remarks about the 'moral advice' in this poem, with special attention to the earlier section (lines 1–33a), see Howie 1989: 55ff.
8. Hornblower 2004: 233ff.
9. Davies 1997: 49. Note how many *Pythian* odes feature in this paper: was Pindar specially aware of the moral aspect when celebrating victories at

Delphi? For his possible awareness and imitation of the so-called Delphic precepts, see Hornblower 2004: 361 and n. 29.

10. The 'good king' theme is expressed in other, striking, ways as well. Note Homer's description of Agamemnon as ὀλβιοδαίμων, 'attended by a beneficent daimon': *Iliad* 3.182, with Dietrich 1965: 321.
11. Silk 1974: 30.
12. Segal 1989: 189ff.; cf. Finley 1955: 82.
13. On Pindar *Olympian* 12 and liberated Himera, see Barrett 1973 and Lloyd-Jones 1990: 59.
14. *SEG* 41.778–95; 42.846, with Murray 1997: 493–504.
15. Rose 1992: ch. 3.
16. Cameron 1995: 23, citing Gildersleeve 1885: xxvi. Contrast Finley 1968: 38–43.
17. Croiset 1880: 137, 158.
18. Bundy 1986: 14–15. Bundy 15 n. 39 goes on to compare the final sentence of Lys. 2.2 (land/sea) with *Nemean* 6.47–55.
19. Hornblower 1982: 294, cf. 333–4 for the occasion.
20. But for scepticism about the Orphic character of the fragment see Holzhauser 2004.
21. Silk 2001.
22. *Gorg.* 484b, 488b, cf. *Laws* 690b, 715a, 890a. See Ostwald 1965 and Pavese 1967; Rutherford 1995: 163.
23. Nightingale 1995.

CHAPTER 11

The comic Pericles

James McGlew

Tyranny made a thunderous entrance when it stepped onto the political stage of archaic Greece in the seventh century BC; it has every right to the prominent place it is given in most accounts of the archaic Greek city-state. But the language of tyranny, the ways Greeks understood and remembered tyrants, continued to play a significant role in Greek political culture even after the changing social and economic conditions of Greek cities made tyrants, as Greeks first knew them, increasingly improbable. The survival of the language and representations of tyranny provided a kind of discursive continuity which allowed later generations to re-envision and resist political oppression in new forms and contexts. This survival is particularly evident in fifth-century Athens, when the sort of tyranny that Greek cities, including Athens, experienced in the archaic period was no longer a 'clear and present danger'. Long after Pisistratus' death, which, as his unfortunate sons learned, marked tyranny's end as a viable political institution in Athens, the tyrant served as an important and flexible concept for movements of political resistance. This chapter highlights the part that Attic comedy played in this political and cultural effort to keep the idea and image of tyranny alive and well and to use it as a political tool.

We can best appreciate comedy's special role in sustaining and politicising the memory of tyranny, if we begin with the comic image of Pericles. This is not an easy task. Many contemporary scholars are uncomfortable treating Attic Old Comedy as a political medium, and comedy's ribald treatment of the august figure of Pericles has seemed particularly puzzling. While no one can miss the extraordinary freedom comic authors enjoyed in lambasting and caricaturing the personal and political behaviour of political figures like Pericles, such comic political characterisation now seems so outlandish that scholars sometimes find it difficult to believe that Athenian audiences took it seriously or that comedy, which positively revelled in such material, exerted real political significance.[1] Comic freedom, from this perspective, was hardly an exercise of genuine political speech: the raucousness of the occasion, the irony of the genre made it something else entirely. I do not agree.[2] The comic Pericles, I will argue, was a powerful political construction that demonstrates comedy's political role in Athens as well as the significance that the memory of tyranny continued to hold.

In the decade before his death, Pericles commanded a lion's share of Old Comedy's attention; a considerable effort in comic imagination went into representing the leader as a tyrant. Surviving fragments show that the tyrannical Pericles was a fixture in Telecleides and Cratinus. Telecleides, as Plutarch reports, represents Pericles lording over most affairs of Athens:

> Πόλεών τε φόρους αὐτάς τε πόλεις τὰς μὲν δεῖν τὰς δ' ἀναλύειν,
> λάϊνα τείχη τὰ μὲν οἰκοδομεῖν, τὰ δ' αὐτὰ πάλιν καταβάλλειν,
> σπονδάς, δύναμιν, κράτος, εἰρήνην, πλοῦτόν τ' εὐδαιμονίαν τε.

> Regarding the tributes of allies, which to impose and which to
>   forgive,
> which stone walls to build, and which to tear down,
> and treaties, power, might, sovereignty, peace and wealth and
>   human happiness. (45KA)

Both Telecleides and Cratinus give the tyrannical Pericles mythological credentials; as a Zeus-like creature, Pericles wields great powers which are matched only by the personal discretion he enjoys in exercising them. Telecleides describes the mythologised Pericles, sitting heavy-headed,

> μόνον ἐκ κεφαλῆς ἑνδεκακλίνου θόρυβον πολὺν ἐξανατέλλειν.

> alone causing great disturbance to rise from his eleven-chambered
>   head. (47KA)

Similarly in Cratinus' *Thrattai* a character recognises a hybrid of Pericles and Zeus:

> ὁ σχινοκέφαλος Ζεὺς ὁδὶ προσέρχεται
> ὁ Περικλέης, τῷδεῖον ἐπὶ τοῦ κρανίου
> ἔχων, ἐπειδὴ τοὔστρακον παροίχεται.

> Here's the squill-headed Zeus coming along,
> namely Pericles, wearing the Odeion on his head,
> since the danger of ostracism has passed. (73KA)

Thrattai itself must have been about Thracian women, or about Athenian women behaving as Thracian women were thought to behave, and the new cult of Bendis. While this Pericles-Zeus seems to have stood on the periphery of the play's action and no fragment must necessarily have been spoken by him, this kind of cameo appearance may only prove how easy it was for comedy to conjure up the tyrannical Pericles. The same creature recurs through Cratinus' extant fragments. The *Cheirones* gives him an appropriately jaded genealogy:

> Στάσις δὲ καὶ πρεσβυγενὴς
> Χρόνος ἀλλήλοισι μιγέντε
> μέγιστον τίκτετον τύραννον
> ὃν δὴ κεφαληγερέταν
> θεοὶ καλέουσι.

> Stasis and ancient Chronos
> lay with each other and
> bore the greatest tyrant,
> whom the gods call
> Head-collector. (258KA)

The play also traced his line into the next generation with the birth of his consort:

> Ἥραν τέ οἱ Ἀσπασίαν τίκτει Καταπυγοσύνη
> παλλακτὴν κυνώπιδα.

> And Lechery bore him Hera-Aspasia,
> the dog-eyed slut. (259KA)

Cratinus' penchant for comic mergers of Pericles and Zeus (and for ridiculing Pericles' oddly shaped head) is apparent also in the *Nemesis* where Pericles, represented as divine, is summoned with the following invocation:

> μόλ' ὦ Ζεῦ ξένιε καὶ καραιέ.

> Come, Oh Zeus, patron of strangers and heads. (118KA)

According to Pericles' biographical tradition, this sort of characterisation had an effect on Pericles from early in his life, from when Pericles as a young man, according to a small nonsensical story Plutarch transmits, feared that his resemblance to Pisistratus in his physical appearance and voice was an obstacle on the road to political prominence (Plut. *Per.* 7.1). But according to Plutarch, this was malice unjustified by anything Pericles did. Pericles' quick dismissal reflects his conviction (entirely foreign to the fifth-century Athenian democracy) that considerable individual power is bad only if it is corrupt. For Plutarch, too, the war with Sparta and the considerable demands of the Athenian Empire made it absolutely necessary for the Athenians to be guided by the strong leadership skills of a single wise and meritorious leader. Plutarch also includes the somewhat less non-sensical account of Pericles' appropriation of the Athenians' anxieties about tyranny at a crucial point of his career (14–15). When the Athenians, incited by the comic poets and Thucydides son of Melesias, become disturbed by the expense of Pericles' building pro-gramme, Pericles offered to reinscribe the dedications in his own name, instead of the Athenians'. Of course the Athenians could not permit this. Their immediate and unanimous response was that he should use the public funds in whatever ways he thought would best serve the city. For Plutarch, Pericles raises the spectre of tyranny in order to turn the Athenians into partners and competitors in pro-moting the city's interests. A somewhat less generous reading goes like this: Pericles' gambit allowed the Athenians the illusion of preventing their leader from competing with them as the city's dominant power; they, in turn, allowed him free reign to control public policy and deci-sions short of establishing a tyranny – a demarcation that his politi-cal manipulation in fact establishes. The result, according to Plutarch, is clear: from this point 'the city became equable and unified' ($\tau\hat{\eta}s$ $\pi\acute{o}\lambda\epsilon\omega s$ $o\acute{i}o\nu$ $\acute{o}\mu\alpha\lambda\hat{\eta}s$ $\kappa\alpha\grave{\iota}$ $\mu\iota\hat{\alpha}s$ $\gamma\epsilon\nu o\mu\acute{\epsilon}\nu\eta s$), while Pericles' own powers were augmented and consolidated (*Per.* 15.1). Thucydides' ostracism soon followed and the transformation of Pericles' role in Athens, from appeasing the Athenian *dêmos* to leading it.

The account, however one reads it, suggests that tyranny (and the residual fear of tyranny) played some role in Pericles' political self-rep-resentation and that comic poets were on to something. Cratinus' *Dionysalexandros* is helpful here. Although none of the few surviving fragments names Pericles, the hypothesis to the play (*P.Oxy.* 663), if reliable, finds him implicated throughout the plot. *Dionysalexandros*, according to the surviving portions of the hypothesis, borrowed from the famous story of the Judgement of Paris and its catastrophic con-sequences, the rape of Helen and the Achaean expedition to Troy. The element of burlesque lay in Dionysus' assumption of the role trad-itionally assigned to Paris. Cratinus has Dionysus instead of Paris awarding the prize to Aphrodite, stealing Helen, and bringing her to Troy; when the Achaeans arrive to get revenge, he hides Helen and dis-guises himself to escape the real Alexander, who has discovered the impostor. Yet, as the conclusion of the hypothesis makes apparent, things are still more complicated than a simple comic parody of Dionysus' attempt to appropriate the pleasures of Paris and escape his trials. Beneath mythological travesty there is political allegory full of contemporary allusions. In the place of Paris, the Athenian audience got Dionysus, and, at the same time, in Dionysus they were invited to recognise Pericles:

κωμῳδεῖται δ' ἐν τῷ δράματι Περικλῆς μάλα πιθανῶς
δι' ἐμφάσις ὡς ἐπαγηοχὼς τοῖς Ἀθηναίοις τὸν πόλεμον.

Pericles is very persuasively attacked in the play by insinuating
that he brought the war on the Athenians. (38.44–8 KA)

At first glance allegorical suggestion (ἔμφασις) may seem less over-whelming as a form of comic attack than the more direct *onomasti kômôdein of* Cratinus' other plays. A. M. Bowie argued that the sub-tlety of the play's attack on Pericles makes it important that scholars not exaggerate the political character of the play or its reception.[3] But the allegory of *Dionysalexandros* may well have been transparent, and no less politically effective than *onomasti kômôdein*, the form of political criticism that dominates in most modern treatments of Aristophanes. Cratinus was certainly equipped with dramatic tools to bring this about. While the attack in *Dionysalexandros* is indirect and the hypothesis cannot be supported by fragments, leaving many dra-matic questions unresolved (for example, how exactly Cratinus mingled the identities of Paris and Dionysus), it is extreme to con-clude that the hypothesis exaggerates the political character of the play or that Cratinus' audience would have had trouble seeing the ref-erences to Pericles in this behaviour of Dionysus-Paris and the devel-opment of the play. Certainly the vengeance that the Greeks take against Troy (πυρπολεῖν τὴν χώραν: Cratinus 38.24–5 KA) had to remind the Athenians of the incursions of Sparta at the start of the Peloponnesian War and to suggest Pericles' own role in it.

This is only the most obvious of a series of double entendres in which Cratinus invokes and reshapes mythological precedents to recall and ridicule Pericles. More important perhaps is Cratinus' transformation of the famous Judgement of Paris into a comic Judgement of Pericles. Near the start of its surviving portion, the hypothesis describes what seems to have been the opening scene of *Dionysalexandros*: the three divine contestants appear to make their respective offers to the disguised god. Hera offers him 'unshakable tyranny' ($\tau\upsilon\rho\alpha\nu\nu\grave{\iota}s$ $\dot{\alpha}\kappa\acute{\iota}\nu\eta\tau os$), Athena promises 'good fortune in war' ($\epsilon\grave{\upsilon}\tau\upsilon\chi\acute{\iota}\alpha$ $\kappa\alpha\tau\grave{\alpha}$ $\pi\acute{o}\lambda\epsilon\mu o\nu$), and Aphrodite offers to make him 'lovely and attractive' ($\kappa\acute{\alpha}\lambda\lambda\iota\sigma\tau\acute{o}\nu$ $\tau\epsilon$ $\kappa\alpha\grave{\iota}$ $\dot{\epsilon}\pi\acute{\epsilon}\rho\alpha\sigma\tau o\nu$). Of course, Pericles' decision (like Paris') is really more about himself than the contestants. Scholars have seen that all three offers have a particular relevance for Pericles: tyranny, as the dominant leader of an entire generation; success in war, as an advocate of war with Sparta; personal beauty, for the peak-headed, notoriously amatory comic Pericles. Success in war will obviously benefit Athens as well as Pericles. The same might be argued for Hera's offer of an 'unshakable tyranny' – for if *tyrannis* typically meant a personal power exercised at the city's expense, Pericles himself could use it to describe Athens' power over its allies. But whether it suggests the city's power or Pericles' own, Hera's gift obviously interests the Pericles of *Dionysalexandros* no more than Athena's. At this crucial point in the play, Cratinus' Pericles reveals his comic nature; given an opportunity to make Athens supreme in the Greek world and perhaps to make himself supreme in Athens, he instead abandons the good of the city and makes his political actions gratify pleasures that are all his own.

The rest of the play seems to have built on the dual characterisation of Pericles as a lover and an impostor; he is a man committed to private pleasures despite his apparent interest in public matters and in that respect is a perfect composite of Paris and Dionysus. Helen, though apparently unmentioned in the judgement scene, now emerges as the reward for Dionysus' decision and the immediate cause of the Greeks' retribution. In the course of this transition from crime to punishment and from pleasure to pain, the characters of Paris and Dionysus are separated: Paris discovers Dionysus' ruse and seeks to turn him over to the Greeks, but Dionysus finds a new disguise (a ram), and apparently escapes with the help of satyrs. Helen may been intended to suggest Aspasia, Lechery's daughter, in *Cheirones* (259 KA); Pericles' political supporters (the 'Pisistratids' elsewhere) were probably the Satyrs. But the hypothesis makes clear that the point of the allegory is Pericles himself who, as the play suggests, found war useful to indulge and screen his desires.

What do we make of this allegory? It is likely that Plutarch, if he had known the play, would have used it as further proof of the malice in comic representations of Pericles. In his account, Pericles' mastery of his own private desires seems related to his expertise at manipulating the desires and emotions of his fellow citizens. To win their support at an early point in his career, he bribes the mass of Athenians with their own money. Throughout his life, Pericles uses the 'hopes and fears' of the people like rudders to check their ambitions – playing their hopes against their fears and their fears against their hopes. Pericles' greatest success in this respect (and also the principal reason Plutarch paired his biography with Fabius') was the self-control and high-mindedness that made him able to resist the anger, insistence and entreaties of the Athenian *dêmos* to allow them to meet the Spartan and Boeotian armies that attacked Attica at the start of the Peloponnesian War.

Of course, Plutarch did not have problems with the political asymmetry that comes with strong leaders (compare Plut. *Per.* 16.2); power, like any other possession, is a good thing to have if it is not abused. His *Life of Pericles* is an account of a good, though certainly not perfect, man, who exercises extraordinary political power and influence with great benefits for his city, if also a few for himself. Thucydides, Plutarch says (16.1), tells how much power Pericles had; Plutarch himself is more interested in giving an account of the relationship between the man and his power. His representation of the personal motivations in the crucial months and years before the onset of the Peloponnesian War may complicate the picture of Pericles' character but does not fundamentally change it. Personal hostilities and desires, wanting power or fearing its loss may have led him to commit acts detrimental to Athens. But his great service, none greater than keeping the Athenians from attacking the superior infantry of the Spartans – a testament to his independence and determination – and the fact that Pericles does ultimately pay for his arrogance (37.5), make him, at the end of Plutarch's *Life of Pericles*, most deserving of his readers' admiration.

Not all of this should be taken to reflect fifth-century history or fifth-century perceptions of political power. The legal attacks and rumours directed at Pericles, Aspasia and his associates, which Plutarch recounts in some detail, must be largely fictional. If we want to find some historical reality, we cannot expect to be satisfied with Pericles' behaviour; we must instead look to Pericles' political self-representation – the image of leadership utterly uncorrupted and immune to influence.

It follows then that Cratinus was not in the business of creating or destroying moral role models. While Pericles' private desires are made the driving engine behind the mythological adventures described in the hypothesis of *Dionysalexandros*, corruption is not the ultimate target here; rather Cratinus, I am suggesting, objected to the way

Pericles sought to obscure the personal dimensions of his own – indeed, of all power. If this account of his play is accurate, Cratinus may deserve more credit than he usually gets. His characterisation of Pericles is calculated but subtle; if we are lulled to sleep by our own complaints about fairness and accuracy or if we think Cratinus is simply attacking privilege whenever he encounters it, we may miss most of what he has to offer. In fact Pericles was the perfect object of Cratinus' sort of attack, not because he was so dominant, nor because of any exceptionally corrupt behaviour on his part (we really have to trust Thucydides and Plutarch on this point), but rather because Pericles built his public persona on the radical subordination of private desires. We have to believe, then, that Cratinus' audience laughed at his comic Pericles because they recognised in him something of the political persona of the real Pericles. This does not imply that the Athenians found extraordinary venality in Pericles but rather that they believed he possessed the same sort of desires, hopes and expectations that they recognised in themselves. Comedy, then, did not undertake to destroy Pericles but to control him: it is in fact arguable that the Athenians were able to re-elect Pericles and make use of his extraordinary talents as a leader precisely because they continually exposed (or pretended to expose) his private life, in effect making their own, completely un-Periclean division between Pericles' abilities and his rhetorical self-representation.

Comedy did not wield the distinct punitive power of the Athenian courts, but comic fantasy and humour had a certain kind of political power – power perhaps not so very different from the kind Pericles might draw from the praise his 'Funeral Oration' lavished on the war dead – a passage where we can appreciate the political image that Pericles crafted for himself. Praise and ridicule are similarly infectious: they share a certain quality of psychological coercion and in groups they work to elicit crescendos of sympathetic feeling. Pericles, in praising the war dead as he presides over their funerals, exerts control over their story, making that story about the city and making the city the judge of its truth. So too Cratinus, when he ridicules Pericles in *Dionysalexandros* for the private motives that underlie his policies, establishes a certain measure of control over Pericles' image. To be sure, even Cratinus' invention, the Paris-Dionysus-Pericles of *Dionysalexandros*, was not a particularly vile creature: in fact, by preferring Aphrodite to Hera and Athena, sexual delights to power and war, Cratinus' Pericles repeats a mistake that was disastrous but understandable; it was certainly supported by good mythological credentials. In fact, Cratinus seems to 'out' Pericles by positioning him closer to thoughts and desires of Athenian audience. This is the point: in rendering him common in his desires and behaviour, Cratinus punctures Pericles' ideology and self-representation. The thrust of *Dionysalexandros* thus seems very simple: 'you claim that you are exemplary and you insist that we become like you,' Cratinus assumes comedy's characteristic role as spokesman for the common citizen to tell Pericles, 'but you are really just like us.' And yet, as simple as it is, it is hard to imagine a more effective attack on the Pericles who constructed a model of citizenship in the 'Funeral Oration', and scripted his political image career on a radical disjunction of private desire and public virtue. For as long as it lasted and for those who heard it and enjoyed it – and ridicule is not inherently more fleeting than praise – Cratinus' *Dionysalexandros* offered a new image of Athens' dominant leader, not necessarily as corrupt, but as secretive and arrogant.

Cratinus is not, then, complaining about Pericles' policies; nor is he claiming that the war is all bad, let alone that Pericles' policies and decisions should be reversed. Focusing instead on the nature of Pericles' power and his persona in Athens, his play pretends to expose private motivation and a personal narrative pervading that power. There is truth here, but despite the medium of expression, it is general and universal, not specific. Moreover, it is easy to locate the political consequences – which do not in any way depend on whether Cratinus' representation of Pericles in *Dionysalexandros* is a work of fiction or a product of genuine investigation. In Cratinus' vision of the Athenian–Spartan hostilities, private desires replace public virtues; neither the war nor the demands that war makes on Athenian life are axiomatic or inevitable. Instead they are interested, subject to scrutiny, and, for that reason, political.

Much of this sort of imaginative exposure can still be found in Attic comedy after death robbed Cratinus and his fellow comedians of the 430s of their favourite target. For Old Comedy in Cratinus' generation and later, bad politics is largely the consequence of the personal vices of leaders. This seems to support contemporary scholars in their efforts to find the political limits of comedy: comedy lets itself be distracted from democracy's structural flaws by its own intense interest in the misdeeds of its leaders. While this is a better criticism than the older insistence that comedy made its audience laugh not think, it is also misleading. Because comedy focuses on the intersection between political and personal life, comedy enjoys a uniquely external perspective on the workings of the Athenian democracy. Cratinus contends that Pericles too possesses a private life; in fact, Pericles' personal desires show through his political persona, despite everything he does to conceal them.

AFTER PERICLES

Pericles' death might seem a natural end to tyranny's ideological force, at least until his ward helped revive it – albeit by cultivating and advertising, not suppressing, the link between the personal and polit-ical. In fact, comedy certainly reserves the grand image of the *tyran-nos* for nobler material than it found in Pericles' most important successor in the 420s and Aristophanes' target in *Knights*. In that play Cleon is portrayed as a Paphlagonian slave in the household of Demos, a disguise that every member of Aristophanes' audience would have seen through, and he is attacked in relatively simple terms. Serving as the principal domestic servant in the household of Demos, Cleon is represented as a vicious but common thief and a pan-derer. Even when the domestic analogy at the start of *Knights* seems played out, Demos is the only *tyrannos* in Knights (1114) – the Paphlagonian slave's vices are rather unimpressive.[4]

Then what is the sudden flare-up of the language of tyranny such a short time later in *Wasps*? In that play, Bdelycleon, as he is laying out arguments why his father should give up jury duty, forcefully complains about the chorus's indiscriminate accusations of tyranny:

> ὡς ἅπανθ᾽ ὑμῖν τυραννίς ἐστι καὶ ξυνωμόται,
> ἤν τε μεῖζον ἤν τ᾽ ἔλαττον πρᾶγμά τις κατηγορῇ,
> ὡς ἐγὼ οὐκ ἤκουσα τοὔνομ᾽ οὐδ᾽ πεντήκοντ᾽ ἐτῶν·
> νῦν δὲ πολλῷ τοῦ ταρίχους ἐστὶν ἀξιωτέρα,
> ὥστε καὶ δὴ τοὔνομ᾽ αὐτῆς ἐν ἀγορᾷ κυλίνδεται.

Everything for you is tyranny and conspiracies
whether a guy takes on a big case or a small one;
I hadn't heard the word for fifty years
but now it is more current than salted fish.
So the word is even circulating in the agora. (488–92)

Bdelycleon is exaggerating: the ghost of tyranny had not vanished quite as completely as he claims, nor has it re-emerged so fully. The real point must be that the image of the tyrant is undergoing some significant changes, which, in fact, *Wasps* documents very clearly. In the chorus's hyperbolic anxiety, there is no real or pretended fear of a single figure with tyrant-like power. Linked now specifically to *synômotai*, itself a relatively new label for bands of wealthy young men who are hostile to the democracy, tyranny is something different from the βαρυτέρα ὑπεροχή in Pericles that Telecleides saw as a threat to Athens (Plut. *Per.* 16.1).

This is worth noting. While Pericles might be tarred with the brush of the 'new Pisistratids', and though Cratinus's *Dionysalexandros* sees him as underhand and hypocritical, the primary force of his characterisation as a tyrant does not seem to have much to do with conspiracy. He rises above his associates. But in *Wasps* the chorus smell a tyranny, although they do not name him: 'tyranny secretly attacks me unawares' (464–5). Bdelycleon is himself attacked for being a 'lover of monarchy' (474): their mission is to resist 'whoever you are who wants to establish a tyranny over us' (487), but no specific action on Bdelycleon's part is offered to support these vague accusations. Their inability or unwillingness to make their charges concrete – even to name clearly the individual who is striving to make himself tyrant – almost makes their claim stronger: in his invisibility and deviousness lies the greatest threat.

What was Aristophanes' own view of tyranny? Berve's view a generation ago was that Aristophanes shared with Thucydides a hostility to the 'Massenpsychose' that Cleon first aroused in the Athenian *dêmos* – the period, during which, Berve believed, 'die Demokratie sich übersteigerte'.[5] Berve's view of Aristophanes is not necessarily undercut by his unsympathetic view of the Athenian democracy of the 420s – that it lost the discipline of a strong leader of Pericles' ilk – but it certainly cannot draw on that view for support. For Aristophanes, I think, the danger is not primarily the charge of tyranny but the consequences: the loss of good leaders to the uncontrolled envy of the many in pressing times, as seems to have been Thucydides' principal worry. And what makes this new tyranny dangerous is not fictional charges and the confused reactions of the Athenian *dêmos*, but a political climate of secrecy.

This is supported by what *Wasps* actually does with tyranny. When Bdelycleon complains that charges of tyranny are bandied about indiscriminately, we can be pretty sure that Aristophanes' audience laughed, but that does not justify putting Aristophanes (or his audience) in Thucydides' camp: the historian was totally earnest when he treats such political accusation as a political and military disaster, but there is no reason to think this was true of most Athenians. This is not to question Bdelycleon's rhetorical success in countering the chorus's charges; in fact, Bdelycleon reaches beyond the play to make something of a political statement. But that reach to contemporary political rhetoric serves to characterise him and his rhetoric more than it defines comedy's own political position, much as the chorus's own charges characterise them. Bdelycleon's words certainly fit him. He is a wealthy man with clear social aspirations. He does not like his father's plebeian interests, and he is anxious to persuade his father to give up his association with the likes of the chorus.[6] Bdelycleon, much like the chorus's modern critics, views such charges as a bit déclassé. 'Leave politics to the experts,' we almost hear Bdelycleon saying; 'the rest of us should mind our own business.'

From this perspective, the chorus's charge and Bdelycleon's response (although neither is particularly substantive) reflect some emerging sense in the 420s that politics in Athens was being made in private by small, exclusive groups.[7] Tyranny's face is given a make-over to fit what is (or what is perceived to be) a new political threat to democracy: insidious, concerted, secret actions against the *dêmos*. I suggest that Aristophanes' treatment is pervaded by the view that the sort of charges made by the chorus of *Wasps* and vigorously rejected by Bdelycleon are politically awful if they are false, and even more awful if true. Aristophanes would likely agree with the message behind Thucydides' description of the political chaos that followed the discovery of the mutilation of the Herms and the imitation of the Eleusinian Mysteries in 415 (5.53.2): it was easier to make such charges than to defend against them. But it is unlikely that Aristophanes shared Thucydides' view that the Athenians' fear and suspicion reflected their bad memories of the Pisistratid tyranny, in particular their inability to convince themselves that they themselves had much to do with getting rid of the Pisistratids:

ἐπιστάμενος γὰρ ὁ δῆμος ἀκοῇ τὴν Πεισιστράτου καὶ τῶν παίδων τυραννίδα χαλεπὴν τελευτῶσαν γενομένην καὶ προσέτι οὐδ᾽ ὑφ᾽ ἑαυτῶν καὶ Ἁρμοδίου καταλυθεῖσαν, ἀλλ᾽ ὑπὸ τῶν Λακεδαιμονίων, ἐφοβεῖτο αἰεὶ καὶ πάντα ὑπόπτως ἐλάμβανεν.

Because the Demos knew from accounts that the tyranny of Pisistratus and his children had been brought to an end with con- siderable difficulty and that, moreover, its fall was not their work and the work of Harmodius, but of the Lacedaemonians, they feel fear constantly and view everything with suspicion. (6.53.3)

Athenian political history after 415 suggests that Aristophanes may well have been on the right track. When, within a decade, oligarchy emerged as political reality capable of displacing democracy, its appearance was careful and insidious rather than sudden, dramatic or overt. The coup of 411 was set into motion by a series of deliberate and apparently legal moves. It seems that Antiphon and his co-authors clearly planned it to look like a revision rather than a replacement of the *dêmos*. The *dêmos* would still function; the Pnyx was not slated to become a relic of an abandoned regime. This certainly made the change easier for the Athenians to swallow, but, paradoxically, it may also have made the coup more radical. It was a remaking of the Athenian citizen more than a restructuring of the political constitution.

Aristophanes was probably not alone among comic playwrights in focusing on the re-emerging discourse of tyranny and new political realities that gave it force. Pherecrates, who rivalled Aristophanes'enthusiasm for fantasy, seems to have anticipated his use of the image of tyranny as insidious and anonymous. This notion apparently underlay his play *Tyrannis*, which anticipated Aristophanes' city of women citizens in *Assemblywomen*. In *Tyrannis*, tyranny is something each citizen is liable to encounter in his own home. Yet Aristophanes gives this fear a more explicitly political slant. Tyranny's new face – secret, conspiratorial, everyday – has an obvious relevance for the new Athenian oligarchy, whose political work seems to have been conducted far from the agora and political assemblies, at dinner parties in private homes and in conversations in the gymnasia frequented by rich and idle young men. There are hints that oligarchy's enemies exploited the power of tyranny's newly revived image. The law of 410 against tyranny which Andocides mentions in 'On the Mysteries' (1.96) is one: tyranny appears there as the all-inclusive opposite of democracy; not only the tyrant but those complicit with him – broadly defined as all who participate in a non-democratic government – are liable to be treated as tyrants. Of course, the law did not stop the Thirty, but that does not mean it was meaningless. The image on which it was based may still have played some role in helping the Athenians label and resist them. The intriguing but elusive expatriate Polycrates the Sophist certainly had no trouble calling the Thirty 'tyrants' – a label that, if not already current in the time of the Thirty, puts an appropriate name to their horrendous behaviour, substituting for notions of oligarchic virtue the idea of self-interested, and now also devious and underhand, power.

NOTES

1. On Cratinus' treatment of Pericles in relation to Aristophanic politics, see more fully McGlew 2002: ch. 1, parts of which are taken up again in this paper.
2. This, I think, misconstrues political speech as much as comedy: political discussion is effectively isolated from other aspects of daily life. For very different views of comedy politics to those I offer here, see MacDowell 1995 and Heath 1987.
3. Bowie 2000. See also Koerte 1904: 491 and Heath 1990: 144–7.
4. On tyranny and Aristophanes, see the recent papers Kallet 2003 and Henderson 2003.
5. Berve 1967: I.198.
6. The chorus of wasps of course continues to accompany Philocleon as he samples the life of the Athenian rich and famous, but they are now clarified as a personal retinue rather than as fellow devotees of the Athenian courts.
7. Whether this was any more true in the late fifth century than in the great age of ostracism, when small political groups were clearly caucusing in support of or against particular political figures, is an interesting question but one that does not belong here.

CHAPTER 12

Tyrannical oligarchs at Athens

Lynette Mitchell

In his description of the events of 415 BC, Thucydides says that the Athenians were afraid because they thought that those who carried out the mutilation of the Herms and the profanation of the Mysteries were aiming at oligarchy and tyranny and the overthrow of democracy (Thuc. 6.60.1), and in the fourth century the story was still current that Alcibiades desired oligarchy and tyranny (Isoc. 16.36–8).[1] Concern about tyranny and the conceptual link between oligarchy and tyranny is also reflected in the law against tyranny passed in 410 after the oligarchic coup of the previous year (Andoc. 1.96–8).[2]

Athens had known tyrants in the sixth century, and ostracism, the *Ath. Pol.* tells us, was first instituted as a measure to prevent tyranny at Athens (*Ath. Pol.* 22.3–4). Yet that fear of tyranny was still a live concern at the end of the fifth century is puzzling, as neither Alcibiades nor any one else actually demonstrated any inclination outside popular rumour to seize unconstitutional rule. Just as surprising is the close association of tyranny and oligarchy in popular thought – in the late fifth century in Athens at least it was assumed that oligarchies would appeal to the ultimate tyrant, the Persian king (though Herodotus (6.35) told the story with some surprise that the Persian Mardonius had converted tyrannies in Ionia to democracies). In fact, by the fourth century it was assumed that early tyrants had arisen as champions of the people against a ruling elite (e.g. Arist. *Politics*, 1305a7–28; cf. *Ath. Pol.* 13.4).

In this chapter I want to investigate the second of these two issues, and will argue that oligarchy was linked to tyranny because in the development of Greek political theory, both at the popular and more reflective and philosophical levels, tyranny informed and even provided the analytical framework for understanding constitutional forms. In a conceptual and ideological world where definitions of constitutional forms were neither fixed not clearly defined, tyranny represented a fixed point against which other types of constitution could be formulated, analysed and criticised. In order to look at the way in which tyranny became the point of critical analysis in constitutional theorising, we need to consider the development of constitutional theory in both popular and philosophical fields, and the ways in which they had an impact on each other.

From perhaps as early as the late sixth century, the discourse of 'tyranny' had been important to popular definitions of Greek constitutional government by defining it through opposition and developing the notion of the slavery of tyranny and its opposite, the rule of law. At Athens, as the myth of the Tyrannicides began to flourish, the Athenians (or at least some of them) sang that Harmodius and Aristogeiton slew the tyrant and gave Athens 'political equality' (*isonomous t' Athênas epoiêsatên*: PMG 893 [Page]).[3] Outside Athens, in the sixth century, Xenophanes of Colophon reviled the 'hateful tyranny' (*stygera tyrannis*) of the Lydians (DK 21 F 3), and the Persian invasions of the Greek mainland had been quickly seen in the pseudo-Simonidean epigram celebrating the Greek victory as deliverance from 'hateful slavery' (*doulosynê stygera*: Diod. 11.33.2 = [Simonides] XVII (b) Page). Aeschylus fused the notion of tyranny and slavery in the *Persae* of 472 both in Atossa's dream and in the contrast between Persian autocratic slavery and Athenian rule by the assembly (Aesch. *Pers.* 176–99, 241–2, 584–96), and in the second half of the fifth century Herodotus contrasted the 'rule of law' (*despotês nomos*) with the slavery of rule by one man (Hdt. 7.104.4, 135.3, cf. 3.142–3). At Athens, this contrast was given a specifically Athenian twist, when in about 460, at the same time as the Athenians first became 'self-consciously' democratic,[4] significant shifts in the representation of 'tyrants' and 'Persians' in Athenian vase-painting suggest that tyranny, and Persian tyranny in particular, had crystallised as the explicit opposite of Athenian democracy in Athenian representations of themselves and their political system.[5]

In fact, by the late fifth century (in Athens at least) a tyrant was a standard type. Herodotus says in the constitutional debate (3.80) that a tyrant does anything he wants without responsibility or control, and is not accountable to anyone.[6] He is corrupted by wealth and power, and typically is full of envy and pride, both of which vices lead to savagery and violence. The tyrant overturns traditional law, rapes women and puts men to death without trial. For Thucydides, on the other hand, the tyrant was only interested in his own security and interests (1.17),[7] while for Euripides, tyranny was a 'barbarian' constitution (*Heracleid.* 423); and the tyrant held control through flattery for private profit (*Supp.* 409–25), stood outside common laws (*koinoi nomoi*), and removed equality (*ison*). In the discourse of fifth-century democratic Athens, then, the tyrant ruled in his own interest, stood outside the law, inhibited equality, and prevented freedom.[8] The tyrant represented everything democracy did not, and the prime example of the tyrant was the Persian king.

In the fourth century, among thinkers less positive towards democracy, the tyrant equally stood outside law. For Plato (for whom democracy must result in tyranny) the would-be tyrant, 'having complete control of a persuaded mob, does not refrain from shedding the blood of his people, but by bringing the customary unjust accusation, brings a man into court and assassinates him, blotting out the life of a man, and tasting with unholy tongue and mouth the murder of kinsmen, and by driving out exiles, killing, and hinting at the wiping out of debt and the dividing up of land' (*Rep.* 8.565e–566a). Xenophon, on the other hand, who gives an ostensibly more positive account of the tyrant in the *Hieron*, says that all harbour evil thoughts against the tyrant (1.15), that the tyrant can never be sure he is loved rather than feared (1.32–8, 3.1–9, 7.5–10, 8.8–10), that for the tyrant praise is flattery (1.15), and that he cannot enjoy luxury because of its excess (1.17–30, 4.6–11); he is forced to have an armed and foreign bodyguard in his own country (2.7–11, 5.3, 6.5), and lives in a continual state of fear (1.11–13, 2.16–18, 4.1–5, 5.1–4, 6.5–8). [9]

This opposition between constitutional government and tyranny also affected other attempts at classifying and defining constitutions. The model of the 'three constitutions', the rule of the one, the few and the many, had been current from at least the second quarter of the fifth century and is reflected in Pindar's second *Pythian*.[10] By the time that Herodotus is writing his constitutional debate, 'rule of the many' refers to Athenian democracy, and he uses the term *oligarchia* for the rule of few. The rule of the one, Herodotus calls *monarchia* or *tyrannis*, which has at least a negative aspect since it is implicit in the debate that one-man rule will always slide into stereotypical and violent tyranny (so that the rule of Cyrus – which brings 'freedom' for the Persians (Hdt. 1.127.1, 210.2, 3.82.5) – becomes the 'enslaving' rule of Cambyses, and his successors).[11]

Having made the point that *monarchia* is inevitably tyranny, the opposition between tyranny, and democracy (here *plêthos*) underpins much of the rest of the debate. Even the discussion of *oligarchia* (the rule of the 'best men' (*aristoi*)) is framed in terms of the rule of the tyrant (*tyrannos*) and the rule of the multitude (*plêthos*), and the argument for oligarchy is based largely on the vices of the other two. The case against oligarchy, on the other hand, is that it ends in *stasis*, which inevitably leads to monarchy, as indeed does democracy since (according to Herodotus' Darius) the wickedness and wicked men who thrive in democracy are overcome by the people's champion, who is made *monarchos*. Darius' argument then, like Plato's in the *Republic*, is that all constitutions end in tyranny (although we know that in the case of Darius and his son monarchy will not produce freedom).

In the fourth century, the model of the three constitutions was further developed into 'good' constitutions and their perversions, and 'tyranny' provided the framework for this conceptual development. Isocrates seems to suggest the importance of the concept of tyranny to his good and bad forms of constitution when he says that oligarchy, democracy and monarchy could all provide a good and just management of affairs if the most competent (*hikanôtatoi*) people were in power, but in those constitutions where the rulers think only of their own interests and ambition (*pleonexia*) 'the cities . . . will be administered in a manner similar to the roguishness of their leaders' (Isoc. 12.132–3). Plato, on the other hand, explicitly uses the principle of rule inside and outside law in the *Politicus* (e.g. 302c–e) when he says that the rule of the one, the few and the many is divided into its good forms (kingship, aristocracy and a positive form of 'democracy'), which are rule according to law, and the perversions (tyranny, oligarchy and the 'bad' form of democracy), which are rule outside law.

This elaborated form of the three constitutions is of course then picked up and developed further by Aristotle, for whom the defining characteristics of the perverted forms are that they rule in their own interests rather than the interests of the whole people (*Politics* 1279a25–32, 1279b4–10), and that they rule outside of law. For Aristotle, while kingship (*basileia*) under law is possible (it is the Spartan form of kingship he approves of most: *Pol.* 1285a2–8), the form of monarchy 'which seems especially to be tyranny . . . rules without any kind of accountability (*anupeuthunos*) over all his equals (*homoioi*) or superiors (*beltiones*) and for its own interest, but not in the interests of those who are ruled. For this reason it is rule over the unwilling. For none of those who are free (*eleutheroi*) willingly endure such a constitution' (*Pol.* 1295a19–23). Likewise, the worst form of oligarchy is where the magistrates rule, not the law (*Pol.* 1292b5–7), and, although positive forms of democracy are possible where the poor (*aporoi*) are not sovereign over the rich (*euporoi*), and where equality (*isotês*) and freedom (*eleutheria*) obtain, the worst form of democracy is where the *plêthos* are sovereign and not law; in this kind of constitution the *dêmos* is a *monarchos*, decrees are like the dictats of a tyrant, and flatterers are honoured (*Pol.* 1291b30–1292a23). While the worst forms of *oligarchia* and *dêmokratia* are here equated with tyranny, the basic model which informs the classification of constitutions distinguishes between lawful constitutions and tyranny, which stands outside law.

However, in addition to this polarity between constitutions under law and tyranny, at some point between the 460s and the writing of the Old Oligarch's treatise on the *Constitution of the Athenians* (which is variously dated between the 440s and the early fourth century), a new opposition developed in Athenian political theorising between democracy and oligarchy.[12] As a result, the Old Oligarch contrasts life under an oligarchy with life under a democracy (e.g. 1.4, 2.20), and Thucydides describes the *stasis* in (and between) the Greek cities during the Peloponnesian War as arising out of the opposition between democracy and oligarchy (e.g. 3.82.1).

Rather than replacing the opposition between tyranny and democracy, oligarchy was generally assimilated to tyranny. Thucydides is the first to make explicit the link between oligarchy and tyranny, and describes oligarchy at Thebes during the Persian Wars as tyrannical (as compared with *isonomos oligarchia* and *dêmokratia*: 3.62.3). Likewise Xenophon describes the Thirty at Athens of 404/3 as 'acting tyrannically' (Xen. *Hell.* 2.4.1), and at some point during the fourth century the name the Thirty Tyrants was coined (e.g. Arist. *Rhet.* 1401a35–6; cf. (for example) Diod. 14.2.1, 4). For Isocrates and Demosthenes oligarchy has tyrannical values: oligarchy enslaves (Isoc. 8.125), is driven by *pleonexia* (Isoc. 7.60), and is opposed to equality (7.61); it is brutal (Dem. 22.52, 24.24), and brings wealth to its adherents (Dem. 20.15); it is opposed to the rule of law, and those who choose to live under it are cowards and slaves (Dem. 24.75–6); war with oligarchs is ideological war or a war about freedom, and oligarchy is equal to slavery (Dem. 15.17–18). Indeed, oligarchs (like the Persian king) are the common and natural enemy: 'When men overthrow democracies and change to oligarchies', Demosthenes says, 'I recommend you consider them to be the common enemies of all who desire freedom (*eleutheria*)' (Dem. 15.20). Aeschines, on the other hand, makes a direct reference back to the three types of constitution: 'it is agreed that there are three types of constitution, tyranny, oligarchy and democracy. Tyrannies and oligarchies are managed after the fashion of those in authority, but the cities which are democracies are according to the laws' (Aesch. 1.4; cf. 1.5, 3.6). Further, for

Aeschines, oligarchs like tyrants need protection from bodyguards. Because of this threat from those who stand outside law (that is, from Aeschines' political opponents), it is an important democratic right, Aeschines says, to prosecute anyone who proposes an illegal decree (Aesch. 3.7). For fourth-century rhetoricians, then, oligarchy assimilated the language of tyranny, so that oligarchy was a kind of tyranny, and could be opposed to the right (in the Athenian popular context) form of constitution, Athenian democracy.

It is often argued that the demonisation of oligarchy and the link between oligarchy and tyranny arose out of the violence of the oligarchic coups at Athens at the end of the fifth century. Certainly, the violence of the Thirty in 404/3 cannot be denied, and Thucydides describes the seizure of the assembly at Colonus by the Four Hundred in violent terms, as well as the series of events which led to the downfall of the oligarchs.[13] On this level, the assimilation of violent oligarchy to stereotypically violent tyranny seems natural enough. But the opposition between democracy and oligarchy was not natural, since neither oligarchy nor democracy, 'the rule of the few' and the 'rule of the many', were necessarily formal or ideological opposites. Certainly, it is true that when oligarchy and democracy were defined by class they could be constructed as opposite constitutional forms. The Old Oligarch, for example, defines oligarchy as the rule of the 'best' (*chrêstoi* or *beltistoi*), and democracy as the rule of the *dêmos*, by whom he means the 'poor' (*penêtes*) (e.g. 1.4). Likewise, in his description of *stasis* in the cities, Thucydides describes the struggle as between the champions of either the political equality (*isonomia politikê*) of the masses or prudent aristocracy (*sôphrôn aristokratia*) (Thuc. 3.82.8), but champions neither since both groups were working in their own interests.

However, democracy was not always defined in this way, and the *dêmos* was not always limited to the lower sections of society. Thucydides' Pericles in the Funeral Oration offers instead an inclusive definition of democracy which disregards class:

> Our constitution is called a democracy (Pericles says) because we give the management of affairs not to the few (*oligoi*) but to the many (*pleiones*). In private disputes there is equality (*to ison*) for all according to the law (*nomoi*). There is also a claim based on worth, as each man is distinguished in something, he wins preferment in the state not on the basis of rotation but from merit (*aretê*). Again no one is prevented from taking part by the obscurity of his public position if he is able to do some good thing for the city. (Thuc. 2.37.1)[14]

In fact, the formal difference between democracy and oligarchy was not always great. The Athenians in 411 did not necessarily see much difference between the oligarchy that would bring them Persian support and democracy, and were persuaded by Peisander to adopt a form of constitution which was 'having democracy not in the same way' (Thuc. 8.53.1), though it was called 'oligarchy', and was limited to 5,000 (Thuc. 8.65.3), and defined in the period after the fall of the Four Hundred as 'those who bore arms' (Thuc. 8.97.1; one might compare Pindar's rule of the 'rowdy army' in *Pythian* 2).[15]

Indeed, the flexibility and variability of this constitutional nomenclature and the values ascribed to it are indicated by the variety of reactions to the Spartan constitution. Thucydides unequivocally classes the Spartan constitution as an oligarchy, but Aristotle describes it as a mixed constitution (*Pol.* 1294b6–40), and Isocrates says in the *Areopagiticus*:

> In most of the speeches I have made I have condemned oligarchy and *pleonexia*, and commended *isotês* and democracy, not all of them, but those which are established on a good basis, and not indiscriminately, but justly and with reason. For I know that our forefathers in this constitution far excelled the rest. The Spartans too for this reason conduct themselves politically in the best way, because they happen to be particularly democratic. In the selection of magistrates, in their daily life, and in other habits we can see among them *isotês* and *homoiotês* have greater influence than among others. Oligarchies are hostile to these principles, while well-ordered democracies use them continually. (Isoc. 7.60–1)

While Isocrates is clearly buying into the model of democracy versus oligarchy/tyranny, he is also obviously running against the grain of political thought by identifying the democratic slogans of 'equality' and 'egalitarianism' with Sparta (and so making Sparta anti-oligarchic).

Isocrates, however, has his own agenda, and his own ideas about what constituted democracy, or at least the best form of democracy. Although concerned that he will be branded an oligarch and an enemy of the people (*misodêmos*) (Isoc. 7.57), he condemns the democracy of his own day and argues that the democracy instituted first by Solon and re-established by Cleisthenes ('who drove out the tyrants') should be restored (7.16–18). He says that what made these earlier forms of democracy better managers of the state was that they recognised two kinds of equality, one which gives the same to all, and one which gives each man what is fitting, and on this basis did not select officials by lot, but elected the best (*beltistoi*) and most appropriate (*hikanôtatoi*) men. For Isocrates, the element of democracy is in the *dêmos*'s ability to act as a *tyrannos* and to appoint magistrates, to punish those magistrates who had done wrong, and to judge in the disputed cases (7.26). In Isocrates' democracy those who have leisure and sufficient means of livelihood look after the rest, and are praised by them when they do well, but punished when they make mistakes (7.26–7): 'How could one find a democracy more stable or just than this, in which those who are most able manage affairs, but which makes the *dêmos* sovereign (*kyrios*) over them?' But the sort of sovereignty Isocrates is imagining is certainly not the sort imagined by other theorists, and his comparison with Sparta where the assembly was able to comment on policy but not necessarily formulate it is an apt one.

For Isocrates oligarchy was a bad word and was the opposite of democracy. However, in order to force and structure a contrast between democracy and oligarchy, Isocrates and others used the implicit assimilation of tyranny and oligarchy. Not only was oligarchy placed outside law, but also the practically unclear and morally neutral relationship between democracy and oligarchy on the constitutional spectrum was obscured. While there were certainly oligarchies among the Greek cities which were ideologically at the opposite pole to Athens – at Chios, for example, the council (*bolê*) seems to have held executive power and there is no sign of an assembly[16] – not all constitutions which called themselves or were called oligarchies were radically opposite in their conception or operation to some democracies, not even the democracy at Athens.[17] Nor were all oligarchs in Athens the natural enemies of democracy, but oligarchy became a rhetorical devise to describe and demonise any who opposed the prevailing political view in Athens and placed them outside law and beyond popular consideration.

So, in conclusion, this chapter has tried to do three things. First, (at the level of the implicit) it has tried to show how popular ideas about the nature of Greek constitutions and more reflective and serious political theorising were in dialogue with each other, and that the simple opposition between the rule of law and tyranny affected the development of constitutional theory. Second, it has argued that oligarchy was assimilated to tyranny in order to force a contrast between oligarchy and democracy which could not be sustained in terms of the constitutional forms themselves. Finally, it has tried to provide one answer, or an answer on one level, to why the Athenians were so concerned about tyranny. It was not in the fifth and fourth centuries because they were afraid that a tyrant really would overthrow their constitution, but because tyranny provided a natural opposite of democracy, against which they could measure and analyse not only other constitutions, but democracy itself.

NOTES

1. Cf. Rhodes 2000, esp. 136 where he notes: 'In the fifth century Ephialtes and his supporters campaigned openly for democracy; they were opposed by aristocrats who disapproved of democracy, and this opposition persisted into the 440s and was more serious than is sometimes allowed. After that our next trace of oligarchy is in the pamphlet of the Old Oligarch, but what the new-style demagogues claimed to be keeping at bay was not oligarchy but tyranny.'

2. Note also *Ath. Pol.* 16.10 with Rhodes 1993: 220–2; see also McGlew 1993: 184–90.

3. On *isonomia*: Vlastos 1981. The date of the *skolia* is unknown, as is the date of the initial dedication of Antenor's statue groups which also appear to celebrate Harmodius and Aristogeiton as Tyrannicides, although a *terminus* of 480 for the statue group is provided by its transfer to Susa by Xerxes. This original group was later replaced by the statue group of Nesiotes. Ostwald (1969: 131–3) opts for a date soon after 507, but a substantial objection to a date in the first years after the expulsion of Hippias is that it is unclear how a claim that was so manifestly wrong could have been made so soon after the event (cf. Thuc. 1.20.2, 6.54–9; *Ath. Pol.* 18), an objection Ostwald tries to deal with by suggesting Cleisthenes was happy to encourage this as propaganda (cf. Raaflaub 2004: 94–5). Nevertheless, Podlecki's date of 477 has to minimise the impact of the first statue group (Podlecki 1966), as Ostwald objects. Thompson and Wycherley 1972: 155 note that '[the Antenor group] may have been made some years later, but we must allow a sufficient interval between them and their replacements to account for the fact that Pausanias characterised Antenor's work as obviously "older".'

4. For 'self-conscious' democracy at Athens, see Rhodes, *CAH²* V.62–95 at 67–77.

5. Miller 1988; 1995; 2000.

6. In most analyses, the 'constitutional debate' is considered to be basically ironic in the sense that Greek political theory is given to Persians to delineate. For a recent interpretation, however, which does not see irony in this aspect of the debate, though it does want to find elaborate overlays of subtlety, see Pelling 2002.

7. This is also true of the tyrant city: see esp. Thuc. 6.85.1, but compare 1.75.3 with 1.76.2; note also that both Cleon's and Diodotus' speeches (esp. 3.40.4 and 44.2) in the Mytilene debate also advocate self-interest (and Thucydides' Cleon, of course, makes firm the link with tyranny already suggested by his

Pericles: 3.37.2), though they differ in their interpretations of what consti-
tutes Athens' best interests. For the lengthy bibliography regarding this
complex and in many ways paradoxical pair of speeches, see Hornblower
1991– : 2.420–2. Note, however, that Cleon, although he recognises that
Athens *is* a tyrant city, also advocates that the Athenians act according to
law (3.37.3–4 – which he identifies with the decree of the assembly: on these
difficult passages, see Hornblower 1991– : 2.423–5), whereas Diodotus
(3.44–7) argues that the Mytileneans should not be punished with death
because (a) although they are acting contrary to law (by revolting) they are
acting according to nature, and (b) the issue is not what is just but what is
expedient (see also Macleod 1983: 92–100). Cleon, then, ironically insists
that a tyrant city act according to law, while Diodotus urges the Athenians
to disregard law and maintain the Mytileneans' freedom (that is, he urges
the Athenians by setting aside law not to act tyrannically by enslaving them).
Thucydides here seems to be experimenting with and testing ideas of law and
tyranny and the relationships between them.

8. For 'Freedom' (*Eleutheria*) as a peculiarly fifth-century (and post-Persian
Wars) idea, see Raaflaub 2004.

9. The notion of the foreign bodyguard is at least at one level construct, since
the argument runs that a tyrant needs a bodyguard of foreigners since he
stands outside law; on the other hand, a monarch who rules according to
law is able to draw his bodyguard from among the citizens who themselves
stand in fear of law: Arist. *Pol.* 1285a16–29; cf. Xen. *Hieron* 6.9–10.

10. For the date of about 468, see Bowra 1964: 410. Burton 1962: 113–15 gives
a date of 470. For Pindar's tripartite classification, which Ostwald thinks
is likely to pre-date Pindar, see Ostwald 2000: 15–17 and Hornblower,
Chapter 10, this volume.

11. Xenophon and Plato attribute the decline from the 'good' king Cyrus to the
later bad kings of Persia to the introduction of luxury (Xen. *Cyropaed.*
8.8.15; *Laws* 3. 694a–696a). See also Briant 2002a. Herodotus also suggests that luxury is at the root of Persian decline: Hdt. 9.122.3, cf. 1.126.

12. Bowersock 1966 (445–441 BC); Forrest 1970 (424 BC); Rhodes 2000: 128
(431–424 BC); Hornblower 2000: 365–76 (early fourth century, either
c. 393 BC or c. 380 BC).

13. Although note Taylor 2002.

14. See Hornblower 1991– : 1.300–1.

15. Rhodes forthcoming. cf. Hornblower, Chapter 10 in this volume,
pp. 209–11.

16. *IGA* (Roehl) 381, Michel 707, *SEG* 35.923, Rhodes with Lewis 1997: 230.

17. For an overview, see Mitchell forthcoming.

CHAPTER 13

Plutarch and the Sicilian tyrants

Claude Mossé

Plutarch's *Parallel Lives* are a mine of information for specialists of classical antiquity, in that the biographer was able to draw on sources that have not come down to us. It is nevertheless important to examine this information with a critical eye: Plutarch was writing at the end of the first century AD in a world dominated by Rome and, as he reminds us at the start of the *Life of Alexander*, his intention was not to write a work of history but rather to present exemplary lives of great men from the history of Greece and Republican Rome.[1]

Two of these *Lives* – those of Dion of Syracuse and Timoleon of Corinth – unfold against the background of the history of Sicily in the fourth century BC. Both Dion and Timoleon attempted, with varying degrees of success, to free Sicily from the yoke of tyranny, and specifically from the two Dionysii who ruled over Syracuse and part of the island for much of the period – Dionysius the Elder from 406 to 367, and Dionysius the Younger (with interruptions of varying length) from 367 until his ultimate fall in 344. It may therefore be of interest to trace the image of tyranny we find in these two *Lives*.[2]

In writing the biographies of his two heroes, Plutarch could draw on numerous sources: the narratives of the historians Ephorus and Theopompus, who lived through these events, and especially the *History of Sicily* by Philistus, a personal friend of Dionysius the Elder, and that of Timaeus, a bitter enemy of the tyrants, written during the first third of the third century.

But Plutarch is interested in these two figures in the history of fourth-century Syracuse, and therefore in the tyranny of the two Dionysii, mainly because Plato, the founder of the Academy, was linked to these events. The Athenian philosopher is said to have stayed in Syracuse on three separate occasions, first during the reign of Dionysius the Elder around 388–387, then twice more under Dionysius the Younger, and at his invitation. These visits are mentioned in letters attributed to Plato, which are addressed to different participants in the life of Syracuse, among them Dionysius the Younger himself (*Letters* 1, 2 and 3), Dion (*Letter* 4) and, after the latter's death, some of his friends (*Letters* 7 and 8). The authenticity of most of these letters has been contested by many commentators, who regard them as scholastic exercises. But the authenticity of *Letter* 7 is acknowledged by a number of editors of Plato's works;[3] and it is this letter that contains most information about Plato's time in Syracuse. As we shall see, Plutarch drew heavily on *Letter* 7 in his description of Syracusan tyranny and of the climate that reigned in the tyrants' entourage.

We must, however, take into account another aspect of Plato's influence. Plutarch was in fact a pupil at the Academy and therefore familiar with Plato's works, in particular the great dialogues like the *Gorgias* and the *Republic*, in both of which Plato had constructed an image of the tyrant and of the tyrannical man. It is certainly true that in creating this image, he took over earlier representations of tyranny dating back to the fifth century, which were already present in the works of Herodotus and the tragedians. Among these concepts were the idea that the tyrant's power was illegitimate, obtained by relying on the support of the lower classes at the expense of the aristocracy and maintained by the use of mercenaries, and the notion that the tyrant showed contempt for the laws of the city and ruled entirely according to his whims and desires. Because he was above the law, he practised polygamy, which contributed to problems of succession and led to interminable conflicts. Polycrates of Samos, Cypselus of Corinth, Cleisthenes of Sicyon and to a lesser extent Pisistratus and his sons in Athens exemplified this type of tyrant. But Plato gave these representations of tyranny a philosophical underpinning and a more rigorous dimension, and this is no doubt due in part to his experiences in Syracuse.[4]

It is important to keep this in mind if we want to gain a deeper understanding of the image of the Sicilian tyrants in the *Lives* of Dion and Timoleon. Plato's influence is particularly perceptible at the start of the *Life of Dion*. Plutarch describes the milieu in Syracuse in which Dion lived as a place of depravity: 'he had nevertheless grown up in a moral environment corrupted by tyranny; a way of life dominated by injustice and fear, nouveau-riche ostentation, vulgar luxury, an existence in which beauty was sought in pleasure and excess' (*Dion* 4.3). We find in this description an echo of what Plato says about his first voyage in *Letter* 7:

> Once I had arrived, the life that over there was considered to be happy
> because the tables were provisioned in the Italian and Syracusan style

> did not appeal to me in any way. Stuffing oneself twice a day and
> never being alone in bed at night, not to mention all the habits engen-
> dered by that way of life – these things would prevent any man in the
> world who had practised them from childhood from becoming wise.
> (*Letter* 7.326c)

Although he had been raised in this milieu and was brother-in-
law of the tyrant, Dion had succeeded in maintaining his independence. He became convinced that Plato's influence could be beneficial
to Dionysius and took advantage of the philosopher's presence in
Syracuse to arrange a meeting between the two men. But Plato's discourse on the just man and the unjust man (a theme explored more
fully in the *Gorgias*) is said to have angered the tyrant.[5] He allowed
Plato to leave Syracuse freely, but had the ship on which he was sailing
diverted towards Aegina, where the unfortunate philosopher was sold
as a slave. This story, which we also find in Diogenes Laertius, is of
very doubtful accuracy; but Plutarch takes pleasure in recording it as
a black mark against Dionysius the Elder, the tyrannical man par
excellence. Plutarch completes the portrait of Dionysius the Elder
with a series of anecdotes in Chapter 9 of the *Life of Dion*: Dionysius'
imprisonment of his son, the future tyrant, so that the latter would
not be tempted to conspire against him; his morbid fear of an attempt
on his life, which led him to have his hair singed for fear of the
barber's scissors; his insistence that all visitors remove their clothes,
to ensure that they were not concealing a weapon; the execution of
anyone who seemed to be a danger to him, even in his dreams!

Plutarch does not dwell on the death of Dionysius the Elder who,
according to certain traditions, is supposed to have died of joy on
hearing that one of his tragedies had won the prize at Athens.[6] He
does, however, show more interest in Dionysius the Younger, for the
obvious reason that the latter, unlike his father, had genuinely wanted
Plato to come to Syracuse. Once again, Dion was the instigator of the
visit. In *Letter* 7, Plato mentions this intervention on the part of Dion,
who thought he might thereby manage to divert the young man from
the excesses of tyranny:

> He described the empire of Italy and Sicily and the power that he
> himself possessed there, mentioning also Dionysius II's youth and his
> great passion for philosophy and study. He explained to me again how
> easily his nephews and relatives could be won over to the doctrine and
> the way of life that I unceasingly advocated and maintained that they
> could easily join forces to exert pressure on Dionysius II. So if ever the

hope that the same men could be both philosophers and rulers of a great city was to be realised, this was the time. (*Letter* 7.327e)

Dion had indeed remained an influential figure at the tyrant's court. He tried to induce the young prince to renounce the excesses that had marked his father's reign and to become Plato's pupil:

> As soon as Plato arrives, he said, you will let him regulate your character according to the principles of virtue so that you will come to resemble the most divine and most beautiful model of being, the guide whom the whole universe obeys as it changes from disorderly chaos into an ordered world. He will bring both you and your fellow-citizens great happiness, for everything that they now grant you reluctantly and under compulsion, you will be able to obtain through wisdom and justice tempered with benevolence; you will rule with paternal authority and instead of being a tyrant, you will become a king. (*Dion* 10.2–3)[7]

Plutarch had earlier taken care to emphasise that 'by nature' (*physêi*) the young Dionysius did not belong to the category of the worst tyrants. Dion's words inspired in Dionysius 'a violent and passionate desire to hear the philosopher and to spend time with him' (*Dion* 11.1).

Thus Plato was welcomed in Syracuse with the greatest of honour. And Plutarch adds that very soon the extent of his influence could be measured:

> The sense of propriety that reigned at banquets, the decorum of the court and the mildness shown by the tyrant himself in all his dealings gave the citizens great hopes of change. There was a general enthusiasm for letters and philosophy; it was said that the tyrant's palace was filled by a cloud of dust, so great was the number of people there drawing geometrical figures. (*Dion* 13.3–4)

But Dion's enemies had not given up. They accused him in Dionysius' hearing of wanting to seize power in order to pass it on to his nephews, the sons of his sister Aristomache, second wife of Dionysius the Elder.[8] Young Dionysius was not yet sufficiently influenced by Plato's teachings to remain deaf to such accusations. He banished Dion and seized his family and part of his property. As for Plato, he was allegedly put under guard to prevent him embarking with Dion. Once again, Plutarch reproduces the account we find in *Letter* 7: the tyrant had succumbed to an all-consuming passion for the philosopher, combined with pathological jealousy of Dion's friendship with him. Plato was, however, able to go back to Athens, thanks to a war of which we know nothing.

Dionysius had promised Plato that he would recall Dion, but he did nothing of the sort. At the same time, though, he did not give up the ambition

> to surpass everyone in debate . . . Therefore he began to miss Plato, blaming himself for not having profited from his presence and properly understood all the fine things he had said. And since, like any tyrant, he was always at the mercy of his desires and ready to be carried away by his various enthusiasms, he decided at once to send for Plato again and made every effort to persuade the Pythagorean Archytas to vouch for his good faith and to summon Plato. (*Dion* 18.4–5)

In *Letter* 7, Plato talks of his hesitations and of Archytas' intervention and his agreement to it, and gives a lengthy account of the conditions of his last stay in Syracuse.[9]

Plutarch, on the other hand, returns to his main subject, Dion, who was preparing to land in Sicily. As for Plato, he 'remained aloof from the conflict out of respect for the ties of hospitality binding him to Dionysius, and because of his age'. This is not the place to relate the main events of the history of Syracuse at that time; what concerns us here is the image Plutarch gives of Dionysius' behaviour, which is an entirely negative one. Dionysius at first fled to Italy, leaving his friend Timocrates, to whom he had given Dion's wife in marriage, with the task of defending the city. Then when Dion had captured the city, Dionysius returned to Syracuse, where the Acropolis had remained in the hands of his mercenaries. At this point Plutarch makes a point of emphasising the duplicity shown by Dionysius, who made false promises to the Syracusans in order to win them away from his adversary; then, having taking the city's envoys prisoner, 'at dawn, having gorged his mercenaries with undiluted wine, he drove them headlong against the Syracusans' fortifications'. Dionysius' manoeuvres only added to the complexity of the situation in Syracuse, where three groups confronted one another: Dion and his followers, a group of Syracusans who had rallied to Heracleides, and the mercenaries fighting for Dionysius, who once again fled to Italy.

Shortly afterwards Dion was assassinated on the orders of the Athenian Callippus.[10] At the start of the *Life of Timoleon*, which Plutarch wrote before the *Life of Dion*, the biographer summarises in a few sentences the situation in Syracuse just after Dion's death:

> As soon as he had driven out the tyrant Dionysius, Dion was treacherously murdered and those who had helped him liberate the people

of Syracuse were divided amongst themselves. Control of the city passed continually from one tyrant to another and it suffered so many misfortunes that it became almost a desert. As for the rest of Sicily, one part was completely devastated as a result of war and left without any cities; those that survived were mostly occupied by barbarians of all races and by unpaid soldiers who readily accepted any change of regime. Ten years later, Dionysius gathered together some mercenaries, drove out Nysaeus who was at that time ruler of Syracuse, seized power and became tyrant once again. Against all expectations, he had been deprived by a few men of the most powerful tyranny the world had ever seen; now, after having been exiled and humiliated, he became, even more unexpectedly, the master of those who had driven him out. The Syracusans who had remained in the city found themselves slaves of a tyrant who had never shown moderation and whose soul had by then become cruel as a result of his misfortunes. (*Timoleon* 1.2–5)

The young prince who had been eager to study philosophy under Plato but had, through jealousy of Dion, adopted a duplicitous policy that had cost him power, returned from exile full of hatred and ferocity and assumed, as it were, the traditional mantle of the tyrant. And yet this same brutal tyrant was to behave towards Timoleon with a certain nobility of character that Plutarch mentions several times. Timoleon had come from Corinth, the mother city of Syracuse, in response to appeals by the Syracusans who had suffered the loss of their liberties since Dionysius's return, but who were equally fearful of the threat of Carthage. They could not expect much help against Carthage from Hicetas, the ruler of Leontini, who was himself of Syracusan origin and perhaps wished to exploit the Carthaginian threat in order to seize power in Syracuse.[11]

The crucial point here is Dionysius' attitude, as described by Plutarch. When Timoleon's soldiers succeeded in capturing the citadel and the tyrant's palace, where they found horses, instruments of war, projectiles and armour, Dionysius put up no resistance and surrendered to Timoleon the two thousand soldiers he still had under his command. Plutarch sums up in a couple of sentences the unhappy fate of this tyrant for whom (we surmise) he feels a kind of pity:

He went to Timoleon's camp, where for the first time he was seen reduced to a state of deprivation and humiliation. He was sent to Corinth with a single ship and some meagre possessions. This, we should remember, was a man who had been born and raised under the most famous and powerful tyranny there had ever been, who had himself been tyrant for ten years and then, for twelve years after Dion's expedition, had been buffeted by struggles and conflicts. The misfortunes that he suffered were even greater than those he had inflicted on others when he was tyrant. He saw his sons die in their prime, his virgin daughters raped, and his sister (who was also his wife) physically abused by his enemies to gratify their basest pleasures when she was alive, then murdered together with her children and finally thrown into the sea. (*Timoleon* 13.8–10)

Plutarch then describes the miserable life led by the former tyrant at Corinth: he spent his days in taverns, visited common prostitutes and made a living by giving singing lessons. The biographer says that in some people's view Dionysius behaved thus in order to convince the Corinthians that he was nothing but a contemptible and dissolute individual, and that there was no reason to fear that he would return to power in Syracuse. But Plutarch does not seem to share this view. Instead, he makes a point of citing 'certain remarks that seem to show that he bore his misfortunes with a degree of nobility' (*Timoleon* 15.1). These remarks show that he had once been a pupil of Plato. To a foreigner who asked him what good Plato's wisdom had done him, Dionysius is reputed to have replied: 'Do you really think that Plato taught me nothing when you see how I endure the change in my fortunes?'

Although Dionysius had not been the philosopher king Plato dreamed of when he went to Syracuse, he had at least distinguished himself from his father – the autocratic and all-powerful tyrant who had made Syracuse tremble for almost forty years – by his wisdom and humanity in the face of misfortune, which proved that he had benefited from his association with Plato. But Plutarch is perhaps influenced here by the idea that Plato could not have shown such interest in the young Dionysius – going so far as to visit Syracuse a third time, even though his disciple and friend Dion was still in exile – if the young ruler had not possessed real qualities. In *Letter* 7, Plato writes that these qualities were negated by the bad influence of treacherous advisers. Thus Plutarch could hold to the view that once the tyrant had been divested of power and reduced to a humiliating condition, these qualities could have re-emerged, thus explaining Dionysius' ability to endure his misfortunes with a certain nobility of spirit.

Plutarch does not concentrate primarily on the history of the Dionysii. His two heroes, Dion and Timoleon, are in a sense oppositional figures. But in placing them in the context of the turbulent history of fourth-century Syracuse, he could not but take account of the personalities of the two tyrants. As a faithful admirer of Plato, Plutarch chose to characterise tyrannical power by drawing on representations created in the fifth century and taken over in the schools of philosophy, like the Academy. But because there was a tradition, based on letters by Plato that everyone took to be genuine, that the philosopher had visited Syracuse three times, it had to be assumed that the aim of these visits – inducing the tyrant to adopt the wisdom of the philosopher – implied that those who held tyrannical power retained some humanity and a genuine interest in philosophy. That assumption quickly proved unfounded in the case of Dionysius the Elder, but the situation is more complicated with regard to Dionysius the Younger: on the one hand, he was a worthy successor to his father, but he was also to some extent a young man with a great love of knowledge and ultimately an unfortunate victim of the vagaries of Fortune.

Plutarch's verdict on the tyranny of the two Dionysii has more to do with morality than with historical analysis. That does not, however, make it any less valuable to the historian of representations attempting to understand the construction of an image of tyranny that was to endure throughout the centuries.

NOTES

1. On Plutarch, see Hartog 2001: Preface. All translations in this article are based on the French version by A.-M. Ozanam in Hartog's edition.
2. On Syracusan tyranny in the fourth century, see Mossé 2004: 99–120.
3. On the *Letters* of Plato, see Brisson's introduction: Brisson 1994: 9–56, and the Notes to *Letter* 7, 210–32.
4. See Mossé [1969] 2004: 133–45.
5. See especially the dialogue between Polus and Socrates (*Gorgias* 468c–479e), where the problem is discussed in relation to a tyrant, Archelaos, who had illegally seized power in Macedonia.
6. If Athens seems at first to have been hostile to Dionysius, this changed from the 370s onwards. See especially the honorary decree in favour of Dionysius and his sons (Tod 133) dating from 368, and the alliance concluded the following year, shortly before Dionysius' death (Tod 136). On Dionysius' victory at the Lenaia, see Diodorus 15.74.
7. The theme of the opposition between king and tyrant is treated in particular detail in the political literature of the fourth century. See Mossé 1962: 375–99.
8. At the start of the *Life of Dion*, Plutarch mentions Dionysius' first marriage, with the daughter of Hermocrates, then after her suicide his double marriage, on the same day, to the Locrian Doris and the Syracusan Aristomache

(daughter of Hipparinus and sister of Dion). Dionysius the Younger was the son of Doris, who was the first to give birth to a son – to the great disappointment, Plutarch adds, of the majority of Syracusans, 'who would have wanted the native woman to win out over the foreigner'.

9. Archytas of Tarentum was a scholar, philosopher and musical theorist, who seems to have had real political authority at Tarentum, acting as *stratêgos* for seven consecutive years. In *Letter* 7, Plato mentions the ties of friendship he (supposedly) helped establish between Archytas and the Tarentines, and Dionysius.

10. During his exile in Athens, Dion had stayed with Callippus who, as Plutarch is careful to remind us, was not a pupil at the Academy. Callippus had taken part in Dion's expedition but after the death of Heracleides he left to take command of the 'popular party' opposed to Dion. Corrupted by the latter's enemies (he supposedly received twenty talents for his treachery), he instigated a plot against his former friend. Plutarch gives a lengthy account of this plot, ascribing a sacrilegious and quasi-religious dimension to Dion's murder (*Dion* 54–6). Callippus became ruler of Syracuse for a time, but was himself murdered shortly afterwards.

11. On Timoleon, see Sordi 1961 and Talbert 1974.

CHAPTER 14

Reckoning with tyranny: Greek thoughts on Caesar in Cicero's Letters to Atticus in early 49

Ingo Gildenhard

> Die Tyrannis ist eine der ganz unvermeidlichen Formen der griechi-
> schen Staatsidee und in jedem begabten und ehrgeizigen Griechen
> wohnte ein Tyrann und ein Demagog. (Jacob Burckhardt)[1]

Greek history and literature are rife with figures in quest, or in the possession, of omnipotence. The fascination with absolute power in the
hands of an individual is a constant in Greek thought. In the wake of
the intensified Hellenisation of Roman society in the second and first
centuries BC, the figure of the tyrant also became, first, part of Rome's
political discourse and then a dire fact.[2] This chapter reviews one
episode in this complex and fascinating story of acculturation, exploring how Cicero, in his correspondence with Atticus from the winter
and spring of 49, reacted to the outbreak of civil war and Caesar's rise
to power. In these letters he resorts repeatedly to Greek precedents to
cope with and to position (and reposition) himself vis-à-vis the ever-
changing face of Roman *Realpolitik*. In fact, it is possible to trace the
mental trajectory that Cicero underwent in those crucial months,
which took him from shock to fear, from indecision to regret, to,
finally, accommodation, by looking at the themes, figures and quotations that he drew from the Greek discourse on tyranny.

SHOCK

Already at the end of 50, Cicero anticipated that the impending civil
war would lead to tyranny – whatever the outcome.[3] A few weeks later,
the worst-case scenario started to become reality. Caesar had crossed
the Rubicon and was advancing on the capital with lightning speed.

All dates are BC. Translations of Cicero's correspondence with Atticus are those
of Shackleton Bailey 1965–70 (hereafter SB); all others are my own.

Rumours from the theatre of operation in Northern Italy floated to
Rome. A letter from Cicero to Atticus (Cic. *Att.* 7.11.1 = 134 SB;
Formiae (?), 21 January (?) 49) conveys the ensuing confusion in
the capital. Its opening consists of a string of desperate questions and
bits and pieces of disjointed news: 'Pray, what's all this? What is going
on? I am in the dark. "We hold Cingulum, we've lost Ancona, Labienus
has deserted Caesar".' *Labienus discessit a Caesare* – the name of
the offender initiates a change in stylistic registers. Cicero now opts for
a more analytic mode of discourse. In the next few sentences, he steps
back to reflect on the enormity of Caesar's actions. The array of
images and ideas to which he resorts amounts to a creative reckoning
with the individual who is in the process of destroying his world, the
res publica libera:

> utrum de imperatore populi Romani an de Hannibale loquimur? o
> hominem amentem et miserum, qui ne umbram quidem umquam τοῦ
> καλοῦ viderit! atque haec ait omnia facere se dignitatis causa. ubi est
> autem dignitas nisi ubi honestas? honestum igitur habere exercitum
> nullo publico consilio, occupare urbis civium quo facilior sit aditus
> ad patriam, χρεῶν ἀποκοπάς, φυγάδων καθόδους, sescenta alia
> scelera moliri, 'τὴν θεῶν μεγίστην ὥστ' ἔχειν τυραννίδα'?

> Is it a Roman general or Hannibal we are talking of? Deluded
> wretch, with never in his life a glimpse of even the shadow of Good!
> And he says he is doing all this for his honour's sake! Where is
> honour without moral good? And is it good to have an army without
> public authority, to seize Roman towns by way of opening the road
> to the mother city, to plan debt cancellations, recall of exiles, and a
> hundred other villainies, 'all for that first of deities, Sole Power'?

The first salvo in Cicero's assault consists of a thoroughly Roman
device of abuse: the invocation of an *exemplum malum*. Caesar, who
is invading Italy from his strongholds in Gaul, follows in the footsteps
of Hannibal, Rome's most pernicious enemy ever.[4] Then follows a cultural code switch. Cicero's next conceptual manoeuvre is distinctly
Platonic. He situates Caesar in a sort of ontological limbo, at two
removes, that is, from the realm of Plato's ideas. In the end, the
warlord is worse off than the troglodytes of the *Republic*, the ordinary, unenlightened mortals, who, while being consigned to lives in the
shadows, are at least able to grasp the reflections of transcendental
verities.[5] Caesar's actions, Cicero insinuates, are so evil that, unlike
Plato's cave-dwellers, he could not possibly have ever had even an
intimation of the idea of the good.

The allusion to Plato is only the beginning of a barrage of Greek ideas that Cicero marshals to denounce Caesar. Thus he counters Caesar's (Roman) argument that he was justified to march on Rome in defence of his *dignitas* with a philosophical veto.[6] *Dignitas*, he claims, is not to be had without *honestas*. This definition of *dignitas*, which grounds social esteem in a normative ethics, departs from common usage, but allows Cicero to transform Caesar's *contentio dignitatis* into criminal licence. He begins his list of charges with undeniable facts, pointing to Caesar's illegal possession of his army and his invasion of Italy. But his terms of reference soon become decidedly literary. The themes of χρεῶν ἀποκοπάς, the remission of debts, and φυγάδων καθόδους, the return of the banished, belong to a specifically Greek discourse: the discourse of tyranny.

Cicero flags the broader discursive affiliations of his polemic by switching into the Greek. A direct allusion to Plato's *Republic* is possible, though the ominous prospect of remission of debt was a commonplace in anti-populist rhetoric.[7] Appropriately, his chain of Greek associations culminates in an allusion to Euripides' *Phoenissae*: τὴν θεῶν μεγίστην ὥστ᾽ ἔχειν τυραννίδα (*Phoen.* 506). Caesar, Cicero asserts, behaves just like one of those characters in Greek drama who worship (the deified concept of) Absolute Power. His climactic use of a citation from Euripides in the context of politico-philosophical musings is not accidental. Tragedy, in both its Greek and Roman guise, notoriously obsessed about the figure of the tyrant. From Plato onwards, philosophers drew on tragic imagery to endow their argument with special vividness. Suffice it to mention *Republic* 577b1 where the tyrant appears as the theatrical man par excellence, who in public puts on a show but in private turns literally into an emperor without clothes, and [Plato] *Letter* 1, 309d2–310a, where the author enhances the plausibility of his diatribe against Dionysius with choice quotations from tragic scripts.[8]

In all, the Greek themes and citations in Cicero's letter amount to the suggestion that Caesar, in crossing the Rubicon, underwent a metamorphosis. He turned from a fellow-senator and *civis Romanus* into a *monstrum*, an unnatural entity in the Roman order of things, a political criminal made in Greece, that is, who has ceased to act in accordance with the normative expectations that sustained the Roman republic. Far from being driven by any concerns for his constitutional rights, Caesar's actions manifest the perverse and perverted psychology of the tyrant.[9]

FEAR

What is a tyrant? A standard, cerebral definition, taken from *Merriam Webster's Collegiate Dictionary*, s.v., runs: 'an absolute ruler unrestrained by law or constitution'. In the *Gorgias*, Plato brings home in more visceral fashion what tyrannical power entails. Reacting to Socrates' preference for suffering, rather than committing, injustice, Polus enquires whether he would therefore refuse to become a tyrant if the chance offered itself. Socrates replies that this would indeed be the case if, that is, Polus has the same understanding of what it means to be a tyrant as he does. To clarify matters, Polus gives the following definition (*Gorg.* 469c): 'Of course what I mean is what I said just now, namely to be able to do anything in the city that one deems fit – to kill, to exile, to do everything according to one's fancy.'

A tyrant, then, is someone who can do whatever he wants, who has no need to limit the range of his radius of action in any way. For his environment this means radical uncertainty. Under tyranny, anything may happen to you at any time. Put differently, the tyrant is contingency personified. The prospect of random misfortune, ranging from exile to death, is bound to cause fear: it takes a Stoic sage to face with equanimity a social environment that is utterly unpredictable. With the outbreak of civil war and Caesar's military success precisely this sort of contingency re-entered Roman politics. The expectations that had hitherto sustained the universe within which Cicero lived were by the way, or at least put in temporary abeyance. No one knew how the fledgling despot would behave. Atticus at least was filled with dire foreboding; his fear gave rise to a deft neologism, poignant enough to capture in a single phrase the potential of the tyrant to inflict unspeakable outrage on his subjects (*Att.* 7.12.2 = 135 SB; Formiae, 22 January 49):

> As for the man whose Phalarism you dread, I expect nothing but atrocities from him. Neither the suspension of business nor the departure of Senate and magistrates nor the closure of the Treasury will put a brake on him. But as you say, we shall know shortly.

Atticus fears Caesar's Φαλαρισμός – tyrannical behaviour, that is, resembling that of Phalaris, the notorious tyrant of Acragas, who roasted people on a whim in an iron bull, taking pleasure from their 'bellowing' groans of anguish. No anecdote from the rich store of tyrannical lore better illustrates the wickedness and perversity to which absolute power is prone, and in Greek literature Phalaris had long since become a proverbial byword for tyrannical cruelty.[10] However, what is as interesting as Atticus' choice of the Greek notion 'Phalarism' is Cicero's reply. True, he believes that Caesar will act most hideously in *everything* – the *omnia* flags the endless possibilities of outrage at the disposal of the tyrant. Significantly, though, the specific instances of Caesar's transgressive conduct he cites all concern his utter disregard for traditional institutions, not cruelty against individuals. Despite the fact that the war was only a few days old, Cicero might already have guessed that Caesar would ride roughshod over the constitution of the *res publica libera* but spare its representatives.

The inability to predict what Caesar would do recurs as the thematic focus of Cicero's following letter. Once more, he seems mainly preoccupied with Caesar's constitutional arrangements.[11] For the first time, we also get a pointer to the consequences of Caesar's rise to power for traditional religion. Via an allusion to Greek tragedy, Cicero half-jokingly entreats his friend to foretell the future: 'Everyone tells me what *has* happened, from you I expect things to come. "He prophesyeth best . . .".'[12] While the Republic was working, Rome's ruling elite relied on established procedures to communicate with the gods, which revolved around the interpretation of divine signs. These were taken by magistrates of the Republic or qualified experts or, in the case of *prodigia*, had to be accepted as valid by the senate. What the signs meant was a matter for debate which could involve the consultation of various religious bodies (such as the soothsayers or the college of fifteen in charge of the Sibylline books) but had its centre in the senate.[13] Throughout the Republic, those in power frowned upon charismatic individuals (so-called *vates*, or, in Greek, μάντεις) who sidestepped constitutional protocols by claiming direct, privileged access to the supernatural realm and hence the future.[14] With Caesar, the traditional procedures of figuring out the will of the gods were of course by the way – at just the time when the brave new world he brought into being must have increased the desire to preview an ever more uncertain future. Unsurprisingly, once Caesar had firmly established his hold on power, Cicero came to explore alternative means of divining the future, such as Platonic tyrannology.[15]

INDECISION

While Cicero soon developed a good intuition of what he could expect from Caesar (disregard for Republican traditions, but mercy towards his opponents), he still found himself faced with an unenviable dilemma. Simultaneously opposed to the civil war and an arch-Republican, he was unsure of whether he should join the forces of Pompey who was retreating to Brindisi and then to Greece, yielding Rome and Italy to the quickly advancing Caesar, or whether he should stay in Italy, in the secret hope of playing mediator between the two warring parties. His correspondence with Atticus chronicles the musings and mood-swings that he underwent on a well-nigh daily basis. One of the constants in his efforts at analysis of the current political situation and his personal choices are references to the Greek experience with tyranny.

Thus, on 5 February 49, he penned a brief note to Atticus from Capua, where he was supposed to organise the Republican resistance to Caesar, in which he outlined the pros and cons of whether or not he should join Pompey's forces.[16] If Pompey were to make a stand in Italy, he would be willing to die with him (*ego autem in Italia 'καὶ συναποθανεῖν'*). But in case Pompey took flight, Cicero was unsure of what to do. The season (winter), his desire to celebrate a triumph for his military success as governor of Cilicia, and the amateurish conduct of the war by the Republican leaders pushed him towards staying. His friendship with Pompey, the justness of the cause, and the moral disgrace of associating with a tyrant were the factors that predisposed him towards taking flight: *ad fugam hortatur amicitia Gnaei, causa bonorum, turpitudo coniungendi cum tyranno; qui quidem incertum est Phalarimne an Pisistratum sit imitaturus.*[17] That Caesar is a tyrant is beyond dispute – what remains to be seen is whether he turns out to be a member of the species that might just be endured (Pisistratus, an *exemplum bonum* as far as tyrants go, 'the type of a benevolent despot'[18]) or a genuine monster in human form (Phalaris, indisputably an *exemplum malum*). Two Greek names serve Cicero to flesh out the spectrum of possibilities with pithiness and ease.[19]

Cicero, then, found himself in a complicated situation, all the more so since the advice he received from his partner in correspondence seems to have been inconsistent. At first, Atticus counselled Cicero to stick around and see how matters evolved. But in one letter of early February, he must have insisted that, if Pompey abandoned Italy, Cicero too would have to go. Despite his renewed protestation that he would gladly die for Pompey (*ego pro Pompeio libenter emori possum*), Cicero disagrees (*Att.* 8.2.4 = 152 SB; Formiae, 17 February 49):

> For you suggest, somewhat out of keeping with your previous atti-
> tude, that you think I ought even to leave Italy if Pompey does so.
> Now *I* do not think this would be in the public interest or in that of
> my children, nor yet right and honourable. Follows the question (?):
> 'Can you then bear the sight of a tyrant?' As though it mattered
> whether I hear of him or see him, or as though I needed a better prece-
> dent than Socrates, who never put a foot outside the gates when there
> were thirty tyrants in Athens!

Cicero here lists the personal and philosophical considerations that
influence his decision: the advantages or disadvantages that might
accrue to the state and to his children and ethical criteria of a universal nature: what would be *rectum* and *honestum*?[20] He now believes
that he is well advised to stay in Italy on both counts. Atticus' objection that this course of action will inevitably bring him in contact with
a tyrant Cicero counters with a Greek *exemplum*. Just like Socrates
during the reign of the Thirty, he plans to sit out Caesar's time in
power at home.

About a month later, the situation has not significantly changed.
Cicero is still biding his time. In order to distract himself, he uses the
current state of affairs to debate with himself in both Greek and
Latin.[21] His language of choice, however, for setting out his themes
for Atticus is Greek, and each of his theses contains the t-word. All
pinpoint a crucial dilemma Cicero had to ponder. The way in which
he formulates his theses hints at his preference for a course of action
that was decidedly unpopular in the Republican camp. Implied in all
is a choice between unconditional resistance to tyranny and a course
of compromise. Cicero seems to argue for the viability of a position
that would allow him to uphold his commitment to the Republic,
without following in the footsteps of Pompey – despite the fact that
this entails living within the remit of a tyrant.

REGRET

As soon as it had become clear that Cicero was committed to
staying in Italy, regret set in. Immobilised under despotism and
considered a coward and a traitor by the Republican die-hards,
Cicero tried his best to ennoble his wretched terms of existence in
his correspondence with Atticus. Plato came to his aid (although
possibly his perusal of Plato's *Letter* 7 was also a factor in making
him stay). With a learned allusion, Cicero evokes a fateful symmetry
between his own situation and that of the Greek philosopher at the

court of Dionysius of Syracuse (*Att.* 9.10.2 = 177 SB; Formiae, 18 March 49):

> But now my affection comes to the surface, the sense of loss is unbearable, books, writing, philosophy are all to no purpose. Like Plato's bird I gaze out over the sea day and night, longing to take wings.

Tamquam avis illa is a reference to Plato, *Letter* 7. 347e–48a, where the philosopher, kept in town at the tyrant's bidding, likens himself to a bird that gazes out of its cage, longing to fly off and away. Apart from likening Cicero's fate to that of Plato, the intertextual gesture, which is so subtle that it could only have worked if Atticus was thoroughly familiar with the text of reference, was probably also designed as a comment on the relation of the tyrants (Dionysius, Caesar) to their prisoners (Plato, Cicero). Immediately after the bird simile, Plato complained that Dionysius, despite his coercive policies, managed to convey the impression that he and his Athenian guest were the best of comrades ($\dot{\epsilon}\tau\alpha\hat{\imath}\rho o\iota$) – likewise, Caesar, too, tried his best to entertain good relations with the former *pater patriae*. It is this aspect upon which Cicero elaborates a few days later (*Att.* 9.13.4 = 180 SB; Formiae, 23 March 49):

> qua re ita paratus est, ut, etiam si vincere non possit, quo modo tamen vinci ipse possit non videam. ego autem non tam γοητείαν huius timeo quam πειθανάγκην. 'αἱ γὰρ τῶν τυράννων δεήσεις' inquit Πλάτων, 'οἶσθ' ὅτι μεμιγμέναι ἀνάγκαις'.

> So his resources are such that even if he cannot win I do not see how he can be beaten. I personally do not fear his beguilements so much as his *force majeure*. 'For the requests of despots', says Plato, 'have, you know, an element of compulsion.'

Again, we are dealing with an allusion to Plato, *Letter* 7 (329d). In the pretext, Dionysius had realised that the imminent departure of his intellectual guests would discredit him and he accordingly put on a great show of begging, pleading and consoling to change their minds. Plato saw right through the charade but notes dryly: τὰς δὲ τῶν τυράννων δεήσεις ἴσμεν ὅτι μεμειγμέναι ἀνάγκαις εἰσίν . . .: 'As we all know, the requests of tyrants are mixed with compulsions . . .'. Cicero found himself in virtually identical circumstances. In a re-enactment of Dionysius' wooing of Plato, Caesar tried to get into his good graces, hoping, no doubt, that the disempowered consularis would, if he chose to rejoin Rome's daily political life, add a

Republican veneer to his regime. Like Plato, Cicero considered himself immune to the rhetorical dimension of the tyrant's plea, but knew very well that the wishes of those in power combine persuasion with compulsion.[22]

ACCOMMODATION

There is no reason to doubt that, on one level, Cicero's regret at not having gone with Pompey was genuine.[23] Nevertheless, the allusions to Plato also indicate that, on another level, Cicero started to adjust to the new realities of power created by Caesar. Plato's writing offered him the means of staking out a position for himself in the Caesarian universe as well as hope for its imminent end.

The two allusions to Plato's *Letter* 7 in his correspondence with Atticus show that Cicero was (re-)reading this text at the time. The reason is obvious: in Plato's experiences with Dionysius, he detected clear parallels to his own situation. Just like the Athenian philosopher, Cicero found himself under the sway of a despot, who tried to exploit the close affiliations with respected figures for his regime. Plato's letter must have appealed to Cicero on a very existential level: the text is an attempt to justify the decision to remain in contact with a tyrant in the hope of exercising some influence, perhaps even to bring him to abrogate his unlawful position and re-establish the rule of law within constitutional government. Plato's stints in Syracuse offered a model for the man of the word, who courageously tried to put his philosophical principles into political practice by advising those in power.

Cicero fancied a similar role, cherishing the hope that he could act as mediator between the two warring parties. At the same time, one should not overlook that the parallel between him and Plato is not exact, especially in terms of background and standing. Cicero was Caesar's peer, whereas what we find outlined in Plato's letter is the Greek configuration of the philosopher in the entourage of the tyrant. The philosopher and the tyrant are complementary figures in Greek thought, the one endowed with absolute power, the other with the means of coping with it. Complementarity does not necessarily mean antagonism: the philosopher, as someone who insists on speaking truth to power, endows the tyrant with a veneer of legitimacy.[24] Cicero's Platonic self-fashioning thus implies a social formation foreign to Rome and simultaneously condemns and encourages complicity with power.

That Cicero did in fact look to Plato for instruction on how to handle a tyrant emerges clearly from another letter (*Att.* 10.8.6–7 = 199 SB; Cumae, 2 May 49):

> And yet, my dear Atticus, I am also urged in this direction by a sure hope I have in certain auguries, not those of our College inherited from Attus, but Plato's on the subject of tyrants. As I see it, Caesar cannot last very long without falling by his own impulse, even though we are ineffective . . . you will soon see that this reign can hardly last six months.

Attus Navius was the legendary founder of the college of augurs, but his discipline ceased to be of use with Caesar in charge. With the *res publica libera* in ruins, her gods (and the signs they produced) were rendered defunct or meaningless as well.[25] Cicero, at least, preferred Plato's political philosophy as a medium for gazing into the future. What he read in the *Republic* offered hope. In Plato's theory, the tyrant is a creature prone to self-destruction.

EPILOGUE

Even before Caesar's grab for autocracy, the spectre of tyranny had started to loom large in Rome's political imagination. Cicero in particular deemed the tyrant good to think with. In his literary *oeuvre* this Greek figure is a constant point of reference, from the *De Republica* to the *Tusculan Disputations* to the *De Officiis*. If the tyrant featured as the notional other in the 50s, as the antithesis not just of the *princeps* but the very commonwealth,[26] he soon after became a dire reality. From the first news of Caesar's advance to Rome, Cicero assessed his antagonist, the unfolding events and his own role within them with reference to the Greek discourse on (absolute) power. This is not to say that Greek figures of thought were Cicero's one and only conceptual resort. *Exempla* from Roman history, such as Sulla, served both parties to define themselves and others.[27] But the categories provided by Greek thinking on tyranny offered more profound and radical means of reflecting, on a very basic level, what Caesar's actions meant for the Republican constitutions and the citizens of Rome.

Cicero's hope of 49 that the fall of the tyrant was imminent turned out to be misplaced. Caesar achieved a resounding victory over his Republican foes and managed to consolidate his position at the head of the Roman state for the foreseeable future. Politically marginalised, Cicero picked up his indefatigable pen and started to reckon more systematically with Caesar. His late *philosophica*, starting with the *Brutus* and the *Paradoxa Stoicorum*, offer a sustained meditation on what it meant to live under a form of government which he branded as tyranny. This body of work culminated in the *Tusculan Disputations*, a work written in the summer and fall of 45, at the height, that is, of Caesar's power and Cicero's despair. His final reckoning with Caesar came in the *De Officiis*, where he sets out to vindicate the violent elimination of Caesar as legitimate tyrannicide.[28]

NOTES

1. Burckhardt 1902: 166.
2. A particularly influential conduit for the influx of Greek ideas into Rome was the adaptation of tragedy by Latin playwrights. The tragic tyrants in turn inspired orators and historiographers who stigmatised their opponents as literary monsters who had come alive. See Dunkle 1967.
3. *Att.* 7.5.4 = 128 SB (end of 50): *ex victoria cum multa mala tum certe tyrannus exsistet.*
4. The insult recurs at *Phil.* 13.11.25, where Cicero addresses Antonius as *novus Hannibal.* See Opelt 1965: 145.
5. Cicero was fond of playing with images derived from Plato's theory of ideas and the allegory of the cave. See *Orat.* 9–10, *Tusc.* 3.5, *Off.* 3.69. The notion of 'the good' (in Latin: *honestum*) recurs at *Att.* 8.8.2 = 158 SB (Formiae, 23 February 49) with reference to Pompey, whom Cicero also deems blinded to its implications: *fulsisse mihi videbatur* τὸ καλὸν *ad oculos eius* [sc. Pompei], *et exclamasse ille vir qui esse debuit* 'πρὸς ταῦθ' ὅ τι χρὴ καὶ παλαμάσθων / καὶ πάντ' ἐπ' ἐμοὶ τεκταινέσθων· / τὸ γὰρ εὖ μετ' ἐμοῦ.' *at ille tibi* πολλὰ χαίρειν τῷ καλῷ *dicens pergit Brundisium.* See also *Att.* 2.19.1 = 39 SB (Cicero about himself in 59): *me miserum! cur non ades? nihil te profecto praeteriret. ego fortasse* τυφλώττω *et nimium* τῷ καλῷ προσπέπονθα.
6. Cicero omits to mention whom Caesar in fact purported to reinstall at Rome: the *tribuni plebis* who had fled the city. See in general Raaflaub 1974.
7. See Plato *Rep.* 566a with the note ad loc. by Adam 1907.
8. On these passages, see further Wohl 1998.
9. For Caesar's 'Greek' behaviour, see *Off.* 3.82, where Cicero relates the (apocryphal?) anecdote that Caesar was in the habit of citing two lines from Euripides' *Phoenissae* that encapsulated his political principles: εἴπερ γὰρ ἀδικεῖν χρή, τυραννίδος πέρι / κάλλιστον ἀδικεῖν, τἄλλα δ' εὐσεβεῖν χρεών (524–5). Cf. Suet. *Jul.* 30.5.
10. Already Pindar assumed that everybody knew the story of the bull (*Pyth.* 1.95–6). Cicero recounts the anecdote at *Verr.* 4.73 and uses Phalaris as

tyrannical exemplar at *Rep.* 3.31. For a version of events that slightly differs from the orthodox account, see Diod. 9.19.1.

11. *Att.* 7.13.1 = 136 SB (Minturnae, 23 January 49).
12. *Att.* 7.13.4 = 136 SB: *nam acta omnibus nuntiantibus a te exspecto futura*; 'μάντις δ'ἄριστος . . .' The verse continues ὅστις εἰκάζει καλῶς and is most likely Euripidean. See Pease 1923: 369, on *Div.* 2.12 where Cicero translates the line into Latin.
13. North 2000a: 28.
14. North 2000b: 92–107.
15. See below. Further passages that illustrate the devastating impact of Caesarian despotism on the civic theology of the Roman republic are *Fam.* 6.6.8 = 234 SB (October 46, to Caecina) and *Fam.* 6.14.2 = 228 SB (November 46, to Ligarius). See Gildenhard forthcoming a.
16. *Att.* 7.20 = 144 SB.
17. *Att.* 7.20.2 = 144 SB.
18. Shackleton Bailey ad loc. He compares *Ath. Pol.* 16.2.
19. By then Cicero must have been fairly certain which way Caesar was heading, even though Atticus remained unconvinced. If any brutalities should occur, he was sure that they would be caused by Caesar's advisers, not himself. See *Att.* 7.22.1 = 146 SB (Formiae, 9 February 49). At this point, at any rate, the warlord's wooing of the vacillating *consularis* was already in full swing. See e.g. *Att.* 7.21.3 = 145 SB (Cales, 8 February 49): *ipse me Caesar ad pacem hortatur.* Shame replaced fear as the primary emotion against staying in Italy. Cicero managed to overcome it.
20. On the philosophical background of these two terms, see Leonhardt 1995.
21. *Att.* 9.4 = 173 SB. Cf. *Att.* 9.9.1 = 176 SB.
22. Cicero might have picked up the paradoxical notion of πειθανάγκη (compulsion under the disguise of persuasion) from Polybius, who uses it at 21.42.7 and fr. 194.
23. See also *Att.* 10.4.2 = 195 SB (16 April 49), where Cicero fumes that Caesar no longer objects, indeed demands, to be called a tyrant and *Att.* 10.12a.1 = 204 SB (6 May 49), where he wishes Caesar's henchmen to inflict on him some injury, however bad, so he can credibly dissociate himself from the despot.
24. See Haake 2003.
25. The best formulation of this point I know of is an epigram transmitted in the scholia to Persius' second satire: *marmoreo Licinus tumulo iacet, at Cato parvo,/Pompeius nullo: credimus esse deos?*
26. See *Rep.* 3.31: *ergo ubi tyrannus est, ibi . . . dicendum est plane nullam esse rem publicam.*
27. See *Att.* 9.7C.1 = 174C SB (c. 5 March 49, Caesar to Oppius and Cornelius): . . . *L. Sullam, quem imitaturus non sum*; *Att.* 9.10.3 = 177 SB (Formiae, 18 March 49; Cicero quoting Pompey): '*Sulla potuit, ego non potero?*' Further references to Sulla occur at *Att.* 9.11.3 = 178 SB (Formiae,

20 March 49); *Att.* 9.14.2 = 182 SB (Formiae, 24 or 25 March 49); and *Att.* 9.15.2 = 183 SB (Formiae, 25 March 49). On Sulla, see Thein, Chapter 17 in this volume.

28. For the argument and bibliography, see Gildenhard forthcoming b and (for the *De Officiis*) Gildenhard forthcoming c.

PART IV

The limits of tyranny

CHAPTER 15

The violence of the Thirty Tyrants

Andrew Wolpert

The Thirty carried out a systematic campaign of political murder unparalleled in the history of classical Athens. Although it may not be surprising that the oligarchs remained in power for such a brief period of time, it is difficult to understand how the Thirty thought that they could maintain their grip on Athens through such means. What led the Thirty onto a path of violence until they eventually set out against Eleusis to execute as many of its inhabitants as they could apprehend? What did the Thirty hope to accomplish from such despotism? These questions are hard to answer in part because the regime lasted less than a year, and therefore it is difficult to determine what their long-range goals were. So too, it is difficult for us to reconstruct the oligarchs' aims since the Athenians subsequently attributed motives to them that served the political necessity of post-civil-war Athens, and these motives were mapped onto the historical narratives of the oligarchy. Although most ancient testimony emphasises how lawlessness, greed and licentiousness caused the Thirty to embark on a reign of terror, our sources also stress how the Thirty became more and more violent as opposition intensified. These explanations are not mutually exclusive, and there is certainly a significant degree of truth to both of them. The oligarchs personally benefited from the atrocities that they committed, and in the process, they caused more opposition that they had to confront. Still, these explanations are unsatisfactory because they imply that the violence could have been avoided if only the oligarchs and their supporters had not been morally bankrupt, or if the regime had not sparked so much opposition. Elsewhere I have suggested that we can better understand the rule of the Thirty once we recognise that such violence was systemic to the regime. Violence was a necessary and integral part of their rule that was inevitable once the Thirty plotted to overthrow the democracy and replace it with a narrow oligarchy.[1] Here, I will further expand on this notion by drawing upon modern political theories on authoritarian regimes. The Thirty used violence, repression and terror to reconfigure the political landscape of Athens from a broad-participatory democracy to a narrow oligarchy. The violence of the Thirty was not irrational, senseless or pathological; rather it was, in a perverse sense, constructive. The Thirty could only build up their regime by tearing down the democracy. Violence provided them the means of doing so. But first, it is necessary to examine the explanations that are prevalent in our sources.

In his speech against Eratosthenes Lysias vividly describes how far the Thirty were willing to go to enrich themselves. With the city bankrupt from the war, the Thirty were in desperate need for cash to maintain their control of Athens. Theognis and Peison, therefore, proposed that they finance their expenses from the arrest of ten metics and that they intentionally select two poor metics so that they could claim that the men were arrested because of their opposition to the government, and not because the Thirty wanted to confiscate their property. This plan met with wide approval among the Thirty, who, according to Lysias, did not hesitate to commit murder for the sake of money. Sharing responsibility for the arrests, the Thirty then set out against the metics. A group of them were chosen to go to Lysias' home where they found him entertaining guests. The guests were driven away, and Lysias was placed in Peison's custody while the rest went to Lysias' workshop. In their absence, Lysias asked Peison if he would accept a bribe, and Peison replied that the sum would need to be substantial. Lysias offered Peison a silver talent provided that he swear an oath, and Peison agreed. The oath, however, did not deter Peison from seizing the entire contents of a chest, which included three silver talents, four hundred Cyzicene staters, one hundred Persian darics and four silver cups. Lysias pleaded with Peison to leave him some money for travelling, to which Peison curtly replied that Lysias was lucky to be alive (5–11). As Lysias and Peison left the house, Melobius and Mnesitheides came upon them and instructed Peison to continue with his confiscations while they took Lysias to Damnippus' house where Theognis was guarding some others. Lysias beseeched Damnippus to help him escape. Damnippus agreed and offered money to Theognis. Fearing that Theognis might not accept the bribe, Lysias fled the house while Damnippus and Theognis were discussing terms, and he made it safely out of Athens (12–16). Lysias' brother, Polemarchus, was not so fortunate. Eratosthenes seized Polemarchus in the streets and took him immediately to prison where he was later forced to drink hemlock. While Polemarchus was imprisoned, Melobius entered his home and had the indecency not only to appear in the presence of

Polemarchus' wife, but also to snatch earrings that she happened to be wearing, though the jewellery was of only modest value compared to the wealth that had already been seized (16–19).[2] Lysias' message to the jury is unmistakable: the oligarchs were so greedy for money that they were willing to violate all laws, customs and rights no matter how longstanding or universally held they might be among the Greeks. Lysias also emphasises that the oligarchs were united behind the proposal of Theognis and Peison. None of the Thirty objected when it was first proposed, and all helped carry it out, a point which he drives home by giving us the names of the five oligarchs who were involved in his and his brother's arrests. The manner in which they carried out the arrests is also striking. They acted without hesitation, without reluctance and without any regret, as though their actions were mundane.

Metics were, undoubtedly, easy targets, but the Thirty also went after wealthy Athenians. In Lysias 18, the nephew of Nicias asserted that the Spartans began to sympathise with the democratic exiles when they saw that the Thirty were harming not the worst, but those Athenians who ought to have been honoured for their birth, wealth, and other fine qualities. The speaker implied that Thirty targeted these men because of such attributes. They were eliminated in part because they could have created an effective base of opposition thanks to their social standing and in part because the Thirty coveted their wealth (cf. Lys. 34.4). So too litigants insisted that the Thirty encouraged others to plot against the wealthy, so that it was a time when those who never before committed crimes were tempted to do so.[3] As the speaker of Isocrates 21 declared, 'It was worse at that time to be wealthy than to harm others; for the latter were taking the possessions of others while the former were deprived of their own' (12).

The Attic orators, as has been frequently noted, are not the most reliable sources for political events, and there are certainly many instances when speakers misrepresented the civil war.[4] However, Xenophon, the *Ath. Pol.* and Diodorus Siculus all support this portrayal of the oligarchs as greedy and avaricious.[5] Xenophon stands out in particular because his exile from Athens, his association with Sparta and his possible involvement in the rule of the Thirty made him that much more likely to give a sympathetic account of the oligarchy. And yet he is perhaps as critical of the Thirty as Lysias, if not more so. Four times, Xenophon interrupts his narrative of the civil war to explain that the Thirty eliminated opposition so that they could do as they pleased. Once in power, they requested a Spartan garrison from Lysander. Although they told the Spartans that the garrison was needed to remove the *ponêroi*, Xenophon explains that the Thirty requested the garrison so that they could rule the city however they wanted (*Hell*. 2.3.13). Once Callibius arrived in Athens to serve as harmost, the Thirty courted him so that he would approve of all that they wanted to do (*Hell*. 2.3.14). They then killed any Athenian who might be powerful enough to oppose them. Next, they reviewed all the Athenians in the city and took away the weapons of those who were not on the roll of the Three Thousand. Free to do whatever they wanted, the Thirty killed many either because of personal enmity or to obtain their property (*Hell*. 2.3.20–21). And finally, the execution of Theramenes permitted the Thirty to rule as tyrants without fear (*Hell*. 2.4.1). Waiting to describe the Thirty as tyrannical until the trial of Theramenes, Xenophon presents his death as their last obstacle and marks the last period of their rule as a time of limitless licentiousness. With Theramenes out of the way, the Thirty evicted from Athens all who were not on the roll of the Three Thousand, so that they and their friends could have the property of the disenfranchised. In Xenophon, it was only after the expulsion of the disenfranchised that Thrasybulus seized Phyle, followed by the attack on Eleusis. And while Xenophon begins his account of the arrests of the Eleusinians by saying that the Thirty wanted to secure a place for retreat, he concludes it by saying, 'These measures were pleasing to those citizens whose thought only about their own gain' (*Hell*. 2.4.10). So even in his account of Eleusis, greed was a driving force for the actions of the Thirty.

As Dillery has pointed out, the Thirty serve in Xenophon as a 'paradigm of the bad community that fails'.[6] Step by step, they methodically tightened their grip on Athens, committing greater and greater crimes until they were surrounded by enemies on all sides. First they killed democratic leaders, next they disarmed all who were disenfranchised and finally they executed Theramenes, even though he was a fellow oligarch. It was the brutality of the Thirty which accelerated opposition and not vice versa. Xenophon can be accused of overly simplifying the motives of the oligarchs, rendering them mere caricatures, in order to support this paradigm of the bad community.[7] But although his portrayal of the Thirty lacks subtlety, his narrative of their rule offers a complex and even sophisticated treatment on the nature of power. For Xenophon, it was because the Thirty could not control their desires and because their desires grew only greater as they tightened their grip, that opposition to their rule continued to grow as well as their own fear of opposition.[8] They were, as a result, forced to widen their net until they eventually searched for and found enemies from within their own ranks. Thus, their rule became more unstable even as their ability to assert their power grew stronger. Lack of restraint allowed the Thirty to seize control of Athens and to do as they wished to the city and its inhabitants, but without restraint they could not keep their power. So, for Xenophon, the lesson of the Thirty is that true power requires self-restraint.

Balot infers from the ancient testimony that the Thirty were 'acting out the ideas and ideals of the discourse on greed' that had been developed in previous decades.[9] Rejecting conventional morality, Critias and his associates seized power to pursue their 'acquisitive desires'. While this explanation draws attention to important questions previously overlooked, it under-theorises the political goals of the Thirty. None of the sources suggests that principles or ideals caused the Thirty to steal from their fellow citizens; rather they engaged in these crimes because of a lack of principles and lack of character. They embarked upon a campaign of lawlessness, licentiousness and depravity because they were utterly corrupt, and through their actions they proved that they, and not their victims, were the true *ponêroi*. Greed was merely one manifestation of their moral bankruptcy. The speaker of Isocrates 20, for example, accused Lochites of having the same character as the oligarchs, who were willing to become the slaves of the enemy in order to commit *hybris* against their fellow citizens. And although the speaker conceded that Lochites was too young to have participated in the oligarchy, he warned the jury that conspirators might again take control of Athens unless they punished the *ponêroi* (10–11). But why was Lochites on trial? What offence did he commit that made him the same as the Thirty? It was not theft, but battery. According to the speaker, Lochites' social position and wealth made him hybristic so that he would not adhere to the laws of Athens, which is how Lochites resembled the Thirty. If our sources emphasise the greed of the Thirty, it is not because they believed that greed was the oligarchs' primary motive. Rather, the Athenians thought that the wealthy were least likely to violate the laws for the sake of financial gain since they had sufficient resources to support themselves and their families.[10] It was, therefore, particularly shocking and disturbing that the Thirty killed for the sake of wealth. Thus the ancient testimony recounts the greed of the Thirty in order to illustrate their utter depravity. From this perspective, then, the violence of the Thirty was senseless, even pathological.[11] It was caused by a group of men who lacked self-restraint because they respected neither divine law nor human conventions. They were guided not by a philosophy or doctrine of greed, but by an utter lack of principles and a complete lack of control. As a result, they could never be reformed nor ever see the errors of their ways. They could only be stopped if confronted by a stronger force, which brings us to the second explanation for the violence.

Given the sheer number of citizens and metics executed by the Thirty, it was easy for the Athenians to conclude that the oligarchy collapsed under the weight of wide-scale opposition. As the candidate of Lysias 25 said:

> When you heard that the men of the city were in agreement, you had little hope of return since you considered our harmony to be the greatest obstacle to you in your exile. But when you learned that the Three Thousand were divided, the rest of the citizens had been banished from the city, the Thirty were quarrelling, and more feared on your behalf than were fighting against you, then you expected to return and punish your enemies. (21–2)

Even litigants who spoke against the men of the city supported such an image of dissent (e.g. Lys. 26.17–20). In his speech against Eratosthenes, Lysias claimed that the Ten were elected with the mandate to reconcile with the democratic resistance.[12] Speakers, however, failed to provide concrete evidence of such dissent. We hear of no specific acts of opposition carried out by the Three Thousand, except for the expulsion of the Thirty. But once in power, the Ten did not begin negotiations, but requested more troops from Sparta to use in their war against the exiles. Rather than believe that the Ten duped the Three Thousand, it is more reasonable to conclude that the men of the city continued the war against the exiles, if not because they approved of the oligarchy, then because they feared reprisals should the exiles return to Athens.[13] Critias, after all, had the Three Thousand condemn the Eleusinians precisely so that the men of the city would be forced to remain committed to the oligarchy.

Other apologetic narratives are more controversial, such as the dating of the Spartan garrison. Xenophon places the arrival of the Spartan garrison before the disarming of the disenfranchised, after which followed the execution of Theramenes and the democratic seizure of Phyle (*Hell.* 2.3.14, 20, 4.1–2). In the *Ath. Pol.*, the order is reversed. The democratic seizure of Phyle appears first, followed by the execution of Theramenes, then the disarming of the disenfranchised and finally the arrival of the Spartan garrison (37.1–2).[14] The effect of this chronological discrepancy is striking. In the *Ath. Pol.*, the Spartan garrison was installed, not so that the Thirty could carry out a campaign of terror, but in response to Thrasybulus. The Thirty eliminated Theramenes and disarmed the disenfranchised not so that they could rule as tyrants, but because they feared the success of the democratic exiles and needed to take necessary precautions. The *Ath. Pol.*'s sequence of events also serves to remove Theramenes from the Thirty before they disarmed the disenfranchised and committed some of their more notorious actions.[15]

But, for our purposes, it is most interesting that the *Ath. Pol.*'s version is clearly incorrect. The Thirty could only have carried out their violent policies with the military assistance that Sparta provided, and thus the garrison must have been installed early in the regime.[16] The *Ath. Pol.*'s mistake, however, was not innocent; rather it was made for ideological and political reasons. Immediately after the civil war, some Athenians attempted to rehabilitate Theramenes in order to justify their own involvement in the rule of the Thirty, as Lysias' speech against Eratosthenes shows. The positive depictions of Theramenes which appear in Xenophon, the Theramenes papyrus, the *Ath. Pol.* and Diodorus, though differing widely in content and form, must also ultimately derive from the political turmoil of post-civil-war Athens and the controversies that the reconciliation sparked.[17] The *Ath. Pol.* offers perhaps the most sympathetic account of the Thirty. Since it presents much of the violence as a response to the growing opposition, the *Ath. Pol.* makes it easier for others to take the next step and blame the opposition for the violence.[18] The *Ath. Pol.* does not redeem the Thirty, but it makes the violence more understandable.

Of course, none of our sources relies on a single explanation for the violence of the Thirty. Just as Lysias mentions that violence accelerated because of opposition, so the *Ath. Pol.* draws our attention to the greed of the Thirty. They differ primarily in emphasis, and I have focused on the differences in order to explore the ideological significance of their explanations. Still, we must bear in mind that there was much agreement. While there was some debate over Theramenes, the sources agree about Critias and the moral bankruptcy of the Thirty. Perhaps the greatest difficulty in the narratives of the civil war lies not with the political agenda of the sources nor the emphasis that they place on the Thirty's motives, but with their lack of an explicit theoretical framework to explain the nature of the oligarchic regime. Modern political theories on authoritarian regimes can help us understand the violence of the Thirty in two ways.

First, opposition and repression of opposition are inevitable in such polities. As Dahl explains, dissent and disagreement over political preferences exists in any form of government. Those governments which permit only a narrow group to set policy must place the most severe limits on expression, and as a result, they create a self-fulfilling prophecy:

> Since all opposition is potentially dangerous, no distinction can be made between acceptable and unacceptable opposition, between loyal and disloyal opposition, between opposition that is protected and opposition that must be repressed. Yet if all oppositions are treated as dangerous and subject to repression, opposition that would be loyal if it were tolerated becomes disloyal because it is not tolerated. Since all opposition is likely to be disloyal, all opposition must be repressed.[19]

Relying primarily on modern theories about political representation and the role of political parties, unions and the press in the industrial world, Dahl considers authoritarian and totalitarian regimes unstable because they prohibit the expression of opposition.

For the ancient Greeks, political legitimacy depended on a perceived sense of consensus among the citizen body. Greek writers could speak of 'the Athenians' or of 'the Corinthians' when referring to actions carried out on behalf of those cities because supreme power was thought to reside in the citizens regardless of whether the *polis* was a democracy or an oligarchy.[20] The Thirty, however, could not claim to embody the will of the entire community. In fact, it is imprecise and even somewhat misleading to label their regime merely an oligarchy. The Thirty more closely resembled the *dynasteia* which, as described by the Thebans in the debate over the fate of Plataea, was a 'system furthest removed from law and restraint but closest to a tyrant' (trans. Ostwald), and therefore fundamentally different from oligarchy.[21] The Thirty had usurped power and restricted participation so narrowly that the regime lacked the legitimacy which most contemporary democracies and oligarchies could claim. As a result, the Thirty could not tolerate opposition, and anyone who disagreed with the oligarchs or who attempted to reform the oligarchy, whether from within or without, was a threat. Hence the debate between Theramenes and Critias in Xenophon focuses on questions concerning loyalty and treachery (*Hell.* 2.3.9–56).[22] Should the Thirty have yielded to Theramenes' suggestions, the regime would have had to extend participation, and then it would have suffered the same fate as the Four Hundred. But by killing Theramenes, the Thirty were forced to become more repressive and create more opposition. Thus it is not the case that repression caused opposition or vice versa; rather the Thirty were responsible for both repression and opposition. And it was only a matter of time until their rule came to an end.

Second, modern political theories show that violence in authoritarian regimes has a constitutive function. Violence serves not only to eliminate opposition and potential opposition, but also to recondition the population so that it accepts its new role as political subjects.[23] Given that Athens was a broad-participatory democracy and that most citizens participated fairly regularly in politics, the shift to the narrow oligarchic regime of the Thirty necessitated a well-planned campaign of terror. They removed the visible markers of the democracy from the landscape of Athens by tearing down the laws of Ephialtes, and they mocked democratic practices by conducting trials where votes were cast in full view. Property was confiscated to enrich the oligarchs and to pay for the expenses of the regime. But confiscations and banishments also served as a way for the Thirty to assert that the disenfranchised were no longer citizens. It was not enough to exclude the disenfranchised from politics. The Thirty had to take away from them rights that were reserved for citizens. If the Thirty, as many believe, sought to model their government after Sparta, Athens could not have been 'laconized without violence'.[24] And their government would never have been stable given the number of Athenians who had to be disenfranchised for Athens to become a second Sparta. Perhaps, the Thirty had such an ambitious plan, but it was not the reason for the acceleration of violence. Once they seized power, violence was needed both to destroy the democracy and to construct their regime.

The constitutive function of violence also helps us understand why so few Athenians joined Thrasybulus at Phyle. Certainly, the odds against the democratic resistance were great. The democrats had few resources while the oligarchs had the cavalry and the Spartan garrison to assist them. But the Athenians had in the past been willing to take on enormous risks. They had abandoned the city during the Persian Wars. Then during the Peloponnesian War, they abandoned their fields and allowed the Spartans to ravage their crops without a fight, and even after numerous setbacks, they continued to hold out against Sparta. So it is also doubtful that the Athenians failed to rally behind the exiles simply because of exhaustion from the many years of fighting the Peloponnesian War. The Thirty had killed too many

Athenians for their relatives just to give up. Instead, the Thirty had successfully reconditioned many Athenians, at least temporarily, through their acts of terror and repression so that few had the wherewithal to resist the oligarchs. Perhaps we should not be surprised that the Thirty faced little opposition, but it was still a particularly embarrassing fact, which the Athenians had to confront after the democracy was restored.

The ancient testimony draws our attention to the repression and opposition that occurred during the rule of the Thirty, focusing on the character of the oligarchs and the actions of their opponents. The sources vary in their emphasis, with some giving more attention to the moral bankruptcy of the Thirty and others to the oligarchs' efforts to crush the opposition. They teach a lesson of how the Thirty – because of their moral faults, because of their abuse of power, because of the opposition that they sparked – turned to violence, which ultimately doomed them. This explanation is partially correct, but it is incomplete since it renders the brutality exterior to the regime and fails to address the structural nature of the violence embedded within the political system that the Thirty created. Violence was a necessary condition for the rule of the Thirty. It both made the regime possible and caused its demise. It both emanated from the oligarchs and was ingrained within the regime itself. The Thirty were the utter villains described in the sources, but the conduct of most of them prior to the civil war could not have prepared the Athenians for what was to come. The associates of Critias were not doomed to become members of the Thirty nor were they simply pathological criminals; rather they chose to embark upon a path from which they could not turn back.

NOTES

1. Wolpert 2002.
2. Wooten 1988; Borthwick 1990; Bons 1993.
3. Lys. 7.27; Isoc. 18.17; 21.3, 7.
4. For problems of interpreting Attic oratory, see Dover 1974: 8–24; Ober 1989: 43–9; Todd 1990; Hunter 1994: 5–7. For selective remembering of the civil war, see Wolpert 2002.
5. See Krentz 1982: 80–1; Balot 2001: 219–25.
6. Dillery 1995: 147.
7. Krentz 1982: 140; Ostwald 1986: 483; Dillery 1995: 143–4.
8. Cf. Balot 2001: 224–5, 232–3.
9. Balot 2001: 223.

10. For bribery and corruption, see Harvey 1985; Taylor 2001a, 2001b.
11. Diodorus describes the Thirty as driven by *aponoia* (14.5.b).
12. Lys. 12.54–5, 58; cf. *Ath. Pol.* 38.1; Diod. 14.33.5.
13. Cloché 1915: 71–6; Krentz 1982: 93.
14. Adeleye 1976.
15. Rhodes 1981: 422: 'The effect of *A.P.*'s distortion (lost in his own account, which does not admit that Theramenes was one of the Thirty) is that most of the outrages of the Thirty are placed after Theramenes' death, and he therefore cannot be made to share the blame for them.'
16. Cloché 1915: 4–7; Hignett 1952: 384–9; Rhodes 1981: 410–22; Munn 2000: 413 n. 15. Contra: Krentz 1982: 131–51; Ostwald 1986: 481–3.
17. e.g. Xen. *Hell.* 2.3.56; *Ath. Pol.* 28.5, 32.2; Diod. 13.38.2, 42.2, 14.5.4. For the Theramenes papyrus, see Merkelbach and Youtie 1968; Henrichs 1968; Andrewes 1970; Engels 1993.
18. Krentz concludes, 'If Thrasybulus had not acted, one suspects that far, far fewer than 1,500 would have died' (1982: 130).
19. Dahl 1973: 13.
20. Brock and Hodkinson 2000: 11.
21. Thuc. 3.62.3. See Ostwald 2000: 25–6.
22. See Gray 1989: 94–9.
23. Corradi 1982; O'Donnell 1986; Perelli 1994.
24. Ostwald 1986: 487.

CHAPTER 16

The politics of Persian autocracy, 424–334 BC

Stephen Ruzicka

Thanks to Greek interest and involvement in Persian affairs and Persian involvement in Greek affairs during the fourth century BC, we know a good deal about various fourth-century Persian military enterprises and diplomatic activities. From time to time we hear also about revolts by leading Persian officials. This is important because it reminds us that Persian politics are always there whether we see them in our sources or not, and we may suspect they have a bearing on all the other developments we are trying to reconstruct.

I want to ask if there is a story of Persian politics in the fourth century BC that can be reconstructed. If so, how does it illuminate other events? Another way to put this is to ask: does Persian autocracy have a history? More specifically, does it have a distinctive fourth-century history? We may be encouraged that we are dealing only with the equivalent of two and a half kingships in the fourth century; subtract the ephemeral reign of Arses/Artaxerxes IV (338–337) and the brief, beleaguered reign of Darius III (336–331), and we are down to just two – those of Artaxerxes II (404–359) and his son Artaxerxes III (359–338). We may be discouraged, however, by the paucity and the episodic nature of our sources. Let us see.

The revolt of Cyrus the Younger might be a good place to start if we are looking for the beginning of a fourth-century story. His *anabasis* took place in 401, right on the eve of the fourth century BC and at the beginning of the reign of Artaxerxes II, the king who ruled for nearly half of the century. I think, however, that we may be able to see the basic elements of a useful narrative if we go further back to the previous succession struggle – the one which began in 424 with the death of Artaxerxes I.

Ctesias (44–56) documents the confusion and conflict of the succession struggle, and there are no obvious reasons to doubt his account here.[1] By his Persian wife, Artaxerxes had one son, Xerxes, who

followed him as king (Xerxes II) in 424. By Babylonian and other con-
cubines, Artaxerxes had seventeen additional sons. Such sons might
hold all manner of high positions, but their parentage normally dis-
qualified them from consideration as potential successors. However,
Xerxes had been king for only forty-five days when one of his 'illegitimate' half-brothers, Sogdianos, with the connivance of a couple of
court officials, murdered him and claimed the kingship (evidently at
Susa). This initiated a broad and prolonged struggle. Sogdianos had
no better claim than any other of Artaxerxes' 'illegitimate' sons, and,
as it turned out, not much backing. Ochus, another of the 'illegitimate'
sons, got the support of troops at Babylon and (perhaps because of
this) the backing of such powerful figures as Arsames, satrap of Egypt,
grandson of Darius, and apparently the senior Achaemenid, and the
Paphlagonian eunuch Artoxares, an intimate of Artaxerxes I. Wrongly
expecting clemency and lacking military support, Sogdianos yielded to
Ochus, who had troops. By February 423 Ochus was recognised as
king, employing the throne name Darius (II). But Darius II then faced
a challenge from his own full brother Arsites, based in Syria. Darius'
forces lost twice to Arsites' commander Artyphius, son of Megabyzus,
until Darius' general bribed away Arsites' Greek mercenaries and
seized Arsites and Artyphius.

Matters remained fluid. Because there was no solid basis for a
claim to the kingship beyond power itself and there remained fourteen coequal offspring of Artaxerxes I, as power might seem to move,
so might the support of former allies. This is well illustrated by the
affair of Teritouchmes, son of Hydarnes, and his family. In search of
allies at an early date, Darius II had contracted an important marriage
connection to the 'house of Hydarnes', giving his daughter Amestris
and the satrapy of Hyrcania to Hydarnes and marrying his son
Arsaces (the later Artaxerxes II) to Hydarnes' daughter Stateira – all
pointing to a solid, mutually beneficial political merger. Subsequently,
however, as Ctesias reports, after Hydarnes had died and his son
Teritouchmes became satrap of Hyrcania, Teritouchmes came to hate
Amestris, ended up putting her in a sack, and with 300 of his men
stabbed her to death. Ctesias then follows Darius' retaliation: the execution of Teritouchmes and most of his relatives (not including
Stateira, who was spared because of Arsaces' pleas) (Ctes. 53–56).
What we clearly have here behind the gory details is evidence of a
major defection well after the original stage of the succession struggle on the part of the family of important early supporters of Ochus
and allies of that family. Artoxares, an original backer of Darius, also

turned against him at some point, according to Ctesias (53), and sought the throne for himself.

We are by this time down to 418 at least,[2] and if Ctesias is trustworthy regarding Artoxares, then Artoxares' ambition reflects the perception that even six years or so after his original recognition as king Darius II was vulnerable. The problem was that there was no other Xerxes II – son of the king and a Persian mother – and the passage of time had not, it appears, made Darius II's claim unassailable. This probably explains why in the early 410s Darius II dispatched a sizable army with three commanders, including Tissaphernes, to the west to seize Pissuthnes, satrap of Lydia and a grandson of Darius I, who from the relative security of Sardis had evidently withheld recognition of Ochus/Darius II as king. Victory came once again as a result of bribing away Greek mercenaries (Ctesias 52; Thuc. 8.26–8).

The usual succession mess, we might observe, with just a few more details in this case, thanks to Ctesias' inside information. Perhaps. But this succession struggle was more long-lasting than normal. It involved, it appears, a greater number of authentic contenders, and, probably, as the number of losers piled up, a greater number of exterminated families. (Ctesias does not furnish all such details, but we can be sure that each contestant had ranked behind him more supporters than just the leading figures Ctesias names; for example, Darius' retaliation certainly targeted not just Teritouchmes and various family members but also the 300 men and their relatives who had joined with Teritouchmes.) Ochus' choice of the throne name Darius was surely calculated to conjure up the memory of kingship interrupted, refounded, and freshly legitimised.[3] Facing the situation in a straightforward way, Ochus/Darius said in effect, 'Yes, I am a new sort of king, but remember the last one (Darius I).' And if people did not remember, then early in his reign Darius II commissioned the copying on papyrus and in Aramaic of Darius I's Bisitun inscription, Darius' boasting account of his succession, including his victories over 'liar-kings' (DB 52–5).[4]

While Ochus as Darius II did link himself to Darius I for various reasons, there was a very big difference between the two. Darius II had no group of powerful families who worked with and for him on a sustained basis. There were no 'Seven Families' this time. Darius II's original supporters were men of Artaxerxes' era, and when they died (Hydarnes, Arsames) or turned against him (Artoxares), Darius was relatively isolated. He had won the succession struggle, or at least all the conflicts so far, but he had not gained much renown in the process.

There had been no great military victories, just successful briberies and captures through false promises. He reached out early for important alliances – the Hydarnes marriages – but what he ultimately got from this was a heightened sense of suspicion and mistrust. Darius II and Parysatis may have hoped to produce a throng of offspring who might reliably staff important posts, but childhood deaths took away all but three sons (Ctes. 49). In the absence of trust (blood- or favour-based), Darius as ruler seems to have employed what might be called the politics of insecurity – playing officials off against each other (Pharnabazus and Tissaphernes in Anatolia), using multiple commanders in the same enterprise (Tissaphernes, Spithridates and Parmises sent to suppress Pissuthnes), perhaps amplifying use of the 'King's Eye' (Artasyras).[5]

The succession troubles of this reign had repercussions well beyond the circle of Persian families drawn into the succession struggle. We can see a chain of events starting now in connection with the succession struggle and leading ultimately to the big problems of the fourth century, the independence of Egypt in particular and the various Spartan and Athenian aggressions. The suppression of Pissuthnes, the satrap of Lydia, left his son Amorges a rebel in western Anatolia, and Athenian cooperation with Amorges at the time of the Sicilian expedition turned Darius against Athens, determining him to restore imperial authority over the Anatolian Greek cities left alone since 449 (Thuc. 8.54.3; Andoc. 3.29).[6] This drew the Spartans into Persian affairs as the satraps Tissaphernes and Pharnabazus sought assistance in accomplishing this. Revived Athenian hostility toward Persia and evidence of a lack of royal aggressiveness may have encouraged always restive Libyan dynasts in the Egyptian Delta – including descendants of the mid-century rebels – to move into active revolt by striking Persian estates, including those of Arsames in the Delta in 410.[7]

It may have been this Egyptian development which persuaded Darius to push for real victory in the west by providing adequate and sustained support for Sparta and to send one of the two or so figures he may have trusted or had to trust, his younger son Cyrus, to accomplish this (though here too Darius used a watchdog in the form of Tissaphernes) (Xen. *Hell.* 1.4.3; *Anab.* 1.9.7). Here too Darius may have been employing the politics of insecurity to encourage zealous effort, with Cyrus and Arsaces as competitors and the implied prize being the promise of succession.

Cyrus arrived in Anatolia in 408/7 with an enormous, supersatrapal command. Cyrus seems right from the beginning to have aimed at kingship. He executed two relatives for not employing the appropriate royal greeting gestures (Xen. *Hell.* 2.1.8), and when Darius died in 404, although Cyrus' older brother Arsaces had been designated as successor, Cyrus (who had been summoned back east) seems to have planned to assert himself as king at Pasargadae (the scene of burial and coronation ceremonies) in the interval of mourning before the next reign officially began. He may have planned to seize control of Darius' body and direct funeral procedures as custom required of the dead king's successor, but he was prevented from doing so and then nearly executed by his brother before managing to return to western Anatolia (Xen. *Anab.* 1.1.3; Ctes. 57; Plut. *Artox.* 3.1–5). This was no resolution, and, despite subsequent signs of compliance by Cyrus, the issue of the succession was still really up in the air. The question after Darius' death was why anyone should support Cyrus, a mere youth (probably in his early twenties at this time), instead of his much older, experienced brother.

Cyrus himself seems to have sought now as previously to answer this question by modelling in his person and policies a distinct mode of autocracy that contrasted at virtually every point with his father's practices and what (without any time to discover evidence to the contrary) everyone might expect would be Artaxerxes' practices. Cyrus built up his following on the basis of close personal ties, using charm, friendship, extravagant generosity and expressions of trust to win over capable men. The descriptions of his behaviour leave little doubt about the effort to display a distinct alternative to the ruling style of Darius II. For example, according to Xenophon (*Anab.*1.9.18), 'whenever he saw that a man was a skilful and just administrator, not only organizing well the country over which he ruled, but producing revenues, he would never deprive such a man of territory, but would always give him more besides.' The examples of gift-giving spill out endlessly (see *Anab.* 1.9.7–18). Cyrus also seems to have been at pains to establish a reputation for clemency, forgiving defections (such as those of the repeated offender Orontas), and restoring defectors to table companionship (Xen. *Anab.* 1.6.6). Cyrus was, of course, too young to employ marriage alliances (or even the promise of such), but he was the source of unflagging solicitude and largesse, both of which communicated his great personal concern for others – his openness as opposed to isolation. Set next to the stingy and precautionary practices of Darius, Cyrus' many generous practices seemed to promise a return to the favour allocation customs of the past and to a degree of predictability where merit was applauded and rewarded.

There were undoubtedly many notable Persians who had a vested interest in the Darius-Artaxerxes model. Tissaphernes and Pharnabazus, for example, had built their careers on it. But Cyrus gained a great number of very devoted supporters, and the attraction of his model seems to have extended throughout the empire, well beyond the scope of his immediate contacts in western Anatolia. Plutarch reports that Cyrus depended on those of the interior as much as those of his own coastal region when he began the war against Artaxerxes (*Artox.* 6.2). Xenophon is explicit about the motivation of supporters:

> many went over from the king to Cyrus after the two had become enemies (these being, moreover, the men who were most highly regarded by the king), because they thought if they were deserving, they would gain a worthier [more fitting] reward with Cyrus than with the king. (*Anab.* 1.9.29)

The battle of Cunaxa, where Cyrus perished in 401 in battle with Artaxerxes, decided the succession once and for all. But it did not decide what model of autocracy would prevail. Artaxerxes II fostered and jealously guarded the story that he had been the Cyrus-killer, that he had delivered the fatal blow (putting to death other men who had been responsible and were not keeping their mouths shut) (Plut. *Artox.* 16.1–4). He also sealed the claim of victory by arresting and executing Cyrus' Greek mercenary commanders (Xen. *Anab.* 2.5.31–6.1). The suppression of Greek mercenary commanders (albeit through bribery rather than execution) had decided Darius II's victories over his brother Arsites and over Pissuthnes. Artaxerxes could profitably have used Cyrus' mercenaries himself (and Clearchus offered their services for the expected Egyptian campaign: Xen. *Anab.* 2.5.13), but Artaxerxes evidently saw greater profit in re-enacting the pattern of Darius II's successes, literally and figuratively decapitating Cyrus' mercenary force, and thereby certifying his own claim to the kingship. This must have pointed to what might be called a Darian kingship.

But at the same time Artaxerxes signalled his affirmation of a 'Cyrean' kingship with measures that reflected the 'royal virtues' of trust, lavish reward and clemency modelled by Cyrus. Tissaphernes and Pharnabazus, though they might have been faulted for failure to deal successfully with Athens and Sparta at the end of Darius' reign, were confirmed in their satrapies, certainly on the basis of their displays of unwavering loyalty to Artaxerxes in recent years. Artaxerxes heaped honours on figures such as Tiribazus and Orontes – younger men – who had performed valiantly at Cunaxa. To Orontes went marriage to Artaxerxes' daughter, and to Tiribazus a promise of marriage. Clemency was likely broadly applied. We hear of no retaliatory measures by Artaxerxes, and in the case of Ariaeus, commander of Cyrus' 'barbarian' force, we can see Artaxerxes using Ariaeus' family members to encourage reconciliation on the part of Ariaeus and his clients and ultimately bestowing satrapal power on him (*Anab.* 2.4.1). There may be a hint of Artaxerxes' adoption of additional 'Cyrean' practices; Plutarch has a whole passage about Artaxerxes' character as king early in his kingship:

> In the beginning he seemed to be altogether emulous of the gentleness of the Artaxerxes whose name he bore, showing himself very agreeable in intercourse, and bestowing greater honours and favours than were really deserved, while from all his punishments he took away the element of insult or vindictive pleasure, and in his acceptance and bestowal of favours appeared no less gracious and kindly to the givers than to the recipients. There was no gift so small that he did not accept it with alacrity. (*Artox.* 4.3–4, Loeb translation)

This could almost be a description of Cyrus' manner. Plutarch places it before his account of Cyrus' challenge to Artaxerxes, but if we accept Xenophon's account of the reasons many chose Cyrus over Artaxerxes, it is hard to see that there would have been a greater prospect of rewards from Cyrus than from the Artaxerxes Plutarch describes. More generally, we may see Artaxerxes' unusually accessible dining behaviour and his encouraging his wife Stateira to allow herself to be seen by parting the curtains on her carriage as an expression of Cyrus-like openness (Plut. *Artox.* 5.3).

Bits of evidence thus suggest that Artaxerxes II tried to become Cyrus. But either he could not sustain it (that is, actually trust) or was not very good at it (that is, he did not engage a sizeable number of trustworthy adherents). Darius II seems to have exterminated many families without replacing them, out of paranoia, making an autocracy even more autocratic. Cyrus seems to have promised an abandonment of such policies and adoption of a policy of fostering the rise and enhancing the roles of additional new families or of restoring other, traditionally significant, families. Artaxerxes II's policy of clemency indicates a determination to reconstitute a large body of 'followers'. But this does not seem to have happened.

What is striking about Artaxerxes' reign, stretching as it does over more than forty years, is the relatively small number of leading officials we find or, to put it another way, how we find the same figures again and again for decades.[8] Notable newcomers are non-Persians – the Hecatomnids, Glos, Datames – who acquire important positions. If Artaxerxes was indeed displaying a calculated leniency in the hopes of broadening the participation of Persians, as Ariaeus' appointment suggests, why was there not greater participation? Why does the Cyrean model disappear?

What we need most to remember in order to attempt an answer is that for the whole of the fourth century up to his death in 359, Artaxerxes was continuously at war. In this whole time, there is not a single year in which, just in the eastern Mediterranean, campaigning or preparations for campaigning are not under way. Consider the list:

400–391	At war with Sparta, both land and naval operations (Xen. *Hell.* 3.1.3–4.8.19; Diod. 14.35.6–39.6, 14.79.1–86.4, 94.1–4, 97.1–4)
391–390	Enterprise against Evagoras of Salamis (Diod. 14.98.1–4)
389–387	Invasion of Egypt (Isoc. *Paneg.* 140)[9]
387	Fighting against Athens (Xen. *Hell.* 5.1.28–9)
386–380	Preparations, then new war against Evagoras, with land and naval operations in Cilicia and Phoenicia as well (Diod. 14.110.5, 15.2.1–4.3, 8.1–9.5
379–373	Preparations for renewed invasion of Egypt and invasion (Diod. 15.41.1–43.6)
372–371	New preparations for Egyptian campaign (Nep. *Datames* 3.5)
371–	Datames' revolt (Nep. *Datames* 5.2–6; Diod. 15.91.2)
367–	Ariobarzanes' revolt (Dem. 15.9–10; Xen. *Ages.* 2.26)
365–	Beginning of Great Satraps' Revolt (Diod. 15.90.1–91.1)
361–	War with Egyptian king Tachos (Diod. 15.90.2, 92.1–5)

Circumstances thus conspired (a) to privilege a very short list of officials – men already experienced, with special skills and knowledge (working with Greeks or overseeing maritime operations, for example), and proven political reliability, since the undertakings assigned them were large-scale military enterprises, not just holding operations or diplomatic activity; and (b) to exclude new men from important posts since there was simply not time for probation.

The list was headed initially by a few figures from Darius II's era: Tissaphernes, Pharnabazus and Abrocomas, who had been unwavering supporters of Artaxerxes against Cyrus. Tissaphernes and Pharnabazus naturally got responsibility for confronting the Spartan incursions in the 390s; they were after all familiar with Spartans from their dealings with them in the Peloponnesian War. What Artaxerxes did in an effort to have the war proceed as expeditiously as possible was to create a single command, which went to Tissaphernes. When Spartan naval operations proved effective, the Persian response was familiar: use another Greek force or at least one headed by a Greek, in this case the veteran Athenian Conon, overseen and paid by a figure used to such arrangements – Pharnabazus. Tissaphernes lasted only through 395 when Artaxerxes grew impatient and (perhaps to please Persian land-holders sick of depredations, perhaps also to please Parysatis) had him executed. This reduced by one the already small number of proven and knowledgeable figures Artaxerxes could employ. The other veteran, Pharnabazus, now exercised sole command. The open satrapy was soon filled by the appointment of one of the younger, but already estab-lished favourites, Tiribazus (though Tiribazus' philo-Laconian policy would soon prompt his recall and replacement by Autophradates) (Xen. *Hell.* 3.1.3, 2.13, 4.25; 4.8.12).

When the Spartans ceased operations in Anatolia and Artaxerxes finally resumed operations against Egypt which had been broken off by Cyrus' *anabasis*, he turned here too to veterans: Abrocomas, the original commander of the aborted campaign of 401, Tithraustes, the chiliarch who had skilfully accomplished Tissaphernes' murder, and Pharnabazus, the long-time satrap and loyalist, rewarded for support and service by marriage to a daughter of Artaxerxes.[10] No new men here. The campaign was a disaster, eclipsing for a time at least the rep-utation of these veteran officials. This removed three more men from the already small group of dependable veterans.

There was hardly a moment's break in hostilities. Evagoras had been busy during the Egyptian campaign, aggrandising himself by seizing territory on the Cilician and Phoenician coasts opposite Cyprus. This raised the spectre of the 450s when Persia had been con-stantly distracted from recovery of Egypt by problems on Cyprus. With the discrediting eclipse of veteran commanders, the door was now open for newcomers. Yes, but only in a limited sense. Artaxerxes turned to younger men, but 'men of Cunaxa', that is, proven loyalists: Orontes, satrap of Armenia, and Tiribazus, men with Anatolian experience, and in Tiribazus' case also maritime experience (at least in shipbuilding operations in the early 380s) and familiarity with Greeks, who would furnish ships for the expedition. Unfortunately, both were over-anxious and competitive; Orontes was probably especially impatient to prove his worth some fifteen or more years after Cunaxa and marriage to Artaxerxes' daughter. When Tiribazus with his son-in-law and fleet commander the Egyptian Glos ended up winning battles and preparing the final settlement with Evagoras, Orontes falsely accused Tiribazus of collusion with Evagoras, prompting Tiribazus' arrest and removal from command and from Cyprus. Glos revolted, taking the Greek fleet with him, and entering into alliance with the Egyptian king and allegedly with Sparta. Artaxerxes, lacking other commanders with appropriate skills, acquitted Tiribazus, ending Glos's defection but not returning Tiribazus to service. When Orontes' accusations against Tiribazus proved intentionally false, Orontes lost his standing, 'struck from the list of royal "friends" ' (Diod. 15.10.1–11.2). The Cyprus commands had probably been a sort of tryout for Egyptian campaign commands. But with Tiribazus and Orontes discredited, Artaxerxes could not employ this 'younger generation' of experienced loyalists. Two more men were subtracted.

No one else with appropriate attributes was now available but Pharnabazus. Advanced in years, Pharnabazus compensated by employing the Athenian commander Iphicrates – significantly, not a Persian. This was a version of the 390s arrangement involving Pharnabazus and Conon. But Iphicrates received a greater role, *stratêgos* instead of something like *hêgemôn*, and seems to have functioned as virtual commander during the 373 invasion. Nevertheless, another failure ensued; Iphicrates then fled to avoid the anticipated burden of blame (Diod. 15.41.1–43.6).

Right after mentioning the failure of Pharnabazus and Iphicrates in Egypt, when they fell into *stasis*, Plutarch goes on to narrate the Cadusian war which Artaxerxes led in person and which turned out to be a big disaster (*Artox.* 24.1). (This most likely preceded the Egyptian campaign.[11]) Plutarch's point is that Artaxerxes was losing everywhere, both through others and when he himself commanded. But Artaxerxes' assumption of sole command suggests that he held no one else fit to do this. If that bespeaks a limited pool of potential commanders, the pool was much further diminished when Artaxerxes put to death many of his 'first men' after his disastrous Cadusian campaign (Plut. *Artox.* 25.3).

After the 373 failure in Egypt, Artaxerxes quickly set in motion preparations for a third Egyptian campaign, probably in 372. With

Pharnabazus defeated in Egypt for the second time and the leading figures of the next generation, Orontes and Tiribazus, suspect, Artaxerxes finally brought in a new figure – but a non-Persian, Datames, the half-Carian satrap of Cappadocia. He had participated and performed splendidly in the recent Cadusian War, and seemed to have the initiative and resourcefulness that the Egyptian enterprise clearly needed. Following Pharnabazus' previous practice, Datames hired an Athenian as *stratêgos*, Conon's son Timotheus.

Here we have reached an important point: Persian enterprise was entirely in non-Persian hands. Military exigencies, one after another since 400, had compelled Artaxerxes to use the same men again and again, excluding a whole generation of Persians from high commands and status rewards. Now he had put to death many leading figures and then given over command to non-Persians. Was this the end of opportunities for Persian grandees? Would war-making be contracted out to non-Persians? Many at court evidently feared so, and to judge by what Datames learned from a letter delivered secretly to him, jealous court officials were determined to bring about his death at the first sign of setbacks (that is, when he might best be brought under Artaxerxes' scrutiny). This was enough to convince Datames that Artaxerxes was not in control of all matters. Now Datames withdrew from expedition preparations and began consolidation of defences in Cappadocia/Paphlagonia. Datames left a proxy commander in place, Mandrocles of Magnesia – significantly, another Greek (Nep. *Datames* 5.2.6; Dem. 49.25).

Day-to-day control over Persian enterprise has fallen out of Persian hands and the king cannot control those who are in charge: the Persian effort to regain Egypt had to be abandoned. This was a low point; but worse was to come.

Datames' was the first in a wave of 'revolts' that broke out through the rest of Artaxerxes' reign. What are they? We are certainly not talking about attempts to gain independence. We may get a clue from a gesture of Datames during the initial stage of his revolt. Besieging Sinope on the Black Sea as part of his effort to consolidate power in the face of anticipated suppression, he reportedly received a letter from Artaxerxes commanding him to break off the siege, and, kissing the letter, he complied (Polyaen. 7.21.2, 5; cf. Nep. *Datames* 5.6). We are not told what the letter said, but obviously it served to conciliate Datames (at least for the moment). So the dynamic is revolt – royal response – reconciliation. In other words, the revolt functions as a means of negotiation; it is leverage. Ariobarzanes, a brother of

Pharnabazus left as satrap of Hellespontine Phrygia in about 390 when Pharnabazus became one of the commanders of the first Egyptian campaign, followed suit shortly after when Artaxerxes sent his own grandson (son of his daughter and Pharnabazus) to take up Pharnabazus' old satrapy (Dem. 23.154). The only way to deal with this was to employ loyalist satraps to wage war, which is what two of them, Autophradates, the Lydian satrap, and Mausolus, the Carian satrap, did in 366. But what would happen if all nearby satraps and officials chose to seek leverage for one reason or another and cease to comply with royal orders? Military response would be impossible. Concessions by the king would be inevitable.

This is just what happened in the late 360s: the so-called Great Satraps' Revolt – a coalition of rebel satraps and officials headed ultimately by Orontes, the quondam son-in-law of Artaxerxes and nemesis of Tiribazus, who had resurfaced by this time. Orontes' defection seems to have been precipitated by the ascendancy of Tiribazus as intimate adviser of Artaxerxes' designated heir Darius. A kind of unholy coalition then formed which included, in addition to Orontes, the already rebellious Ariobarzanes and his recent adversaries Autophradates, satrap of Lydia, and Mausolus, satrap of Caria. The whole of the western empire, satrapies and subject peoples, ended up in revolt (Diod. 15.91.1–2). There is no credible evidence of fighting in connection with this revolt, just very explicit information about the amassing of funds, the hiring of great numbers of mercenaries, the links with other disaffected figures or peoples – all calculated, it seems, to provide the appearance of a great threat and thereby establish a strong bargaining position.[12]

If a good definition of autocracy is to be found in Darius I's words in the Bisutun inscription (DB 19–20), 'what was said by me, night and day, it was done', then Artaxerxes II had by 362/1 ceased to be an autocrat. He had run out of commanders; he had not raised up any more; and his attempts now to arrange for the future by designating Darius as heir had only alienated powerful figures who had a vested interest in the status quo. Artaxerxes II had no choice but to agree to demands. The politics of autocracy had set all this – the collapse of autocracy – in motion a half-century and more earlier. Artaxerxes II, or at least his authority as king, was the ultimate victim of the succession struggle that had begun in 424.

Ironically, however, it was not the near-collapse of autocracy that set the stage for the ultimate demise of the Persian empire or of Persian kingship, but rather the restoration of autocracy by Artaxerxes II's youngest son and successor, Ochus/Artaxerxes III. Having come to power through palace intrigue (he was the youngest son, and not originally Artaxerxes' choice as successor), Artaxerxes III was determined not to face any intrigue or challenge himself, and to prevent this he had dozens of male relatives murdered (Plut. *Artox.* 26.1–27; 30.1–5; Curt. 10.5.23). To remove the possibility of revolts (meaning leveraged negotiations) he commanded that all mercenary forces in the employ of Persian officials be dismissed (Schol. Dem. 4.19). (Note how legitimacy is established again by the destruction or neutralisation of Greek mercenary forces.) He himself assumed personal, direct command of all military enterprises. This backfired at first, as he failed in person in his first Egyptian campaign and then faced revolts in Phoenician cities and elsewhere as he pressed forward urgently with new preparations. Artaxerxes finally retook Egypt in 343/2 (Diod. 16.51.2–3). Then he set about reordering affairs everywhere. He aimed at re-establishing a system in which 'what was said by me, night and day, it was done'.

In typically systematic fashion, Artaxerxes created two great commands under two commanders: the west under Mentor, the proven Rhodian commander, and the 'upper satrapies' under Bagoas (Diod. 16.52.2; Strabo 13.1.57), significantly, a Greek and a eunuch. Clearly, Artaxerxes was taking no political chances. These commanders were to suppress once and for all troublesome peoples and independent dynasts in their respective general areas of authority. In the west this meant Hermias of Atarneus and other quasi-independent local potentates (Diod. 16.52.4–6), and in the upper satrapies certainly the Cadusians, and possibly also the Medes. Mentor did a rapid and thorough job in the west. No source tells us of Bagoas' performance. Instead, we find him accomplishing the murder through poison of Artaxerxes III in late 338 (Diod. 17.5.3). It is plausible to see his killing of Artaxerxes as a self-preserving move as he anticipated punishment (humiliation) for military failure.

If Artaxerxes' revived, effective kingship promised swift and decisive punishment for failure (despite earlier achievements), Bagoas must have anticipated disgrace or worse for his failed enterprise. The ensuing disarray – Artaxerxes III's youngest son Arses became king only to be murdered along with most of the rest of Artaxerxes III's family after a year or so (Diod. 17.5.3) – gave the distant observer Philip of Macedon enough evidence of Persian vulnerability reminiscent of the situation in the late 360s to make revival of the Egyptian king Tachos' plans seem reasonable. We know the outcome of Philip's observations.

Is there a story of Persian politics in the fourth century BC that can be reconstructed? Perhaps not a detailed narrative, but at least a sketch. If we start with the last quarter of the fifth century and bring in Darius II and Cyrus the Younger, we have a coherent story that might be titled 'The Politics of Autocracy' – a three-generations-long story in which the succession crisis beginning in 424 ends up leading in a direct line to the different sort of crisis of 334.

NOTES

1. Reconstructions based on Ctesias may be found in Briant 2002b: 588–91; Dandamaev 1989: 258–60; Cook 1983: 129–30; Lewis 1977: 70–82. See also Stolper 1983.
2. Lewis 1977: 81.
3. Briant 2002b: 591.
4. Tavernier 2001.
5. Artasyras as king's Eye: Plut. *Artox.* 12.1.
6. Darius seems not to have dared endow anyone else with extensive military resources. He himself commanded against Median and Cadusian rebels (who had perhaps been emboldened by the weakness of Darius' satraps) in 407 and 405 (Xen. *Hell.* 1.2.19, 2.1.13; Briant 2002b: 596), and gave satraps in the west only intermittent financial support to accomplish their objectives.
7. Damages to Arsames' estates: Driver 1954: nos 5, 7, 8. On the possible circumstances, see Driver 1954: 4–5; Briant 2002b: 597. Some scholars argue for an earlier dating and thus different circumstances; see Dandamaev 1989: 242–3.
8. Since our sources are entirely Greek, we are informed only about affairs and officials in the western part of the empire. Conclusions are therefore based on admittedly partial knowledge of the whole situation. See the cautionary remarks of Briant 2002b: 596.
9. Some date the Egyptian campaign to the late 380s. See, e.g., Reid 1974; Shrimpton 1991.
10. Isoc. 4 (*Paneg.*) 140.
11. Plut. *Artox.* 24.1–25.3.
12. Interpretation of the Satraps' Revolt has swung from seeing it as a large-scale insurrection culminating in an offensive pushing as far as Syria (this from Trog. *Prol.* 10) to seeing it as a collection of localised disturbances of limited scope and significance. Cf., for example, Hornblower, 'Persia', *CAH²* VI.86–7; Hornblower 1982: 180 and Weiskopf 1989. My view is that it was essentially a staged affair funded in large part by the Egyptian king Tachos; see Diod. 15.90.1–92.1.

CHAPTER 17

Sulla the weak tyrant

Alexander Thein

As dictator, Sulla was labelled a 'tyrant' by Plutarch and Appian, but this Greek term was also applied to Sulla by Latin writers such as Cicero and Sallust. Important studies by Laffi and Hinard have shown that the potential for contemporaries to have viewed Sulla as a tyrant existed during his lifetime, but that the hostile image, especially of Sulla's cruelty, was only fully activated during the civil war that began in 49, as Pompey came to be configured, by Caesar and even by his own public comments, as a 'second Sulla'.[1] In the years after Actium Antony was cast in the role of a 'second Sulla' as architect of the triumviral proscriptions, and in the early Julio-Claudian period Sulla emerged as the archetype of cruelty and the subject of colourful invention. Hinard aptly describes the civil war victories of Caesar and Augustus as two 'accidents' which fuelled the hostile tradition on Sulla.[2] In earlier years Cicero had alluded to Sulla's cruelty and tyranny, yet his criticisms were always guarded and balanced by a positive appreciation for Sulla's politics.[3]

Scholarship on Sulla's posthumous image has concentrated on the genesis of the negative tradition and how it was conditioned by the politics of the Late Republic. But the trajectory of Sulla's reception has not been traced beyond the early Julio-Claudian period, and the definition of what it meant for Sulla to be a 'tyrant' has been largely confined to its hostile nuances. The ancient response to Sulla's abdication lets us address both issues. It was at the end of the first century AD, as Sulla's cruelty could be taken for granted, that the reception of Sulla's memory came to be dominated by a new question, to which

My first thanks go to Sian Lewis for inviting me to contribute a chapter to this volume. I would also like to express my debt to the exchange of ideas with Richard and Michal Bosworth at the British School at Rome during my tenure of a Rome Scholarship in 2002–3. Special thanks are also due to Lothar Haselberger for reading a draft of this chapter. Any shortcomings of course remain my own.

there seemed to be no satisfactory answer: why did he abdicate? This was not a question that troubled the Republican mind, but Imperial writers wondered why Sulla had not been the first emperor. The establishment of the Empire and institution of the emperor was another 'accident' which influenced Sulla's reception.

Sulla's portrayal as a tyrant and proto-emperor implies unprecedented powers and the unlimited exercise of political free will. It is this familiar image of Sulla's dictatorship that I wish to challenge. Above all, I wish to separate Sulla's powers from his political effectiveness, and to evaluate Sulla's dictatorship in terms of its 'strength' and 'weakness'. I have derived this analytical model from the historiography of the major dictatorships of the twentieth century. Mussolini's Italy provides the most striking contrast between the public image of the 'strong' dictator projected by the propagandists of the regime, and the ineffectiveness of the *Duce*'s leadership throughout the period of the 'Fascist Revolution' down to its ignominious end in the Second World War. Stalin was able to bring about a revolution on a scale only promised by Mussolini, but he remained (rightly) suspicious of deception by the state bureaucracy and hostility from the population at large. In Hitler's Germany, the widespread acceptance of the '*Führer* cult' was combined with endemic dissatisfaction with the Nazi party and its functionaries throughout the national-socialist period, and paradoxically, decision-making in the 'totalitarian' state operated without the day-to-day involvement of Hitler himself.[4]

In the Preface to his *Sulla the Fortunate*, published in 1927, the biographer G. B. Baker argued that 'with Mussolini dominating Italy, Primo del Rivera ruling Spain, and Pilsudski Poland, and with a Dictatorship of the Proletariat reigning in Russia . . . [we] can understand Sulla better, because we live in an age more like his own.'[5] The dictatorship of the Roman Republic was far-removed from these twentieth-century dictatorships, yet Sulla nevertheless resembles his modern successors in some respects. Sulla's rise to power was defined by the cultivation of an image of *felicitas* which raised him above the many rivals who had as much or as little to offer as he did. In the 1920s contemporaries of Mussolini were struck by his 'charisma'. The same personal energy underscored Sulla's *felicitas*. Both men were noted for their piercing gaze.[6] Sulla's public image was the projection of a strong persona. Indeed, he was not just *felix*, but also *fortis* – brave or strong.[7] However, the contrast between the image and the realities of power in twentieth-century dictatorships encourages us to be sceptical, and to look for the 'weak' Sulla beneath the image of strength.

The following analysis provides an introduction to the problem of Sulla's political 'strength' and 'weakness'. It focuses on the reception of Sulla's abdication in the High Empire, but also looks back to Republican sources such as Cicero and Sallust. There was a general acceptance at all periods in antiquity that Sulla's powers had been exceptional, and though there was also a recognition that Sulla's political effectiveness was subject to well-defined limitations, this was never more than a substratum in the general portrayal of Sulla. The image of the 'weak' Sulla never dominates, but conversely, it is never entirely absent from the picture, and emerges clearly even in Appian's characterisation of Sulla's formal powers, political personality and power-base – the most coherent and systematic exposition of the 'strong' Sulla in antiquity.

SULLA'S POWERS

Appian stresses that no one before Sulla voluntarily stepped down from sole power, except as part of a dynastic arrangement.[8] Silius Italicus has Scipio shown future Romans in the Underworld by the Sibyl, among them Sulla: 'he will be the first to seize complete power (*imperium*), but there is glory in his wrongdoing, for he alone will give it back, nor will there be anyone of such greatness who will choose to follow Sulla's lead.'[9] This is praise indeed, especially in the Imperial era. Not even Augustus chose to become a 'second Sulla' in this respect, though he frequently dreamed of retirement from his public duties; it was a common goal, seldom achieved even by lesser men, to pass one's final years in *otium*.[10] Sulla was both willing and able to retire, and Appian looked to this as proof of his *felicitas*.[11]

Sulla's abdication was simple. He gave a speech in the Forum in which he offered to give a formal account of his term of office on request. He then dismissed his lictors and his entourage of clients.[12] It was an unexpected event and the antithesis of Sulla's earlier ambition, yet Sulla did not explain his motives. Martial creates the conceit that Sulla abdicated due to the divine intervention of a bronze statuette of Hercules which graced his banquets and which had been crafted by Lysippus and previously owned by Hannibal and Alexander.[13] In the schools of rhetoric Sulla's abdication speech was a popular choice for practice compositions and ranked alongside Priam's words to Achilles.[14] Quintilian, meditating on Sulla's moral legacy, expresses the view that Sulla cannot have taken up arms to exercise tyranny if he resigned the dictatorship.[15] Caesar rejected any similar appeal to posterity and famously stated, according to Suetonius, that Sulla did not know his political ABC.[16] The problem of Sulla's abdication was identified by Silius Italicus, Martial and Quintilian in the last decades of the first century, and taken up by Suetonius and Appian in the second century. In each case the response was conditioned by surprise, and this reflects the belief that Sulla had stepped down from a position of unparalleled political strength.

Sulla's dictatorship was indeed unprecedented. Plutarch, in the early second century, describes unlimited, almost 'totalitarian' powers: 'He was voted . . . the power of life and death, of confiscation and colonisation, of founding and destroying cities, of taking away kingdoms, and of granting favours to anyone he chose.' Appian records a letter from Sulla to the *interrex* L. Valerius Flaccus recommending the appointment of a dictator 'not for a fixed period of time, but until he should restore order to the city, Italy and the entire empire'.[17] Appian judged that under Sulla the dictatorship 'for the first time became limitless and thus a complete tyranny' (because it was no longer limited to six months). Dionysius of Halicarnassus, focusing on Sulla's acts of cruelty rather than his powers, and reflecting the Augustan vilification of Sulla, felt contemporaries then realised for the first time that the very institution of the dictatorship was a tyranny. As far as Plutarch was concerned, Sulla might be consul or dictator, but he was always a tyrant.[18] Even at Sulla's Mithridatic triumph in January 81 there was a lively debate among the soldiers – within the framework of apotropaic mockery expected on such occasions – as to whether Sulla's dictatorship was more akin to kingship or tyranny.[19] These varied judgements reveal no sign of a 'weak' Sulla.

Eight years after Sulla's death Cicero offered a qualified condemnation of the excessive powers of Sulla's dictatorship: 'Since the foundation of the city there has only been one man – let the immortal gods see to it that there be no other! – to whom the Republic has surrendered itself completely, driven by the circumstances of the times and domestic troubles, and that man was Lucius Sulla.'[20] As consul in 63, he described the *lex Valeria* as the most unjust of all laws, though a product of its times. Paradoxically, it 'imposed a tyrant on the Republic by law'. Sulla may have been a tyrant, but he was a legal tyrant.[21] In the *Philippics* Sulla's *dominatio* develops from the *potentia* of Cinna and heralds Caesar's *regnum*. This trio eclipsed the entire Republic, but Antony with his bodyguard was nevertheless worse.[22] The memory of Sulla enhances Cicero's rhetorical repertoire in his speeches against Verres in 70, Rullus in 63 and Antony in 44–43. Criticism was often mixed with appreciation for Sulla's 'restoration of the Republic'.[23] In a letter to Atticus of August 47 Cicero expresses the widespread opinion in antiquity that Sulla's victory was a 'good thing' marred by the violence of the proscriptions: 'You compare the state of affairs under Sulla, in which everything was in and of itself most admirable, but not sufficiently tempered by moderation.'[24] As a negative *exemplum*, however, Sulla was by necessity constructed as a 'strong' ruler.

SULLA'S PRESCIENCE

Appian ends his account of Sulla's abdication with an apocryphal illustration of Sulla's prescience. Sulla wandered around the Forum for a long time without his entourage and revelled in the stunned amazement of the watching crowd. When he left for home he was subjected to a torrent of verbal abuse from a small boy, but no one stopped him. Sulla was followed and abused by the boy all the way back to his house, but he apparently showed none of his familiar rage, and is credited only with the calm and prophetic response as he stepped through his front door, 'that this child will prevent another man who holds such power from laying it down'. Appian finds confirmation in the fact that Caesar extended his dictatorship to a life term.[25] In fact it was this idea that Sulla was a proto-Caesar that persuaded him that Sulla's dictatorship had also been for life.[26]

The idea that Sulla foresaw Caesar's future career was perhaps based on the fact that the young Caesar had been proscribed. Sulla was persuaded to pardon him, and it was on this occasion that he is said to have remarked that Caesar would destroy the *optimates*, and that there was many a Marius inside him (*nam Caesari multos Marios inesse*).[27] Sulla is also credited with specific warnings, either to the *optimates* or Pompey, 'to beware the ill-girt boy' (*ut male praecinctum puerum caverent*), a reference to Caesar's idiosyncratic style of dress.[28] Sulla's prescience was recognised by Appian, Plutarch and Suetonius, and came to be a well-established trope. Dio, in the Several period, tells us that Sulla was unable to predict the civil war between the consuls of 87, 'in spite of the fact that he was most gifted in perceiving the inner thoughts of men and calculating the future course of events'.[29] Only one prediction has any conceivable historical basis, and that is Sulla's warning to Pompey that he had 'strengthened his own opponent' by supporting Lepidus in the consular elections of 79 for 78. Its fulfilment in the revolt of Lepidus came one year later, soon after Sulla's own death.[30]

Sulla's reputation for prescience finds a useful parallel in Tacitus' treatment of the Imperial succession after Tiberius:

> Now he was uncertain of mind and physically weak and he left to fate a decision that he was unable to make himself, but he nevertheless let certain comments slip from which it was clear that he was able to see into the future; for he rebuked Macro in unambiguous terms for deserting the setting and looking to the rising sun, and when in random course of conversation he heard Gaius Caesar mocking Lucius Sulla, he foretold that he would have all Sulla's vices and none of his positive virtues.[31]

Tiberius could read the future. He perceived that Caligula, the 'rising sun' which attracted the allegiance of Macro, the praetorian prefect, would become a 'second Sulla'. He then predicted that Caligula would kill his rival Tiberius Gemellus but himself fall victim to eventual assassination.[32] Tiberius' prescience was more than intuition. He learned the art of Chaldaean astrology from Thrasyllus in Rhodes, and this enabled him to predict that Galba, consul in AD 33, would have a short taste of empire in old age (after Nero's suicide).[33] Tiberius could thus predict future emperors, yet he was unable to determine the succession after his death. He was physically and emotionally weak (*mox incertus animi, fesso corpore*) and was forced to leave his decisions to fate (*consilium cui impar erat fato permisit*).[34] The portrayal of Tiberius in Tacitus combines prescience with impotence. The same paradox underscores the prophecies associated with Sulla.

At the end of the first century AD it appeared that Sulla prefigured Imperial rule, and by the start of the second century, the notion began to circulate that Sulla had himself predicted the inevitability of sole rule under the Caesars. The fiction of Sulla's prescience fostered a sense of continuity between Sulla and his Imperial successors, even if Sulla's opposition to Caesar and the anomaly of his abdication marked him as an antithesis to the Caesars. Sulla could 'foresee' that his own career provided a dangerous precedent for the future of the Republic, and that Caesar would ultimately destroy his political legacy. This pessimism parallels Tacitus' portrayal of Tiberius and provides a useful corrective to the view held by some scholars that the Sullan reforms were conceived as a 'last attempt' to prevent the fall of the Republic.[35] The 'prescient' Sulla was 'weak', frustrated by the limitations of his unprecedented executive powers, and resigned to the ultimate futility of his reforms.

FEAR AND SILENCE

Sulla's abdication was greeted with stunned silence.[36] At Sulla's funeral some of the onlookers were afraid of his body (and his veterans) but grudgingly acknowledged the fear that he inspired even in death and the *felicitas* that he brought to his own faction.[37] Fear and silence are a common response to Sulla. One may note the shocked reaction of the senators meeting with Sulla in the temple of Bellona who were told to ignore the screams emanating from the nearby Villa Publica as the Samnites were massacred after their defeat at the Colline Gate.[38] The same reaction greeted Sulla's announcement in a *contio* that he had ordered the murder of Q. Lucretius Afella at the elections for the consulship of 81. Afterwards he is said to have 'ruled as he pleased'.[39] Appian viewed terror as a weapon of a 'strong' tyrant able to impose his will on his subjects, and despite the many thousands (carefully enumerated by Appian) who had been killed in the civil war or in the hour of victory, Sulla was himself 'afraid of nothing'.[40]

The natural question was why no one could be found to kill the tyrant. Cato is said to have posed the question as a boy when he saw severed heads being brought into the *atrium* on a visit to Sulla's house for the morning *salutatio*. Plutarch attributes Cato's pedagogue, Sarpedon, with the response: 'Because they fear him, my boy, more than they hate him.' Afterwards he watched his charge closely, and even frisked him before taking him to Sulla's house.[41] The weakness of an autocracy based on fear and hatred was also recognised by Cicero with regard to Caesar: *Quem metuunt, oderunt, quem quisque odit periisse expetit*, 'They hate the man they fear, and anyone who hates such a man also wishes him dead.'[42] These words derive from Ennius' treatment of Atreus in his *Thyestes*. Accius provided a variation in his *Atreus*: 'Let them hate as long as they are afraid' (*Oderint dum metuant*).[43] When Seneca cited this line he claimed that it was written under Sulla (*Sullano scias saeculo scriptam*).[44] No doubt Seneca knew that the line originated with Ennius and Accius, yet he felt that the dynamic of a tyranny based on fear and hatred was epitomised best in the dictatorship of Sulla. Even Appian recognised that the ideal was to be 'feared' ($\varphi o\beta\epsilon\rho\delta s$) but also 'fortunate' ($\dot{\epsilon}\pi\iota\tau\nu\chi\dot{\eta}s$), a verdict that he applied to both Sulla and Augustus.[45]

SULLA'S POWER-BASE

Appian's disbelief at Sulla's retirement from politics stems from his conviction that Sulla was still at the height of his power. He provides a clear exposition of Sulla's power-base at three crucial points in his narrative dealing with the Sullan dictatorship. The first of these passages illustrates the punishment of the Italian municipalities at the end of 82:

> In most of them he settled those who had served in his army so that he might have garrisons throughout Italy, confiscating land and houses and distributing these to his soldiers, whom he thus made especially loyal to himself even after his death. As they could not retain these holdings securely unless Sulla's entire legacy remained secure, they were zealous on his behalf even after he had passed away.[46]

Appian again mentions Sulla's veteran settlements in connection with the dictatorial reforms, and states that Sulla added 300 knights to the senate and 10,000 former slaves of the proscribed to the people. These were the 10,000 Cornelii and, according to Appian, had been chosen for their youth and strength as a ready source of muscular support for Sulla among the *plebs*.[47] In his account of Sulla's retirement from Rome to Cumae, Appian once again emphasises the continuing solidity of Sulla's power-base:

> There were twelve times ten thousand men throughout Italy, who had recently served in his army and had received large rewards and much land from him; the ten thousand Cornelii in the city were ready for anything; and there were also the many members of his faction, who were loyal to him and remained a source of fear to his enemies. As for what they all had done together with Sulla, they relied on Sulla's survival for their own security.[48]

By citing the enfranchisement of slaves and redistribution of land, Appian configures Sulla as a classic Greek tyrant of the 'revolutionary' type. In addition it is implied that his veterans formed garrisons to uphold his power throughout Italy, and that the 10,000 Cornelii served Sulla's interests in the city of Rome. In both respects Appian is followed by modern commentators who emphasise the coercive nature of the veterans and freedmen.[49] Yet there are signs of weakness even in Appian's portrayal of strength, for the veterans, the 10,000 Cornelii and the Sullani were all burdened by a guilty conscience.

Appian argues that the veterans in particular were bound to uphold Sulla's legacy. In the speech of Brutus and Cassius after the death of Caesar he elaborates on this theme. The veterans settled by Sulla and

Caesar could neither enjoy peace nor live without fear, for the dispossessed were continually looking for revenge. Colonisation followed the logic of tyranny. Its aim was not simply to provide land, but to create 'strong guards' and willing partners in an unjust regime, 'since the bond between bodyguards and tyrants grows out of crimes and fears in common'.[50] The dynamic of guilt also applied to the leading Sullani. Sallust's Lepidus admits to being a profiteer but configures himself as a victim of the regime and argues that Sulla's aim was to create loyalty through a common sense of guilt: 'This is indeed the greatest of his crimes, that neither I nor anyone would have been sufficiently safe if we had conducted ourselves justly.'[51] The Sullan land transfers created a culture of fear and insecurity throughout Italy, as recognised by Sallust in the triumviral period and by Cicero in 63. Shameless largesse (*impudens gratificatio*) was contrasted with bitter personal loss (*acerba iniuria*), but the winners still had grounds for apprehension (*scrupulum*) and the losers retained some hope (*spes*).[52]

Sulla's strategy of divide and rule between the winners and losers of the *victoria Sullana* was based on mutual fear and insecurity. Yet he was successful in finding 'willing' accomplices to share the guilt of his regime and this ensured that his power enjoyed at least the appearance of strength. Appian differs from Sallust and Cicero only in the degree that he was willing to recognise the underlying weakness of Sulla's regime. As the precursor of the principate, Sulla's dictatorship was necessarily strong, but it also suited Appian, as an advocate for the virtues of Imperial government, to associate Sulla with the violence and insecurity of the collapsing Republic. Appian's portrayal of Sulla is simultaneously 'strong' and 'weak', notably in the final explanation that he gives for the abdication. Appian stresses that Sulla was physically fit and in the prime of life when he retired to his villa at Cumae, yet he also feels that Sulla was weary of power and tired of Rome.[53]

CONCLUSION

Sulla generally enjoyed a posthumous reputation as a 'strong' tyrant, and it is only when we read these sources 'against the grain', notably in Appian's discussion of Sulla's power-base, that we begin to isolate complexities in the model. The image of the 'weak' tyrant which emerges from the ancient characterisation of Sulla allows, moreover, for a revision in the standard view of politics in the Sullan period. Cicero's *Pro Roscio Amerino*, from the year of Sulla's second consulship, illustrates the rewards of this approach. In 44 BC Cicero recalled having delivered this speech 'against the powerful interests of Lucius Sulla, who was acting as our master' (*contra L. Sullae dominantis opes*).[54] Scholars who accept this statement at face value and admire the 'courage' of the young Cicero implicitly ascribe to the view of the historical Sulla (not just Cicero's Sulla) as a 'strong' leader.[55] Sulla was all-powerful and opposition was dangerous. Certainly this reflects the fear and lack of freedom of speech to be found in other characterisations of the Sullan period, notably Appian, but it does not reflect normal Republican politics, even under the Sullan dictatorship. One may compare Tacitus' reflections on the glory days of free speech under the Republic, 'when many eloquent speakers did not spare even Publius Scipio, Lucius Sulla or Gnaeus Pompeius'. Sulla was one of the *principes viri* noted by Tacitus as favourite targets of attack.[56] Cicero's exceptionality as the defender of Sextus Roscius disappears, and with it part of the literary image of Sulla the 'strong' tyrant.

The historical Sulla can remain a 'strong' ruler only if we can prove that he was able to make effective use of his wide powers as dictator and his immense *auctoritas* as civil war victor. Yet this was not always the case. As dictator, Sulla brought a motion to the *comitia centuriata* to deprive Volaterrae and other *municipia* of their lands and citizenship. The confiscation of lands was ratified, but not the clause on citizenship. Cicero's concluding words in his discussion of this bill – *civitatem eripere non potuit* – emphasise the restrictions on Sulla's constitutional authority and power as dictator.[57] We may even turn to Sulla's own testimony in his memoirs on the reality of his power and influence, namely that he considered his *amicitia* with Metellus Pius, his colleague in the consulship of 80, to be an example of divine *felicitas*.[58] These are not the words of a 'strong' tyrant. Sulla recognised that his consulship would entail politics as usual, with all its difficulties and uncertainties. The politics of the Sullan period did not revolve around Sulla.

Notes

1. Laffi 1967: 258, 266–70; Hinard 1984: 91; 1985: 278.
2. Hinard 1984: 93–4; 1985: 282. Cf. Laffi 1967: 274–7. Commodus, Septimius Severus and Caracalla all became violent 'second Sullas'. See *SHA, Comm.* 8.1, *Pesc. Nig.* 6.4, *M.Ant.* 4.10.
3. Hinard 1984: 90; 1985: 280; 1988: 95, drawing from Laffi 1967: 265–6, 274.
4. See Bosworth 2002, esp pp. 1–12; Kershaw 1987; Harris 2003, esp. 375–9.

5. Baker 1927: 6.
6. See Bosworth 2002: 77, 97–8, 139, 184, 194, 207–13. Cf. Plut. *Sull.* 2.1.
7. Sall. *Jug.* 95.4, cf. Val. Max. 6.9.6, Cic. *Mur.* 38. See Balsdon 1951: 3.
8. App. *B.C.* 1.3, 1.103.
9. Sil. *Pun.* 13.858–60, cf. Amp. 18.16.
10. Sen. *Dial.* 10.4.3, cf. 10.3.5, 10.4.1, Cic. *Agr.* 2.9.
11. App. *B.C.* 1.104.
12. App. *B.C.* 1.3, 1.103, cf. Plut. *Sull.* 34.3.
13. Mart. 9.43.10, cf. Stat. *Silv.* 4.6.86–8.
14. Quint. *Inst.* 3.8.53.
15. Quint. *Inst.* 5.10.71.
16. Suet. *Jul.* 77.
17. Plut. *Sull.* 33.1, App. *B.C.* 1.98. The letter derives from Sulla's memoirs.
    See Bellen 1975: 556–9, 568–9.
18. App. *B.C.* 1.99; DH 5.77.4–5, Plut. *Lys. Sull.* 1.4.
19. App. *B.C.* 1.101, with Hinard 1985: 235–6. On the importance of
    apotropaic mockery at the triumph, see Simon 1995: 122–4.
20. Cic. *Verr.* 2.3.81.
21. Cic. *Agr.* 3.5. The paradox is stressed by Hinard 1985: 275; 1988: 90–2.
22. Cic. *Phil.* 2.108, 5.17.
23. Cic. *Har. resp.* 55. Cf. Cic. *Rosc. Am.* 132, 139; *Brut.* 227, 311; *Dom.* 79.
24. Cic. *Att.* 11.21.3. Cf. Sall. *Jug.* 95.4, *Cat.* 11.4, Cic. *Off.* 2.27, Livy *Per.* 88,
    Vell. Pat. 2.17.1, 2.25.3, Val. Max. 9.2.1.
25. App. *B.C.* 1.104.
26. App. *B.C.* 1.3, 1.4.
27. Suet. *Jul.* 1.3, cf. Plut. *Caes.* 1.2.
28. Suet. *Jul.* 45.3, Macr. *Sat.* 2.3.9.
29. Dio 30–5.102.4.
30. Plut. *Sull.* 34.5, *Pomp.* 15.2.
31. Tac. *Ann.* 6.46.
32. Tac. *Ann.* 6.46, cf. Suet. *Cal.* 11.
33. Tac. *Ann.* 6.20, Dio 57.19.4, cf. Suet. *Tib.* 14.4, 62.3, 69.1. Sulla's memoirs
    reveal a corresponding interest in Chaldaean astrology, though his concern
    was to learn his personal destiny, not to become a practitioner himself.
    See Plut. *Sull.* 5.5–6, 37.1, cf. Vell. Pat. 2.24.3.
34. Tac. *Ann.* 6.46.
35. Valgiglio 1956: 228–9; Hackl 1982: 253; Christ 2000: 228.
36. App. *B.C.* 1.3, 1.104.
37. App. *B.C.* 1.106.
38. Plut. *Sull.* 30.3, Sen. *Clem.* 1.12.2, Strabo 5.4.11, Dio 30–5.109.6–7.
39. App. *B.C.* 1.101, cf. Plut. *Lys. Sull.* 2.4.
40. App. *B.C.* 1.103.
41. Plut. *Cat. min.* 3.2–4, Val. Max. 3.1.2.
42. Cic. *Off.* 2.23, cf. 1.97.

43. See Dyck 1996: 255–6, 393–4.
44. Sen. *Ira* 1.20.4, cf. *Clem.* 1.12.4.
45. App. *B.C.* 1.106, cf. 1.5.
46. App. *B.C.* 1.96.
47. App. *B.C.* 1.100.
48. App. *B.C.* 1.104.
49. Citing only those who adopt both parts of Appian's scheme: Lewis 1991: 517; Eder 1997: 189–90; Bleicken 1999: 74.
50. App. *B.C.* 2.141.
51. Sall. *Hist.* 1.55.18, cf. 1.55.23.
52. Cic. *Agr.* 3.6.
53. App. *B.C.* 1.104, cf. 1.3.
54. Cic. *Off.* 2.51.
55. Buchheit 1975: 574; Ridley 1975: 85; Diehl 1988: 50.
56. Tac. *Dial.* 40.1.
57. Cic. *Dom.* 79.
58. Plut. *Sull.* 6.6.

Bibliography

Adam, J. (1907), *The Republic of Plato edited with critical notes, commentary and appendices, vol. 2, books vi–x and indexes*, Cambridge: Cambridge University Press.

Adamesteanu, D. (1962), 'L'ellenizzazione della Sicilia nel momento di Ducezio', *Kokalos* 8, pp. 167–98.

Adeleye, G. (1976), 'Theramenes: the end of a controversial career', *Museum Africum 5*, pp. 9–22.

Agostiniani, L. (1992), 'I modi del contatto linguistico tra greci e indigeni nella Sicilia antica', *Kokalos* 34–5, pp. 167–206.

Albanese-Procelli, R. M. (1996), 'Greeks and indigenous people in eastern Sicily: forms of interaction and acculturation', in R. Leighton (ed.), *Early Societies in Sicily*, London: Accordia Research Centre, pp. 167–76.

—— (2003), *Sicani, Siculi, Elimi: Forme di identità, modi di contatto e processi di trasformazione*, Milan: Longanesi.

Alcock, S. E. (1993), *Graecia Capta: The Landscapes of Roman Greece*, Cambridge: Cambridge University Press.

Amado Araceli, G. (1991), 'Algunas precisions sobre el "golpe de estado" de Agatocles de Siracuse', *Polis* 3, pp. 111–19.

Amandry, P. (1987), 'Les trépieds de Delphes et du Péloponnèse', *BCH* 111, pp. 79–131.

Ameling, W. (1993), *Karthago*, Munich: Beck.

Andrewes, A. (1956), *The Greek Tyrants*, London: Hutchinson.

—— (1970), 'Lysias and the Theramenes papyrus', *ZPE* 6, pp. 35–8.

Antonaccio, C. (1997), 'Urbanism at archaic Morgantina', *Acta Hyperborea* 7, pp. 167–93.

—— (2001), 'Ethnicity and colonization', in I. Malkin (ed.), *Ancient Perceptions of Greek Ethnicity*, Cambridge, MA: Harvard University Press, pp. 113–57.

Antonaccio, C. and Neils, J. (1995), 'A new graffito from archaic Morgantina', *ZPE* 101, pp. 261–77.

Arnold-Biucchi, C. (1983), 'Appunti sulla zecca di Messana dal 480 al 450 a. C.', *NAC* 12, pp. 49–64.

Asheri, D. (1966), *Distribuzioni di terre nell'antica Grecia*, Turin: Accademia delle Scienze di Torino.

Asheri, D. (1980), 'Rimpatrio di esuli e ridistribuzione di tere nelle città siceliote ca. 466–461 a.C.', in *Miscellanea di studi classici in onore di Eugenio Manni*, vol. 1, Rome: Giorgio Bretschneider, pp. 145–58.

—— (1991/2), 'The art of synchronization in Greek historiography: the case of Timaeus of Tauromoenium', *SCI* 9, pp. 52–89.

Aubet, M. (2001), *The Phoenicians and the West: Politics, Colonies and Trade*, trans. M. Turton, 2nd edn, Cambridge: Cambridge University Press.

Babelon, J. (1958), 'Le roi Pyrrhos', in H. Ingholt (ed.), *Centennial Publication of the American Numismatic Society*, New York: American Numismatic Society, pp. 53–71.

Bacci, G. M. (1995), 'Messana in età ellenistica', in M. Caccamo Caltabiano (ed.), *La Sicilia tra l'Egitto e Roma: la monetazione siracusana dell'età di Ierone II* (*Atti della Accademia peloritana dei pericolanti* 69 Suppl. 1), Messina: Accademia peloritana dei pericolanti, pp. 427–30.

Bacci, G. M. and Tigano, G. (eds) (1999), *Da Zancle a Messina: un percorso archeologico attraverso gli scavi*, vol. 1, Palermo: Assessorato dei beni culturali e ambientali e della pubblice instruzione.

Baker, G. P. (1927), *Sulla the Fortunate*, London: John Murray.

Balot, R. (2001), *Greed and Injustice in Classical Athens*, Princeton: Princeton University Press.

Balsdon, J. P. V. D. (1951), 'Sulla Felix', *JRS* 41, pp. 1–10.

Barcelo, P. (1993), *Basileia, Monarchia, Tyrannis: Untersuchungen zu Entwicklung und Beurteilung von Alleinherrschaft im vorhellenistischen Griechenland* (*Historia Einzelschriften* 79), Stuttgart: Steiner.

Barrett, W. S. (1973), 'Pindar's Twelfth *Olympian* and the fall of the Deinomenidai', *JHS* 93, pp. 23–35.

Basile, M. (1978), 'Analisi e valore della tradizione sulla *Rogatio Cassia Agraria* del 486 a.C.', *MGR* 6, pp. 277–98.

Bayet, J. (1966), *Tite Live Histoire Romaine liv. VI*, Paris: Les Belles Lettres.

Beard, M. (1993), 'Looking (harder) for Roman myth: Dumézil, declamation and the problems of definition', in F. Graf (ed.), *Mythos in mythenloser Gesellschaft: Das paradigma Roms*, Stuttgart and Leipzig: Teubner, pp. 44–64.

Bell, M. (1999), 'Centro e periferia nel regno siracusano di Ierone II', in G. Vallet et al. (eds), *La Colonisation grecque en Méditerranée occidentale*, Rome: École Française de Rome, pp. 257–77.

Bellen, H. (1975), 'Sullas Brief an den Interrex L. Valerius Flaccus: Zur Genese der sullanischen Diktatur', *Historia* 24, pp. 555–69.

—— (1991), 'La monarchia nella coscienza storica dello stato repubblicano. Un problema di continuità della storia romana', *Athenaeum* 79, pp. 5–15.

Beloch, K. J. (1927), *Griechische Geschichte*, 2nd edn, vol. 4.1, Berlin and Leipzig: de Gruyter.

Bengtson, H. (1956), 'Aspetti storico – universali del mondo ellenistico', *PP* 11, pp. 161–78.

—— (1975), *Herrschergestalten des Hellenismus*, Munich: Beck.

Béranger, J. (1935), '*Tyrannus*', *REL* 13, pp. 85–94.

Berger, S. (1988), 'P.Oxy. XXIV, 2239 and the opposition to Agathocles', *ZPE* 71, pp. 93–6.

—— (1991), 'Great and small poleis in Sicily', *Historia* 40, pp. 129–42.

—— (1992), *Revolution and Society in Greek Sicily and Southern Italy*, Stuttgart: Steiner.

Bernabò Brea, L. (1966), *Sicily Before the Greeks*, rev. edn, New York: F. A. Praeger.

Berve, H. (1953), *Die Herrschaft des Agathokles*, München: Bayerischen Akademie der Wissenschaften.

—— (1954), 'Das Königtum des Pyrrhos in Sizilien', in R. Lullies (ed.), *Neue Beiträge zur klassischen Altertumswissenschaft. Festschrift zum 60. Geburtstag von Bernhard Schweitzer*, Stuttgart: Kohlhammer, pp. 272–7.

—— (1967), *Die Tyrannis bei den Griechen*, Munich: Beck.

Bettini, M. (1988), 'Il divieto fino al "sesto grado" incluso nel matrimonio romano', *Athenaeum* 76, pp. 69–98.

Bitto, I. (2001), *Le iscrizioni greche e latine di Messina I*, Messina: Dipartimento di Storia Antica.

Bleicken, J. (1999), *Geschichte der römischen Republik*, Munich: Oldenbourg.

Blum, H. (1998), *Purpur als Statussymbol in der griechischen Welt*, Bonn: Habelt.

Boedeker, D. and Raaflaub, K. A. (eds) (1998), *Democracy, Empire and the Arts in Fifth-Century Athens*, Cambridge, MA and London: Harvard University Press.

Boehringer, C. (1968), 'Hierons Aitna und der Hieroneion', *JNG* 18, pp. 67–97.

Bons, J. A. E. (1993), 'Lysias 12, 19: the earrings again', *Hermes* 121, pp. 365–7.

Borba Florenzano, M. B. (1992), 'The coinage of Pyrrhus in Sicily: evidence of a political project', in T. Hackens (ed.), *The Age of Pyrrhus: Archaeology, History and Culture in Early Hellenistic Greece and Italy (Brown University 1988)*, Louvain-la-Neuve: Collège Érasme and Providence: Brown University, pp. 207–23.

—— (1993), 'Political propaganda in Agathocles' coins', in T. Hackens et al. (eds), *Actes du XIe Congrès International de Numismatique (Bruxelles 1991)*, Louvain-la-Neuve: Association Professeur M. Hoc, pp. 71–7.

Borthwick, E. K. (1990), 'Two emotional climaxes in Lysias' *Against Eratosthenes*', *CW* 84, pp. 44–6.

Bosworth, R. J. B. (2002), *Mussolini*, London: Arnold.

Botsford, G. W. (1909), *The Roman Assemblies*, New York: Macmillan.

Bowersock, G. W. (1966), 'Pseudo-Xenophon', *HSCP* 71, pp. 33–55.

Bowie, A. M. (2000), 'Myth and ritual in the rivals of Aristophanes', in D. Harvey and J. Wilkins (eds), *The Rivals of Aristophanes: Studies in Athenian Old Comedy*, London: Duckworth and Classical Press of Wales, pp. 317–39.

Bowra, C. M. (1964), *Pindar*, Oxford: Oxford University Press.

Braccesi, L. (1998), *I tiranni di Sicilia*, Roma-Bari: Editori Laterza.

Brett, A. B. (1950), 'Athena Alkidemos of Pella', *ANSMN* 4, pp. 55–72.

Briant, P. (2002a), 'History and ideology: the Greeks and "Persian decadence"', trans. A. Nevill, in T. Harrison (ed.), *Greeks and Barbarians*, Edinburgh: Edinburgh University Press, pp. 193–210 (originally published (1989) as 'Histoire et idéologie: les Grecs et la "décadence perse"', in M.-M. Mactoux and E. Geny (eds) *Mélanges P. Lévêque II*, Besancon, pp. 33–47).

—— (2002b), *A History of the Persian Empire*, trans. P. T. Daniels, Winona Lake, IN: Eisenbrauns.

Brisson, L. (1994), *Platon: Lettres*, 2nd edn, Paris: Garnier-Flammarion.

Brock, R. (2000), 'Sickness in the body politic: medical imagery in the Greek polis', in V. M. Hope and E. Marshall (eds), *Death and Disease in the Ancient City*, London and New York: Routledge, pp. 24–34.

Brock, R. and Hodkinson, S. (eds) (2000), *Alternatives to Athens*, Oxford: Oxford University Press.

Brunt, P. A. (1988), '*Libertas* in the Republic', in *The Fall of the Roman Republic and Related Essays*, Oxford: Clarendon Press, pp. 281–350.

Bruun, C. (2000), ' "What every man in the street used to know": M. Furius Camillus, Italic legends and Roman historiography', in C. Bruun (ed.), *The Roman Middle Republic: Politics, Religion and Historiography c. 400–133 BC*, Rome: Institutum Romanum Finlandiae, pp. 41–68.

Buchheit, V. (1975), 'Ciceros Kritik an Sulla in der Rede für Roscius aus Ameria', *Historia* 24, pp. 570–91.

Buckler, J. (1980), *The Theban Hegemony*, Harvard: Harvard University Press.

—— (2003), *Aegean Greece in the Fourth Century*, Leiden: Brill.

Buda, V. (1969–70), 'Le emissioni siracusane negli ultimi due decenni del IV sec. a.C. e il significato della riforma monetale di Agatocle', *Helikon* 9–10, pp. 192–231.

Bundy, E. L. (1986), *Studia Pindarica*, Berkeley: University of California Press.

Bunnens, G. (1979), *L'Expansion Phénicienne en Méditerranée*, Brussels/Rome: Institut historique belge de Rome.

Burckhardt, J. (1902), *Griechische Kulturgeschichte*, vol. 1, Berlin and Stuttgart: Spemann (= Burckhardt, *Gesammelte Werke*, vol. 5).

Burkert, W. (1985), 'Das Ende des Kroisos: Vorstufen einer Herodoteischen Gegischtserzälung', in C. Schaüblin (ed.), *Catalepton: Festschrift für*

Bernhard Wyss zum 80. Geburtstag, Basel: Seminar für Klassische Philologie der Universität Basel, pp. 4–15.

Burton, R. W. B. (1962), *Pindar's Pythian Odes*, Oxford: Oxford University Press.

Cabanes, P. (1976), *L'Épire de la mort de Pyrrhos à la conquète romaine*, Paris: Belles Lettres.

Caccamo Caltabiano, M. et al. (1995), 'Il sistema monetale ieroniano: cronologia e problemi', in M. Caccamo Caltabiano (ed.), *La Sicilia tra l'Egitto e Roma: la monetazione siracusana dell'età di Ierone II (Messina 1993)*, Messina: Accademia peloritana di pericolanti, pp. 195–274.

—— (1997), *Siracusa ellenistica: le monete "regali" di Ierone II, della sua famiglia e dei Siracusani*, Messina: Di. Sc. A. M.

Cairns, F. (1989), *Virgil's Augustan Epic*, Cambridge: Cambridge University Press.

Callataÿ, F. de (2000), 'Un "octobole" de Pyrrhus surfrappé sur un statère de type corinthien: réflexions sur les masses monnayées par Pyrrhus en or et en argent', *AIIN* 47, pp. 189–213.

Cameron, A. (1995), *Callimachus and his Critics*, Princeton: Princeton University Press.

Cantilena, R. (1993), 'L'emissione dei "pegasi" nelle zecche siciliane', in A. Stazio et al. (eds), *La monetazione corinzia in Occidente. Atti del IX Convegno del Centro Internazionale di Studi Numismatici (Napoli 1986)*, Rome: Instituto italiano di numismatica, pp. 61–85.

Carey, C. (1981), *A Commentary on Five Odes of Pindar*, New York: Arno Press.

Carlier, P. (1984), *La Royauté en Grèce avant Alexandre* (Études et travaux 6), Strasburg: AECR.

Carradice, I. and Price M. (1988), *Coinage of the Greek World*, London: Seaby.

Carroccio, B. (1994), *La monetazione aurea ed argentea di Ierone II*, Turin: Circolo Numismatico Turinese.

Castrizio, D. (1995), 'La destinazione dei pegasi agatoclei', in M. Caccamo Caltabiano (ed.), *La Sicilia tra l'Egitto e Roma: la monetazione siracusana dell'età di Ierone II (Messina 1993)*, Messina: Accademia peloritana di pericolanti, pp. 295–302.

Caven, B. (1990), *Dionysius I: Warlord of Sicily*, London and New Haven: Yale University Press.

Cawkwell, G. L. (1995), 'Early Greek tyranny and the people' *CQ* 45, pp. 73–86.

Cazenove, O. de (1989), 'Sp. Cassius, Cérès et Tellus', *REL* 67, pp. 93–116.

—— (1990), 'Le sanctuaire de Cérès jusqu'à la deuxième sécession de la plèbe', in *Crise et Transformation des Sociétés archaïques de l'Italie antique au Ve siècle av. J.-C.*, Rome: École Française de Rome, pp. 373–99.

Chassignet, M. (2001), 'La "construction" des aspirants à la tyrannie: Sp. Cassius, Sp. Maelius et Manlius Capitolinus', in M. Coudry and T. Späth (eds), *L'Invention des Grands Hommes de la Rome antique*, Paris: De Boccard, pp. 83–96.

Chisoli, A. (1993), 'Diodoro e le vicende di Ducezio', *Aevum* 67 (Jan.–Apr.), 21–9.

Chrisostomou, P. (1994), Ηλατρεία του Διόνυσου στη Θεσσαλία και ειδικότερα στις Φερές, in D. Karaberopolous (ed.), *Hypereia* 2: *Proceedings of the Second Symposium 'Pherai-Velestino-Regas'*, Athens: Epistemonike Hetaireia Meletes 'Pheron-Velestinou-Rega', pp. 113–49.

Christ, K. (2000), *Krise und Untergang der römischen Republik*, Darmstadt: Primus.

Classen, C. J. (1965), 'Die Königszeit im Spiegel der Literatur der römischen Republik', *Historia* 14, pp. 385–403.

Cloché, P. (1915), *La Restauration démocratique à Athènes en 403 avant J.-C.*, Paris: E. Leroux.

Coarelli, F. (1982), 'La pugna equestris di Agatocle nell'Athenaion di Siracusa', in L. Beschi (ed.), *Aparchai: nuove ricerche storico-archeologiche sulla Magna Grecia e la Sicilia antica in onore di P.E. Arias*, Pisa: Giardini, pp. 547–57 (= F. Coarelli, *Revixit ars: arte e ideologia a Roma. Dai modelli ellenistici alla tradizione repubblicana*, Rome 1996, pp. 85–101).

—— (1988), *Il Foro Boario*, Rome: Quasar.

Coby, J. P. (1999), *Machiavelli's Romans: Liberty and Greatness in the Discourses on Livy*, Lanham, MD: Lexington.

Coli, U. (1951), 'Regnum', *SDIII* 17, pp. 1–168 (= Coli, *Scritti di diritto romano*, 1, Milan: Giuffre, 1973, pp. 321–483).

Connor, W. R. et al. (eds) (1989), *Aspects of Athenian Democracy* (*C&M* Dissertationes 11), Copenhagen: Museum Tusculanum.

Consolo Langher, S. N. (1976), 'Agatocle: il colpo di stato. "Quellenfrage" e ricostruzione storica', *Athenaeum* 54, pp. 383–429.

—— (1980), 'La Sicilia dalla scomparsa di Timoleonte alla morte di Agatocle', in E. Gabba and G. Vallet (eds), *La Sicilia antica*, vol. 2.1: *La Sicilia greca dal VI secolo alle guerre puniche*, Naples: Società editrice storia di Napoli e della Sicilia, pp. 289–342.

—— (1992), 'Tra Falaride e Ducezio', *Kokalos* 34–5, pp. 229–63.

—— (1993), 'Il messaggio monarchico sulle monete di Agatocle', in T. Hackens et al. (eds), *Actes du XIe Congrès International de Numismatique (Bruxelles 1991)*, Louvain-la-Neuve: Association Professeur M. Hoc, pp. 78–81.

—— (1996a), 'Cartagine e Siracusa: due imperialismi a confronto. Problemi archeologici e storici della spedizione agatoclea nella Libye', *Kokalos* 42, pp. 237–62.

—— (1996b), *Siracusa e la Sicilia Greca tra età arcaica ed alto ellenismo*, Messina: Società Messinese di Storia Patria.

Consolo Langher, S. N. (1999a), 'Aspetti giuridici del potere regale in Sicilia', in M. Barra Bagnasco et al. (eds), *Origini e incontri di culture nell'antichità: Magna Grecia e Sicilia. Stato degli studi e prospettive di ricerca*, Messina: University of Messina, pp. 331–49.

—— (1999b), 'Zankle-Messana in età Greca', in G. M. Bacci and G. Tigano (eds), *Da Zancle a Messina: un percorso archeologico attraverso gli scavi*, vol. 1, Palermo: Assessorato dei beni culturali e ambientali e della pubblice instruzione, pp. 31–44.

—— (2000), *Agatocle: da capoparte a monarca fondatore di un regno tra Cartagine e i Diadochi*, Messina: Di. Sc. A. M.

Cook, J. M. (1983), *The Persian Empire*, New York: Schocken Books.

Cook, R. M. (1958), 'Speculations on the origins of coinage', *Historia* 7, pp. 275–92.

Cordano, F. (1986), 'Le leggi calcidesi di Monte San Mauro di Caltagirone', *Miscellanea Greca e Romana* 10, pp. 33–60.

Cornell, T. J. (1978), '*Principes* of Tarquinia', *JRS* 68, pp. 167–73.

—— (1986), 'The value of the literary tradition concerning archaic Rome', in K. Raaflaub (ed.), *Social Struggles in Archaic Rome: New Perspectives on the Conflict of the Orders*, Berkeley: University of California Press, pp. 52–76.

—— (1995), *The Beginnings of Rome: Rome and Italy from the Bronze Age to the Punic Wars (c.1000 to 264 BC)*, London: Routledge.

—— (2003), 'Coriolanus: myth, history and performance', in D. Braund and C. Gill (eds), *Myth, History and Culture in Republican Rome: Studies in Honour of T. P. Wiseman*, Exeter: University of Exeter Press, pp. 73–97.

Corradi, J. (1982), 'The mode of destruction: terror in Argentina', *Telos* 54, pp. 61–76.

Corvisier, J. N. (1999), 'La succession royale Molosse', in P. Cabanes (ed.), *L'Illyrie méridionale et l'Épire dans l'Antiquité – III (Chantilly 1996)*, Paris: De Boccard, pp. 395–401.

Costabile F. (1978), 'Strateghi e assemblea nelle *politeiai* di Reggio e Messana', *Klearchos* 20, pp. 19–57.

Crane, G. (1996), 'The prosperity of tyrants: Bacchylides, Herodotus, and the contest for legitimacy', *Arethusa* 29, pp. 57–85.

Crawford, M. H. (1974), *Roman Republican Coinage*, Cambridge: Cambridge University Press.

Cristofani, M. (1990), *La Grande Roma dei Tarquini*, exhibition catalogue, Rome: L'Erma di Bretschneider.

Croiset, A. (1880), *La Poésie de Pindare et les lois du lyrisme grec*, Paris: Hachette.

Cusumano, N. (1996), 'Sul lessico politico di Diodoro: *synteleia*', *Kokalos* 42, 303–12.

Dahl, R. (ed.) (1973), *Regimes and Oppositions*, New Haven: Yale University Press.

Dandamaev, M. (1989), *A Political History of the Achaemenid Empire*, trans. W. J. Vogelsang, Leiden: Brill.

Davies, J. K. (1997), 'The moral dimension of Pythian Apollo', in A. Lloyd (ed.), *What is a God? Studies in the Nature of Greek Divinity*, London: Duckworth, pp. 43–64.

—— (2000), 'A wholly non-Aristotelian universe: the Molossians as ethnos, state, and monarchy', in R. Brock and S. Hodkinson (eds), *Alternatives to Athens: Varieties of Political Organization and Community in Ancient Greece*, Oxford: Oxford University Press, pp. 234–58.

Davis, N. and Kraay, C. M. (1973), *The Hellenistic Kingdoms, Portrait Coins and History*, London: Thames and Hudson.

De Angelis, F. (1998), 'Ancient past, imperial present: the British Empire in T. J. Dunbabin's *The Western Greeks*', *Antiquity* 72, pp. 539–49.

—— (2003), 'Equations of culture: the meeting of natives and Greeks in Sicily (ca. 750–450 BC), *Ancient West and East* 2.1, pp. 19–49.

De Francisci, P. (1959), *Primordia civitatis*, Rome: Apollinaris.

De Martino, F. (1972), *Storia della costituzione romana*, vol. 1, 2nd edn, Naples: Jovene.

De Sensi Sestito, G. (1977), *Gerone II: un monarca ellenistico in Sicilia*, Palermo: Editrice Sophia.

—— (1980), 'La Sicilia dal 289 al 210 a.C.', in E. Gabba and G. Vallet (eds), *La Sicilia Antica*, vol. 2.1. *La Sicilia greca dal VI secolo alle guerre puniche*, Naples: Società editrice storia di Napoli e della Sicilia, pp. 343–70.

—— (1995), 'Rapporti tra la Sicilia, Roma e l'Egitto', in M. Caccamo Caltabiano (ed.), *La Sicilia tra l'Egitto e Roma: la monetazione siracusana dell'età di Ierone II (Messina 1993)*, Messina: Accademia peloritana di pericolanti, pp. 17–57.

de Ste. Croix, G. E. M. (1981), *The Class Struggle in the Ancient Greek World*, London: Duckworth.

De Vido, S. (1997), 'I dinasti dei Siculi: il caso di Archonides', *Acme* 50.2, pp. 7–37.

Demand, N. H. (1990), *Urban Relocation in Archaic and Classical Greece: Flight and Consolidation*, Norman and London: University of Oklahoma Press.

Dench, E. (1995), *From Barbarians to New Men: Greek, Roman and Modern Perceptions of People from the Central Apennines*, Oxford: Clarendon Press.

Dewald, C. (1987), 'Narrative surface and authorial voice in Herodotus' *Histories*', *Arethusa* 20, pp. 147–70.

—— (2002), ' "I didn't give my own genealogy": Herodotus and the authorial persona', in E. Bakker et al. (eds), *Brill's Companion to Herodotus*, Leiden: Brill, pp. 267–89.

Dewald, C. (2003), 'Form and content: the question of tyranny in Herodotus', in K. A. Morgan (ed.), *Popular Tyranny: Sovereignty and its Discontents in Ancient Greece*, Austin: University of Texas Press, pp. 25–58.

Di Salvatore M. (1994), 'Richerche sul territorio di Pherai. Insediamenti, difese, vie e cofini', in *La Thessalie: quinze années de recherches archéologiques 1975–1990*, Athens: Editions Kapon, 93–124.

Di Vita, A. (1996), 'Urbanistica della Sicilia greca' in G. Pugliese Carrattelli (ed.), *I Greci in Occiendente*, Milan: Bompiani, pp. 263–308.

—— (2002), 'L'urbanistica nella Sicilia del IV sec. a.C.', in N. Bonacasa et al. (eds), *La Sicilia dei due Dionisî*, Rome: L'Erma di Bretschneider, pp. 139–47.

Diehl, H. (1988), *Sulla und seine Zeit im Urteil Ciceros*, Hildesheim: Olms-Weidemann.

Dietler, M. (1989), 'Greeks, Etruscans and thirsty barbarians', in T. Champion (ed.), *Centre and Periphery: Comparative Studies in Archaeology*, London: Unwin Hyman, pp. 127–41.

—— (1999), 'Consumption, cultural frontiers, and identity: anthropological approaches to greek colonial encounters', in *Confini e frontiera nella Grecità d'Occidente: Atti del 37 convegno di studi sulla Magna Grecia*, Taranto: Istituto per la storia e l'archeologia della Magna Grecia, pp. 475–501.

Dietrich, B. C. (1965), *Death, Fate and the Gods: the Development of a Religious Idea in Greek Popular Belief and in Homer*, London: Athlone Press.

Dillery, J. (1995), *Xenophon and the History of His Times*, London: Routledge.

Dougherty, C. (1993), *The Poetics of Colonization: From City into Text in Archaic Greece*, Oxford and New York: Oxford University Press.

Doulgeri-Intzesiloglou A. (1994), 'Οι νεοτερες αρχαιολογικές επευνες στην περιοχή των αρχαίων Φερών', in *La Thessalie: Quinze années de recherches archéologiques 1975–1990*, Athens: Editions Kapon, pp. 71–92.

Dover, K. J. (1974), *Greek Popular Morality in the Time of Plato and Aristotle*, Oxford: Blackwell.

Drews, R. (1983), *Basileus: The Evidence for Kingship in Geometric Greece*, New Haven and London: Yale University Press.

Driver, G. R. (1954), *Aramaic Documents of the Fifth Century* BC, Oxford: Clarendon Press.

Dunbabin, T. J. (1948), *The Western Greeks: The History of Sicily and South Italy from the Foundation of the Greek Colonies to 480* BC, Oxford: Oxford University Press.

Dunkle, J. R. (1967), 'The Greek tyrant and Roman political invective of the late republic', *TAPA* 98, pp. 151–71.

Dyck, A. R. (1996), *A Commentary on Cicero*, De Officiis, Ann Arbor: University of Michigan Press.

Dyer, L. (1905), 'Olympian treasuries and treasuries in general', *JHS* 25, pp. 284–319.

Eckstein, A. M. (1980), 'Unicum subsidium populi Romani: Hiero II and Rome, 263–215 B.C.', *Chiron* 10, pp. 183–203.

Eder, W. (1997), 'Lucius Cornelius Sulla Felix', *Der Neue Pauly*, vol. 3, Stuttgart: J. B. Metzler, pp. 186–90.

Engels, J. (1993), 'Der Michigan-Papyrus über Theramenes und die Ausbildung des "Theramenes-Mythos" ', *ZPE* 99, pp. 125–55.

Erskine, A. (1991), 'Hellenistic monarchy and Roman political invective', *CQ* 61, pp. 106–20.

Evans, A. J. (1894), 'Contributions to Sicilian numismatics', *Num. Chron.*, p. 237.

Feldherr, A. (1998), *Spectacle and Society in Livy's History*, Berkeley and London: University of California Press.

Figueira, T. (1998), *The Power of Money: Coinage and Politics in the Athenian Empire*, Philadelphia, PA: University of Pennsylvania Press.

Finley, J. H. (1955), *Pindar and Aeschylus*, Cambridge, MA: Harvard University Press.

Finley, M. I. (1968), 'Silver tongue', in M. I. Finley, *Aspects of Antiquity*, London: Chatto and Windus, pp. 38–43.

—— (1979), *Ancient Sicily to the Arab Conquest*, Totowa, NJ: Rowman and Littlefield.

—— (1981), 'Debt-bondage and slavery,' in B. Shaw and R. Saller (eds), *Economy and Society in Ancient Greece*, London: Chatto and Windus, pp. 150–66.

Flower, H. I. (1996), *Ancestor Masks and Aristocratic Power in Roman Culture*, Oxford: Clarendon Press.

Forrest, W. G. (1970), 'The date of the pseudo-Xenophontic *Athenaion Politeia*', *Klio* 52, pp. 107–16.

Forsythe, G. (1994), *The Historian L. Calpurnius Piso Frugi and the Roman Annalistic Tradition*, Lanham, MD and London: University Press of America.

Fraser, P. and Matthews, E. (1997), *A Lexicon of Greek Personal Names*, vol. IIIA, Oxford: Oxford University Press.

Frederiksen, M. W. (1984), *Campania*, London: British School at Rome.

Freeman, E. A. (1891), *The History of Sicily from the Earliest Times*, Oxford: Clarendon Press.

Frolov, E. D. (1974), 'Die späte Tyrannis im Balkanischen Griechenland', in E. C. Welskopf (ed.), *Hellenische Poleis: Krise – Wandlung – Wirkung*, 1, Berlin: Akademie, pp. 231–400.

—— (2001), *Греция в эпоху поздней классики. Общество. Пичность. Власть*. St Petersburg: Izdatel'skii tsentr "Gumanitarnaia akademiia".

Fuscagni, S. (1975), 'Callistene di Olinto e la vita di Pelopida di Plutarco', in *Contributi dell'Istituto di Storia Antica 3: Storiografia e propaganda*, Milan: Vita e Pensiero, pp. 31–51.

Gabba, E. (1964), 'Studi su Dionigi di Alicarnasso III: la proposta di legge agraria di Spurio Cassio', *Athenaeum* 42, pp. 29–41.

Gabrielsen, V. (1994), *Financing the Athenian Fleet: Public Taxation and Social Relations*, Baltimore and London: Johns Hopkins University Press.

Gallo, L. (1980), 'Popolosità è scarcità: contributo allo studio di un topos', *Annali della Scuole Normale Superiore di Pisa* ser. 3.10, pp. 1233–70.

Galvagno, E. (1991), 'Ducezio "eroe": storia e retorica in Diodoro', in E. Galvagno et al. (eds), *Mito Storia Tradizione: Diodoro Siculo e la storiografia classica*, Catania: Edizioni del Prisma, pp. 99–124.

—— (2000), *Politica ed economia nella Sicilia Greca*, Rome: Carocci.

Gammie, J. G. (1986), 'Herodotos on kings and tyrants: objective historiography or conventional portraiture', *JNES* 45, pp. 171–95.

Garbini, G. (1996), 'The Phoenicians in the Western Mediterranean (through the fifth century B.C)', in G. Carratelli (ed.), *The Greek World: Art and Civilization in Magna Graecia and Sicily*, New York: Rizzoli, pp. 121–32.

Garnett, G. (2004), 'How the Normans did an English' (review of H. M. Thomas, *The English and the Normans*), *Times Literary Supplement* July 30, p. 11.

Garnsey, P. (1988), *Famine and Food Supply in the Graeco-Roman World: Responses to Risk and Crisis*, Cambridge: Cambridge University Press.

Garraffo, S. (1995), 'Problemi della monetazione siracusana da Agatocle a Ierone II', in M. Caccamo Caltabiano (ed.), *La Sicilia tra l'Egitto e Roma: la monetazione siracusana dell'età di Ierone II (Messina 1993)*, Messina: Accademia peloritana di pericolanti, pp. 453–63.

Gauthier, P. (1966), 'Le parallèle Himère-Salamine au Ve et IVe siècle av. J-C', *REA* 68, pp. 5–31.

Gehrke, H. J. (1986), *Stasis: Untersuchungen zu den inneren Kriegen in den griechischen Staaten des 5. und 4. Jahrhunderts v. Chr.*, Munich: Beck.

Gentili, B. (1953), 'I tripodi di Delfi e il Carme III di Bacchilide', *PP* 8, pp. 199–208.

Georgiadou, A. (1996), 'Pro-Boiotian traditions in the fourth century BC: Kallisthenes and Ephoros as Plutarkhos' sources in the "Pelopidas"', *Boeotia Antiqua* 6, pp. 73–90.

—— (1997), *Plutarch's Pelopidas: A Historical and Philological Commentary*, Stuttgart: Steiner.

Gernet, L. (1981), 'Marriages of tyrants', in *The Anthropology of Ancient Greece*, trans. J. Hamilton and B. Nagy, Baltimore: Johns Hopkins University Press, pp. 289–302.

Gianelli, G. (1980–1), 'Il tempio di Giunone Moneta e la casa di Marco Manlio Capitolino', *BCAR* 87, pp. 7–36.

Giesecke, W. (1923), *Sicilia Numismatica*, Leipzig: Hiersemann.

Gildenhard, I. (forthcoming a), 'Gelegenheitsmetaphysik: religiöse Semantik in Reden Ciceros', in A. Bendlin and J. Rüpke (eds), *Form und Funklion religioser Diskurse in der lateinischen Literatur des I. Jahrhunders v. Chr.* (2005/6).

—— (forthcoming b), *Paideia Romana: the design and purpose of Cicero's Tusculan Disputations*, in the supplement series of the Proceedings of the Cambridge Philological Society.

—— (forthcoming c), 'Greek auxiliaries: tragedy and philosophy in Ciceronian invective', in the Proceedings of the conference 'The Language and Style of Ciceronian Invective', Swansea, 2001.

Gildersleeve, B. (1885), *Pindar: the Olympian and Pythian Odes*, London: Macmillan.

Giorgini, G. (1993), *La citta e il tiranno: il concetto di tirannide nella Grecia del VII–IV secolo a.c*, Milan: Giuffre.

Giua, M. A. (1967), 'La valutazione della monarchia a Roma in età repubblicana', *Studi classici e orientali* 16, pp. 308–29.

Giuliani, A. (1995), 'Le migrazioni forzate in Sicilia e in Magna Grecia sotto Dionigi I di Siracusa', in M. Sordi (ed.), *Coercizione e mobilità umana nel mondo antico*, Milan: Vita e Pensiero, pp. 107–24.

Glinister, F. (1995), 'The Roman Kingship in the Sixth Century BC', PhD thesis, University College London.

Gray, V. (1989), *The Character of Xenophon's Hellenica*, Baltimore: Johns Hopkins University Press.

Gray, V. J. (1996), 'Herodotos and images of tyranny', *AJP* 117.3, pp. 361–89.

Grimal, P. (1986), 'Les éléments philosophiques dans l'idée de monarchie à Rome à la fin de la République', in H. Flashar and O. Gigon (eds), *Aspects de la philosophie hellénistique (Fondation Hardt, Entretiens sur l'antiquité classique* 32), Geneva: Vandoeuvres, pp. 233–81.

Gruen, E. S. (1985), 'The coronation of the Diadochoi', in J. W. Eadie and J. Ober (eds), *The Craft of the Ancient Historian: Essays in Honor of Chester G. Starr*, Lanham, MD: University Press of America.

—— (1996), 'Hellenistic Kingship: puzzles, problems and possibilities', in P. Bilde et al. (eds), *Aspects of Hellenistic Kingship* (Studies in Hellenistic Civilization VII), Aarhus: Aarhus University Press, pp. 116–25.

Guarino, A. (1948), 'Notazioni romanistiche: la genesi storica dell'*auctoritas patrum*', in V. Arangio-Ruiz (ed.), *Studi in onore di S. Solazzi*, Naples: Jovene, pp. 21–31.

Gutberlet, D. (1985), *Die erste Dekade des Livius als Quelle zur gracchischen und sullanischen Zeit*, Hildesheim and New York: Olms-Weidmann.

Haake, M. (2003), 'Warum und zu welchem Ende schreibt man *peri basileias*? Überlegungen zum historischen Kontext einer literarischen Gattung im Hellenismus', in K. Piepenbrink (ed.), *Philosophie und Lebenswelt in der Antike*, Darmstadt: Wissenschaftliche Buchgesellschaft, pp. 83–138.

Hackl, U. (1982), *Senat und Magistratur in Rom von der Mitte des 2. Jahrhunderts v. Chr. bis zur Diktatur Sullas*, Kallmünz: Verlag Michael Lassleben.

Hall, J. (2002), *Hellenicity: Between Ethnicity and Culture*, Chicago: University of Chicago Press.

Hammond, N. G. L. (1967), *Epirus*, Oxford: Clarendon Press.

Hansen, M. H. (1999), *Athenian Democracy in the Age of Demosthenes*, 2nd edn, Bristol: Bristol Classical Press.

Harrell, S. (2002), 'King or private citizen: fifth-century Sicilian tyrants at Olympia and Delphi', *Mnemosyne* 55, pp. 439–64.

Harris, J. (2003), 'Was Stalin a weak dictator?', *The Journal of Modern History* 75, pp. 375–86.

Harrison, C. (2002), 'Numismatic problems in the Achaemenid West: the undue modern influence of "Tissaphernes"', in V. B. Gorman (ed.), *Oikistes: Studies in Constitutions, Colonies and Military Power in the Ancient World, Offered in Honour of A. J. Graham*, Leiden: Brill, pp. 301–19.

Hartog, F. (2001), 'Plutarque entre les Anciens et les Modernes', in Plutarque, *Vies parallèles*, Paris: Gallimard Quarto, pp. 9–49.

Harvey, F. D. (1985), '*Dona ferentes*: some aspects of bribery in Greek politics', in P. A. Cartledge and F. D. Harvey (eds), *Crux: Essays in Greek History Presented to G. E. M. de Ste. Croix*, London: Duckworth, pp. 76–117.

Head, B. V. (1874), 'On the chronological sequence of the coins of Syracuse', *Num. Chron.*, pp. 56–8.

—— (1911), *Historia numorum: A Manual of Greek Numismatics*, 2nd edn, Oxford: Clarendon Press.

Heath, M. (1987), *Political Comedy in Aristophanes* (*Hypomnemata* vol. 87), Göttingen: Vanderhoeck and Ruprecht.

—— (1988), 'Receiving the *komos*: the context and performance of epinician', *AJP* 109, pp. 180–95.

—— (1990), 'Aristophanes and his rivals', *G&R* 37, 143–58.

Helly, B. (1995), *L'État Thessalien: Aleuas le Roux, les Tétrades et les Tagoi*, Lyons: Collection de l'Orient Mediterranéen.

Henderson, J. (2003), 'Demos, demagogue and tyrant', in K. Morgan (ed.), *Popular Tyranny: Sovereignty and its Discontents in Ancient Greece*, Austin: University of Texas Press, pp. 155–79.

Henrichs, A. (1968), 'Zur Interpretation des Michigan-Papyrus über Theramenes', *ZPE* 3, pp. 101–8.

Herman, G. (1987), *Ritualised Friendship and the Greek City*, Cambridge: Cambridge University Press.

Hermon, E. (2001), *Habiter et partager les terres avant les Gracques*, Rome: École Française de Rome.

Herring, E. (2000), ' "To see oursels as others see us!" The construction of native identities in southern Italy', in E. Herring and K. Lomas (eds), *The Emergence of State Identities in Italy in the 1st Millennium* BC, London: Accordia Research Institute, pp. 45–78.

Hignett, C. (1952), *A History of the Athenian Constitution to the End of the Fifth Century B.C.*, Oxford: Clarendon Press.

Hinard, F. (1984), 'La naissance du mythe de Sylla', *REL* 62, pp. 81–97.

—— (1985), *Sylla*, Paris: Fayard.

—— (1988), 'De la dictature à la tyrannie: réflections sur la dictature de Sylla', in F. Hinard (ed.), *Dictatures*, Paris: De Boccard, pp. 87–96.

Holzhauser, J. (2004), 'Pindar und die Orphik: zu Fr. 133 Snell/Maehler', *Hermes* 132, pp. 20–36.

Homolle, T. (1897) 'Les trépieds de Gélon', *BCH* 21, pp. 588–90.

—— (1898), 'Les offrandes Delphiques des fils de Deinoménes et l'epigramme de Simonides', in *Mélanges Henri Weil*, Paris: Thorin, pp. 207–24.

Hornblower, S. (1982), *Mausolus*, Oxford: Clarendon Press.

—— (1991–), *A Commentary on Thucydides*, Oxford: Oxford University Press.

—— (2000), 'The *Old Oligarch* (Pseudo-Xenophon's *Athenaion Politeia*) and Thucydides. A fourth-century date for the *Old Oligarch*?', in Flensted-Jensen, et al. (eds), *Polis and Politics: Studies in Ancient Greek History*, Copenhagen: Museum Tusculanum, pp. 363–84.

—— (2004), *Thucydides and Pindar: Historical Narrative and the World of Epinikian Poetry*, Oxford: Oxford University Press.

Howie, G. (1989), 'Greek polytheism', in G. Davies (ed.), *Polytheistic Systems (Cosmos 5)*, Edinburgh: Edinburgh University Press.

Hunter, V. J. (1994), *Policing Athens: Social Control in the Attic Lawsuits, 420–320 B.C.*, Princeton: Princeton University Press.

Huss, W. (1980), 'Neues zur Zeit des Agathokles: einige Bemerkungen zu P. Oxy. XXIV 2399', *ZPE* 39, pp. 63–71.

Jaeger, M. (1997), *Livy's Written Rome*, Ann Arbor: University of Michigan Press.

Jenkins, G. K. (1966), *Coins of Greek Sicily*, London: British Museum Press.

—— (1972), *Ancient Greek Coins*, London: Barrie and Jenkins, and New York: Putnam.

Kallet, L. (2003), '*Dêmos Tyrannos*: wealth, power and economic patronage', in K. A. Morgan (ed.), *Popular Tyranny: Sovereignty and its Discontents in Ancient Greece*, Austin: University of Texas Press, pp. 117–53.

Kallet-Marx, L. (1993), *Money, Expense and Naval Power in Thucydides' History 1–5.24*, Berkeley, Los Angeles and Oxford: University of California Press.

Kershaw, I. (1987), *The 'Hitler Myth': Image and Reality in the Third Reich*, Oxford: Oxford University Press.

Keyt, D. (1999), *Aristotle* Politics *Books V and VI*, Oxford: Clarendon Press.

Kinzl, K. H. (1979), *Die ältere Tyrannis bis zu den Perserkrieg: Beiträge zur griechischen Tyrannis (Wege der Forschung 510)*, Darmstadt: Wissenschaftliche Buchgesellschaft.

Kirsten, E. (1941), 'Ein politisches Programm in Pindars Erstem Pythischen Gedicht', *RhM* 90, pp. 58–71.

Knapp, R. (2002), 'Greek coinage, mercenaries and ideology', *Eulimene* 3, pp. 183–96.

Knoepfler, D. (1989), 'Tétradrachmes attiques et argent "alexandrin" chez Diogène Laërce', *Mus. Helv.* 46, pp. 193–230.

Koerte, A. (1904), 'Die Hypothesis zu Kratinos' *Dionysalexandros*', *Hermes* 39, pp. 481–98.

Kraay, C. M. (1976), *Archaic and Classical Greek Coins*, London: Methuen.

Krasilnikoff, J. A. (1995), 'The power base of Sicilian tyrants', in T. Fischer-Hansen (ed.), *Ancient Sicily* (*Acta Hyberborea* 6), Copenhagen: Museum Tusculanum Press, pp. 171–84.

Krentz, P. (1982), *The Thirty at Athens*, Ithaca: Cornell University Press.

Krumeich, R. (1991), 'Zu den goldenen Dreifüssen der Deinomeniden in Delphi', *JDAI* 106, pp. 37–62.

Kuschel, B. (1961), 'Die neuen Münzbilder des Ptolomaeus Soter', *JNG* 11, pp. 9–18.

La Bua, V. (1980), 'La spedizione di Pirro in Sicilia', *MGR* 7, pp. 179–254.

Laffi, U. (1967), 'Il mito di Silla', *Athenaeum* 45, pp. 177–213, 255–77.

Last, H. (1945), 'The Servian reforms', *JRS* 35, pp. 30–48.

Lateiner, D. (1989), *The Historical Method of Herodotus* (Phoenix Suppl. 23), Toronto and London: University of Toronto Press.

Le Rider, G. (1981), 'Une drachme d'Alexandre de Phères surfrappée en Crète', in L. Casson and M. J. Price (eds), *Coins, Culture and History in the Ancient World. Studies in Honor of B. L. Trell*, Detroit: Wayne State University Press, 43–5.

Lehmann, C. M. (1981), 'The striding god of Zancle-Messana', *RBN* 127, pp. 19–32.

Leifer, F. (1931), *Studien zum antiken Ämterwesen 1. Zur Vorgeschichte des römischen Führeramts* (*Klio* Beiträge 23), Leipzig: Dieterich.

Leighton, R. (2000), 'Indigenous society between the ninth and sixth centuries BC: territorial, urban and social evolution', in C. Smith and J. Serrati (eds), *Sicily from Aeneas to Augustus: New Approaches in Archaeology and History*, Edinburgh: Edinburgh University Press, pp. 15–40.

Lentini, M. C. (2002), 'Testimonianze della prima metà del IV secolo a.C a Naxos', in N. Bonacasa et al. (eds), *La Sicilia dei due Dionisî*, Rome: L'Erma di Bretschneider, pp. 223–41.

Leonhardt, J. (1995), 'Theorie und Praxis der *deliberatio* bei Cicero: der Briefwechsel mit Atticus aus dem Jahre 49', *ACD* 31, pp. 153–71.

Lévêque, P. (1957), *Pyrrhos*, Paris: De Boccard.

Lewis, D. M. (1977), *Sparta and Persia*, Leiden: Brill.

Lewis, R. G. (1991), 'Sulla's Autobiography: Scope and Economy', *Athenaeum* 69, pp. 509–19.

Lewis, S. (2000), 'The tyrant's myth', in C. Smith and J. Serrati (eds), *Sicily from Aeneas to Augustus: New Approaches in Archaeology and History*, Edinburgh: Edinburgh University Press, 97–106.

—— (2004), 'καὶ σαφῶς τύραννος ἦν: Xenophon's account of Euphron of Sicyon', *JHS* 124, pp. 65–74.

Linderski, J. (1990), 'The auspices and the Struggle of the Orders', in W. Eder (ed.), Staat und Staatlichkeit in der frühen römischen Republik, Stuttgart: Steiner, pp. 34–48.

Lintott, A. W. (1970), 'The tradition of violence in the annals of the early Roman Republic', *Historia* 19, pp. 12–29.

Liou-Gille, B. (1996), 'La sanction des *leges sacrata* et l'adfectatio regni: Spurius Cassius, Spurius Maelius et Manlius Capitolinus', *PP* 51, pp. 161–97.

Lloyd-Jones, H. (1990), *Greek Epic, Lyric and Tragedy: Academic Papers*, Oxford: Clarendon Press.

Lomas, K. (1993), *Rome and the Western Greeks, 338 BC – AD 200: Conquest and Acculturation in Southern Italy*, London: Routledge.

—— (2000), 'The *polis* in Italy: ethnicity and citizenship in the western Mediterranean', in R. Brock and S. Hodkinson (eds), *Alternatives to Athens: Varieties of Political Experience and Community in Ancient Greece*, Oxford: Oxford University Press, pp. 167–85.

Luraghi, N. (1994), *Tirannidi Archaiche in Sicilia e Magna Grecia*, Florence: Olschki.

Lyons, C. L. (1996), 'Sikel burials at Morgantina: defining social and ethnic boundaries', in R. Leighton (ed.), *Early Societies in Sicily: New Developments in Archaeological Research*, London: Accordia Research Centre, pp. 167–76.

Maas, B. (1888), 'Διόνυσος πελάγιος', Hermes 23, pp. 70–80.

MacDowell, D. M. (1995), Aristophanes and Athens: *An Introduction to the Plays*, Oxford and New York: Oxford University Press.

Macleod, C. (1983), 'Reason and necessity: Thucydides III 9–14, 37–48', in *Collected Essays*, Oxford: Oxford University Press, pp. 88–102 (= (1978), 'Reason and necessity: Thucydides III 9–14, 37–48', *JHS* 98, pp. 64–78).

Mafodda, G. (1979), 'Aspetti e problemi di storia siceliota dalla morte di Agatocle all'insediamento mamertino in Messana', *Kokalos* 25, pp. 197–204.

Magdelain, A. (1964), '*Auspicia ad patres redeunt*', in M. Renard and R. Schilling (eds), *Hommages à J. Bayet (Collection Latomus 70)*, Brussels: Latomus, pp. 427–73.

—— (1968), *Recherches sur l'"imperium". La loi curiate et les auspices d'investiture*, Paris: Presses Universitaires de France.

—— (1973), 'Remarques sur la *perduellio*', *Historia* 22, pp. 405–22.

Mallwitz, A. (1972), *Olympia und seine Bauten*, München: Prestel.

Maniscalco, L. et al. (2003), 'The Sanctuary of the Divine Palikoi (Rocchicella di Mineo, Sicily): fieldwork from 1995 to 2001', *AJA* 107, pp. 145–80.

Manni, E. (1984), 'Teossena. Una principessa fra Alessandria e Siracusa', in N. Bobacasa and A. di Vita (eds), *Alessandria e il mondo ellenistico-romano. Studi in onore di Achille Adriani*, Rome: L'Erma di Bretschneider, pp. 480–3 (= Manni, E., *Sikelika kai Italika: Scritti minori di storia antica della Sicilia e dell'Italia meridionale*, Rome 1990, pp. 289–94).

Martin, P.-M. (1982–94), *L'Idée de royauté à Rome* (2 vols), Clermont-Ferrand: Adosa.

—— (1990), 'Des tentatives de tyrannies à Rome aux Ve–IVe siècles?', in W. Eder (ed.), *Staat und Staatlichkeit in der frühen römischen Republik*, Stuttgart: Steiner, pp. 49–72.

Martin, T. R. (1983), 'The chronology of the fourth-century B.C. facing-head silver coinage of Larissa', *ANSMN* 28, pp. 1–34.

—— (1985), *Sovereignty and Coinage in Classical Greece*, Princeton: Princeton University Press.

Massner, A. (1973), 'Zur Interpretation der Münzbildnisse des Hieronymos von Syrakus', *Schw. Munz.* 23, pp. 41–7.

McGlew, J. F. (1993), *Tyranny and Political Culture in Ancient Greece*, Ithaca and London: Cornell University Press.

—— (2002), *Citizens on Stage: Comedy and Political Culture in the Athenian Democracy*, Ann Arbor: University of Michigan Press.

McKechnie, P. (1989), *Outsiders in the Greek Cities in the Fourth Century B.C.*, London and New York: Routledge.

Meadows, A. and Williams, J. (2001), 'Moneta and the monuments: coinage and politics in Republican Rome', *JRS* 91, pp. 27–49.

Mehl, A. (1980–1), '*ΔΟΡΙΚΤΕΤΟΣ ΧΩΡΑ*. Kritische Bemerkungen zum "Speererwerb" in Politik und Völkerrecht der hellenistischen Epoche', Ancient Society 11–12, pp. 173–212.

Meiggs, R. (1972), The Athenian Empire, Oxford: Clarendon Press.

Meister, K. (1967), *Die Sizilische Geschichte bei Diodor*, Diss. Munich.

Mele, A. (1981), 'Il Pitagorismo e le populazioni anelleniche d'Italia', *Annali di Archeologia e Storia Antica*, Napoli: Istituto Universitario Orientale, pp. 61–96.

Merkelbach, R. and Youtie, H. C. (1968), 'Ein Michigan-Papyrus über Theramenes', *ZPE* 2, pp. 161–9.

Meyer, R. (1970), *History of Purple as a Status Symbol in Antiquity*, Brussels: Latomus.

Michel, C. (1900–27), *Recueil d'inscriptions grecques*, Brussels: Lamertin.

Mildenberg, L. (1985), *The Arthur S. Dewing Collection of Greek Coins*, New York: American Numismatic Society.

Miller, H. F. (1984), 'The practical and economic background to the Greek mercenary explosion', *Greece and Rome* 31, pp. 153–60.

Miller, M. C. (1988), 'Midas as the Great King in Attic fifth-century vase-painting', *AntK* 31, pp. 79–89

—— (1995), 'Persians: the oriental Other', *SOURCE: Notes in the History of Art* 15.1 (*Special Issue: Representations of the 'Other' in Athenian art, c. 510–400 BC*), pp. 39–44.

—— (2000), 'The myth of Bousiris: ethnicity and art', in B. Cohen (ed.), *Not the Classical Ideal: Athens and the Construction of the Other in Greek Art*, Leiden: Brill, pp. 413–42.

Millino, G. (2003),'Ierone II, Roma e l'Adriatico', in L. Braccesi (ed.), *Hesperìa* 17: *Roma, l'Adriatico e il mondo ellenistico (Venezia 2001)*, Rome: L'Erma di Bretschneider, pp. 105–27.

Mitchell, L. G. (1997), *Greeks Bearing Gifts: The Public Use of Private Relationships in the Greek World*, Cambridge: Cambridge University Press.

—— (forthcoming), 'Greek government', in K. Kinzl (ed.), *Blackwell Companion to the Classical Greek World*, Oxford: Blackwell Publishing.

Mitchell, R. E. (1990), *Patricians and Plebeians: The Origin of the Roman State*, Ithaca and London: Cornell University Press.

Momigliano, A. (1936), 'Due punti di storia romana arcaica', *SDHI* 2, pp. 373–98 (= *Quarto Contributo* 329–61).

—— (1967), 'Osservazioni sulla distinzione fra patrizi e plebei', in E. Gjerstad (ed.), *Les Origines de la république romaine* (*Fondation Hardt, Entretiens sur l'antiquité classique* 13), Geneva: Vandoeuvres, pp. 199–221.

Mommsen, T. (1864–79), 'Sp. Cassius, M. Manlius, Sp. Maelius, die drei Demagogen der älteren republikanischen Zeit', in T. Mommsen, *Römische Forschungen* vol. 2, Berlin: Weidmann, pp. 153–220.

—— (1908), *The History of Rome*, vol. 1, London: Macmillan.

Mooren, L. (1983), 'The nature of Hellenistic monarchy', in E. Van't Dack et al. (eds), *Egypt and the Hellenistic World*, Louvain: Studia Hellenistica, pp. 205–40.

Moreno, P. (1998), 'Elementi di pittura ellenistica', in A. Rouveret, *L'Italie méridionale et les premières experiences de la peinture hellénistique (Rome 1994)*, Rome: École Française de Rome, pp. 6–67.

Moretti, L. (1953), *Iscrizioni agonistiche greche*, Rome: A. Signorelli.

Morgan, K. (1993), 'Pindar the professional and the rhetoric of the *komos*', *CPh* 88, pp. 1–15.

Morgan, K. A. (ed.) (2003), *Popular Tyranny: Sovereignty and its Discontents in Ancient Greece*, Austin: University of Texas Press.

Mørkholm, O. (1991), *Early Hellenistic Coinage from the Accession of Alexander to the Peace of Apamea (336–186 BC)*, Cambridge: Cambridge University Press.

Morris, I. (1994), 'Archaeologies of Greece', in I. Morris (ed.), *Classical Greece: Ancient Histories and Modern Archeologies*, Cambridge: Cambridge University Press, 8–47.

Morris, I. (2003), 'Mediterraneanization', *Mediterranean Historical Review* 18.2, pp. 30–55.

Morris, I. and Raaflaub, K. A. (eds) (1997), *Democracy 2500? Questions and Challenges* (Archaeological Institute of America Colloquia and Conference Papers 2), Dubuque, IA: Kendall/Hunt.

Morris, I., Jackman, T., Blake, E. and Tusa, S. (2002), 'Stanford University excavations on the Acropolis of Monte Polizzo, Sicily, 2: Preliminary report on the 2001 season', *Memoirs of the American Academy in Rome* 47, pp. 153–98.

—— (2003), 'Stanford University excavations on the Acropolis of Monte Polizzo, Sicily 3 Preliminary report on the 2002 season', *Memoirs of the American Academy in Rome* 48, pp. 343–415.

Mossé, C. (1962), *La Fin de la démocratie athénienne*, Paris: Presses Universitaires de France.

—— (1969, rev. 2004), *La Tyrannie dans la Grèce antique*, Paris: Presses Universitaires de France.

—— (1999), 'Timoléon et la recolonisation de la Sicile grecque (Plutarque, Vie de Timoleon, XXII, 4 s.)', in G. Vallet et al. (eds), *La Colonisation grecque en Méditerranée occidentale*, Rome: École Française de Rome, pp. 249–56.

Mullen, W. (1982), *Choreia: Pindar and Dance*, Princeton: Princeton University Press.

Munn, M. H. (2000), *The School of History: Athens in the Age of Socrates*, Berkeley: University of California Press.

Murray, O. (1997), 'Rationality and the Greek city: the evidence from Kamarina', in M. H. Hansen (ed.), *The Polis as an Urban Centre and as a Political Community (Acts of the Copenhagen Polis Centre* 4), Copenhagen: Munksgaard, pp. 493–504.

Murray, R. J. (1964–5), 'The attitude of the Augustan poets toward *rex* and related words', *CJ* 60, pp. 241–6.

Mustakallio, K. (1994), *Death and Disgrace: Capital Penalties with* post mortem *Sanctions in Early Roman Historiography*, Helsinki: Suomalainen Tiedeakatemia.

Musti, D. (1992), 'Tradizioni letterarie', *Kokalos* 34–5, pp. 209–26.

Nenci, G. (1953), *Pirro: Aspirazioni egemoniche ed equilibrio mediterraneo*, Turin: University of Turin.

Nichols, J. J. (1967), 'The content of the Lex Curiata', *AJP* 88, pp. 257–78.

Niemeyer, H. G. (1990), 'The Phoenicians in the Mediterranean: a non-Greek model for expansion and settlement in antiquity', in J.-P. Descoeudres (ed.), *Greek Colonists and Native Populations*, Oxford: Oxford University Press, pp. 469–89.

Nightingale, A. W. (1995), *Genres in Dialogue: Plato and the Construct of Philosophy*, Cambridge: Cambridge University Press.

North, J. A. (2000a), *Roman Religion (Greece & Rome New Surveys in the Classics* 30), Oxford: Oxford University Press.

—— (2000b), 'Prophet and text in the third century BC', in E. Bispham and C. Smith (eds), *Religion in Archaic and Republican Rome and Italy: Evidence and Experience*, Edinburgh: Edinburgh University Press, pp. 92–107.

Oakley, S. P. (1997), *A Historical Commentary on Livy VI–X*, vol. 1, Oxford: Clarendon Press.

Ober, J. (1989), *Mass and Elite in Democratic Athens: Rhetoric, Ideology, and the Power of the People*, Princeton: Princeton University Press.

—— (1996), *The Athenian Revolution: Essays on Ancient Greek Democracy and Political Theory*, Princeton: Princeton University Press.

Ober, J. and Hedrick, C. W. (1996), *Demokrateia: A Conversation on Democracies, Ancient and Modern*, Princeton: Princeton University Press.

Ober, J. and Hedrick, C. W. (eds) (1993), *The Birth of Democracy: An Exhibition Celebrating the 2500th Anniversary of Democracy at the National Archives, Washington, D.C. June 15, 1993–January 2, 1994*, Princeton: American School of Classical Studies at Athens.

O'Donnell, G. (1986), 'On the fruitful convergences of Hirschman's *Exit, Voice, and Loyalty* and *Shifting Involvements*: reflections from the recent Argentine experience', in A. Foxley, M. McPherson and G. O'Donnell (eds), *Development, Democracy, and the Art of Trespassing: Essays in Honor of Albert O. Hirschman*, Notre Dame: University of Notre Dame Press, pp. 249–68.

Ogden, D. (1997), *The Crooked Kings of Ancient Greece*, London: Duckworth.

Ogilvie, R. M. (1965), *A Commentary on Livy Books 1–5*, Oxford: Clarendon Press.

Opelt, I. (1965), *Die lateinischen Schimpfwörter und verwandte sprachliche Erscheinungen: Eine Typologie*, Heidelberg: Winter.

Orioles, V. (1992), 'Bilinguismo e biculturalismo nella Messana mamertina', *Studi linguistici e filologici offerti a Girolamo Caracausi*, Palermo: Centro di studi filologici e linguistici Siciliani, pp. 331–45.

Orlandini, P. (1958), 'La rinascita della Sicilia nell'età di Timoleonte', *Kokalos* 4, pp. 24–30.

Osborne, R. G. (1996), *Greece in the Making*, London: Routledge.

—— (1998), 'Early Greek colonisation? The nature of Greek settlement in the West', in N. Fisher and H. van Wees (eds), *Archaic Greece: New Approaches and New Evidence*, London: Duckworth/Classical Press of Wales, pp. 251–67.

—— (2003), 'Changing the discourse', in K. A. Morgan (ed.), *Popular Tyranny: Sovereignty and its Discontents in Ancient Greece*, Austin: University of Texas Press, pp. 251–72.

Ostwald, M. (1965), 'Pindar, *Nomos* and Heracles', *HSCP* 69, pp. 109–38.
—— (1969), *Nomos and the Beginnings of Athenian Democracy*, Oxford: Oxford University Press.
—— (1986), *From Popular Sovereignty to the Sovereignty of Law: Law, Society, and Politics in Fifth-Century Athens*, Berkeley: University of California Press.
—— (2000), *Oligarchia: The Development of a Constitutional Form in Ancient Greece* (*Historia* Einzelschriften 144), Stuttgart: Steiner.
Panitschek, P. (1989), 'Sp. Cassius, Sp. Maelius, M. Manlius als *exempla maiorum*', *Philologus* 133, pp. 231–45.
Parke, H. W. (1933), *Greek Mercenary Soldiers from Earliest Times to the Battle of Ipsus*, Oxford: Oxford University Press.
Parker, V. (1998), '*Τύραννος*: the semantics of a political concept from Archilochus to Aristotle', *Hermes* 126, pp. 45–72.
Parlangèli, O. (1956), 'Le iscrizioni osche (mamertine) di Messina', *Bollettino Centro di Studi Filologici e Linguistici di Sicilia* 4, pp. 28–38.
Parry, A. (1989), *The Language of Achilles and Other Papers*, Oxford: Clarendon Press.
Pavese, C. (1967), 'The new Heracles poem of Pindar', *HSCP* 72, pp. 47–88.
Pearson, L. (1987), *The Greek Historians of the West: Timaeus and his Predecessors*, Atlanta: Scholars Press.
Pease, A. S. (1923), *M. Tulli Ciceronis de divinatione liber secundus*, Urbana: University of Illinois.
Pedley, J. G. (1990), *Paestum: Greeks and Romans in Southern Italy*, London: Thames and Hudson.
Pelagatti, P. (1972), 'Naxos II. Ricerche topografiche e scavi, 1965–70: Relazione preliminare', *Bolletino d'Arte* 57, pp. 211–20.
Pelling, C. B. R. (2002), 'Speech and action: Herodotus' debate on the constitutions', *PCPS* 48, pp. 123–58.
Perelli, C. (1994), '*Memoria de Sangre*: fear, hope, and disenchantment in Argentina', in J. Boyarin (ed.), *Remapping Memory: The Politics of TimeSpace*, Minneapolis: University of Minnesota Press, pp. 39–66.
Pfeijffer, I. (1999), *Three Aeginetan Odes of Pindar* (*Mnemosyne* Suppl. 197), Leiden: Brill.
Pfiffig, A. J. (1965), *Uni-Hera-Astarte. Studien zu den Goldblechen von S. Severa-Pyrgi mit etruskischer und punischer Inschrift* (Österreich. Akad. d. Wissensch., Phil. Hist. Kl. 88), Vienna: H. Böhlaus.
Philipp, H. (1994), 'Olympia, die Peloponnes und die Westgriechen', *JDAI* 109, pp. 77–92.
Pinzone, A. (1999), 'Per la storia di Messana Mamertina', in A. Pinzone, *Provincia Sicilia*, Catania: Edizini del Prisma, pp. 121–72 (= *Archivio Storico Messinese* 32, 1981, 5–54).
Podlecki, A. J. (1966), 'The political significance of the Athenian "tyrannicide"-cult', *Historia* 15, pp. 129–41.

Prandi, L. (1985), *Callistene: Un storico tra Aristotele e i rei Macedoni*, Milan: Jaca.

Prestianni Giallombardo, A. M. (1995), 'Aspetti istituzionali e segni di regalità della basileia di Ierone II', in M. Caccamo Caltabiano (ed.), *La Sicilia tra l'Egitto e Roma: la monetazione siracusana dell'età di Ierone II (Messina 1993)*, Messina: Accademia peloritana di pericolanti, pp. 495–509.

Pritchett, W. K. (1969), 'The battle of Kynoskephalai in 364 B.C.', in W. K. Pritchett, *Studies in Ancient Topography*, vol. 2, Berkeley: University of California Press, pp. 112–19.

—— (1974), *The Greek State at War*, vol. 2, Berkeley: University of California Press.

Purcell, N. (2003), 'Becoming historical: the Roman case', in D. Braund and C. Gill (eds), *Myth, History and Culture in Republican Rome: Studies in Honour of T. P. Wiseman*, Exeter: University of Exeter Press, pp. 12–40.

Raaflaub, K. (1974), *Dignitatis contentio. Studien zur Motivation und politischen Taktik im Bürgerkrieg zwischen Caesar und Pompeius*, Munich: Beck.

—— (2003), 'Stick and glue: the function of tyranny in fifth-century Athenian democracy', in K. Morgan (ed.), *Popular Tyranny: Sovereignty and its Discontents in Ancient Greece*, Austin: University of Texas Press, pp. 59–93.

—— (2004), *The Discovery of Freedom in Ancient Greece*, Chicago: Chicago University Press (translation and revision of *Die Entdeckung der Freiheit: Zur historischen Semantik und Gessellschaftsgeschichte eines politischen Grundbegriffes der Griechen*, Munich: 1985).

Raccuia, C. (1981), 'Messana, Rhegion e Dionysius I dal 404 al 398 a.C.', *RSA* 11, pp. 15–32.

Raffone, L. (2001), 'Per una lettura di P.Oxy. XXIV 2399. Sulla campagna d'Africa di Agatocle e la situazione politica di Siracusa', *Minima Epigraphica et Papyrologica* 6, pp. 209–28.

Redfield, J. (2003), *The Locrian Maidens: Love and Death in Greek Italy*, Princeton: Princeton University Press.

Reid, C. I. (1974), 'Ephorus Fragment 76 and Diodorus on the Cypriote War', *Phoenix* 28, pp. 135–43.

Rhodes, P. J. (1981, rev. 1993), *A Commentary on the Aristotelian* Athenaion Politeia, Oxford: Clarendon Press.

—— (2000), 'Oligarchs in Athens', in R. Brock and S. Hodkinson (eds), *Alternatives to Athens: Varieties of Political Organization and Community in Ancient Greece*, Oxford: Oxford University Press, pp. 119–36.

—— (forthcoming), 'Fourth-century oligarchs', in Chieti conference proceedings.

Rhodes, P. J. with Lewis, D. M. (1997), *The Decrees of the Greek States*, Oxford: Oxford University Press.

Ribbeck, O. (1875), 'Ueber einige historische Dramen der Griechen', *RhM* 30, pp. 156–9.

Ridley, R. T. (1975), 'Cicero and Sulla', *WS* 9, pp. 83–103.

Ritter, H.-W. (1965), *Diadem und Königherrschaft. Untersuchungen zu Zeremonien und Rechtsgrundlagen des Herrschaftsantritts bei den Persen, bei Alexander dem Grossen und im Hellenismus*, Munich: Beck.

Rizzo, F. P. (1970), *La repubblica di Siracusa nel momento di Ducezio*, Palermo: U. Manfredi.

Roisman, J. (1985), 'Maiandrios of Samos', *Historia* 34, pp. 257–77.

Rose, P. W. (1992), *Sons of the Gods, Children of Earth: Ideology and Literary Form in Ancient Greece*, Ithaca: Cornell University Press.

Rosivach, V. (1988), 'The tyrant in Athenian Democracy', *QUCC* 30, pp. 43–57.

Ross Holloway, R. (1969), *The Thirteen-Months Coinage of Hieronymos of Syracuse*, Berlin: de Gruyter.

—— (1979), 'The bronze coinage of Agathocles', in O. Mørkholm and N. M. Waggoner (eds), *Greek Numismatics and Archaeology. Essays in Honour of M. Thompson*, Wetteren: Editions NR, pp. 87–95.

—— (1991), *The Archaeology of Ancient Sicily*, London: Routledge.

Rutherford, R. B. (1995), *The Art of Plato: Ten Essays in Platonic Interpretation*, London: Duckworth.

Rutter, N. K. (1997), *The Greek Coinages of Southern Italy and Sicily*, London: Spink.

—— (ed.) (2001), *Historia Nummorum: Italy*, London: British Museum Press.

Salmon, J. (1977), 'Political hoplites', *JHS* 97, pp. 84–101.

—— (1997), 'Lopping off the heads: tyrants, politics and the *polis*', in L. G. Mitchell and P. J. Rhodes (eds), *The Development of the Polis in Archaic Greece*, London and New York: Routledge, pp. 60–73.

Sanders, L. J. (1987), *Dionysius I of Syracuse and Greek Tyranny*, London and New York: Croom Helm.

Scanlon, T. (1987), 'Thucydides and tyranny', *ClAnt* 6, pp. 286–301.

Schwenk, C. J. (1985), *Athens in the Age of Alexander: The Dated Laws and Decrees of 'the Lykourgan era', 338–322 BC*, Chicago: Ares.

Scibona, G. (1986), 'Punti fermi e problemi di topografic antica a Messina: 1966–1986', in *Atti del 26° Convegno di Studi sulla Magna Grecia*, Taranto: Istituto per la Storia dell'Archeologia della Magna Grecia, pp. 433–58.

Seaford, R. (2003), 'Tragic tyranny', in K. Morgan (ed.), *Popular Tyranny: Sovereignty and its Discontents in Ancient Greece*, Austin: University of Texas Press, pp. 95–115.

Segal, C. (1971), 'Croesus on the pyre: Herodotus and Bacchylides', *WS* n.s. 5, pp. 39–51.

Segal, C. (1989), 'Choral lyric in the fifth century', in P. E. Easterling and B. M. W. Knox (eds), The *Cambridge History of Classical Literature* vol. 1, Cambridge: Cambridge University Press, pp. 181–203.

Seltman, C. T. (1955), *Greek Coins: A History of Metallic Currency and Coinage Down to the Fall of the Hellenistic Kingdoms*, London: Methuen.

Shackleton Bailey, D. R. (1965–70), *Cicero's Letters to Atticus* (6 vols), Cambridge: Cambridge University Press.

Shepherd, G. (1999), 'Fibulae and females: intermarriage in the Western Greek colonies and the evidence of the cemeteries', in G. Tsetskhladze (ed.), *Ancient Greeks West and East*, Leiden: Brill, pp. 267–300.

Shipley, G. (1987), *History of Samos, 800–188 BC*, Oxford: Clarendon Press.

Shrimpton, G. (1991), 'Persian strategy against Egypt and the date for the battle of Citium', *Phoenix* 45, pp. 1–20.

Signes Codoñer, J. (2002), 'Ἐπιστολαί ο λόγοι? Problemas en torno a las cartas I, VI y IX de Isócrates', *Materiali e discussioni per l'analisi dei testi classici* 48, pp. 77–110.

Silk, M. (1974), *Interaction in Poetic Imagery*, Cambridge: Cambridge University Press.

Silk, M. S. (2001), 'Pindar meets Plato: theory, language, value and the classics', in S. J. Harrison (ed.), *Texts, Ideas and the Classics: Scholarship, Theory and Classical Literature*, Oxford and New York: Oxford University Press, pp. 26–45.

Simon, E. (1995), 'Spott zum Schutz vor Nemesis', in G. Alföldy et al. (eds), *Römische Lebenskunst*, Heidelberg: Winter, pp. 119–30.

Sjöqvist, E. (1973), *Sicily and the Greeks*, Ann Arbor: University of Michigan Press.

Skinner, Q. (2002), *Visions of Politics* (3 vols), Cambridge: Cambridge University Press.

Small, A. (2004), 'Some Greek inscriptions on native vases from South East Italy', in K. Lomas (ed.), *Greek Identity in the Western Mediterranean*, Leiden and Boston: Brill, pp. 267–85.

Smith, C. J. (1996), *Early Rome and Latium: Economy and Society c. 1000–500 BC*, Oxford: Clarendon Press.

—— (1997), 'Servius Tullius, Cleisthenes, and the emergence of the *polis* in central Italy', in L. G. Mitchell and P. J. Rhodes (eds), *The Development of the* polis *in Archaic Greece*, London: Routledge, pp. 208–16.

—— (2005), *The Roman Clan: The* gens *from Ancient Ideology to Modern Anthropology*, Cambridge: Cambridge University Press.

Smith, R. R. R. (1988), *Hellenistic Royal Portraits*, Oxford: Clarendon Press.

—— (1994), 'Spear-won land at Boscoreale: on the royal paintings of a Roman villa', *JRA* 7, pp. 100–28.

Sommerstein, A. (1989), *Aeschylus* Eumenides, Cambridge: Cambridge University Press.

Sordi, M. (1958), *La lega tessala fino ad Alessandro Magno*, Rome: Bardi.
—— (1961), *Timoleonte*, Palermo: Flaccovio.
—— (1980), 'Il IV e III secolo da Dionigi I a Timoleonte (336 a.C.)', in E. Gabba and G. Vallet (eds), *La Sicilia Antica*, Naples: Società editrice storia di Napoli e della Sicilia, vol. II.1, pp. 207–87.
—— (1981), 'Ermocrate di Siracusa, demagogo e tiranno mancato', in L. Gasperini (ed.), *Scritti sul mondo antico in memoria di Fulvio Grosso*, Rome: Giorgio Bretschneider, pp. 595–600.
—— (1992), *La* dynasteia *in Occidente (Studi su Dionigi I)*, Padova: Editoriale Programma.
Spaeth, B. S. (1996), *The Roman Goddess Ceres*, Austin: University of Texas Press.
Spoerri, W. (1966), 'Prosopographica', *Mus. Helv.* 23, pp. 44–57.
Sprawski, S. (1999), *Jason of Pherae*, Kraków: Jagiellonian University Press.
—— (2003), 'Philip II and the freedom of the Thessalians', *Electrum* 9, 55–66.
—— (2004), 'Were Lycophron and Jason tyrants of Pherae?', in C. Tuplin (ed.), *Xenophon and his World*, Stuttgart: Steiner, 437–52.
Starr, C. G (1982), 'New specimens of Athenian coinage 480–449', *Num. Chron.* 142, pp. 129–34.
Staveley, E. S. (1954), 'The conduct of elections during an *interregnum*', *Historia* 3, pp. 193–211.
—— (1956), 'The constitution of the Roman Republic, 1940–1954', *Historia* 5, pp. 74–122.
—— (1972), *Greek and Roman Voting and Elections*, New York: Thames and Hudson.
Stewart, A. (1993), *Faces of Power: Alexander's Image and Hellenistic Politics*, Berkeley and Oxford: University of California Press.
Stolper, M. (1983), 'The death of Artaxerxes I', *AMI* 16, pp. 22–36.
Stroheker, K. F. (1958), *Dionysios I: Gestalt und Geschichte des Tyrannen von Syrakus*, Wiesbaden: Steiner.
Stylianou, P. J. (1998), *A Historical Commentary on Diodorus Siculus Book 15*, Oxford: Clarendon Press.
Tagliamonte, G. (1994), *I Figli di Marte. Mobilià, mercenari e mercenariato italici in Magna Grecia e Sicilia*, Rome: Giorgio Bretschneider.
Talbert, R. J. A. (1974), *Timoleon and the Revival of Greek Sicily (344–317)*, London: Cambridge University Press.
Tavernier, J. (2001), 'An Achaemenid royal inscription: the text of paragraph 13 of the Aramaic version of the Bisitun Inscription', *JNES* 60, pp. 161–76.
Taylor, C. (2001a), 'Bribery in Athenian politics part i: accusations, allegations, and slander', *G&R* 48, pp. 53–66.
—— (2001b), 'Bribery in Athenian politics part ii: ancient reactions and perceptions', *G&R* 48, pp. 154–72.

Taylor, M. C. (2002), 'Implicating the *demos*: a reading of Thucydides on the rise of the Four Hundred', *JHS* 122, pp. 91–108.

Thompson, H. A. and Wycherely, R. E. (1972), *Athenian Agora XIV. The Agora of Athens: The History, Shape and Uses of an Ancient City Centre*, Princeton: Princeton University Press.

Thompson, S. M. (1999), 'A central Sicilian landscape: settlement and society in the territory of Morgantina (5000 BC–AD 50)', PhD Thesis, University of Virginia.

Thomsen, R. (1980), *King Servius Tullius*, Copenhagen: Gylendal.

Todd, S. C. (1990), 'The use and abuse of the Attic orators', *G&R* 37, pp. 159–77.

Torelli, M. (1975), *Elogia Tarquiniensia*, Florence: Sansoni.

—— (2003), 'The frescoes of the Great Hall of the Villa at Boscoreale: iconography and politics', in D. Braund and C. Gill (eds), *Myth, History and Culture in Republican Rome: Studies in Honour of T. P. Wiseman*, Exeter: University of Exeter Press, pp. 217–56.

Treves, P. (1941), 'Herodotus, Gelon, and Pericles', *CPh* 36, pp. 321–45.

Trumpf, J. (1958), 'Stadtgründung und Drachenkampf (Excurse zu Pindar, Pythien I)', *Hermes* 86, pp. 129–57.

Trundle, M. (2004), *Greek Mercenaries from the Late Archaic Age to Alexander the Great*, London and New York: Routledge.

Turchetti, M. (2001), *Tyrannie et tyrannicide de l'Antiquité à nos jours*, Paris: Presses Universitaires de France.

Ure, P. N. (1922), *The Origin of Tyranny*, Cambridge: Cambridge University Press.

Valgiglio, E. (1956), *Silla e la crisi repubblicana*, Florence: La nuova Italia.

Valvo, A. (1975), 'Le vicende del 44–43 a. C. nella tradizione di Livio e Dionigi su Spurio Melio', in M. Sordi (ed.), *Storiografia e propaganda* (CISA 3), Milan: Vita e Pensiero, pp. 92–106.

—— (1983), *La sedizione di Manlio Capiolino in Tito Livio* (Memorie dell'Istituto Lombardo Accademia di Scienze e Lettere xxxviii.1), Milan: Istituto lombardo di scienze e lettere.

Vanotti, G. (1995), 'Leontini nel V secolo, cittàdi profugi', in M. Sordi (ed.), *Coercizione e mobilità umana nel mondo antico*, Milan: Vita e Pensiero, pp. 89–106.

Vassallo, S. (2000), 'Abitati indigeni ellenizati della Sicilia centro-occiden-tale dalla vitalità tardo-arcaica alla crisi del V. sec. a.C.', in A. Corretti (ed.), *Terzo Giornate Internazionali di Studi sull'area Elima, Atti* vol. 2, Pisa-Gibellina: Scuola Normale Superiore di Pisa, pp. 985–1008.

Vattuone, R. (1994), ' "Metoikesis". Trapianti di popolazioni nella Sicilia greca fra VI e IV sec. a.C.', in M. Sordi (ed.), *Emigrazione e immigrazione nel mondo antico*, Milan: Vita e Pensiero, pp. 81–113.

Venturini, C. (1988), s.v. '*Rex*', *Enciclopedia Virgiliana* 4, Rome: Istituto della Enciclopedia italiana, pp. 466–8.

Vetter, E. (1959), *Handbuch der italischen Dialekte*, Heidelberg: Winter.

Vigourt, A. (2001a), 'L'intention criminelle et son châtiment: les condamna-
tions des aspirants à la tyrannie', in M. Coudry and T. Späth (eds),
L'Invention des Grands Hommes de la Rome antique, Paris: De Boccard,
pp. 271–88.

—— (2001b), 'Les *adfectores regni* et les normes sociales', in M. Coudry and
T. Späth (eds), *L'Invention des Grands Hommes de la Rome antique*,
Paris: De Boccard, pp. 333–40.

Virgilio, B. (1998), ' "Basileus". Il re e la regalità ellenistica', in S. Settis (ed.),
*I Greci. Storia, Cultura, Arte, Società. 2. Una storia greca. III.
Trasformazioni*, Turin: Einaudi, pp. 107–76.

—— (2003), *Lancia, diadema e porpora: Il re e la regalità ellenistica*, 2nd
edn, Pisa: Giardini.

Vlastos, G. (1981), '*ΙΣΟΝΟΜΙΑ ΠΟΛΙΤΙΚΗ*', Platonic studies, Princeton:
Princeton University Press, pp. 164–203.

von Reden, S. (1995), *Exchange in Ancient Greece*, London: Duckworth.

von Ungern-Sternberg, J. (1986), 'The end of the conflict of the orders', in
K. Raaflaub (ed.), *Social Struggles in Archaic Rome: New Perspectives on
the Conflict of the Orders*, Berkeley: University of California Press,
pp. 353–77.

Walbank, M. B. (1978), *Athenian Proxenies of the Fifth Century B.C.*,
Toronto: Stevens.

Wallace, W. (1987), 'The Origin of Electrum Coinage', *AJA* 91, pp. 385–97.

Walsh, P. G. (1961), *Livy: His Historical Aims and Methods*, Cambridge:
Cambridge University Press.

Walt, S. (1997), *Der Historiker C. Licinius Macer: Einleitung, Fragmente,
Kommentar*, Stuttgart and Leipzig: Teubner.

Wartenberg, U. (1994), 'The history and coinage of Alexander of Pherae', in
D. Karaberopolous (ed.), *Hypereia 2: Proceedings of the Second
Symposium 'Pherai-Velestino-Regas'*, Athens: Epistemonike Hetaireia
Meletes 'Pheron-Velestinou-Rega', pp. 151–9.

Waters, K. H. (1971), *Herodotus on Tyrants and Despots: A Study in
Objectivity*, Wiesbaden: Steiner.

Weiskopf, M. (1989), *The So-called 'Great Satraps' Revolt', 366–360 BC*
(*Historia* Einzelschriften 64), Stuttgart: Steiner.

Westlake, H. D. (1935), *Thessaly in the Fourth Century*, London: Methuen.

—— (1952), *Timoleon and his Relations with Tyrants*, Manchester:
Manchester University Press.

White, M. (1955), 'Greek tyranny', *Phoenix* 9, pp. 1–18.

Whittaker, C. R. (1978), 'Carthaginian imperialism in the fifth and fourth
Centuries', in P. Garnsey and C. R. Whittaker (eds), *Imperialism in the
Ancient World*, Cambridge: Cambridge University Press, pp. 59–90.

Williams, R. T. (1976), *The Silver Coinage of the Phocians*, New York:
American Numismatic Society.

Wirszubski, C. (1950), *'Libertas' as a Political Idea at Rome during the Late Republic and Early Principate*, Cambridge: Cambridge University Press.

Wiseman, T. P. (1979), 'Topography and rhetoric: the trial of Manlius', *Historia* 28, pp. 32–50 (= T. P. Wiseman, *Roman Studies: Literary and Historical*, Liverpool: Cairns 1987, pp. 225–43).

—— (1996), 'The Minucii and their monuments', in J. Linderski (ed.), *Imperium sine fine: T. Robert S. Broughton and the Roman Republic* (*Historia* Einzelschriften 105), Stuttgart: Steiner, pp. 57–94 (= Wiseman 1998, pp. 90–105).

—— (1998), *Roman Drama and Roman History*, Exeter: University of Exeter Press.

—— (2002), 'Roman history and the ideological vacuum', in T. P. Wiseman (ed.), *Classics in Progress: Essays on Ancient Greece and Rome*, Oxford and New York: British Academy and Oxford University Press, pp. 285–310.

Wohl, V. (1998), 'Plato avant la lettre: authenticity in Plato's Epistles', *Ramus* 27, pp. 60–93.

Wolpert, A. (2002), *Remembering Defeat: Civil War and Civic Memory in Ancient Athens*, Baltimore: Johns Hopkins University Press.

Wooten, C. W. (1988), 'The earrings of Polemarchos' wife (Lysias 12.19)', *CW* 82, pp. 29–31.

Yavetz, Z. (1983), *Julius Caesar and his Public Image*, London: Thames and Hudson.

Young, D. C. (1968), *Three Odes of Pindar: A Literary Study of* Pythian 2, Pythian *3 and* Olympian 7, Leiden: Brill.

Youroukova, I. (1976), *Coins of the Ancient Thracians*, Oxford: British Archaeological Reports.

Zambon, E. (2000), 'Finzia, i Mamertini e la seconda distruzione di Gela', in L. Braccesi (ed.), *Hesperìa 12: Studi sulla Grecità d'Occidente*, Rome: L'Erma di Bretschneider, pp. 303–8.

—— (2001), 'Le tirannidi nella Sicilia post-agatoclea: il caso di Agrigento', in L. Braccesi (ed.), *Hesperìa 14: Studi sulla Grecità d'Occidente*, Rome: L'Erma di Bretschneider, pp. 179–89.

—— (2004), ' "Κατὰ δὲ Σικελίαν ἦσαν τύραννοι": notes on the tyrannies in Sicily between the death of Agathocles and the coming of Pyrrhus (289–279 B.C.)', in K. Lomas (ed.), *Greek Identity in the Western Mediterranean. Papers in Honour of Professor Brian Shefton* (*Mnemosyne* Supplements 246), Leiden: Brill, pp. 455–72.

—— (forthcoming), *Tradition and Innovation: The Greeks of Sicily between Hellenism and Rome*.

Ziolkowski, A. (1993), 'Between geese and the *auguraculum*: the origin of the cult of Juno on the *arx*', *CPh* 88, pp. 206–19.

Index